MANAGING WORLD ECONOMIC CHANGE
INTERNATIONAL POLITICAL ECONOMY
Second Edition

ROBERT A. ISAAK

Pace University

Prentice Hall, Englewood Cliffs, New Jersey 07632

Library of Congress Cataloging-in-Publication Data

Isaak, Robert A.
    Managing world economic change : international political economy /
    Robert A. Isaak. —2nd ed.
        p.   cm.
    Rev. ed. of: International political economy. 1991.
    Includes bibliographical references (p.   ) and index.
    ISBN 0-13-181678-0
    1. International economic relations.   I. Isaak, Robert A.
    International political economy.   II. Title.
    HF1411.I76 1995
    337—dc20   94-35289
                                                                        CIP

**To Gudrun, Sonya, and Andrew,
who light up my life**

Editorial/production supervision
    and interior design: Virginia M. Livsey
Acquisitions editor: Charlyce Jones Owen
Buyer: Bob Anderson
Cover design: Wendy Alling Judy
Editorial Assistant: Nicole Signoretti

© 1995, 1991 by Robert A. Isaak
Prentice-Hall, Inc.
A Simon & Schuster Company
Englewood Cliffs, New Jersey 07632

Formerly published as INTERNATIONAL POLITICAL ECONOMY:
MANAGING WORLD ECONOMIC CHANGE

Printed in the United States of America
10 9 8 7 6 5 4 3 2

ISBN 0-13-181678-0

Prentice-Hall International (UK) Limited, *London*
Prentice-Hall of Australia Pty. Limited, *Sydney*
Prentice-Hall Canada Inc., *Toronto*
Prentice-Hall Hispanoamericana, S.A., *Mexico*
Prentice-Hall of India Private Limited, *New Delhi*
Prentice-Hall of Japan, Inc., *Tokyo*
Simon & Schuster Asia Pte. Ltd., *Singapore*
Editora Prentice-Hall do Brasil, Ltda., *Rio de Janeiro*

CONTENTS

CHAPTER EIGHT   STATE STRATEGIES AND STAGES OF DEVELOPMENT   231

CHAPTER NINE   MULTINATIONAL STRATEGIES, ECONOMIC CYCLES, AND DIRECT INVESTMENT   263

PREFACE

This book takes a collective learning approach to the management of global economic change. It utilizes the standard of *laissez-faire,* liberal, free-market ideology as a point of departure in order to see how, why, and when nations and managers depart from this standard or return to it. Collective learning is the social, political, and organizational behavior involved in this process. Global economic change has speeded up in the 1990s. A primacy is now placed in management upon learning how to learn quickly in an organizational context: victory in the global economic race now goes to the quick rather than to the big.

In focusing on the origins of how change is managed in the global economy of the 1990s, the second edition of *International Political Economy* has put its subtitle up front in more ways than one. *Managing World Economic Change* stresses the human, the strategic, and the political dimensions of managing economic change. The text has been simplified to become more accessible and "human," while the focus upon the process of collective learning has been sharpened.

Updating of a number of economic and political transformations in the 1990s has brought home that we are in an era of comparative capitalisms moving rapidly towards what Peter Drucker has called a "postcapitalist society." A postcapitalist society, however, is also a *postliberal society,* which is a fundamental theme throughout this second edition. Specifically, there are not merely trends towards functional globalization economically, but also countertrends towards local and regional autonomy both politically and economically. These countertrends to globalism represent postliberalism in their resistance to (if not transcendence of) liberal market assumptions of self, society, money, and trade. They seek to protect the cultural and ethnic integrity of peoples and their economic and political sovereignty. Thus, on October 12, 1993, President Bill Clinton spoke at the University of North Carolina of a strategic focus upon "security" as the theme that would unite his policy initiatives. He stressed not *freedom*, but *security*: economic security, health security, and personal security. While many formerly statist nations, such as those in Eastern Europe, were moving towards liberal market freedom, Clinton was leading a postliberal security drive away from the classical liberal standard. This direction was epitomized in his campaign for a universal healthcare system in the United States.

Hence, the second edition brings out the tensions between liberal market assumptions and postliberal development: liberated self versus effective social ethics; the stability of independent national monetary management versus the democratic pressures upon politicians to seek to increase exports and employment by devaluing the currency; the classical liberal assumption of free markets and free trade versus the trend towards protecting certain sectors in the emerging knowledge economy for the sake of long-term national development, short-term job preservation, and social welfare. A new chapter on "Post-Cold-War Economics" replaces the former East-West chapter. It discusses the tension between liberal market assumptions and the global trend towards "privatization." It also deals with local and regional reactions against the abstract (yet significant) macroeconomic principles of economic liberals in the form of movements for protection and reassertion of traditional ethnic and ideological identities. In this context, basic concepts of macroeconomic stabilization and economic liberalism are introduced (through the cases of China, Russia, and Poland) so that those without a background in macroeconomics will be able to follow the rest of the book without difficulty. In later chapters, countries participating in the "East Asian miracle" (from Japan to Hong Kong, South Korea to Malaysia) are shown to have mastered macroeconomic principles of low inflation, sound fiscal policies, high domestic savings, heavy investment in education, and openness to foreign technology. At the same time, these countries intervene with government subsidies for targeted lending, tax incentives, and export subsidies for key industries and short-term protectionism.

A second new chapter has been included on North-North competitiveness in the post-cold-war economy. It focuses upon Japan, Germany, and the U.S. and addresses the kinds of industrial policies and learning frameworks that are necessary in order to become an economic superpower. Collective learning is shown to be the vital dynamic link between external opportunity provided by the global environment and domestic organization for the creation of wealth and jobs.

All chapters have been updated and refocused on this continuing theme of liberalism versus postliberalism in managing world economic change in terms of processes of targeted collective learning. Key concepts have been highlighted in **bold type** and summary principles cast into *italics* to make it easier for students and instructors to review what matters most. Thought questions at the end of each chapter have been added to aid "collective learning" in the classroom. This book has been used successfully in macroeconomics, international political economy, international management/business, and international relations courses as well as those focusing on government institutions, business strategy and economic policy.

* * *

Angela Liberatore, William Clark, and others at the International Environmental Institutions Research Seminar at Harvard's Center for Science and International Affairs provided fruitful suggestions on my application of collective learning to economic development and environmental responsibility. I am also indebted to colleagues Edward Weisband, Mark Levy, and Roger Kasperson, who participated in the round-table discussion on this subject at the 1993 International Studies Association meeting in Acapulco. I also benefitted from comments by Kiichi Kageyama and his colleagues at Tokyo Keizai University in Tokyo in October 1993 at the International Symposium on Networking of Human Relations and Technology. Their reactions to my application of collective learning theory to entrepreneurial networking and strategic alliances were most helpful. These arguments were further refined at the "Training for Change" International Seminar held at the *Institut d'Aministration des Enterprises* in Aix-en-Provence, France, in May 1994.

I am grateful to Yogesh Grover, of Winona State University, and Charlotte A. Price, of Sarah Lawrence College, for their review comments on the original text, to Mellani Day, of Schiller International University in Heidelberg, for thought questions based on teaching with the book; to Thomas Weissmann, Alexander Keck (who contributed thought questions), and Ingo Mueller, for their precise research assistance in helping to bring statistics up to date; to Virginia Livsey, Nicole Signoretti, and Charlyce Jones Owen of Prentice Hall; and to my colleague and friend, Larry Bridwell, for helpful suggestions and support.

R.A.I.

INTRODUCTION

Ill fares the land with the great deal of velocity where wealth accumulates and there ain't any reciprocity.

O. Henry, "Supply and Demand"

O. Henry's short story "Supply and Demand" is the tale of a big white man who goes down to "Gaudymala" and uses force and his wits to turn an Indian tribe into slaves. The white man, Patrick Shane, sets himself up as king. He takes the biggest house in the village for himself, and has the natives wash the streams for gold dust that they bring only to him. To keep this colonized political economy going, King Shane, or the "Grand Yacuma," gives the Indians a weekly sermon in the council-house (he is the council) on the law of supply and demand. He praises supply and knocks demand. Teaching them not to desire anything beyond their simplest needs, they bring him all the gold and remain contented on a bit of mutton, cocoa, and fruit. They even make their own clothes.

All goes well until a capitalist laden down with artificial jewelry and mirrors comes into the village on a mule and tempts the local population with Western luxuries in order to get at the gold that is rumored to be in the village. Enlightened by the marketing of the foreign salesman, the natives revolt against their ruler. The king and the capitalist flee for their lives, taking their trinkets with them but leaving behind the gold, which is not worth much if there are no goods to be traded for it.

O. Henry's tale illustrates key elements involved when managing change in the international political economy. Some people have more than others to start with. They use their advantageous position to speed things up, accumulating even more wealth and further increasing the gap between themselves and the poor. The rich, in short, are better positioned and better able to use speed to their advantage. Noting this, they continue to speed things up to increase their holdings.

Wealth does not seem to buy happiness, however. The hectic velocity of materialism combined with the lack of reciprocity in the community leads to a sense of meanness in the quality of life. Leisure becomes hectic and time-starved. There is hardly a moment left for "others." Ultimately, if the gap between the rich and the poor is perceived to be too great, or too "unfair," those in power may see their power base begin to crumble. The political recipe of pushing supply and knocking demand works only as long as the community can be isolated from the infinite variety of goods and services available to consumers on the global market. As the majority of people gain access to information and goods from markets external to the community, a process of collective learning is stimulated. The people suddenly want more than they have and they know what they want. As their leaders adopt the way of foreign elites who bring new knowledge, goods, and opportunities into the community, this process of collective learning accelerates.

The same impulse that leads the wealthy elites to speed up social and economic processes to maximize their own short-term interests forces those down the social scale to accelerate their learning curves in order to adapt and survive in the emerging economy. As the scarcity of resources appears to become less scarce to the general population, they demand more, buy more, and learn faster. **International political economy** is the study of the inequality in power and wealth between peoples and nations and of the patterns of collective learning and positioning that preserve or change this inequality or asymmetry. By focusing upon collective learning in the process of managing economic change, one can target knowledge in order to improve one's own life chances and those of one's family, village, and nation.

What is striking in O. Henry's tale is not so much the inequality between the foreign elite and the natives—which is the nature of the world—but rather the specific ways in which this asymmetrical status quo is at first preserved and then eventually undermined. Nor are the natives necessarily better off when the foreigners leave, despite their freedom. Like Adam and Eve, they have been bitten by knowledge of the world and can never return to ignorant bliss. International political economy is a process of continual disenchantment. But by examining the collective learning patterns of other peoples as they cope with the conditions and rules of the global political economy, individuals can perhaps understand their own disenchantment as a fruitful learning process for themselves and their people. For there are strategies and tactics in this ceaseless struggle of the strong to keep what they have in conflict with the weak who seek to change the international system in their favor. Perhaps, as Antonio Gramsci suggested, one can learn to train the individual will to be optimistic despite the pessimism of the intellect when it is applied to the outcome of the collective behavior of human beings.

Ever since the Industrial Revolution, the gap between industrialized and developing countries has become a central preoccupation of the study of international political economy. Some scholars define international political economy as the interplay between international politics and international economics or business. Others prefer to stress the process of international wealth acquisition and transfer. But the key question of international political economy concerns the essential dynamics that give rise to unequal distributions: *Who gets what, when, and how among different players in the global economy?*

Because such unequal distributions are not immutable or frozen, the most fruitful focus is upon managing change for the sake of specific collective interests. By stressing ongoing collective learning and positioning processes, one can understand how managers of nation-states, multinational corporations, and international organizations are able to outmaneuver each other and can see the consequences for different peoples. It is particularly important to pay attention to nations or multinational companies that are in the process of making innovative breakthroughs. For example, the eight "superstars" of East Asia (Japan, South Korea, Taiwan, Singapore, Hong Kong, Indonesia, Malaysia, and Thailand) increased their income per person almost 6 percent per year over the past twenty-five years. Japanese memory-chip companies set the standard for competitiveness in the field. Are these examples an outgrowth of something uniquely Asian, or have the Asians discovered a transferable recipe—a blend of state subsidy and free-market innovation that is superior to mere free-market-oriented economies, on the one hand, or state-regulated market economies, on the other? Which factors permit the development of such collective capacity for learning or adaptation in the global economy on the part of states or multinational organizations? Are neo-Confucian societies superior in their ability to learn quickly to adapt collectively to global transformations? Which breakthrough models of organization are most worthy of emulation: the complacent Big Blue IBM that almost went under while clinging to its mainframe computer ideology in the mid-1980s, or the decentralized IBM of hit-team consumer targeting, which began with giving a creative group the autonomy to develop the PC (personal computer) without bureaucratic hurdles to jump? Which structures block such innovative learning or adaptation, and why? How can we collectively learn to pick up competitive learnings of others swiftly enough to satisfy the social and economic needs of our own communities?

Here, the focus upon collective learning and positioning of unequal actors in the global economy and upon successful management strategies will be contrasted with other, more conventional approaches or schools of thought. To demystify the differences between competing perspectives, this book will dwell upon the contrast between the assumptions of Western liberalism and its stress upon markets and what will be termed "postliberalism"— "interventionist" reactions to liberalism stemming from older visions such as Marxism, economic nationalism, structuralism, or from newer communitarian visions seeking to transcend liberalism for the sake of the integrity of an existing community's values. As one observes how these perspectives illuminate the explanation of major phenomena in the global economy—such as the world trade and monetary systems—one also senses what has been left out or left in the dark. The observer can only wear one set of glasses at a time, and each set only permits the wearer to see what the lenses were designed to see. The student's suspicion that international political economy is a war of disciplines and ideologies over the same worldly turf is unfortunately accurate.

Yet the turf remains to be explained in some sort of universal and verifiable way—namely, the human use and abuse of the earth and the way people learn to position themselves to improve their collective life chances upon it. The political economist must separate universal (collective) cognitive patterns of learning from specific organizational and cultural modes of behavior. And in this process the picture of the whole earth or global context cannot be lost without ignoring the dominant revolutionary transformation of our times: the evolution of *one global market or economy* that will be managed one way or another by managers with transnational perspectives—whether they be managers of governmental institutions, multinational corporations, or international organizations.

POLITICS VERSUS ECONOMICS
OR LIBERALISM VERSUS POSTLIBERALISM

The "whole earth" approach to political economy—a *world* view—remains the exception and not the rule.[1] Economists note that their discipline was traditionally called "political economy," the queen of the social sciences dating back at least to Adam Smith's *Wealth of Nations,* published in 1776. While more comprehensive than most visions of economists since, Smith's classical laissez-faire view was based on a Western society of small shopkeepers, anticipating the Industrial Revolution but hardly the global consequences of the multinational corporation or the nuclear superpower state. Nevertheless, Smith's classical tenets of **economic liberalism**—that minimal state interference in the economy and maximum reliance upon the market result in business productivity and social wealth—still predominate in Anglo-Saxon cultures today.

The sacrosanct value of individual freedom in the United States, for example, originally depended upon the assumption that economics and politics could be kept separated, that the state should be kept out of people's private "business" lives as much as possible: "That government is best which governs least." But in the 20th century, this "negative" view of the state was modified by a "positive" view of the state intervening to save the private sector from itself in times of potential economic depression and to create equal opportunities for access to the market for the disadvantaged. Nevertheless, the guiding rule of even "positive state" American liberalism was to rely upon the markets as much as possible and to preserve the stability of individual freedom above all else—even collective competitiveness.[2] Americans, "the people of plenty," have been reluctant to accept that there are no clear boundaries between politics and economics within their own society, not to mention in American attempts to impose their liberal ideology upon other societies. But politics and economics always overlap; they are logical spheres that can never be totally separated in the real world.[3]

One of the most influential critiques of the assumption that politics and economics can be separated was offered by the continental theorist Karl Marx in *Das Kapital,* published in 1867. Perhaps a third of the world's population have been taught that Marx's massive critique of laissez-faire capitalism—focusing upon class struggle as the prime mover—is "the economic truth." As American political economist Charles Lindblom noted in *Politics and Markets:* except for the distinction between despotic and libertarian governments, the greatest difference between one government and another is the extent to which market replaces government or government replaces market. Adam Smith understood this. So did Karl Marx.[4] Neither planned (or "control") economic systems, based on Marx, Lenin, and Stalin, nor market economies, based on Smith and Ricardo, can avoid key questions of governmental-market relations where politics and economics overlap. If the Unites States traditionally attempted to embody the ideology of Smith's market economy, the Soviet Union and the People's Republic of China sought to adapt Marx's economic vision to their own distinctive ideological purposes. The relationship between politics and economics thus became the ideological basis for cold wars between would-be superpowers.

Ideology involves falling in love with ideas that further a certain group's or state's concrete interests. Such action-oriented nests of ideas or worldviews serve to shore up the legitimacy of elites in power. The pragmatic individualism and empiricism of Anglo-Saxon thought served as the backdrop of the birth of the Industrial Revolution in the 19th century. More specifically, Adam Smith's classical liberal doctrine of maximizing self-interest was a precondition for the emergence of the Industrial Revolution in Britain.

Students of international political economy often ask themselves concerning the origins of the Industrial Revolution: Why Europe first? Why England? While conditions other than economic ideology are necessary for a sufficient explanation in answering these questions, contemporary historical developments suggest that individual self-interest and organizational efforts to optimize what already exists, which are the engines of motivation behind industrial capitalism, are ideas without which no adequate explanation is possible. The notion of "industrial society" is an ideological objective of Western modernization rooted in ideas of individual and group self-interest, accumulation, and autonomy—with all the positive and negative implications of these priorities.[5]

Of course, another basis of the Industrial Revolution underlying the British development was the birth of technology itself, which dates in its modern sense at least back to the first half of the 18th century. "**Technology**" derives from the Greek word *techne*, meaning skill or craft, combined with "ology"—organized, systematic, purposeful knowledge. By applying knowledge in systematic ways, the Industrial Revolution demystified the secrecy of the craft guilds, where access was limited and "skill" was assumed to be based upon experience. Apprenticeship schools of applied knowledge emerged in Germany. In the last half of the 18th century, Britain shifted its patent system from monopolies for those favored by the monarchy to a system of rewards for inventors applying their work to tools and production processes. Collective learning thus shifted to become applied learning diffused throughout the population—the diffusion of technology that was to make capitalism the dominant form of political economy in the Western world.

The Americans consolidated the economic power of the British by following their Industrial Revolution with a "productivity revolution," which was stimulated by the influence of Frederick Winslow Taylor (1856–1915). Taylor applied knowledge to the analysis of work, inventing "scientific management." While the model British gentleman and aristocrat was schooled to look down upon mere work, Americans celebrated the independence and wealth it promised if properly organized and administered. Taylor attacked the mythology of "skilled work," arguing that there was no "skilled work," just "work," which could be analyzed in the same way through "task studies." Such task studies reduced redundant movements and sought out the most efficient tools for the job. Upsetting both the managerial classes and union leadership, Taylor said that the benefits resulting from his universal workplace efficiencies would be enjoyed primarily by workers—a prediction that ultimately proved to be accurate. Taylor's systematic method of "task studies" enabled the Americans to organize their military machine quickly in order to win World War II. It also permitted the Japanese to mobilize their workforce in order to win the "cold-war peace" economically.[6]

The influence of Anglo-Saxon ideas upon the world economy deepened with the impact of John Maynard Keynes' *The General Theory of Employment, Interest and Money (1936)*, emerging as a therapy for the Great Depression that began in 1929. A father of the "mixed economy," Keynes focused upon the role of capital investment in providing for national economic growth and stability. In bad times, the government was to intervene in the economy by increasing the money supply and government spending to stimulate the demand for production, which in turn would increase employment. In boom times government was to cool down the economy by intervening to tighten up the money supply, thus reducing demand to assure stable growth. Since government spending is more popular with democratic populations than are government austerity measures, Keynesian policy prescriptions, which have predominated in Western industrialized countries, have had an inflationary, debt-creating bias upon the structure of the world economy.

Anglo-Saxon ideology has "structured" much of world economy since the British Empire dominated it in the nineteenth century and the American regime in the twentieth century. *Pax Britannica* was followed up with *pax Americana*. The compatibility of President Ronald Reagan and Prime Minister Margaret Thatcher on policies of political economy was no accident: It was the cultural outcome of a traditional "special relationship."

But the majority of the world's nations and peoples are not of the Anglo-Saxon culture. Yet they find themselves asked to play by its rules of the economic game and to speak its language. For British hegemony—or power domination—was replaced by American hegemony after World War II, epitomized by the system of Western monetary and trade agreements emerging in 1944 in Bretton Woods, New Hampshire. To the victors went the spoils. Only the United States had the military and financial power to enforce its economic will and to attempt to impose its classical liberal vision upon the world economy. As Louis Hartz noted in his classic work *The Liberal Tradition in America* (1955), the United States skipped the feudal stage of history and the revolutionary reaction against feudalism. Since Americans basically know only what they have experienced, they could never really understand the left-wing rebellion against feudalism (socialism) nor the right-wing reaction to socialism (fascism). In short, rugged individualistic liberalism based upon Anglo-Saxon roots was all Americans knew. Their liberal ideology was rigid and dogmatic. Any form of socialist thought, much less fascist thought, was simply incomprehensible. Americans tended to see the world in terms of black-and-white categories of laissez-faire capitalism versus state-controlled, socialist communism.[7]

THE MORAL DILEMMA OF LIBERALISM

Once these black-and-white categories of the cold war collapsed along with the Berlin Wall in 1989, the ideology of American liberalism confronted a moral dilemma: if the self-maximizing principles of democratic liberal markets had "won," what could be the community limits to this self-aggrandizement?

What, in short, could become the basis of social ethics in managing economic and political change?

Political philosopher Michael Sandel argued in *Liberalism and the Limits of Justice* (1982) that American liberalism involves a notion of the "thin self," or minimal self, "free" to satisfy basic needs or lowest common denominator views of what is "good." For, while the ideal vision of liberalism assumes that "justice" or "duty to do the right thing" is more important than what any one person believes is "good" personally, this notion of justice is too abstract to serve as a practical standard in everyday life. As a consequence, people in liberal societies tend to forget about "justice" and to maximize their own views of what is "good"—often defined in terms of their own selfish interests in the short run. Truly ethical human beings of "character," on the other hand, are "thickly constituted selves" with a sense of duty to a specific community, friends, and long-term commitments.

Such ethical human beings are threatened with being swept away in a liberal American economy that seeks to speed up the maximization of individual and corporate interest over everything else for the sake of economic competitiveness. Mobility and quick adaptation are the qualities rewarded in the economy of the "virtual corporation," where society demands instant consumer satisfaction from companies.[8] **Virtual organizations** are collective learning networks which can almost instantaneously produce and deliver products or services at any time, in any place and in any variety to satisfy a specific customer. In contrast, individuals who cling to local communities, friends, and long-term commitments in a specific place risk poverty as the price for their ethical stance. Just consider the example of the barely surviving independent farmer in rural areas of the world.

GLOBAL LOGIC VERSUS COMMUNITY IDENTITY

The moral dilemma of liberalism is becoming a global moral dilemma in the post-cold-war era. The spread of free market capitalism has speeded up and become more diffuse as formerly "socialist" states have attempted to privatize certain industries or institutions in an effort to attract foreign investment and to stimulate economic growth. However, this global logic of world markets is countered by several significant trends. On the one hand, regional blocs are being formed. At the same time, we see movements of local ethnic groups and community resistance to change for the sake of preserving collective identity and cultural traditions. This book will focus on the ways in which communities, organizations, regions, and states use collective learning processes to adapt to the global logic of capitalism, while struggling to preserve their ethical and cultural integrity. The global economic "standard" of free-market liberalism will be used as a point of departure for collective learning that resists or transcends it, or, for collective learning that turns back towards it. Which will it be: more market or more state? (or community?) That nations outside the Anglo-Saxon heritage are often ambivalent about adopting free market liberalism is understandable from a recent historical perspective.

One could not blame the majority of the world's nations and peoples if they were to perceive the hegemony or domination of the Anglo-Saxon culture and its incorporation in American economic liberalism to be self-serving. They look back to the nineteenth century and see colonial expansion by established Western nations, a time when mobility of labor and capital over state boundaries was much more taken for granted, and they discover unfair advantages seized by Western states in building up national wealth and power.[9] By the time that many of the world's nations became politically independent after World War II, most of the earth's prime real estate in terms of resources was already occupied and legal boundaries had been erected between states, which regulated and slowed down the flow of labor and capital among them. The doctrine of classical economic liberalism tracing back to Adam Smith and advocated by the Americans focused upon the more efficient use of the status quo allocation of existing resources, not upon their redistribution or radical restructuring for the sake of the disadvantaged. International law was defined as stable reciprocity in terms of protecting existing ownership and contracts. Classical economic liberalism's assumption that the world economy would become more prosperous and peaceful if each nation used its existing stakes or "comparative advantages" more efficiently did not permit for any redistribution of shares among peoples, more or less guaranteeing a widening gap between the wealth of the rich, established nations and the poor, developing countries.

By the end of 1990 the inequality of income worldwide was striking: Of 185 countries, in terms of income per head, 45 countries had an annual average of $330, 41 countries of $820, 39 countries of $2,400, 11 countries of $4,360 and 50 countries of $19,520. In short, the top 50 countries in terms of income earned more per capita *per week* ($375) than average individuals in the bottom 45 countries earned *per year* ($330).[10]

The inequality among nations and peoples has become more pronounced in the postmodern world economy. Technological development and socioeconomic change have accelerated the tempo of modern life. The gap between the haves and have-nots has grown as those with property were positioned to benefit the most from the opportunities evolving from this historical transformation. As the logic of time seemed to speed up, the logic of space contracted with international communications, transportation, and financial flows. Major events such as the dropping of the gold standard, the 1973 quadrupling of oil prices by OPEC (Organization of Oil Exporting Countries), the rise of Japanese competitiveness, the debt crisis in the developing countries, the collapse of communist regimes in Eastern Europe, the nuclear arms race, and the nuclear accident at Chernobyl demonstrated that postmodern technological and socioeconomic events can only be fully understood in global terms.

The **postmodern sensibility** is one of no-nonsense disenchantment: The Industrial Revolution has come and gone, leaving uncompetitive manufacturers, perforated nation-states, impotent central banks, restructured conglomerates, miseducated youth, the proliferation of waste, and the still undigested split between the real economy (which produces goods) and the capital economy (which speculates on the spreads between borrowing rates and rates of return on investment). Postmodernism is postindustrialism never achieved, narcissism going sour, socialism approaching bankruptcy, and capitalism spreading fast throughout the globe—speeding up the socioeconomic tempo to the disproportionate advantage of the haves. The many parts of the globe that have yet to experience an industrial revolution are often told to forget about it by postmodern opinion-makers for the sake of ecology, if not for their own competitiveness. Quality of life is the postmodern preoccupation: Money is the means, a trophy, an indicator—not the end in itself. Postmodern language is that of "apolitical management"—transforming political and economic issues into technical or administrative black humor. A status job is more important than money, a safe home or maintenance base the prerequisite to entrepreneurial, existential risk-taking and world travel. The world is seen as a whole in postmodern eyes, but the differentiation between parts is more important than the wholeness.

The primacy of global logic does not go to the point of closure of Immanuel Wallerstein, who argues in *The Modern World System* (1974) that neither the sovereign state nor national society constitutes "a social system," that only the world-system constitutes a social system and that one can only speak of social change in social systems. Perhaps the primary characteristic of the postmodern world economy at the end of the twentieth century is its transitional nature between the modern nation-state system and the diffuse world social system that Wallerstein envisions. There *are* social systems that are less than global, but that may not be coterminous with the nation-state—the European Union, for example. Moreover, there are social systems of various sorts within nation-states—the Amish Mennonite community in the United States, for instance. And the anticipation of social change within discrete social systems within nation-states on the one hand and within regional organizations on the other is the critical task for those who would manage global economic change.

The fundamental problem of liberalism and globalism is ethically and politically the same: there is no commitment to *any particular here and now* or local community; all is macro, abstract, future-oriented process. But the content and character of our lives and our community are *always* here and now. Our life chances are grounded at any one point in time.

The grounding of life chances at different places on the globe is made clear when considering that in 1990 about 54 percent of the world's population lived in economies where the gross national product (GNP) per capita was less than $500. Not surprisingly, the people who live in developed countries with GNP per capita over $15,000 have the longest life expectancy at birth (73 years or more), whereas those countries with the lowest GNP have the lowest life expectancy at birth (people in Ethiopia and Sierra Leone, for example, have a life expectancy of less than 50 years).[11] To maximize your life chances, you must be born into a rich country.

But how can one picture in one's mind the extreme economic differences between the richest and poorest countries when there are some 185 of them? One way is to group them.

TIERS

In economic terms, the world can be divided into a number of tiers or layers:

I. **OECD Nations:** members of the Organization for Economic Cooperation and Development (OECD), sometimes referred to as "the rich men's club": The United States, Japan, West Germany, France, and other members of the European Union (EU), Switzerland, the Scandinavian countries, Canada, Australia, and New Zealand.

II. **Newly Industrializing Countries (NICs):** Hong Kong, the Republic of Korea, Singapore, and Taiwan. These are the most upwardly mobile of the developing countries and are characterized by economic growth rates that are often higher than the more established rich countries of the first tier.

III. **Developing Oil-exporting Nations:** a nonhomogeneous group like the others ranging from Saudi Arabia (with the largest oil reserves in the world) to Nigeria and Venezuela.

IV. **Non-oil-producing Developing Nations:** numbering about 100.

V. **"Socialist" Nations:** a heterogeneous mix that appears to be declining in number with the end of the cold war: North Korea, China, and Cuba.

Since the 1930s, about two-thirds of world trade has taken place within the first tier.[12] Compared with the early 1970s, the industrialized nations' share of world trade has shrunk a bit: In 1973 more than 70 percent of total world exports and imports was transacted by industrial countries compared to 68 percent for imports and 66 percent of exports in 1985. By 1992, the value of the industrialized economies' merchandise exports and imports still made up about 70 percent of world trade, increasing about 2 percent in 1991, the smallest increase since 1985. Meanwhile, in 1991, the exports of developing countries increased by some 10 percent in volume and imports by about 9 percent. This trend contrasted with a sharp fall in the volume of trade in the five eastern European countries, where exports fell 10 percent in value.[13]

The first tier of the wealthy OECD countries is where the majority of the world's trade and investment takes place: The majority of foreign direct investment (that is, multinational companies setting up manufacturing facilities abroad) occurs in this arena. And the radical transformation in the world economy toward the importance of financial instruments and away from manufacturing—toward the internationalization of capital—has been initiated by the OECD group. Notwithstanding the rise in manufactured goods originating in the second tier, the increase in oil revenues by the third tier, and the growth in direct bank lending to the fourth tier, the changes most responsible for the present global disequilibrium have come *within* the first tier in the past two decades.[14] The rich, in short, basically trade with and invest in the rich and are the prime movers in determining the direction of change in the postmodern world economy.

MANAGING CHANGE AND ENTREPRENEURIAL RISK

The world political economy can be seen as a lopsided pair of scissors in which the global system represents a large, heavy blade while the individual country, international organization, or multinational corporation represents a thin "counter"-blade. Effective management of change involves human coordination so that the thin, more dependent blade functions in harmony with the predominant global reality.

The thinner and more dependent the small blade—as in the case of the poorest of the developing countries—the more the managers or elites seek control and stability, or the equilibrium that keeps them in power and makes their domestic economy appear predictable enough to merit foreign aid and investment.[15] The wealthier countries and multinational firms, in contrast, can more easily take equilibrium for granted. They can use this base of stability to take risks for entrepreneurship and technological innovation. Their managers can concern themselves with strategies of dynamic equilibrium in coordinating with the large global reality. They can speed up their learning curves.

Many of the wealthy, however, fail to take advantage of this dynamic management potential inherent in their privileged position, preferring instead to minimize their risks for the sake of preserving a status quo which is so friendly to their interests. They fail to save *or* to invest enough. Hence, there is an understandable conservative bias on the part of both rich and poor alike to seek out stability and to optimize the existing equilibrium they perceive in crisis rather than to take long-term risks in order to adjust effectively to the rapidly changing postmodern global political economy. The aim of this book is not only to explain the widespread human failure to take farsighted risks for the sake of adjustment and global economic prosperity, but also to illustrate "breakthrough" models of collective learning and structural positioning that have led to economic and political success in the period since World War II.

In English, "crisis" implies a short-term juncture or turning point. In Italian, it derives from the word "process." And the Chinese symbol for crisis also signifies "hidden opportunity." To manage global change astutely requires a collective philosophy of viewing economic crisis as a long-term learning process in which one systematically takes advantage of hidden opportunities.

HOW THIS BOOK WORKS

This book is divided into five parts: (I) Concepts for Managing Change, (II) The Global Environment, (III) From North-North to North-South, (IV) Domestic Sources of Multinational Behavior, and (V) Conclusions. The parts make up a theory of collective learning defined in terms of reciprocal interactions among global *environment,* domestic sources of multinational *behavior,* and the use of *collective cognitive strategies of management.* For the reader's sake, the parts are further united by a simplifying leitmotif or theme, on the one hand, and a common-sense thesis or recipe for action, on the other. The leitmotif is the global diffusion of the principle of laissez-faire liberalism as the engine for economic growth and the postliberal reactions to this principle and efforts to transcend it. The common-sense prescription for action is simply that human beings can learn collectively to manage economic change by establishing a limited, efficient, risk-reducing maintenance base (or "home base") from which they are able to launch targeted risk-taking entrepreneurial and creative endeavors.

Part One defines the key concepts for managing change using the collective learning and positioning perspective. It then illustrates how these concepts relate to the tensions in the post-cold-war global economy between classical liberal and Keynesian macroeconomic principles, on the one hand, and local and regional efforts to protect cultural and ethnic identity politically, on the other.

Part Two focuses upon the two key areas of the global environment for managing organizational change: namely, the world monetary system and the world trade system.

Part Three contrasts the meaning of competitiveness in the leading industrialized countries of "the North"—Japan, Germany and the United States—with the structures and strategies of North-South relations—from the World Bank to the Lomé Convention to the environmental perspective to the "economic miracles" of East Asia.

Part Four concentrates on the domestic sources of multinational behavior—from elements of collective life chances, education, and socioeconomic

positioning to state strategies of economic development to the direct investment, incentives, and cycles affecting multinational corporations.

Part Five summarizes conclusions that can be drawn from the book,
ending with a list of recipes for collective learning for managers interested in
developing economic competitiveness without sacrificing cultural integrity.
To a great extent we end up where we begin the following chapter—with the
management concepts necessary to cope with the revolutionary changes in
the world economy signaled by the end of the cold war.

THOUGHT QUESTIONS

1. Why does the increase in the speed of globalization matter in the relationship between the rich and the poor? Define "international political
   economy" in comparison with "international relations," "political science," or "economics."

2. What did Adam Smith mean by "liberalism" and what conditions have
   changed the meaning of this concept today? What are the ethical
   morals of liberalism? Of postmodernism? Of postliberalism?

3. How would John Maynard Keynes manage the global economy in a
   time of deep recession? Of economic boom?

4. What does "technology" mean and how did Frederick Taylor apply it to
   management? How does technology relate to (a) how fast people
   learn? (b) average per capita income in different countries?

NOTES

1. Notable among the recent exceptions who do take a global view of political
   economy are: Peter Dicken, *Global Shift: The Internationalization of Economic Activ-
   ity* (New York: The Guilford Press, 1992); Kenichi Ohmae, *The Borderless World:
   Power and Strategy in the Interlinked Economy* (New York: HarperCollins, 1991);
   Wilhelm Hankel, *Weltwirtschaft* (Wien: Econ Verlag, 1977); W. Arthur Lewis, *The
   Evolution of the International Economic Order* (Princeton, NJ: Princeton University
   Press, 1977); Immanuel Wallerstein, *The Capitalist World-Economy* (Cambridge:
   Cambridge University Press, 1979); Independent Commission on International
   Development Issues (Brandt Commission), *North–South: A Program for Survival:
   Cooperation for World Recovery* (Cambridge, MA: MIT Press, 1983); Harold K. Ja-
   cobson and Susan Sidjanski, eds., *The Emerging International Economic Order* (Bev-
   erly Hills, CA: Sage Publications, 1982); Johan Galtung, *The True Worlds: A
   Transnational Perspective* (New York: Free Press, 1980); and Garret Hardin and J.
   Raden, eds., *Managing the Commons* (San Francisco: W.H. Freeman & Co.,
   1977).

2. See R. Isaak, "The Conservative Tradition of American Liberalism," Introduction to *American Political Thinking: Readings from the Origins to the 21st Century*
   (Fort Worth, Texas: Harcourt Brace, 1994).

3. See, for example, Charles E. Lindblom, *Politics and Markets: The World's Political-Economic Systems* (New York: Basic Books, 1977).

4. Ibid., p. ix.

5. See Richard J. Badham, *Theories of Industrial Society* (New York: St. Martin's Press, 1986).

6. Although "productivity" was not used as a concept in Frederick Taylor's era, his *Scientific Management* (Westport, Conn.: Greenwood Press, 1972) aims at the same thing. On Taylor's neglected significance and the impact of his ideas on the world economy, see Peter Drucker, *Post-Capitalist Society* (New York: Harper-Collins, 1993), pp. 32–40. For the need to transcend "Taylorism" in the 21st century, see Yuji Masuda, ed., *Human-Centered Systems in the Global Economy* (London: Springer-Verlag, 1992).

7. Hartz's continuing relevance is demonstrated in Robert A. Packenham, *Liberal America and the Third World* (Princeton, NJ: Princeton University Press, 1973).

8. See William H. Davidow and Michael S. Malone, *The Virtual Corporation: Structuring and Revitalizing the Corporation for the 21st Century* (New York: Harper-Collins, 1992) and R. Isaak, "Virtual Organizations: From Entrepreneurial Networks to Strategic Alliances," a paper presented at the International Symposium on "Networking of Human Relations and Technology" at Tokyo Keizai University, October 25, 1993, Tokyo, and revised for presentation at the International Seminar, "Training for Change," at the *Institut d'Administration des Enterprises,* at Aix-en-Provence, May 5, 1994.

9. See, for example, Mahbub ul Haq, *The Poverty Curtain: Choices for the Third World* (New York: Columbia University Press, 1976).

10. Statistics from *The World Bank Atlas 1991* (Washington, D.C., The World Bank, 1991), p. 10.

11. Statistics from *World Bank Atlas 1991,* pp. 3, 6–9.

12. André Frank, *Crisis in the World Economy* (New York: Holmes and Meier, 1980), p. 4.

13. Statistics from *World Economic Survey 1992: Current Trends and Policies in the World Economy* (New York: United Nations, 1992), pp. 49–52.

14. James M. Cypher, "Global Disequilibrium: The Instability of Interdependent Accumulation," *Economic Forum,* XI (Winter 1980–81): 23.

15. See Stephen D. Krasner, *Structural Conflict: The Third World Against Global Liberalism* (Berkeley: University of California Press, 1985).

CHAPTER ONE

COLLECTIVE
LEARNING
AND POSITIONING

In the knowledge economy, imperfect competition seems to be inherent in the economy itself. Initial advantages gained through early application and exploitation of knowledge (that is, through what has come to be known as the "learning curve") become permanent and irreversible.

Peter Drucker

Knowledge is the orderly loss of information.

Kenneth Boulding

The postmodern world economy is characterized by too much information to digest. "To know" has come to mean to lose as much of this information overload as possible in a systematic way in order to have a few basic principles or categories left over. The managers of the World Bank, IBM, or the U.S. Federal Reserve attempt to cut the quick from the dead in this thicket of data: "News" is some breakpoint in an expected trend or an habitual image of how things usually work. Significant news is often decked over by the superfluous. When it became apparent in the early 1980s, for example, that the nine largest U.S. banks had lent three times the amount they held in equity to developing countries, which had become incapable of paying back the interest on the loans, *The New York Times* published this sensitive news in a small article buried in its least-read Saturday edition. "Knowledge" that suggests "the sky is falling" could send the financial markets into a downward spiral and undermine the Western financial system.

This view of knowledge, however, has a conservative bias. Like Adam Smith's classical notion of capitalism, the motive behind it appears to be to understand the existing equilibrium and to optimize what already exists. In the asymmetrical international political economy, such viewpoints appear to further the interests of the minority of the rich nations rather than the interests of the majority of the poor: Optimizing what exists implies an inevitability in the status quo. Knowledge is limited to how things are. Classical liberal capitalism is concerned with the growth of things that exist, with maintaining them with greater efficiency, productivity, and effectiveness. What *could* exist, be created, or developed is excluded from the view of knowledge as systematically sifted left-over information or from Adam Smith's stress upon optimization.[1]

What is at stake here is the illusion that the classical economic liberalism of Adam Smith is always on the side of "progress." Initially, the private pursuit of self-interest is a powerful motivator, leading individuals and groups to accumulate great stores of private wealth through individual efficiency, rationalization, and productivity. But eventually a point is reached in a capitalist society where so many people have succeeded in creating plump private nest eggs that their interests shift from efficient productivity to risk-reducing maintenance of that which they have already accumulated. The state of rugged individualism becomes the affluent welfare state: Risktaking for future gains is overwhelmed by risk-reducing insurance against possible losses. Or, as economist Joseph Schumpeter suggested, capitalist societies succeed only to do themselves in: The very wealth and leisure that their economic success makes possible provide the means for counterculture lifestyles and motives that undermine the work ethic and efficient rationality that led to the economic success in the first place.[2] From this perspective, the world political economy is characterized by a minority of old, rich capitalist societies conservatively attempting to preserve their past gains (OECD countries); another upcoming minority of "new rich" newly industrializing countries (NICs); a majority of "nonaligned" poor, developing countries without the capital or resources to get their own systems of dynamic economic growth started; and a small, mixed group of socialist states increasingly tempted by the economic success of the old-rich and new-rich nations but ideologically or culturally blocked from moving too fast in the direction of capitalism. The basic theme of this undertaking is the conflict between efficiently maintaining the old versus effectively creating the new in order to adapt to global economic change.

THE ARGUMENT

The argument here is that the only way that individuals, economic organizations, and states can cope effectively with global economic change (and the information overload it implies) is through a process of collective learning and structural positioning. Effective collective learning breaks beyond status quo-conditioned maintenance models to initiate targeted, innovative, strategic risktaking and adaptation.

Collective learning involves three elements: *environment, behavior,* and *strategy*. At any moment in historical time, a group of people find themselves in both an organizational and global environment. Within this environment, they are motivated to act according to cultural habits or patterns of behavior shaped by national and organizational traditions. Finally, in order to survive and to succeed economically, the group must develop managerial or cognitive strategies that enable them to use scarce resources effectively in competition with other groups.

In order to create strategies, the group must first know what it wants to preserve of its cultural tradition and what it is willing to risk for the sake of adaptation, growth, and development. Collective learning is based on a distinction between the organizational maintenance base and entrepreneurial risk. The **maintenance base** maximizes efficiency, stability, and risk reduction inside the organization. **Entrepreneurial risk,** in contrast, stresses effectiveness, risktaking, export growth, and customer and niche creation in the external arena of domestic and global markets. The focus of collective learning is upon the entrepreneurial "breakpoints" or developmental "takeoff" points in corporations or states that result in improved competitive positions in the world economy. "Economic miracles" are assumed *not* to be miracles: they are, rather, effective collective adaptive responses to turbulent change.

Take the cases of West Germany and Japan in the post–World War II period. These nations can be viewed as "tight ships in a storm." The efficient reconstruction of the maintenance base of their political economies was combined with targeted external policies of entrepreneurship and export-oriented growth to create their "economic miracles." Of course, it is significant that the global environment was friendly. The U.S. bankrolled the world monetary system with dollar credits and the 1950s and 1960s were marked with dynamic global economic growth. That West Germany and Japan received a privileged opportunity from their domineering "godfather," the United States (which also took care of their military security), does not distract from their effective collective use of this opportunity. **Hegemony** means domination. A **hegemon** is a state or organization that dominates others in its region or in the world. To the extent that Germany and Japan have become hegemons in their regions, if not at times in the global economy, the most fruitful focus is upon the recipes for hegemony that led to their prosperous condition rather than upon a passive lamentation of the injustices involved in the creation of such superior economic positions. The weak have more to learn from the strong than the strong from the weak if economic competitiveness and full employment are the social objectives sought. While not neglecting the weak, this book will focus upon the recipes of the strong.

In the United States the maintenance base functions differently from that in West Germany and Japan. The ordered chaos of the largest domestic market in the world provides constant economic opportunities and new consumption choices through continuous restructuring within this entrepreneurial, newly rich society: The turbulence of the outside markets is brought home to create jobs through flexible investment opportunities and corporate reorganizations for both the American and global markets. The government serves as the gatekeeper and as a major customer, insuring the heavy debt structure of the society to keep up the cash flow. Dogmatic classical economic liberalism is the basis for the rugged individualism of the American political economy: It may be all the United States knows (as Louis Hartz suggests). But unlike all other societies, given the wealthy endowment of natural resources, it may be all the United States thinks it needs.

However, classical laissez-faire liberalism may be a wasteful, experimental approach to economic problem solving in a technocratic global economy with resource scarcity and payoffs for tightly structured teamwork. The American assumption that each individual will learn mainly from his or her *own* experience (what can be called "learning by burning") implies a multitude of duplicate learning experiences and a host of failures in an uncoordinated trial-by-error approach. The question is whether or not the rest of the world can afford to continue to subsidize the wasteful individualism that is part and parcel of American liberalism. In *The Waste of Nations* (1989), economist Douglas Dowd documents U.S. consumer, military, industrial, agricultural, and human waste and characterizes the style of American hegemony as "an impulsive boyish recklessness."

* * *

Collective learning is a social learning process of distinguishing legitimate patterns of adaptive behavior within an organization in order to manage environmental change without losing cultural integrity.

Albert Bandura of Stanford University defined *social learning theory* as the result of reciprocal interactions among person (or cognition), behavior, and the environmental situation.[3] This is a stimulus-organism-response theory. It assumes that individuals can learn from others vicariously—that is, by *modeling* their own behavior after others whom they have observed.[4] I might, for example, learn by watching a famous tennis player on television always to hit the ball to my opponent's weakest side or backhand. I could learn by watching the tennis celebrity win a tournament using this method. In other words, "learning by burning"—or from one's own experience alone— is not always necessary. It is often cheaper and wiser to learn from others to avoid making the same mistakes oneself. One can learn to manage well by watching other excellent managers in action, and so forth.

Collective learning theory is distinguished from social learning: it is social learning within a specific organizational context and cultural tradition. This cultural tradition is a pattern (or *gestalt*) made up of indigenous **schemata,** that is, prototypes of meaning in a specific culture used for processing information and "branding" it with particular interpretations.[5] To learn within such a cultural tradition involves cognitive change that brings about reframing that eventually can result in new schemata. Such learning can be stimulated from outside the culture, provided that the stimulus is transparent and comprehensible from the viewpoint of the natives within. Such a cultural collectivity or organization has *boundaries* that are marked not by an enveloping membrane but by a behavioral design.[6] Such a behavioral design is characterized by many interacting habits of behavior in conformity to modes of action prescribed by the design. (For example, in Nazi Germany, behaviors included the fascist salute, the goosestep march, and systematic submission to those giving orders up the hierarchy.)

As another example, schemata for the culture of the United States could be identified as including a pattern of perceiving information that stamps all rugged, individualistic actions representing "one-against-the-world" self-sufficiency as "good" and anything else as a form of moral compromise (symbolized by actors John Wayne or Clint Eastwood). However, the stimulus of winning teamwork on the part of Germany and Japan might lead to learning that results in a new schemata—the individual as most respectable as a leader of a winning team (symbolized by Michael Maccoby's *The Gamesman,* showing that the true corporate winners of the 1970s in the U.S. were leaders of winning teams.)[7] A further new schemata may eventually be introduced encouraging all members of the team to think of themselves as potential leaders, thereby making the team less dependent upon any one person. The sooner all members see themselves as important stakeholders in a group, the more effective the collective learning of the team will be.

Learning how to learn is thus a social process structured by organizational relationships between individuals and colored by common cultural assumptions. The cultural tradition or pattern framing the collective learning in Japan, for example, is characterized by a "tight" neo-Confucian hierarchical pattern in which lifelong education represents a dynamic receptivity by the people to new learning, setting them up continually for collective cultural and economic development.[8] The cultural pattern of the German culture is a "work-oriented" socialization process in which the majority of teenagers become involved in hands-on vocational training in targeted apprenticeship programs sponsored by corporate-union-government partnership. Compare the German and Japanese patterns, or networks, of schemata with the U.S. cultural tradition of "loose" laissez-faire individualism, in which the "socialization" of immigrants and young people into American values and civic legal arrangements is the focus of the educational system rather than either hands-on work training or a commitment to lifelong learning for its own sake.[9]

Thus, collective learning in a particular culture legitimates certain models of learning and excludes others. It involves comparing how different groups of people learn how to learn—what anthropologist Gregory Bateson called **deutero-learning.** Bateson observed that democratic societies are based on specific learning contexts or meta-learning patterns. People learn to decide in democratic ways, picking it up as if by osmosis from the structure of the culture in which they live.[10] If the dominant learning models of such cultures become "split" or "polarized," political economic effectiveness breaks down.[11] For example, the elites of highly developed societies (such as England) may come to look down upon mere wealth creation or moneymaking, free-riding upon its "bourgeois" industrial base. Simultaneously, such snobs undermine the authority of hands-on management by declassing its status, legitimacy, and motivation.[12] "High policy" learning models and lifestyles become split off from "low policy" entrepreneurial and maintenance management functions critical for creating economic wealth.

When, eventually, the wealth of the upper class aristocracy declines and this group is declassed by socioeconomic change, as in the case of the downward mobility of the Balinese aristocracy or the samurai of Japan, aristocrats from a feudal tradition often resurrect their entrepreneurial capacities, turning to business to recover their sense of purpose, to create new wealth, and to reverse their decline in status.[13] Thus collective learning involves the shifting legitimacy of various learning modes or models over generations or even centuries with direct economic consequences for the life chances of those in the communities involved. Such generational waves of collective learning or adaptation transcend contemporary ideological movements (such as capitalism and socialism). They also transcend Western dichotomies such as the politics of productivity versus the politics of redistribution, which have been used to characterize shifts in developed political economies during the last half of the twentieth century.[14]

Two things come together to provide the context in which collective learning takes place in the world economy: global capitalism and the nation-state system. Hegemony or competitive dominance in this context is conditioned by both economic and political structures inherited from the past. Economic development, however, is often the measure of breaking beyond these intimidating structures, using them merely as springboards for a particular organization's agenda or a state's own purposes.

CREATIVE DESTRUCTION
AND GLOBAL ECONOMIC DEVELOPMENT

Joseph Schumpeter characterized capitalism as a process of **creative destruction** in which the new incessantly drives out the old. Technological innovation or development led by the dynamism of the entrepreneur is the engine driving this vision of capitalism. "Development" is defined as spontaneous economic change within a nation not forced upon it from without. Development goes beyond mere growth (or the optimization and expansion of what already exists): It implies that something new and distinctive is being produced by spontaneous design or planning that makes a nation (or organization) less dependent upon others. Producers are the agents that usually initiate development, whether they be private entrepreneurs in capitalist systems or apparatchik managers in socialist systems.[15] The dynamic for development emerges from some domestic or national base or other, not from the international system as a whole. Power is homemade.* However, for the overwhelming majority of nations of the world, the economic effectiveness of that power abroad depends upon how national development is managed to fit the markets of the capitalist world economy.

In 1979 Johan Galtung predicted that a new, profoundly capitalist world economy would emerge by the 1990s with the control center in the Orient, not in the West. Even more bluntly, Galtung noted: "Capitalism is not down and out. There is no crisis in capitalism. There is a profound crisis in the Western [read United States and Western Europe] position inside capitalism."[16] The rising economic power of Japan, Taiwan, South Korea, and Hong Kong makes Galtung's prediction ring true, not to mention the competitive difficulties of the Unites States and Western European economies. The British prepared the way for world capitalism with their Industrial Revolution and *pax Britannica*. The United States consolidated the heritage of Anglo-Saxon economic thought, institutionalizing global capitalism at the peak of American hegemony with the Bretton Woods system and *pax Americana*. That some scholars have been surprised that the institutional framework of Bretton Woods (in modified form) has survived as American power has passed its peak may be because they have focused too much upon "institutional inertia" from an American perspective rather than looking at the universal dynamism of capitalism from a global perspective.[17]

The increasing tempo of global social and economic change in the late twentieth century clarifies why international managers and students of international political economy seek some simplifying category or overarching theory to keep the turbulent process of creative destruction in perspective.

---

*And goods, accordingly, should be "homespun" with capital remaining at home to benefit the nation and the nation's working class—argued John Maynard Keynes during the Great Depression. Cf. J.M. Keynes, "National Self-Sufficiency," *Yale Review* 22: 755–69.

Human beings are overwhelmed by future shock and a sense of loss—from the microelectronic revolution to the decay of Western status-order systems that gave hierarchical meaning to the economic world. Perhaps preoccupied with the sense of loss in global status of their own nation since its historical peak following World War II, American students of international political economy often focused upon what they called "hegemonic stability theory" in the 1980s to explain what was happening to them.

HEGEMONIC STABILITY AND IDEOLOGY

Hegemonic stability theory emerged from an interpretation of the Great Depression beginning in 1929, which attributed its width and depth to the absence of a leading country willing and able to bear a disproportionate share of the costs to discharge the responsibilities of a stabilizer. Or, to put the theory positively: a stable world economic system requires the existence of a single great power state or *hegemon* willing and able to furnish an outlet for distress goods, maintain the flow of capital to would-be borrowers, serve as lender of last resort in financial crises, maintain a structure of exchange rates, and coordinate macroeconomic policies. The father of this theory, economist Charles P. Kindleberger, called the key stabilizer nation a "leader," not a "hegemon." He noted that "Political science has now transmuted the concept of leadership into 'hegemony,' a word that makes me uncomfortable because of its overtones of force, threat, pressure."[18] The clearest modern examples of such leaders or hegemons are Great Britain in the nineteenth century (to a limited extent) and the United States after World War II (the historical example *par excellence*).[19]

The hegemon provides stability by disproportionately subsidizing collective or public goods in the world political economy, such as an open market economy based upon an open liberal trading regime, or a stable international currency or an international security system. A *public or collective good* is one that is not reduced for use by other potential consumers even after consumption by an individual, household, company, or state (a road, sidewalk, or ocean, for example). In addition to paying more than its share of the costs, the hegemon has to try to manage the *"free-rider problem,"* namely, the dilemma of so-called cheaters who free-ride upon collective or public goods without paying their "fair share." Thus, with America's decline in hegemony in the late twentieth century, it is little wonder that U.S. managers push their allies for "burden sharing" or picking up more of the economic and security costs of maintaining the global political economic system. From the perspective of the collective learning theory, however, the free-rider strategy is a rational, collective mode of behavior that certain individuals, companies, states, and international organizations utilize in historical situations where they have few other options: The poor, for example, often have little choice about being free riders. In an era of great mobility and economic uncertainty, the free-rider strategy may even appear to be the optimum mode of managing economic change for a majority of people.

However, theorists of hegemonic stability have been surprised by recent history. Since the 1944 Bretton Woods agreement establishing the International Monetary Fund (IMF) and (later) the General Agreement on Tariffs and Trade (GATT) for trade cooperation, American hegemony seemed to decline. And yet the world economy continued to remain basically stable and the institutions emerging from Bretton Woods continued to perform their stabilizing functions. This nest of American-driven institutional arrangements has been referred to as **regimes**—or "principles, norms, and decision-making procedures around which actor expectations converge."[20] And the continuation or effective residue of these regimes despite the relative decline in power of the U.S. hegemon provided the puzzle that seemed most to preoccupy American students of international political economy in the 1980s. That such a preoccupation may be ethnocentric, premature, or understate the actual American economic and military power position remains an often-neglected point of view.[21]

From the standpoint of theory, the hegemonic stability focus is but an unproven historical examination of one exceptional case before the story is over. No other nation will ever be likely to possess the nuclear monopoly enjoyed by the United States after World War II. Nor is it easy to imagine that another nation would have the abundance of resources and large domestic market of the Americans. Even the language of *hegemony* and *regime* has the flavor of a premature attempt to put historical distance between the analyst and the contemporary situation—a somewhat schizophrenic impulse to squeeze the unique quality out of the American case so as to explain continuity or decline in the world political economy. But the conservative bias of this perspective is unmistakable: Global information is being eliminated in an orderly manner to sort out the big fish (the U.S. hegemon) from the little ones (the other some 184 countries and territories for which the annual *World Bank Atlas* lists statistics) even if the big fish should turn out to be as rare as Moby Dick.

The word *hegemony* originated with the founder of the Italian Communist Party, Antonio Gramsci. Gramsci defined hegemony as a form of consciousness in which other social classes or the population as a whole accept an order in which one social class is dominant.[22] The "embedded" liberal economic order, embodied in the institutions, rules and habits of the Bretton Woods system dominated by the United States, is the case in point. The thrust for openness of classical liberalism has become "embedded" in the Bretton Woods hegemony of institutions because of the ongoing compromises this liberalism has made with domestic state demands for social stability and full employment.

Hegemony is usually associated with conservative habits or a "right-wing" ideology. Philosopher Silvan Tomkins defined right-wing ideology or conservatism as the belief that human beings realize themselves only through struggle toward, participation in, and conformity to, a norm, a measure, or an ideal essence basically independent of human beings. "Left-wing" ideology, or liberalism, in contrast considers a human being as "an end in himself, an active, creative, thinking, desiring, loving force in nature."[23] Accordingly, those who believe in sources of value outside of human beings—whether they be members of the "club" of U.S. elite universities, the French Communist Party, or the Catholic Church qualify as "conservatives."

Thus, hegemony has conservative implications when identified as the legitimate ideology of elite classes in the international system. The classic example is the balance-of-power ideology of the dominant European nations—the *ancien régime*—preceding the French Revolution. This balance-of-power hegemony broke down when the ideological elite of the *ancien régime* could no longer communicate with the counterhegemony ideology of Napoleon.[24] Napoleon's drafting of all male citizens and all-or-nothing objectives in war were incomprehensible ideas for the established balance-of-power elites who relied upon mercenary soldiers and limited rules of warfare. The rigidity of both these ideologies—anchoring value in standards outside human individuals in abstract ideals or rules—gave them a brittle, conservative quality, precipitating the breakdown of the equilibrium of the international system. Similarly, the cold war ideologies of neo-conservative *pax Americana* elites and the counterhegemony of the neo-Marxist socialist bloc threatened the stability of the 20th-century international system, until Gorbachev's reforms initiated the breakdown of the socialist bloc. On the global economic level, this ideological conflict was embodied in the defense of the Bretton Woods regime by the developed countries against counterhegemony demands of developing nations for a New International Economic Order.

Both the ideological extremes of Western capitalism and Marxism-Leninism constitute different forms of conservatism, or varieties of economic determinism: The former argues that material self-interest is the engine of economic growth and progress, the latter that class structures and conflicts determine social life. Generally these competing cold war ideologies have served as legitimizing dogmas for established elites, as shields against change in the status quo, rather than as principles of adaptation or innovation. They have tended to function as top-down deterministic rules, outside of human individuals, used to mobilize more efficiency in the existing social equilibrium of the state, not as bottom-up instigators of grass-roots individualism and risk-loving dissent.

Gorbachev attempted to break through the stalemate of the cold war logic of hegemony-counterhegemony. He tried to position himself ideologically on the side of change and of the future through his "New Thinking," leaving the defense of the old to his opponents at home and abroad. Ideologies are born radical, mature into pragmatism, and turn self-righteously in-flexible in old age as those who are heavily invested in them weigh the psy-chic and material costs of change—the **sunk costs.** Gorbachev attempted to symbolize the collective learning he knew his people would have to under-take to restructure their economy to compete in the 21st century. But his policies of reform and his reluctance to use force had the effect of dissolving not only the Eastern socialist bloc but the Soviet Union itself. Gorbachev's re-forms stimulated the spontaneous collective learning of the peoples of Poland, Hungary, Czechoslovakia, East Germany, Rumania, and Bulgaria as a domino series of democratic movements spread in 1989, leading to radical political and economic change. At home, Gorbachev soon found himself out-flanked both on his right and on his left ideologically as he desperately tried to seize the center and hold the Soviet Union together. He failed, setting the stage for the break-away radical reforms of Boris Yeltsin, who succeeded in establishing autonomy for Russia from the other Soviet Republics—Re-publics that also sought independence but with less political and financial capital as means to institutionalize their own forms of collective learning. Each of these would-be nations sought to exploit the regional collective learning dynamism to maximize its own cultural integrity and autonomy. But, many of them then fell back into ideological blinders of the past that blocked their effective adaptation to the demands of global economic com-petitiveness.

ECONOMIC NATIONALISM, LIBERALISM, AND MARXISM

The predominant ideologies that often function as blinders in the world economy of the late twentieth century are economic nationalism (or neo-mercantilism), liberalism, and Marxism. Each of these three ideologies or systematic worldviews represents a total belief system concerning human na-ture and society, which is not easily changed in the minds of true believers by logic or contrary evidence. As political scientist Robert Gilpin has demon-strated in *The Political Economy of International Relations,* while each of these ideologies or paradigms sheds some light on the workings of the world econ-omy, all of them are inherently incapable of being disproven empirically (such as the "truth" of the statement: "Chocolate ice cream *is* best because I *like* it best."). The collective learning approach used here attempts to tran-scend these ideological camps to focus upon which patterns or gestalts of human cultural organization have worked best to foster a harmony of dy-namic economic growth on the one hand, and social equity on the other. The identification of such effective collective learning patterns would benefit the objectives of any of these predominant belief systems—whether to help better target the protectionism of developing or developed countries in vital economic sectors, or to identify how to open markets domestically with least cost to the disadvantaged, or to restructure a socialist state using market incentives for economic and technological competitiveness without losing social consensus or governmental legitimacy. While the collective learning approach is biased toward successes and breakthroughs, it is indifferent as to whether these effective collective behaviors are uncovered in nation-states, multinational corporations, or international organizations.

Each of these three predominant ideologies is a reified or frozen set of beliefs used as a basis for political action in the world economy. Each, in other words, is like a spotlight in a dark amphitheater illuminating a limited part of the reality while inadvertently leaving other parts blacked out in the process.

Economic nationalism—otherwise known as **mercantilism,** statism, and protectionism—spotlights the economic and power interests of a single nation-state in competition with all others, viewing the world economy as a zero-sum game in which that not gained by the state will necessarily be lost to other competitive states. The modern nation-state system emerged from the breakdown of the unity of medieval Christendom and was first officially recognized as the European multistate system with the Peace of Westphalia in 1648 and the Treaty of Utrecht in 1713. The European conception of the sovereign state was one with a concentration of political power within it, which possessed a monopoly on the use of force within its borders.

Following the Industrial Revolution, this consolidation of political power normally corresponded with growing economic power. Economic nationalists are preoccupied with national security and the primacy of military power of the state in the international system, viewing political and economic power as a way to secure national survival. For nationalists or mercantilists, a favorable balance of trade is a prerequisite to national security, and a hard currency is a political weapon in the ceaseless struggle for status and advantage among states. Self-sufficiency, not economic interdependence, is their motto. If every economic system must rest on a secure political base, then in the terms of the collective learning approach used here, economic nationalists are preoccupied with the viability and security of this "maintenance base" defined in geographical and cultural terms. This search by the extreme realist for national unity is epitomized in a negative way by Machiavelli's observation that Italy is not a state but a mere geographical expression.

The lamp that shines from the ideology of **liberalism** looks for the maximization of individual interest and freedom, as often as not expressed in the form of economic profit. Rather than focusing upon the state, the liberal stresses the market. Critical of the zero-sum, conflictual stance of the economic nationalist, which can ultimately culminate in war, the liberal stresses the mutual gain that can come from international cooperation and interdependence: the creation of more economic pie for all through incentives for economic growth, rather than becoming bogged down in the distributional struggle for the pie that already exists (as besets the economic nationalists). The liberal position is critical of the amassing of both military and other forms of power, which can undermine economic efficiency. But the liberal preoccupation with economic success leads to a lopsided focus upon rational, economic individuals in free markets with full information to make their maximizing decisions. Social contexts, "irrational" cultural traditions, collective habits, hierarchical markets, and the normal absence of full information all become "exogenous" variables for liberal economists, variables too easily left out of their equations for not being easily quantifiable or explainable in terms of strict, individualistic, economic rationality. The state is understated, the market overmarketed.

Marxism spotlights the contradictions in the capitalist system that emerge from individuals rationally maximizing their personal interests without regard for the overall consequences for social equity and community well-being. Individual interest maximization leads to overproduction and subsequent economic contraction and unemployment, according to the Marxist thesis. Workers become impoverished and the growing gap between the bourgeois classes and proletariat or working classes will ultimately trigger a revolution and the overthrow of capitalism by a classless, socialist society of equity and solidarity. When he noted that workers within capitalist societies did not become poorer, Lenin argued in 1917 that the fault was in failing to view capitalism as a global phenomenon in which imperialism was the ultimate stage of capitalism: Financial capital in the core developed countries dominated industrial capital, and the law of uneven development assured that the capitalist, colonizing states reap the benefits of economic development, exploiting cheap labor and resources from the developing countries at the periphery of market interactions.

Modern World System theory (represented by Paul Baran, André Gunder Frank, and Emmanual Wallerstein) extends the Leninist interpretation of Marxism. It assumes that the modern world can only be understood as a global system with a single division of labor and multiple cultural systems forming an international hierarchy in the ceaseless struggle of states and classes: the advanced, dominant *core;* the newly industrializing *semi-periphery;* and the dependent, underdeveloped *periphery* (made up of most of the world's people). Modern World System theorists view state and market as epiphenomena of deeper social and economic forces that drive the world economy in a way that integrates the core and periphery so that the "metropolitan" core systematically *underdevelops* the dependent periphery areas both politically and economically.

The (Marxist) World System view, however, is often blind to political and strategic factors that can be as important in interstate relations as economic determinants. (On what basis could it have forecast the democratic uprisings in Eastern Europe in 1989, for example?) Modern World Systems theory is so preoccupied with the market processes of global capitalism—

commercial growth, worldwide recession and the spread of trade and fi-nance—that one could go as far as to suggest that without world capitalism (and its Anglo-Saxon liberal ideology) socialism as an ideology would not exist.

Each of these three ideologies or spotlights of consciousness—the state (economic nationalism), the market (liberalism), and the domestic and in-ternational economic development struggle between the haves and the have-nots (Marxism)—constitutes a different worldview of the same anarchical world. Historically, the anarchy of the international system has always been sufficient to undermine any particular oligarchy or imperial power group that has sought to impose its will upon the system.

The world has remained anarchical and oligarchical: anarchical given the absence of a monopoly of legitimate violence; oligarchical—or hierar-chic—since without civil society, right depends mainly upon might.[25] The dominant oligarchy (or hegemon) is cast in a conservative and defensive role of trying to shore up its power and influence and to maintain the system's equilibrium against inevitable disintegration or entropy. Those outside the oligarchy attempt to change the asymmetrical system in their favor and to keep what autonomy they can. Or as Thucydides observed in ancient Greece: The powerful exact what they can, and the weak grant what they must.

An **oligarchy** is a system of government in which power is invested in a few, whether one is speaking of a domestic or international system of govern-ment. The asymmetry or inequality between powerful oligarchies and weak, dependent peoples has become more pronounced since World War II. The logic of space has become global, or a question of shares of the world mar-ket. The logic of time has speeded up due to global changes in technology, finance, communication and socioeconomic fashions of modeling behavior after the most successful. Most of the advantages of the increasing tempo of technological and financial development have accrued to those best posi-tioned to take advantage of these innovations. *Positioning* is the name of the game in political economy: Rich countries (or people) seek to hold their po-sition while the poor attempt to position themselves more favorably (by join-ing the European Union, for example). *The initial starting position* carries pro-found importance in an anarchical world where physical and economic security are scarce commodities, not to mention the freedom of individual choice.

In the emerging "knowledge" or "postcapitalist" economy, the old as-sumption of "perfect competition" as the basis for the allocation of resources has become obsolete. Imperfect competition has become inherent in the economy itself. Those who gain early access to knowledge and can apply it and monopolize its distribution create what seem to be permanent and irre-versible advantages: They shorten their collective learning curves and are able to accrue the first hold on profits in newly emerging technology and knowledge-based service industries.[26] A secure base is needed, however.

THE CHANGING NATURE OF INSECURITY

During the cold war, the nature of international insecurity was defined by two superpowers that split the world into blocs. Both the U.S. and U.S.S.R. tried to maximize their hegemony, or domination, by preserving the "minimum winning coalition" of allies within their blocs and attempting to head off a global trend towards the dilution of world power into *multipolarity*—a world of many or "multi" power poles or nuclear powers. However, the effect of superpower preoccupation with security was to create an international atmosphere of insecurity—military, technological, economic, and psychological insecurity. The demands for these kinds of security appeared to be insatiable, leading to skyrocketing military and espionage budgets.

Although the cold war has ended, the primacy of insecurity—of the infinite striving for security—has not. Where military security prevails, such as in most industrialized democracies, there has merely been a shift in the form of insecurity to the economic or psychological realms, as nations seek to increase economic competitiveness and to reduce unemployment. The continuing primacy of insecurity as a concern makes the global perspective of political economy inevitably conservative. For, as the simple "balance of terror" between two blocs has fragmented into many countries and factors, the first human task appears to be to order them into a system that is capable of being stabilized in order to prevent system breakdown in the forms either of world war or of global economic depression. As the Director of the U.S. Central Intelligence Agency, James Woolsey, put it in 1993, in referring to the collapse of the U.S.S.R.: "Although the dragon was slain in the forest, there are still a lot of poisonous snakes to be found, which are harder to find and to predict." The chief new threats are spreading nuclear proliferation and terrorism. Clearly, the nuclear powers and the wealthy, developed countries are cast in a conservative role, since they have the most to lose in the event of a breakdown of the world system. Organizations or individuals representing these countries can hardly escape the dominant conservative logic of this maintenance function of preserving the status quo. The United States, as the only remaining military superpower, finds itself specialized in the role of world stabilizer whether the American people like it or not.

Security ultimately means aiming for "unconditional viability"—that is, a party, organization, or nation is considered to be secure if it cannot be absorbed as an independent source of decisions.[27] That this ideal of absolute independence, freedom, or *sovereignty* can no longer be achieved in a nuclear age of international economic interdependence does not mean it is not sought. In the uncertain post–cold-war era, every cultural unit from Latvia to Staten Island seems to want to seek its sovereign independence and security. The more difficult security becomes to achieve technologically and financially, the greater the human desire is to achieve it.

National security or domestic security issues are also useful for elites to solidify their domestic power bases. **Elites,** or those in superior social or political positions ("Those who get the most of what there is to get" according to Harold Lasswell), have an inherent interest in broadcasting the insecurity of the nation in order to help to make themselves appear to be indispensable.

Elites of both developed and developing nations realize that the primacy of security is required for maintaining the nation-state system and their own power position in it. This is how elites in charge of large multinational companies and organizations think as well. What we need is a simple management model that can be used both to analyze how such elites maximize the stability of their organizations and to illustrate how managers take risks for future development from this basis of stability.

THE MAINTENANCE MODEL
OF INTERNATIONAL MANAGEMENT

Given the primacy of one world system, the key question for managing in international political economy is: Which organizational and individual strategies serve best to cope with the creative destruction of global competition and the inevitable insecurity it engenders? Strategies, in turn, flow from the model of economic dynamism used by the strategist: What makes pieces of the world economy move, and how can cycles or trends be anticipated to enable the individual or organization to be positioned the right way at the right time?

* * *

Global economic dynamism begins with technological innovation, with financial power, and with strategic position—of the *rich* countries. For over 60 percent of the world's trade and direct investment takes place among the rich.

Each of these countries can be viewed as a subsystem of the larger world system, as can any of the multinational companies based in them. Each of these subsystems copes with waves of creative destruction, that is, of **entropy,** the disintegration and diffusion of energies, and **syntropy,** the coming together of energies into a new order.

In *Cybernetics,* mathematician Norbert Wiener demonstrated that all systems tend toward entropy or disintegration: The role of the system manager is to sort out critical information or feedback for the environment to help the system adapt to change for the sake of the system's equilibrium—and ultimately its survival. In the high-speed postmodern world, managers coping with disintegrating systems have no choice but to be preoccupied with stabilizing their own subsystems, whether these be states or multinational firms or international organizations.

The maintenance model of management is based upon the distinction between a boundaried *maintenance base* oriented toward internal stability and security "inside" the organization or collective system versus "outside" *entrepreneurship* oriented toward risky adaptation to global market innovation. Typically, the chief maintenance concern is for increasing *efficiency* or security and reducing risk within the home base or headquarters rather than with entrepreneurial *effectiveness* and risktaking to adjust to changing outside markets and conditions.[28] (See Figure 1–1.)

The maintenance model has great explanatory power at different levels of analysis and at various stages of development in international political economy. At the individual level of analysis, for example, the maintenance base in the traditional culture of France is the *foyer,* the family circle or quasi-sacred basis of French civilization. The duty of the head of the French household is to use his wits to take entrepreneurial risks outside the family in order to bring home the goods, much like the hunter bringing back his catch to his cave. In the process the Frenchman is traditionally supposed to keep clear of emotional extremes or entangling alliances that could undermine his will or render him vulnerable.[29]

At the state level, mercantilism—the philosophy of centrally steered economic nationalism—traditionally permits the French President to view France (or, even more accurately, Paris) as the maintenance base from which to take entrepreneurial risks elsewhere for the sake of maximizing French national interests. For example, the French government subsidized the French company launching the Arian rocket abroad so as to help maximize French market share in the highly competitive commercial satellite launching business.

President Bill Clinton learned from mercantilist states such as France and Japan. Within his first year in office he was on the phone to the government of Saudi Arabia requesting that it buy American jets from Boeing to help out the U.S. airline industry.

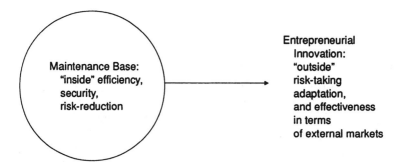

FIGURE 1–1   The Maintenance Base

Strategic Behavior

An examination of individual, corporate, and state economic behavior in the 1970s and 1980s in terms of the maintenance model revealed at least four predominant types of strategic behavior* (expressed here as Weberian ideal types—or characteristic typifications of particular categories of behavior):[30]

1. *Defeatist:* takes as few risks as possible, cutting costs rather than risking assets; past-oriented, passive, defensive, plagued by a fear of loss and a neurotic conservative impulse; thrifty in consumption with a security-oriented, portfolio mix.

2. *Free-rider:* takes high risks at no cost or low cost, specializing in living at someone else's expense; present-oriented with active-passive motivation or *maximin— maxi*mizing individual gains and *min*imizing personal costs; high individual consumption when others pay, low otherwise; portfolio mix centered on cheap money or upon debt at low interest rates.

3. *Maintenance:* takes limited risks at moderate cost to keep up with business cycle and inflation; present-oriented, short-term realism guided by passive-active motivation, seeking to co-opt change in order to assure stability; consumes high quality now before costs go higher; portfolio mix stresses stable returns, liquidity, diversity and flexibility.

4. *Entrepreneurial:* takes high risks even at high costs; aims to come out ahead of inflation and present stage of business cycle; aggressive motivation stemming from tension between perception of handicap and potential advantage; seeks to thrust all energy and resources into direction of highest probable payoff; future-oriented; all-or-nothing consumption: "prince or pauper"; portfolio mix focused upon highest return through astute gambles on the business cycle.

These four types of strategic behavior were derived from analyzing individual, corporate, and state reactions to inflation. But they have wider applicability. For our purposes, they can be consolidated into two basic types, which can then be described in terms of how they are mixed: the maintenance vs. the entrepreneurial. (The "defeatist" type can be dropped as descriptive of "sick" or pathological strategic behavior that does not get us further in terms of knowing what types of positive behavior to adopt.)

The "free-rider" behavior pattern, however, is more interesting. The work of Professor Howard Stevenson at Harvard University implies that the entrepreneur or "promoter" may actually be one particularly creative variety of "free-rider." Stevenson argues that *entrepreneurship is a behavior or process by which individuals pursue opportunities without regard to the resources they currently control.*[31] The wise entrepreneur, in fact, may specialize in taking risks with *other* people's resources. For Stevenson, the contrast with the entrepreneur is the administrative "trustee"—what we call the maintenance man or maintenance mode of behavior. The **maintenance manager** or **trustee** is driven by resources currently controlled, tends towards formalized, promotion-oriented hierarchy in organization, and is security-driven. The **entrepreneur** or **promoter,** in contrast, is driven by the perception of opportunity or value-driven, is often team-oriented, and relies upon performance-based, flat, informal modes of organization.[32]

Now let us illustrate how these two basic types of strategy can be mixed to give a recipe for managing economic change. Economist Paul Samuelson maintained in 1993 that to cure the economic dilemmas of the United States required more savings in order to prepare the way for more investment.[33] Or, translated into our strategy types, by making the maintenance base more efficient through cost-cutting and saving on the part of government and corporate trustees or maintenance managers, more capital can be targeted for investment by entrepreneurs or promoters in order to create new businesses, economic growth, and jobs.

A **strategy** is a blueprint or intentional plan for the future, a cognitive design that can be both personal and organizational. **Strategic behavior,** on the other hand, refers to patterns of individual or collective behavior *after* it has occurred. Strategy stems from the "in-order-to motive" whereas strategic behavior is analyzed from the "because-of motive." Changes in the environment lead to adaptations of strategic behavior as collective learning takes place through the adoption of a series of strategies.

In many cases people do not *choose* a specific type of strategy as much as they *fall into it* as a result of the socioeconomic and information sources available to them at that moment. The maintenance model of management is not a "rational actor model," which always assumes rational choices of individuals before the fact. Rather it is more of a socio-anthropolitical model of the psychology of economic behavior—looking at data after the fact stemming as much from social, economic, and emotional factors as from rational decisions.

For example, in coping with inflation, rich individuals, corporations, and states have overwhelmingly illustrated the *maintenance* strategy. This strategic behavior is probably not due to rational choice (since maintenance is often not the best strategy), but more apt to be due to the future-shock effect of being overwhelmed with more change than can be digested.[34]

Strategies, in short, are symptoms of structural positions in the world economy as much as they are constellations of choice. On the level of the individual, this is what Kierkegaard meant when he said, "I feel like the piece in the chess game that is not allowed to be moved." Decision-makers in Ethiopia and Bangladesh and other developing countries with little structural flexibility can identify with Kierkegaard's remark. Given that almost all human institutions and organizations are being "outpositioned" by the pace of technological and socioeconomic change in the late twentieth century, there are certain times when almost anyone can sense that the strategy they have chosen is the inevitable outgrowth of the structural position in which they find themselves as much as it is due to any freedom of will.

This does not mean that global structures *always* penetrate to individual cognition or that theorists *always* reflect the structural interests of countries from which they emerge. Free will exists, but not in a cultural or structural vacuum. The individual's *strategy* today—that is, his or her future-oriented blueprint or intentional plan—must be distinguished from individual or group *strategic behavior* tomorrow—the actual behavior performed in cultural, structural, and historical context. Effective collective learning can be measured by the extent to which groups of individuals overcome traditional patterns of behavior or habits that have become maladaptive and replace them with effective strategies of adaptation that result in more opportunities for the exercise of free will or autonomy by the company or state in the world economy.

The major American automobile companies, for example, found themselves outpositioned by foreign competition in the late 1970s—they were thrust into the defeatist category by the latest wave of creative destruction in the global economy. Rather than adopting entrepreneurial strategies to escape from their position of structural stalemate and noncompetitiveness, these U.S. companies fell back on defensive maintenance strategies, which blocked their potential adaptiveness. Chrysler even found itself in a free-rider position, accepting subsidies from the U.S. government, which also introduced "voluntary export restraints" (or tariffs by another name) to keep out the Japanese competition until the American companies had time to adapt. The automakers responded with more sophisticated maintenance strategies, forming joint ventures with Japanese car companies so as to be competitively positioned when the export restraints were removed: "If you can't beat them, join them."

The wave of mergers and joint ventures among multinational companies in the 1980s represented maintenance strategies of coping with the creative destruction of global competition. Smaller car companies (American Motors) were taken over by bigger ones.

A similar shakedown occurred in the airline industry with three major airline manufacturers emerging from the competitive trauma: Boeing, McDonnell Douglas, and Airbus. Airbus Industrie illustrates an astute blend between maintenance and entrepreneurial strategies. Founded in 1970 as a consortium of Western Europe's leading aircraft manufacturers (the maintenance base, supported by billions of dollars of state subsidies), the Airbus 320 became the fastest selling plane in aviation history during the 1980s given its technological edge with a fully computerized flight-control system (the entrepreneurial innovation side of the strategic mix).

Nor had the American competitors much grounds for complaint: U.S. government military contracts in the era of American hegemony after World War II enabled Boeing, Lockheed, and McDonnell and Douglas (which had not yet merged) to account for about 90 percent of all airline sales outside the Communist bloc by the late 1960s. Building on the mixed experience of the French-British *Concorde,* Airbus became the European symbol of a joint industrial policy of technological competitiveness to match the *Pentagon Inc.* industrial policy of the United States. As *Pentagon Inc.* was scaled back after the collapse of the U.S.S.R., the Clinton administration began to intervene on the side of the American airline industry in head-to-head industrial policy exchanges with the Europeans.[35] Such differences in industrial policies in reaction to the ebbs (entropy) and waves (syntropy) of the cycles of creative destruction that characterize global capitalism can only be explained by defining the structures that make up these different political economies.

STRUCTURES AND DEPENDENCE

At least five primary structures make up the maintenance base of each state (or multinational organization) in the world economy, which together determine its competitive structural position and relative independence or dependence:[36]

1. **The security structure:** the maintenance of order both within the organization or state and outside—within the international system at large.
2. **The money and credit structure:** the stability and relative value of the currency and the sources and flexibility of short- and long-term finance.
3. **The knowledge structure:** literacy rates, technological competitiveness, training systems, and the distribution of critical economic information and skills throughout the population.
4. **The production structure:** the way resources are organized and the knowledge structure is utilized to determine what is produced.
5. **The value structure:** a cluster of psycho-cultural beliefs and ideological preferences that transcend and color "the rational"—what the people predominantly *choose* to learn. In many cases traditional value structures block states from becoming what Karl Deutsch called "adaptive-learning states" (post-1868 Japan, for example), which are able to change political and economic structures to cope with some major problem in the environment.[37]

Thus, *political economy* can be viewed as the collective capacity of a state or multinational organization to structure payoffs for effective learning or adaptation in the global system—or the study of learning by paying if such adaptation is blocked.[38]

The particular combination of these five primary structures determines the potential power of one state or multinational organization compared to others in the world economy. **Power** is the social capacity to satisfy human needs or wants relative to competitors: It is always increasing or diminishing.[*]

---

[*]This definition stresses the ability of collective consensus to create solutions to adapt to change rather than power as mere materialistic distribution or authoritative allocation of values in the status quo. See R. Hummel and R. Isaak, *Politics for Human Beings*, 2nd ed. (Belmont, Calif.: Wadsworth, 1980), p. 34.

Powerful states, for example, can perhaps best be described in terms of *surpluses in their structural assets*. What sociologist Max Weber might have termed the "ideal type" of Great Power state would be characterized by a surplus of security (nuclear deterrents, armed forces, military preparedness); a surplus of money and credit (a strong international reserve position, a creditor nation); a surplus of production (high gross national product growth, balance of trade surplus, a diverse, competitive industrial capacity); a surplus of knowledge (a deep and wide infrastructure of research and development, high productivity in innovative technologies, a national literacy rate higher than required for most job functions), and a surplus of value consensus (a widespread anti-inflation, pro-savings consensus; absence of ideological polarization; a community spirit that comes together to permit adaptation to new global challenges).

Thus, the world political economy can be envisioned as a hierarchy of states spread between structural surpluses and structural deficits, between relative independence and dependence.

The aim of the nation-state in the world economy is to use its potential power and influence to achieve self-sufficiency and independence with enough surpluses to serve as a buffer against global change. But absolute self-sufficiency or independence is no longer possible to achieve. As political scientist Richard Rosecrance put it: "To be fully independent, an aggressor would now need the oil of the Persian Gulf, the iron ore, bauxite, and uranium of Australia, the chromium of Zimbabwe and South Africa, and the granaries of Canada, Australia and the American West."[39]

The typical cycle of creative destruction or of capitalism is oversimplified for the sake of illustration in Figure 1–2. The cycle begins with creation. For example, in political economies still at the traditional premoney barter stage of trading, the creation of money and credit structures makes possible the technological innovation that is the engine of creative destruction. Historically, financial innovation (through the creation of money and credit structures) precedes technological innovation (or productivity increases in the maintenance base through industrial revolutions). In traditional barter societies, the same individuals perform the functions of producing, saving, and investing—"jacks of all trades." But the creation of money or credit financing through debt permits a splitting off (or "specializing") of producers from savers on the one hand, and of savers from investors, on the other. Individuals who have not earned, saved, or inherited capital can borrow it on credit to make dynamic, risky, innovative investments: the "entrepreneurship" leading to "syntropy" or economic integration in the cycle. **Inflation,** or more money chasing fewer goods, is the inevitable result. Inflation serves as the lubricator for innovative investment and as the liberator of resources held by conservative property-owning individuals through the mechanism of credit.[40] The creation of money and credit structures thus leads to technological innovation, which leads to entrepreneurship, industrial revolution,

FIGURE 1–2 Strategies, Structures, and Cycles of World Economy

and a diffusion of power of the propertied classes. Societies are democratized through inflationary financing (the creation of credit cards, for instance). But as this environment risks becoming "overheated" with economic growth, the "maintenance managers" or "trustees" of organizations and states have to worry about reducing the costs of maintenance of their organizations and about financing entrepreneurial innovation to keep up with the technological state-of-the-art of the global competition. To fail at either of these management functions prevents another positive cycle of economic growth from emerging and leads inevitably to entropy or disintegration, ultimately resulting in the decay of the economic organization.

Managers of all nation-states and multinational organizations have to cope with domestic and global waves of creative destruction simultaneously. Those able to build up surpluses in security, money and credit, knowledge, production and value structures position themselves for a moment of global hegemony. Inevitably their maintenance managers or trustees slip and hegemony begins to slide towards entropy and decay, making space for other states to rise economically, using the stability provided by the declining hegemon as a springboard.

OLIGOPOLIES AND NEOMERCANTILISM

American hegemony prevailed in the world system roughly until 1960. During this post-World War II period, smaller states could pursue **neomercantilist** policies of export-oriented growth in order to increase their structural surpluses, free-riding upon the security structure and economic stability provided by the *pax Americana,* or the maintenance base of the American hegemon.[41] Indeed, following defeat of the Axis in World War II, the United States initially prohibited Germany and Japan from rearming, even writing into the Japanese Constitution that not more than 1 percent of that country's gross national product could be spent on defense. While the Americans reaped many commercial and political benefits from the "public good" of international stability that they provided, when American hegemony began to collapse the Americans found themselves ill-prepared for a more competitive, interdependent environment. Moreover, other leading Western industrial countries (such as West Germany, Switzerland, and Japan) were ill-disposed toward picking up the costs of the "public good" of international stability. The Japanese, for example, wanted nothing to do with nuclear weapons on their soil. And the West Germans and Swiss resisted having their currencies become international reserve currencies to supplement the dollar for fear they would lose domestic control over their own "money constitutions." This fear was justified by the increasing anarchy of the global monetary system, stimulated by the expansion of the "stateless" Eurodollar market.

The decline of American economic domination was marked by a shift from a hegemonic (**unipolar**) global system dominated by one power to an oligopolistic (or **multipolar**) system steered by an **oligopoly** or a system controlled by a few major powers. But it became problematic when all the major states making up the oligopoly focused upon neomercantilist policies or export-oriented trade surpluses at the same time. Someone, after all, has to import what the others export—or to accept trade deficits to permit others to have trade surpluses in the global system. In the 1980s the hegemonic role of the United States was radically transformed from surrogate world banker—providing international credit and liquidity—to major world debtor and borrower—and carrier of trade deficits that the borrowing helped to finance. In the process, the legitimacy of the dollar as the world's key reserve currency was undermined (in no small part by Pentagon-skewed federal budget deficits). Country elites scrambled to create their own exclusive buffer zones against the resulting international instability—from the OPEC cartel of oil-producing developing countries to the 1979 creation of the European Monetary System (or European float against the dollar). Multinational companies formed mergers and bought out competitors. Corporate executives of major firms demanded "Golden Parachute" clauses (giving them luxurious pension benefits in case they were fired in the creative destruction caused by merger buy-outs). Leaders of indebted developing countries threatened with instability (President Jose Lopez Portillo of Mexico, Ferdinand Marcos of the Philippines, and so on) built up private mansions and Swiss bank accounts with money borrowed from the International Monetary Fund. Human activity was focused upon shoring up the maintenance base of vested interests threatened by the inflation and uncertainty of the 1970s, then by the disinflation, deregulation, recession, and privatization trends of the 1980s.

The basic principle of oligopolies is to form minimum winning coalitions (that is, the fewest number of allies or club members required to succeed), since the greater the number of participants, the smaller the share of the economic pie for any one individual or group.[42] The shift away from multilateral to bilateral agreements between nations, for example, illustrates the belief that the payoff is greater and clearer for two partners than for more than two. And it is tempting to explain the crises of cooperation in the OPEC (over oil prices) and European Common Market (over agricultural subsidies) cartels on the basis of numbers alone: These clubs have too many members with too many diffuse interests to easily achieve the universal consensus needed within the organization for effective bargaining with the outside world.

COMPLEXITY, INTEGRITY, AND RESISTANCE

The complexity of the oligopolistic structure of the international political economy is so great that by the time managers understand the rules and structures of the oligopolies at the top of the system they have little time or resources left over to analyze or identify with the majority of the world's developing peoples at the bottom. The conservative bias of conventional Western knowledge assumptions is in part the result of time pressures and the natural human tendency to focus on the two-thirds of the globe where most of international trade and investment take place. Westerners are often fully absorbed in the complexities of their own multiparty democracies and those of nations like their own. Since the managers of oligopolies at the top of the world economic system set both the terms of dialogue and the terms of trade and technological competitiveness, those at the bottom find themselves trapped in the language of dependence if they seek to adapt enough of the cultural integrity of their nations to attract capital investment and support from the developed countries. Third-World leaders lack the security conditions of developed countries and generally seek control over wealth, while aiming for both given their interconnection.[43] Whereas management texts in the Western industrialized countries put the planning function before control, planning is perceived as a luxury in most developing countries where control is the paramount concern.[44]

Not all developing countries are willing to mimic the industrial bias of knowledge typical of the Western countries, the IMF, and GATT. Some, like Papua New Guinea, seek to preserve the integrity of their cultural traditions, even if it means keeping "Stone Age" tribes frozen in a backward stage of development to prevent the extinction of their way of life. Three million people are split into a thousand tribes speaking 700 different languages, yet Papua has managed to create a form of democratic unity through decentralized administrative authority, preserving the integrity of the "large families" that comprise it. Nietzsche presumably once observed: "Character is neurosis." Individuals of character show the strength of their personalities by resisting change or status quo trends for the sake of principles and personal integrity. As with Antigone, who demanded to bury her brother even though it was against the law, their integrity depends upon resistance against what they believe to be unjust norms or conditions. The most idealistic of terrorists may view their armed struggle as a desperate effort on the part of the powerless to upset the rules of the status quo, which have permanently structured their people in a dependent position.

Even within the camp of the wealthy countries, not everyone accepts the priority of materialistic self-sufficiency and economic growth as values (preferences implicit in the dominant maintenance strategy). In his counterculture classic *Small Is Beautiful,* economist E.F. Schumacher argues that the "bigger is better" thrust of the corporate economies of advanced industrial states has contributed to the error of treating capital as income, particularly "natural capital" (such as fossil fuels) as if it were expendable without limits. Developing countries should not aim for this insatiable big business model of capitalist Westernization but wisely accept the limits of nature and the earth's resources, utilizing "intermediate technologies" targeted for their own unique capacities and situations. Economic growth per se is not a higher priority for Schumacher than is the concept of the dignity of man or the respect for the natural environment: "The substance of man cannot be measured by the Gross National Product. Perhaps it cannot be measured at all, except for certain symptoms of loss."[45] Or, to put the case another way, critic Ihab Hassan notes that in the postmodern age, order is rare and precious, but more precious and rare still is human dissent, the so-called crime that is actually the imagination diverging from "everything that is the case" and in the process creating and recreating all there is.[46] The dissent permitted by Western democracy may be an ultimate form of postmodern integrity providing the crucible for imaginative innovations that take us beyond the mere maintenance and optimization of what we already know exists.

IN CONCLUSION

Gross world product grew from about $600 billion in 1900 to over $13 trillion by 1987, spurred by a 12-fold increase in fossil fuel consumption. Even though four-fifths of all the oil discovered in North America has already been burned, energy consumption there remains profligate relative to per capita consumption elsewhere in the world. Free-riding upon the world's finite resources has become habitual despite the negative fallout of acid rain and cancer-causing pollution. By 1989, tropical forests were being cut down globally at the rate of 26 million acres per year (the area of the U.S. state of Pennsylvania). Yet the push for economic growth above all else continued, stimulated by the first dipping in gross global product since World War II. This occurred in 1991, when world output per capita declined by over 2 percent. Negative global changes appeared to reinforce a preoccupation with maintenance or stability.

Inflation fighting and the maximization of economic growth remain primary policy objectives in the maintenance-dominated strategies of wealthy OECD countries. For their numerous property-owning citizens stand to lose their asset value from inflation, and a sovereign sense of national competitiveness, and a theoretical "full employment" from a domestic slowdown in economic growth.

Following the end of World War II, American hegemony served as the international maintenance base for lending capital to rich (or former rich) countries, not to poor ones. Marshall Plan aid went to Western Europe, not Latin America or Africa. Nations already possessing the heritage of the knowledge and value structure for industrial modernization were given the additional asset of U.S. aid and credit for the sake of American security structure priorities in the cold war. By the time most developing countries had achieved political independence and demanded credit and aid to make economic independence possible, American hegemony had declined and the United States was no longer in a mood for altruistic lending: By the 1980s the U.S. position was reversed and the Americans became the world's largest debtor, not creditor, nation. Commercial banks stepped in during the late 1970s to lend capital to the developing countries to help pay for their higher (OPEC-inflated) oil bills. But the banks grew lending-shy in the 1980s when it became apparent that many of these countries could no longer afford to pay the interest on the debt, much less pay back the principal.

Thus, the rich, developed countries benefitted most from the economic growth bonanza of the 1950s and 1960s: By the time the inflationary 1970s and disinflationary 1980s and 1990s arrived, the majority had become wealthy welfare states that sought to maintain and service what they had achieved more than to "risk the pot" on long-term entrepreneurial speculation.

The rich have something to lose from inflation, not the poor who possess nothing of value. Deep-seated, conservative ownership characteristics emerged as masses of people became property owners in the developed countries via the credit innovations that split the savings/production function from the investment function. This, in turn, set the stage for the conservative, risk-shy postmodern era in which inflation is perceived by the influential to be more of a problem than is unemployment, even if the result should be stalemated growth or stagflation. When the peoples of the rich countries had accumulated enough material goods, leisure time became harried and the focus shifted to "positional goods"—status jobs or situations of security and prestige in the social hierarchy, which the elites sought to freeze once they were ensconced.[47] What trade the GATT tried to free up between countries was slowed down and regulated by the union and state hierarchies within them for the maintenance of their aging, position-holding citizens. Consolidation became more important than adjustment given the one-two punches, or threats, of inflation and disinflation in the world economy. Oligopolies emerged to preserve the advantages of the haves—through OPEC, the European Common Market, the North American Treaty Organization, multinational corporate mergers—buffer zones against the economic waves of creative destruction of capitalism, with limited membership so as to preserve larger shares of the economic pie for those in "the club." Winners tried to take all and to keep others from positioning themselves to become potential winners.

Meanwhile, mismanagement of the developed political economies led to a breakdown in their status-order systems and authority structures. Old political elites were upset by young upstarts who promised to help those left behind or to perform the maintenance function even better for those already established. Small, young companies provided the majority of the new jobs with the spread of democratizing financial innovation and information technology. Merger strategies made multinational dinosaurs feel bigger but not necessarily better: The loss of entrepreneurial innovation was no longer made up for in economies of scale given the tempo of competitive change. IBM, for example, could no longer time the introduction of innovations in the computer market as the two-man, garage-spawned Apple Computer Company illustrated in no uncertain fashion. By the early 1990s, IBM realized that its maintenance strategy of focusing on the mainframe computer business had long since been passed by and collective learning was stimulated by crisis. IBM radically decentralized its organization, created joint ventures with almost anyone interested, and attempted to resurrect entrepreneurial growth. The standardized economy had shifted to a customized economy in which the competitive rewards went to the fast rather than the big.[48]

The countries that performed best economically in the postwar period had a stable, predictable maintenance base from which to take entrepreneurial risks for the sake of export growth and international competitiveness. The prime examples are West Germany and Japan: The United States provided stability and capital for both, restricting their entrepreneurial energies to commercial activities (prohibiting them from diffusing their energies in the buildup of military capacity). The social market economy of West Germany was based upon a clear distinction between the limited, state-controlled *economic order* (or maintenance base) and the liberated business sector or *economic process* of the free market (or entrepreneurial innovation).[49]

Similarly, Japan's economic success was based upon a tightly knit, well-organized maintenance base crowned by the collaboration between the employers' organization, the *Keidanren,* and the Ministry of International Trade and Industry (MITI), which together targeted certain areas for national subsidies and development (from automobiles to microchips).[50] Both the West German and Japanese economies were dominated by the concentration of large firms, the superficial attempts of the Americans to break them up after the war notwithstanding. The keys to the West German and Japanese economic miracles were a stable and efficient maintenance base (a "tight ship in the storm" of creative destruction), an imposed free-rider component (the U.S. nuclear umbrella and American financing to shore up allies in the cold war), and well-targeted, entrepreneurial strategies to increase exports and create structural trade and economic surpluses. Low labor costs and a dynamic world economy were no doubt preconditions for this successful maintenance-entrepreneurial strategy mix. But one should not underestimate the astute blending of knowledge, value, and production structures to take full advantage of the free ride provided by the United States in terms of the security and credit structures that absorb most of the time, energy, and resources of less-fortunate countries.

The economic success of the United States was grounded upon the maintenance base of its largest domestic market in the world, refurbished by the technological development stimulated by the World War II effort. Nor should the economic hegemony of the United States be underestimated as the twentieth century comes to an end: Its financial innovations and subsequent ability to attract the lion's share of the world's capital have helped to subsidize a major technological revolution in information processing with unforeseen consequences for international economic competitiveness. Money and credit innovations precede technological revolutions, which make successful entrepreneurial economic developments possible. And the *"limelight effect"* of other nations looking to the U.S. as the international trend-setter gives the Americans marketing advantages.

However, the full recovery of the world economy in the 1990s will depend upon reversing the failure of the United States and other developed countries to create effective, growth-stimulating credit structures for the majority of developing countries, which are supposed to serve as customers for the new services and products that developed countries produce. One must avoid transforming the maintenance strategy, so tempting to developed countries overwhelmed with change, into a rigid *maintenance syndrome*—a risk-shy, efficiency operation aimed just at maintaining the status quo. To avoid this trap, it may help to analyze the economic principles of the emerging post-cold-war economy in order to distinguish between three different national attempts at collective learning that have been at the forefront of the transformation from socialist 'control economies' towards global economic competitiveness.

THOUGHT QUESTIONS

1. Define and contrast the ideologies of economic nationalism, liberalism and Marxism. Which role do the terms zero-sum game, economic pie, and Modern World System theory play in this context?

2. Identify the elements making up the structural position of a state or multinational organization and denote the characteristics of a Great Power according to Max Weber.

3. Describe the four predominant types of strategic behavior and explain in this context the success of Japan and Germany in the post-World-War II era compared to the role of the United States. What is the difference between effectiveness and efficiency in this context? How does the concept of collective learning fit in?

4. What is the linkage between creative destruction, development and hegemonic stability? What is the role of a hegemon? How did the U.S. perform this role? What, by contrast, is meant by oligopolistic structure?

5. What is meant by "entrepreneur" and which kinds of cultural patterns or "schemata" encourage or discourage entrepreneurship?

NOTES

1. This conservative view of knowledge is derived from systems theory. See Kenneth Boulding's lucid, understated interpretation: *The Image: Knowledge in Life and Society* (Ann Arbor: University of Michigan Press, 1956). The associated view of Adam Smith's classical economic liberalism as an optimization of what exists goes back, of course, to Jean-Baptiste Say, only to be picked up in 1911 by Joseph Schumpeter in *Die Theorie der Wirtschaftlichen Entwicklung (The Theory of Economic Dynamics),* and recently contrasted with entrepreneurial innovation in Peter Drucker's *Innovation and Entrepreneurship* (London: Heinemann, 1985). On the "problem-solving" view of knowledge, see Robert Cox, "Social Forces, States and World Orders: Beyond I.R. Theory," in Robert Keohane, *Neorealism and Its Critics* (New York: Columbia University Press, 1986), pp. 208–10.

2. See Joseph Schumpeter, *Capitalism, Socialism and Democracy* (New York: Harper & Row, 1950) and Daniel Bell's recasting of the same thesis in *The Cultural Contradictions of Capitalism* (New York: Basic Books, 1976). What Bell sees as cause for conservative concern—system breakdown due to cultural and technological subversion—Jean-Francois Lyotard finds a cause for celebration in his *La Condi-*

tion Postmoderne (Paris: Les Editions de Minuit, 1979): Paradoxical, cultural language games can lead to imaginative breakthroughs and innovative reconstructions. Compare Lyotard with the less euphoric *Legitimations Probleme in Spät Kapitalismus* of Jürgen Habermas.

3. Albert Bandura, *Social Learning Theory* (Englewood Cliffs, N.J.: Prentice-Hall, 1977), p. 194. "Reciprocal" here is used here to mean mutual action between events rather than referring to its narrower sense of similar or opposite counterreactions.

4. Ibid., pp. 16–53. Also see A. Bandura, "Influence of Models' Reinforcement Contingencies on the Acquisition of Imitative Responses," *Journal of Personality a nd Social Psychology* 1 (1965): 589–95.

5. See David Rumelhart, "*Schemata:* The Building Blocks of Cognition," in R. Spiro et al., eds., *Theoretical Issues in Reading Comprehension* (Hillsdale, N.J.: Lawrence Erlbaum Associates, 1980), pp. 33–58.

6. See Edgar Dunn, *Economic and Social Development: A Process of Social Learning* (Baltimore: The Johns Hopkins Press, 1971), p. 189.

7. Michael Maccoby, *The Gamesman: The New Corporate Leaders* (New York: Simon and Schuster, 1976).

8. See William Theodore de Bary and John W. Chaffee, eds., *Neo-Confucian Education: The Formative Stage* (Berkeley, University of California Press, 1989). The common Confucian culture of China, Japan, Korea, and overseas Chinese communities (and particularly the influence of "progressive" Chu Hsi, whose Sung learning principles were supported by the state) represents a dynamic force in the receptivity of the East Asian people to new learning and their collective capacity for cultural and economic development.

9. See Thomas Janoski, *The Political Economy of Unemployment: Active Labor Market Policy in West Germany and the United States* (Berkeley: University of California Press, 1990).

10. Gregory Bateson, *Steps to an Ecology of Mind* (London: Paladin, 1976), essay on *Deutero-learning.*

11. Ibid., See essay on "National Character."

12. See Charles Hampden-Turner, *Gentlemen and Tradesmen: The Values of Economic Catastrophe* (London: Routledge & Kegan Paul, 1983). And: C. Hampden-Turner & Alfons Trompenaars, *The Seven Cultures of Capitalism* (New York: Currency/Doubleday, 1993).

13. For the case of the samurai, see Everett Hagan, *On the Theory of Social Change* (London: Tavistock Publications, 1964), Chapter 14. For the Balinese, see Clifford Gertz, *Peddlers and Princes: Social Development and Economies in Two Indonesian Towns* (Chicago: University of Chicago Press, 1963).

14. For an example of an interpretation of developed Western economies in terms of the politics of productivity versus the politics of redistribution, see R. Isaak, *European Politics: Political Economy and Policy Making in Western Democracies* (New York: St. Martin's Press, 1980).

15. Some identify Schumpeter as a neoclassical economist, others as a neo-Marxist—evidence of his objectivity. He devotes a chapter to the concept of "creative destruction" in *Capitalism, Socialism and Democracy*, while his conception of development is detailed in *The Theory of Economic Development* (translated from the German by Redvers Opie. Cambridge, MA: Harvard University Press, 1934), pp. 63–65.

16. Johan Galtung made this projection at a conference in Ojai, California, in November 1979: transcribed in W.L. Hollist, "Continuity and Change in the World System," paper presented at the convention of the International Studies Association, Los Angeles, 1980.

17. An influential example of this American preoccupation is found in Robert O. Keohane, *After Hegemony: Cooperation and Discord in the World Political System* (Princeton, NJ: Princeton University Press, 1984).

18. Charles P. Kindleberger, "Hierarchy versus Inertial Cooperation," *International Organization* 40 (Autumn 1986): 841. This article expands the responsibilities of the would-be world stabilizer or "hegemon" initially set out in Kindleberger's *The World in Depression, 1929–1939* (Berkeley: University of California Press, 1973), Chapter 14. Kindleberger's concept of leadership is derived from Frohlich and Oppenheimer who argue that public goods will be underproduced (because of free-riders) unless a leader agrees to bear a disproportionate share of their costs. See Norman Frohlich and Joe A. Oppenheimer, "I Get Along with a Little Help from My Friends," *World Politics* 23 (October 1970): 20, 104.

19. The limitations to interpreting British leadership in the nineteenth century in terms of the hegemony stability thesis, particularly in regard to predicting tariff levels in international trade, are demonstrated in Timothy J. McKeown, "Tariffs and Hegemonic Stability Theory," *International Organization* 37 (Winter 1983): 73–91.

20. This is Stephen Krasner's definition in his "Structural Causes and Regime Consequences: Regimes as Intervening Variables," *International Organization* 36 (Spring 1982): 185.

21. The ethnocentrism implicit in the American fear of international instability due to the decline of U.S. hegemony is noted in Susan Strange, "Cave! Hic Dragones: A Critique of Regime Analysis," *International Organization* 36 (Spring 1982): 299–324. While team-teaching with the late international relations theorist Hedley Bull at The Johns Hopkins Bologna Center in 1980 he told me he thought American economic hegemony was being vastly underestimated. Others who find more continuity than decline in American power include Bruce Russett (Cf. his "The Mysterious Case of Vanishing Hegemony; or, Is Mark Twain Really Dead?" *International Organization* 39 (Spring 1985: 207–31) and, of course, Susan Strange (Cf. her "Still an Extraordinary Power: America's Role in a Global Monetary System," in Raymond E. Lombra and William E. Witte, eds., *Political Economy of International and Domestic Monetary Relations* (Ames: Iowa State University Press, 1982).

22. A. Gramsci, *Quaderni del carere* (Turin: Instituto Gramsci, 1975). For an application of Gramsci's notion of hegemony to the international political economy, see Robert W. Cox, "Production and Hegemony: Toward a Political Economy of World Order," in H.K. Jacobson and D. Sidjanski, eds., *The Emerging International Economic Order* (Beverly Hills, CA: Sage Publications, 1982), pp. 37–58. Cox, in turn, has been applied in James H. Mittelman, "Transforming the International Political Economy: A Crisis of Hegemony in the Third World," paper presented at the International Studies Association, Atlanta, Georgia, March 1984.

23. Silvan Tompkins, "Left and Right: A Basic Dimension of Ideology," in *The Study of Lives*, ed. by Robert W. White (Chicago: Aldine-Atherton, 1971), pp. 391–92. For the origins of "embedded liberalism," see John Ruggie, "International

Regimes, Transactions, and Change," *International Organization,* 36, (No. 2), (Spring 1982: 379–415).

24. See Kyung-Won Kim, *Revolution and International System* (New York: New York University Press, 1970).

25. See Raymond Aron, *Progress and Disillusion: The Dialectics of Modern Society* (New York: Praeger, 1968), p. 160. Robert W. Tucker uses the point of departure of the inevitable anarchy and oligarchy of the international system to defend the existing order or status quo over all else, in which the sovereignty and independence of states are presumably upheld by international law. See Tucker's *The Inequality of Nations* (New York: Basic Books, 1977).

26. See Peter Drucker, *The Post-Capitalist Society* (N.Y.: HarperCollins, 1993).

27. This is Kenneth Boulding's definition of security in his *Conflict and Defense: A General Theory* (New York: Harper and Row, 1963), p. 58. See also Robert Tucker, *The Inequality of Nations* (New York: Basic Books, 1977).

28. The distinction between efficiency preoccupation within the organization and market-oriented effectiveness in the outside environment is the basic dichotomy underlying Peter F. Drucker's *Management: Tasks, Responsibilities and Practices* (New York: Harper & Row, 1973).

29. Substantiated in R. Metraux et al., *Some Hypotheses About French Culture* (New York: Research in Contemporary Cultures, Columbia University, 1950). Also underscored in David C. McClelland, "French National Character and the Life and Works of André Gide," in *Roots of Consciousness* (New York: D. Van Nostrand, 1964) and R. Isaak, "France: An Administrative Economy of Cultural Supremacy," Chapter 3 of *European Politics: Political Economy and Policy Making in Western Democracies* (New York: St. Martin's Press, 1980), pp. 63–98.

30. R. Isaak, Part Three: "Modern Reactions to Inflation: Private and Public Strategies," in Wilhelm Hankel and Robert Isaak, *Modern Inflation: Its Economics and Its Politics* (Lanham, MD: University Press of America, 1983), pp. 91–160. Initial German version: *Die moderne Inflation* (Köln: Bund-Verlag, 1981).

31. See H.H. Stevenson, M.J. Roberts and H.J. Grousbeck, *New Business Ventures and the Entrepreneur* (Homewood, IL: Irwin, 1989).

32. See Michael Warshaw, "The Mind-Style of the Entrepreneur: Q & A: Howard H. Stevenson," *Success* (April 1993): 29–33. The term "entrepreneur" was first introduced by Richard Cantillon (1697–1734), who used it to refer to a specialist in taking on risk, "insuring" workers by buying up their products or labor for resale before consumers have shown how much they are willing to pay for them.

33. Steven Greenhouse, "The Man Who Wrote the Book Suggests Econ 101 for Presidents," *New York Times,* October 31, 1993.

34. The conservative psychological impulse that results in the choice of maintenance strategies due to overwhelming loss or change is perceptively documented in Peter Marris, *Loss and Change* (New York: Pantheon, 1974); also see Isaak, *European Politics.*

35. *"Pentagon Inc"* is the description of contemporary U.S. industrial policy used by Yoshi Tsurumi in *Multinational Management: Business Strategy and Government Policy,* 2nd edition (Cambridge, MA: Ballinger, 1984), p. 8.

36. The primacy of security and then of money and credit among the first four of these structures is propounded by Susan Strange, "Protectionism and World Politics," *International Organization* 39 (Spring 1985): 234.

37. See Karl W. Deutsch, "State Functions and the Future of the State," *International Political Science Review* 7 (April 1986): 209–22.

38. Illustrated in *European Politics*.

39. Richard Rosecrance, "International Theory Revisited," *International Organization* 35 (Autumn 1981): 709.

40. See Wilhelm Hankel and Robert Isaak, *Modern Inflation: Its Economics and Its Politics* (Lanham, MD: University Press of America, 1983), Part Two; initially published in German: *Die moderne Inflation* (Köln: Bund-Verlag, 1981).

41. See Paolo Guerrieri and Pier Carlo Padoan, "Neomercantilism and International Economic Stability," *International Organization* 40 (Winter 1986): 29–42.

42. See Mancur Olson, *The Rise and Decline of Nations* (New Haven, CT: Yale University Press, 1982), pp. 17–74.

43. Illustrated in Stephen D. Krasner, *Structural Conflict: The Third World Against Global Liberalism* (Berkeley: University of California Press, 1985).

44. The primacy of control over planning as a management function in developing countries is substantiated by comparing the cases in the *Columbia Journal of World Business* (Summer 1978), an issue devoted to comparative management. Also see Ramgopal Agarwala, "Planning in Developing Countries," *World Bank Staff Working Paper No. 576,* 1983.

45. E.F. Schumacher, *Small Is Beautiful: Economics as if People Mattered* (New York: Harper & Row, 1973), p. 20.

46. Ihab Hassan, "Desire and Dissent in the Postmodern Age," *The Kenyon Review* V (Winter 1983): 1–18.

47. The wealthy have more things than time to use them, making their leisure seem harried. See Staffan B. Linder, *The Harried Leisure Class* (New York: Columbia University Press, 1970). "Positional goods" are scarce in some absolute or socially imposed sense or are subject to congestion or crowding through more extensive use. See Fred Hirsch, *Social Limits to Growth* (London: Routledge & Kegan Paul, 1978), p. 27.

48. Cf. R. Isaak, "Virtual Organizations: From Entrepreneurial Networks to Strategic Alliances," paper presented at international symposium on "Networking of Human Relations and Technology," at Tokyo Keizai University, October 25, 1993, Tokyo; and in revised form at the "Training for Change" seminar, *Institut d'Administration des Enterprises,* Aix-en-Provence, France, May 5, 1994; and Harry Dent, *The Great Boom Ahead* (New York: Hyperion, 1993).

49. See Graham Hallett, *The Social Economy of West Germany* (New York: Macmillan, 1973), pp. 19–20; and "West Germany: A Social Market Economy," Chapter 2 of *European Politics,* pp. 27–62.

50. See Chalmers Johnson, *MITI and the Japanese Miracle, The Growth of Industrial Policy, 1925–75* (Stanford, CA: Stanford University Press, 1982) and Graham K. Wilson, *Business and Politics* (Chatham, NJ: Chatham House, 1975), Chapter 6, pp. 88–102.

CHAPTER TWO

POST-COLD-WAR ECONOMICS

Better return and make a net, than to go down to the stream and merely wish for fish.

Chinese Proverb

Under the aggressive privatization campaign of the Thatcher era, the U.K. succeeded in privatizing approximately 50 enterprises during the 1980s, roughly 5 firms per year. At the Thatcherite rate (which benefitted from a sophisticated capital market and a large private sector to absorb state firms), the Polish task of privatization would take several hundred years!

Jeffrey Sachs (1992)

Social capital can be transmuted, so to speak, into financial capital: In novelist Amy Tan's Joy Luck Club, *a group of mah-jong playing friends evolves into a joint investment association. China's extraordinary growth over the last decade has depended less on formal institutions than on* guanxi *(personal connections) to underpin contracts and to channel savings and investment.*

Robert D. Putnam (1993)

Once upon a time there was a world more or less divided into black states and red ones—the capitalists and the socialists (or would-be communists). The conflict between them occurred in a world economic market in which the capitalist states attempted to "contain" the progress and power of the communist (or socialist) states. This was the cold-war "containment" doctrine of former U.S. Ambassador to the Soviet Union, George Kennan.

Then, in 1989, down came the Berlin Wall symbolically dividing these states. The Soviet Union disintegrated into numerous ethnic regional political units declaring independence. Communism collapsed as an ideology, along with the cold-war doctrine of "containment" of the capitalists. Presumably, "capitalism" had won the cold war. However, the dominant result was an increasingly global world market in which states per se *seemed* to fall into the background in terms of importance. The cold-war rationale for the legitimacy of states was gone. Governments were being forced to look to economic self-sufficiency and competitiveness—underlaid by domestic security and cultural integrity—for a new rationale for their existence. But most of them were financially, if not intellectually, deeply indebted to cold-war militarism in their industrial and economic structures and were not prepared for this sudden sea change in geopolitics. They needed radical restructuring but they found themselves swamped with habits of the past. Domestic weaknesses, swept under the carpet when the focus was upon cold-war enemies abroad or communist ideologues at home, were now brutally exposed: the emperor suddenly seemed to have no clothes, undermining state **legitimacy**— that deference to elites produced by force and awe.

In the post-cold-war world, "East–West" relations disappeared. Or, to put it more accurately, East–West relations became part of North–South relations—the interdependent network between developed ("North") and developing ("South") nation-states and regions. Although one might identify Cuba, North Korea and the People's Republic of China as exceptions to this rule given their socialist governments, the political economies of these states can be better explained in a North–South context of global economic competitiveness than in the old East–West framework. At the end of the 20th century, only two contexts really matter economically: North–North relations (between competitive, developed, industrialized states) and North–South relations. For the Northern countries, "North–North" relations are always on the front burner, given their domestic self-absorption with economic growth, unemployment, and social security.[1]

One reason for this self-preoccupation among the rich stands out: the massive economic incompetence of their political leaders and political parties. The presumed victory of the capitalists over the communists in the cold war disguised the increasing economic mediocrity of performance in the "victorious" industrialized states. The administrations of Presidents Reagan and Bush won the cold war with defense and technological budgets that broke the financial back of the American political economy, putting the country in a permanent deficit and capital-importing position. It was an expensive victory. Chancellor Helmut Kohl correctly seized the historical moment to reunify Germany. In the process, however, he made economic

promises and established monetary and fiscal policies that effectively mort-
gaged the future of German citizens for years to come.[2] The rest of the world
subsidized German reunification through the high-interest-rate regime the
Germans imposed in trying to contain the domestic inflation caused by their
deficit spending on the Eastern German states. Thus, "victorious" politicians
from the North on the level of short-term geopolitics served up long-term
macroeconomic disasters with which future generations would have to cope.
The intellectual shield of Anglo-Saxon superiority that dominated the West
was coming unraveled at the very moment it was declared officially to have
predominated.[3]

   "Post-cold-war economics" is first and foremost a return to an understanding of

   (a)   economic liberalization,
   (b)   basic macroeconomic principles, and
   (c)   recipes for "privatizing" former state-run industries and institutions.

   Secondarily, but possibly of greater long-term significance, *post-cold-war
economics is concerned with the global expansion of massive unemployment* stemming
from radical restructuring and political efforts to manage this joblessness.
Such unemployment makes scandals among powerful elites in industrial societies intolerable, bringing down governments, as well as chief executive offi-
cers of major corporations from Japan to Italy.

*   *   *

The cold-war era of two superpower blocs after World War II was as much of
an historical aberration as was the incredible global economic growth of the
1950s and 1960s. In the post-cold-war era we must go "back" to the future of
slower "normal" rates of economic growth in industrialized countries and of
diverse multicultural conflict in a multipolar world.[4] In order to understand
these transformations, let us first go back briefly to the origins of the cold
war, beginning with the revolution of Lenin in 1919 and the emergence of
Stalin's model of political economy.

*   *   *

"Imperialism is capitalism at that state of development in which the domination of monopoly and finance capital has taken shape, in which the export of
capital has acquired pronounced importance, in which the division of the
world by international trusts has begun, and in which the partition of all the
territory of the earth by the greatest capitalist countries has been completed."[5] So wrote Lenin in 1916 in *Imperialism, the Highest Stage of Capitalism.*

A year later he took over the Bolshevik Revolution, establishing the Soviet Union on the Marxist-Leninist principle of leadership by an elite, secretive vanguard—a party dictatorship of the proletariat and peasantry for the sake of a revolutionary society. The Communist party assumed total political control, nationalizing industry, organizing the Soviet Youth Movement (Komsomol), proclaiming atheism, making marriage unnecessary, and totally redirecting education. According to Lenin, although the political process decides "what is to be done," state structure specifies "who can do what to whom" (*kto/kovo*) in the state and the economy. Convinced that England and Germany had reached the point of capitalist concentration when their disintegration would begin according to his theory of imperialism, Lenin instructed the Comintern—a network of Communist parties directed secretly by the Soviet Communist Party—to help speed up this process.

While a number of Western intellectuals were attracted by the Russian experiment, the overwhelming majority of Americans and Western Europeans feared the "Red Terror." Diplomatic relations were broken off with the Soviet Union, which was soon isolated in the world community. By 1920 neither the nationalization of factories nor Marxian economic principles helped salvage a Soviet economy that was in desperate shape. Lenin realized that his country could not afford to put through revolutionary principles at home and simultaneously expand the Communist movement into world revolution. Ever the pragmatist, Lenin announced the principle of taking one step backward in order to take two steps forward and postponed the global revolutionary effort. He announced the New Economic Policy, which denationalized industries, praised native millionaires, and invited foreign investment. The West was relieved, believing that the Soviet Union had matured into a normal player in the game of nations. A Soviet nonaggression and mutual trade pact was signed with Germany in 1922 at Rapallo.

But then Lenin died in 1924 and was replaced by Communist party strongman Joseph Stalin, who advocated "socialism in one country," based upon a demanding Five-Year Plan. Industry was nationalized and agriculture was collectivized in the 1930s. Stalin believed that the Soviet Union had to build up its economic and political power in order to become a fortress for future world revolution, and he used whatever authoritarian means necessary to crush political opponents, such as Leon Trotsky, who advocated simultaneous world revolution.

THE STALINIST MODEL: COLLECTIVE LEARNING THROUGH SHORTAGES

Stalin argued that in a period of rapid national modernization, the Soviet Union must exist in peaceful coexistence with the rest of the world, avoiding war and seeking trade until Russia became a great military-industrial power. Moreover, he stressed the total subordination of agriculture to the rapid development of heavy industry, using whatever authoritarian methods were required by the state. Although the Eastern bloc countries did not always subordinate agriculture to heavy industry (Bulgaria, for example, attempted to specialize in agricultural production as its competitive "niche"), the basic structures of the East European hegemony of the USSR largely mimicked the Stalinist model (with the exception of Yugoslavia, which had a market-type of socialism and was only in the shadow of Soviet hegemony). Moreover, recent studies suggest that the domestic structure of East European states was so similar that it was not a determining variable in accounting for the different economic strategies these states adopted in the 1970s and 1980s.[6] The heritage of the Stalinist model in Eastern Europe must be understood in order to assess the meaning of specific national economic reforms that depart from this model. The institutions of Soviet hegemony and similar status as small-resource or capital-poor economic systems in the world economy worked to reinforce this commonality.

Apart from the state ownership of the means of production, the key difference between Communist and capitalist economic mechanisms is that Communist systems rely upon direct controls in the allocation of resources, whereas for most purposes capitalist systems depend upon markets.[*] Until the revolutionary reforms of the late 1980s, the central planning authority or board established output goals for major commodities of Eastern nations, including individual input targets for firms or groups of companies and supply plans specifying where the enterprises were to obtain their nonlabor, material inputs and to whom they were to ship their outputs. The coordination problems in such a regional, collective system of centralized planning were staggering, not to mention the adjustments that eventually had to be made if errors or misjudgments emerged in the planning process (which was inevitable). Given the high priority allocated in socialist systems to full employment (or what some term "overfull" employment), plans tend to be drawn too tightly (with few margins for error or lack of productivity) and projected output targets cannot be achieved with the proscribed inputs. Demand is thus chronically greater than supply, much as with the case of inflation in free-market economies.[7]

Because there is a lack of markets for land and capital in Stalinist political economies, rent, interest and profits are not accurately accounted for, and the pricing system for commodities is called "irrational" by Western economists.[8] This is partly due to the fact that direct controls rather than decentralized markets are used in resource allocation with all the errors and inertia that bureaucratic administration implies. Specifically, both ministries and enterprises are evaluated on the basis of output performance over time according to the central plan, thus motivating managers of ministries and en-

---

[*]Exceptions to this in the United States include government interventions of the Federal Reserve (Central) Bank in the money markets and of the Pentagon in the government procurement contract markets.

terprises to conceal from their superiors both capacity and overorder inputs and to avoid new technology. The Stalinist model is also characterized by *commodity inconvertibility*, meaning that foreigners are not permitted to spend either their own currency or the native currency on commodities within the socialist state (that is, mass intermediate products like coal or machinery, not consumer products purchased by tourists and embassies). Such commodity inconvertibility had the effect of stimulating rigid bilateralism in foreign trade between countries within the socialist bloc. Each socialist country had to keep a balance in trade with every other socialist nation, for to run a surplus would have raised the problem of how to spend it given the restrictions of the Stalinist structure.

Thus the Stalinist model had a dampening effect on interbloc socialist trade, although it had no such effect necessarily on East–West trade where the socialist countries were in hot pursuit of "hard" (convertible) Western currencies.

Finally, the uncertainties involved in expanding the Stalinist nation's trade rendered it more vulnerable to shortages given unpredictable downturns, leading socialist planners into a behavioral pattern of trade aversion, thus dampening growth.[9] *The Stalinist model overemphasizes maintenance strategy by rewarding risk-reduction rather than entrepreneurial growth. Resource shortages and bureaucratic bottlenecks determine economic policy, not prices. And single-party elites, not producers and consumers, create and manage the shortages.*[10]

Stalinist economies result in chronic hard currency deficits. This occurs because the full employment policy drives managers to protect firms rather than letting weak enterprises go bankrupt, reducing their competitiveness through a permanent "greenhouse" treatment or "tenure." The full employment policy yields a seller's market, for there is always surplus demand given endemic shortages. Thus, goods are distributed according to a central plan rather than sold, and "salesmanship" is so unnecessary as to be irrelevant. Tariffs (or "taxes") on international goods are redundant given centralized state control and planning, although they can work as implicit quotas discriminating against countries that do not have most-favored-nation status.[11] From a collective learning perspective, the lack of practice or irrelevance of "selling" leads to poor packaging, poor product quality, and a difficulty in adapting products to fit the consumers in specific foreign markets. With the exception of homogeneous raw materials (with which few Stalinist economies were well endowed), international competitiveness is hard to come by given such maladaptive learning patterns.

POST-STALINIST ECONOMIC GROWTH AND STRATEGIES

Economics is the study of collective choice among alternative uses of scarce resources. Scarcity is the mother of economic value. By rewarding risk-reduction and permitting shortages to determine economic policy, the Stalinist model made scarcity permanent and shortages inevitable. The global transformation towards a post-cold-war economy had the effect of reversing these assumptions, making supply or surplus capacity inevitable as everyone sought to produce many of the same things in anticipation of market demand that might or might not arise. One illustration is the transition from the reliance of East European "satellite" states upon the Soviet Union for trade to the breakup of the Soviet Union and the subsequent decline in Russian demand for East European goods. In the process, the **Comecon**, or Council for Mutual Economic Assistance (CMEA), formed in 1949 to assist in the economic development of Bulgaria, East Germany, Poland, Rumania, USSR, Czechoslovakia, Hungary, and Albania, disintegrated at the end of the 1980s after some significant initial "Eastern bloc" successes.

While Stalin was still alive, the Soviet Union used its centralized power to redirect East European trade from the West (where most of its trade had gone before the war) to the USSR (the Soviet share of East European trade rising from 25 percent in 1947 to 82 percent in 1954). This was a period of Soviet extractions from its East European "satellites": $1 billion each from Rumania and Hungary in goods, 6.5 million tons of coal from Poland, and so on. The value of this extraction by the Soviet Union has been estimated to equal the value of Marshall Plan aid given by the United States for West European reconstruction.[12]

After Stalin's death, Soviet leaders realized they had reached a point of diminishing returns in extractions from their CMEA allies and would have to invest in their growth or be obligated to subsidize them in the future. Some of this investment had already been made in the form of "mixed" companies founded in the East bloc with some of the extracted wealth. But these had caused great local resentment given Soviet control and the disproportionate share of the proceeds that seemed to flow back to the Soviet Union. Some scholars referred to this pattern as the "ghettoization" of Eastern Europe.[13]

In reversing policy, the Soviet Union was motivated by the Eastern European riots of 1953 to cancel debts and extend credits—as long as the CMEA allies continued to buy Soviet goods. This shift in strategy resulted in economic growth in the Comecon countries that outstripped the national income growth in the European Common Market between 1950 and 1980 (7 percent for CMEA excluding the USSR versus 5 percent for the EEC).[14] Thus the Soviets managed to have their hegemonic ghettoization and a pattern of dependent economic development in the East bloc too.[15]

Within the CMEA countries, different foreign policy and economic strategies evolved despite the similarities in domestic structure stemming from the Stalinist model. For example, there was a sharp break even among the most Stalinist of East European states—Rumania and East Germany—in 1968 when Rumania established official diplomatic relations with West Germany without informing any of its East bloc allies. For a quarter of a century (before his violent overthrow in 1989) Nicolae Ceausescu, Secretary General of the Rumanian Communist Party, was able to use an extreme conservative version of the Stalinist model at home to give him the leeway to take independent foreign policy stands—as France did within the NATO alliance (without the Stalinist model at home, of course): It was the first step to the success of Chancellor Willy Brandt's *Ost-politik* of the 1970s, in which West Germany tacitly recognized World War II boundaries in exchange for widespread political and economic cooperation with Comecon countries.[16] Given the desire of the West German people for integration or "unification" with East Germany, the state strategy of West Germany was always different from that of any other NATO member country, tilting heavily toward détente and economic, if not political, integration with East European states. It is no accident, for example, that German banks more than the banks of any other Western country are "held hostage" by Polish debt.

COCOM AND TECHNOLOGY TRANSFER

West Germany's unique position geopolitically between East and West was underscored by the controversy in the early 1980s concerning a West German contract to build a West Europe–Soviet gas pipeline. Anticipated to fill one-third of West Germany's energy needs, the United States feared that the West Germans would become too energy dependent upon the Soviet Union and that the West European, Japanese, and U.S. firms subcontracted in the project would transfer technology with potential national-security implications in the process.

Thus, the Reagan administration prohibited American firms from participating in the project and appealed to the principles of the **Coordinating Committee on Multilateral Export Controls (Cocom)** as a basis for stopping Japan and European NATO allies from exporting to the USSR as well. In addition to the United States, Japan and all members of the NATO alliance except Iceland are members of Cocom, an organization set up in the cold-war atmosphere of 1949 (operating out of a wing of the U.S. consulate in Paris) which coordinates a list of strategic technology prohibited for export to communist countries. However, led by West Germany, the Europeans and Japanese refused to prevent their companies from participating in the gas pipeline project, and the American government was forced to back down and let its firms participate or face the economic costs of losing business to international competitors.[17]

In 1984, the tables were turned when West Germany and France complained about American trade liberalization with the People's Republic of China.[18] Cocom members often circumvent the restrictions by exporting technological goods (such as digital computers) to countries where they are legal and then reexporting them to countries on "the blacklist." Such efforts cause great strains between governments and businesses *within* NATO countries, particularly the United States, as well as conflicts between Cocom member countries. Difficulties in coordination emerge because the export controls in the United States are more stringent than the Cocom list and stricter than the domestic controls of other NATO countries (particularly Germany). These differences were made clear in the late 1980s when the U.S. government protested the sale of technologies and chemicals that enabled Libya to construct a chemical weapons plant: American export restrictions (coordinated by the State, Defense, Energy, and Commerce departments) kept American firms from being involved in such sales, while European countries had much looser restrictions letting such sales sift through. From a global standpoint of legitimacy, it is difficult to prohibit other countries from selling the elements of potential chemical weapons plants when the United States has stockpiled so many chemical weapons itself. By 1990 the Soviet-American détente, the transformation of Eastern Europe and pressures from the business community led the Bush administration to ease up on Cocom restrictions on high-tech sales to the Eastern bloc.

Technology transfer refers to the movement of knowledge or techniques that contribute to the production process across national borders. In a high-tech/high-information, service-sector-dominated age, Benjamin Franklin's principle of sharing all knowledge and techniques with all human beings for the benefit of mankind is a notion considered naive, if not archaic, by leaders of modern nation-states. So technology gaps grow between countries of the North and the South, increasing the gaps in economic production and growth.[19] And, in this sense, often the countries of the East bloc were twice discriminated against: as economic members of the South and as strategic risks of the East.

PERESTROIKA AND THE DEMOCRATIZATION OF RUSSIA

Perestroika (restructuring) and related political and economic reforms announced by Mikhail Gorbachev in the late 1980s represented the most innovative domestic and foreign policy changes in the Soviet Union since the death of Lenin. These ideas did not spring spontaneously from the head of one man, but were carefully developed by a reformist team who patiently kept their blueprints in the drawer until the timing was ripe. Such planning evolved in recognition of the failure of a stalemated socialist economy heavily rooted in the Stalinist model. The 5 percent annual average growth rate in the GNP in the late 1960s fell to 2 percent by the late 1970s and approached zero growth in the late 1980s.[20]

While the USSR's structural economic problems were obvious by the late 1970s, many Western observers did not clearly take their consequences into account until the turnover of a series of aging Soviet leaders in the 1980s. A dark joke circulating in the USSR symbolized the ossification which the Soviet political economy had come to represent: In answer to the question—What is the difference between a crocodile and the Politburo?—comes the reply: The former has forty teeth and four legs, while in the latter the numbers are reversed.

Failures were not only rampant in the economic system but also in the political system. Although the share of the GNP claimed by defense spending had reached 15 to 25 percent (compared to 1 percent in Japan, 3 percent in West Germany and 6 to 7 percent in the United States), Soviet security policy could not prevent a Cessna 172 piloted by a young West German from landing in Red Square or the Afghan rebels from defeating the Soviet army. Moreover, flaws in the Soviet healthcare system had actually led to *reductions* in average life expectancy, unlike any other industrial nation.[21] A series of poor harvests entailed billions of dollars of purchases of grain and food from the West. And since some 80 percent of Soviet export earnings came from the sale of primary energy, when the price of oil unexpectedly dropped and the dollar exchange rate (in which most energy is priced) plummeted, the USSR was suddenly faced with shortfall in annual earnings of hard currency exports of between $8 billion and $10 billion.[22] Since Soviet policy was not to import more than it exports to avoid difficulties with obtaining hard currency for exchange, Soviet trade volume with the West sank about 40 percent. The technological gap between the Soviet Union and leading Western European countries was great, not to mention the gap with Japan and the United States, whose technology in a number of sectors was significantly ahead of that of the Europeans.

Gorbachev was elected Secretary General of the Communist Party of the Soviet Union at the beginning of 1985. There are three key concepts that made up the core of the reforms Gorbachev advocated: *glasnost* (openness), *perestroika* (restructuring), and *uskorenie* (acceleration). Statistics indicate that the first two of these became among the best-known foreign-language terms in the world.[23] Gorbachev used these notions as the basis of what he called "the new thinking."[24]

Perestroika was a strategy of decentralization that aimed to increase the personal responsibility of key managers in Soviet economic organizations and to make them more easily accessible to those in the region which they serviced. A significant portion of the top economic administrators were dismissed when Gorbachev came to power—particularly hard-liners whom he wanted to replace with people who understood his new thinking. But given this philosophy of increased personal responsibility for what goes wrong in the system, there was more turnover of personnel in economic organizations than in the past, when party loyalty and seniority often led to what amounted to lifetime tenure. Moreover, these shifts shook up the complacency of managers of large corporations from abroad who quietly counted upon their "old buddy" ties with comrades in the national bureaucracy, who were replaced or who often had to share authority with newly created regional economic institutions. These economic institutions, in turn, were expected to become "independently operating economic entities" with flexibility and the power to make entrepreneurial decisions. Business firms that operated successfully were no longer to be penalized by having profits skimmed off or by having their production quotas increased. Typically in Stalinesque economies managers with political clout measured success by their ability to reduce their production quotas, giving their workers a better working life.

However, according to the same logic, subsidies will not necessarily be forthcoming for firms that fail: Bankruptcy has become a threat that leads to efficiency. Whether Russian citizens can get used to the possibility of losing a job in a state that used to guarantee them employment is another question. Functional and regional decentralization moved so quickly in some sectors that by 1988, 170 Soviet firms were authorized to make business deals directly with foreign partners in contrast to the old "foreign trade monopoly" system of having all deals go through the Foreign Trade Ministry.

From the viewpoint of collective learning, the acid tests or ultimate models of *perestroika* were supposed to be joint ventures with foreigners which attract capital, transfer technological and organizational know-how, teach Russian managers sales marketing skills, and illustrate day-to-day operations (*glasnost*) as well as the more rapid pace of Western business (*uskorenie*). From the time the Joint Venture Act came into force in January 1987 to March 1988, thirty joint venture deals were approved with Western partners.

But in the early 1990s, the dissolution of the Soviet Union picked up speed. Gorbachev lost power and stepped down. The rise of Boris Yeltsin as the only elected President of Russia and his push for economic liberalism led to political and economic turmoil and rampant inflation. The traditionalists in the Russian parliament revolted. Yeltsin dissolved the parliament, calling for new elections. But the major winner in the elections of December 1993 was ultranationalist Vladimir Zhirinovsky, whose mislabeled "Liberal Democratic Party" overwhelmed Yeltsin's allies, symbolizing a conservative resistance to economic reforms and socioeconomic dislocations.[25] Voters, however, approved Yeltsin's constitution, which increased presidential power. The social trends culminating in these election results served to deter foreign investment as the Gross Domestic Product shrank by 19 percent in 1992, 12 percent in 1993 and by double-digits in 1994, making mass unemployment inevitable.

For example, German companies only invested about 29 million marks ($17 million) in Russia in the years 1991 and 1992, investing a far larger amount into Poland and the former Czechoslovakia (1.3 billion marks).[26] The main reasons: the chronic lack of **hard currencies** (that is, appreciation-tending convertible money) held by Russian customers; excessive Russian bureaucracy; legal uncertainties concerning private property; and the unclear jurisdiction of governmental authorities. The process by which the former

"East bloc" satellites such as Poland and Czechoslovakia positioned themselves for this investment is a fascinating lesson in collective learning.

EAST BLOC REVOLUTION

Philosopher Sören Kierkegaard told the story of a flock of geese kept in a wire cage by a farmer. One day one of the geese looked up and saw there was no top, telling the others excitedly: "Look, there is no top, we may leave and become free!" Few listened or turned their heads to the sky. So he flew away alone. When it became clear that Gorbachev would not use force to put down revolutionary change in his Eastern European satellites in 1989, one Eastern European people after another looked up and saw they were free to express themselves and to throw over their keepers. The top was off the cage and the birds just started to fly.[27]

The politico-economic revolutions in the Eastern bloc are examples *par excellence* of collective learning: one group mimicked another, revolting in domino series until not a single Communist Party monopoly was left standing intact. Within the first six months of 1990 all the nations of East Europe held free elections in one form or another. Actually, the 1989–1990 transformation was just the beginning of a collective learning process in which Eastern Europeans started to unlearn forty years of obedience to Communist one-party rule, of job security in state-run enterprises, and of working along as opposed to working hard given the absence of meaningful individual economic incentives. The revolutions brought widespread social uncertainty, skyrocketing inflation, devalued currencies, rising unemployment, and lack of confidence that newly elected leaders, who often had little experience, could manage the politico-economic crises.

An underground joke in the formerly Communist nations indicates the paradoxes of the economic development of the East bloc. In responding to the question "What is communism?" came the reply: "Communism is the longest and most painful route from capitalism to capitalism." Since all of the East bloc countries were scrambling at once to adopt the liberal assumptions of Western capitalist democracy in what was already becoming a "postliberal" age, it was clear that not all of them would be equally successful in attracting the foreign investment necessary for their successful transformations.

By 1994, foreigners had invested more than $10 billion since 1989 in the twenty-two successor states of the Comecon. Germany and the U.S. were the heaviest investors. Over half of all **foreign direct investment** (that is, the establishing or expanding of corporate operations in a foreign country) in Central and Eastern Europe went to Hungary in this period. Hungarian political stability and clear guidelines concerning private property were drawing cards. The Czech Republic started to rival Hungary as a magnet of foreign direct investment given the credibility of its stringent reforms even after the traumatic split up of Czechoslovakia into two separate nations, the Czech Republic and Slovakia. But let us focus in on the country coming in a distant third in terms of direct foreign investment—Poland.[28]

LIBERALIZATION AND PRIVATIZATION IN POLAND

Even though Poland by late 1993 was the only reformed East bloc country experiencing positive economic growth, it received less foreign investment than Romania on a per capita basis (although a greater absolute amount). An unresolved debt hangover and frequent changes in government due to political crises explain the difficulty Poland has had in attracting the funds it needs. By the end of 1992, in terms of registered foreign direct investment into Poland, the U.S. was responsible for 40 percent, Italy for 25 percent, Germany 15 percent, and France 7 percent. Whereas government approval for such foreign investment is unnecessary in Hungary, in Poland it is necessary for investments in defense, real estate, sea- and airports, and wholesale trade and legal services.[29] Government red-tape deters foreign investment.

It is not just the government that is *there* that brings Poland problems, but the government that is *not:* the coming and going of governments as the country tries to move from political liberalization to economic liberalization makes for an image of uncertainty. For example, when the Italian steel manufacturer Lucchini signed a letter of intent to purchase a majority share of Huta Warzawa, a state-owned Polish steel company in 1991, the Polish Industry Minister resigned the day before the Italians first sought government approval, and two months later the Prime Minister offered to resign the second time approval was requested.[30] Such delays discourage investors.

In 1989 the formerly outlawed Solidarity union movement began the transition into governmental power, initiating the economic reforms. The goal was simple—"to return to Europe." Specifically, the goal was to position Poland to join the prosperous European Common Market, now called the "European Union." But this requires the adoption of some 7,000 legal regulations and the **harmonization** (or matching) of national monetary and tax policies with those of the "Euro-club."

A key post-cold-war strategy of developing states is to position themselves to join a regional economic bloc made up mainly of developed states. In order to be asked to join, they try to learn from the developed states as models, mimicking their behavior—until they are slowed down by a cultural or political reaction at home stemming from threats to traditional perceptions of collective integrity.

By initially deciding to model its political and economic reforms after post-war European states to the west, Poland hoped to cut the costs of experimentation and gain early membership in the Common Market. As Deputy Prime Minister Leszek Balcerowicz described the Polish view of collective learning: "Poland is too poor to experiment. We will therefore follow work-ing models. Let the rich countries experiment if they want."[31]

Poland represents problems typical of most of the East bloc countries: an economy skewed towards the heavy industrialized sector and dominated by state-owned companies; underdevelopment of light industry, the service sector, the distribution and financial networks; plus an archaic agricultural system. Harvard economist Jeffrey Sachs (who advised Polish reformers) identifies three stages in Poland's economic reforms:[32]

(1) **Economic liberalization:** legal and administrative transformation to recognize the right to hold private property and to bring in market competition. This rep-resents reaching for classical economic liberalism.

(2) **Macroeconomic stabilization:** controlling **inflation** (or more money chasing fewer goods: a rise in the general level of prices) by limiting budget deficits, containing growth in the supply of money, and setting up a stable, uniform basis for the exchange of a convertible currency. This represents a mainte-nance strategy to establish economic equilibrium both in **fiscal policy** (the rela-tionship between government spending and taxes or income) and **monetary policy** (the government's policy of controlling the money supply, interest rates, and convertible exchange rates).

(3) **Privatization:** transferring state property to private hands. This represents an entrepreneurial strategy of taking risks for the sake of growth and development beyond the maintenance base of fiscal policy and monetary policy. The limits to privatization, of course, represent limits in the acceptance of classical economic liberalism.

Unlike many other economic reform plans in East Europe, the Polish strategy was to introduce these three stages in reform as quickly as possible. The rationale, as Jeffrey Sachs points out, is the same one that would apply if the British decided to shift from left-hand-side drive to right-hand-side drive on their roads: should the change be gradually introduced by first just putting trucks on the other side of the road, letting the other vehicles drive on the same side as usual? The Poles, in short, went for the "Big Bang" tempo of radical change, pushing through liberalization and stabilization all at once on January 1, 1990, followed six months later with privatization—the most difficult of the three stages given the massive restructuring and attitude changes required. As Sachs notes, if the Poles chose to privatize at the same rate as the British under the policies of Prime Minister Margaret Thatcher (who epitomized the return to Adam Smith's classical economic liberal-ism)—5 firms per year during the 1980s, it would take several hundred years to privatize the some 3,000 Polish industrial firms owned by the state![33]

Polish privatization has succeeded most markedly in the case of small retail businesses (also true in other Eastern states, including Russia), as well as in the trucking, construction, and small industrial sectors. But things have gone much more slowly in the large industrial sector. The plan here has been to distribute a certain number of shares freely to the citizens (a fashionable East European strategy), but given that there is not yet a stock market in the Western sense, it is hard to evaluate the consequences.

Early on, Polish economic reforms appeared successful as exports surged in 1990 and 1991. But imports surged too, as consumer-starved Poles bought Western goods. Prices shot up. On average, though, consumption was somewhat higher than before the reforms. However, of the $25 billion of aid pledged to Poland by the 24 richest nations of the West by 1993, little got to the Poles: advisors got some, some was never sent (due to "risks" in helping small businesses) and much went to the benefit of the donors rather than the donee. Unemployment exploded, hitting 10 percent by 1992—particularly in the small farming and large industrial sectors. Since the reform philosophy behind privatization made it more difficult to subsidize firms in the private sector than in the former publicly owned firms, the legitimacy of the government came under constant pressure by thousands of displaced people. Disenchantment became so great that those representing the Communists were reelected in 1993 as people sought to recover the integrity of their lost past.

Paradoxically, privatization increases growth and the range of choice in society, while imposing losses on beneficiaries in terms of jobs and social security.[34] *The shift from publicly to privately produced goods and services is the key to competitive liberalization economically, but it results in political and cultural attempts to recover lost social status and security. The postliberal era is characterized by cultural and social resistance to liberalism given the joblessness and dislocations that result from the creative destruction that it promotes.*

But "socialist resistance" was not limited to Poland and Eastern Europe. Consider the "socialist market economy" being developed by the Chinese. The Clinton administration took China so seriously that demands for human rights were put on the back burner in order to come to better terms with what could become the world's next geopolitical superpower, if not a key partner for American trade (and source of future U.S. jobs).

CHINA: FROM ECONOMIC REFORMS TO SUPERPOWER?

Ending 1993 with an annual economic growth rate of 13 percent, factory output up 23 percent and exploding retail sales, China appeared to have succeeded not only in its economic reforms, beginning in a shift to free markets in 1978, but to be a potential superpower.[35] When the World Bank recently decided to reorder the economic size of nations in terms of **purchasing power parity** (the ability of average people in a nation to buy the same basket of goods in their own currency), China was ranked number three (despite a per capita income of only about $380). And China *could* pass both number two (Japan) and number one (the U.S.) in two decades. But in order to become "Number One" in purchasing power parity, China will have to move beyond economic liberalization to consolidate its maintenance base with macroeconomic stability and successfully privatize its firms without pro-voking a destabilizing political revolution. To assess its post-cold-war eco-nomic chances more accurately, let us look briefly at Chinese post-World-War-II economic development.

Unlike the Polish case, the People's Republic of China was not con-strained in its *economic* experiments with the possibility of hegemonic inter-vention by a superpower (although there were times in its *political* revolution when Chinese leaders no doubt were concerned with a Soviet invasion as the Chinese turned radically to their own route to socialism). After his victory in the civil war and his establishment of the People's Republic of China in 1949, Mao Zedong turned first to the Stalinist model as a basis for Chinese mod-ernization: politicalization of the economy by the state and an emphasis upon heavy industry at all costs. However, by 1956 widespread famines in China had convinced Mao that the Stalinist model was not appropriate for the Chinese situation. In the Hundred Flowers Campaign, Mao emphasized the importance of agriculture given China's large rural areas as well as light industry, thus taking the focus away from heavy industry as the core of China's modernization. After the Revolution, control had been Mao's con-cern. Now it turned to feeding his people and creating a stable agricultural system. People, not machines, were his priority, he announced (he had more of them, after all). And the modernization of the rural areas became pri-mary, not the Soviet stress on urban centers.[36] Mao initiated the Great Leap Forward, which in many ways established the triumph of the Maoist ap-proach over Soviet modes.[37] The subtle pragmatism of Mao's strategy was not to break entirely with the Stalinist emphasis in the heavy industrial sector of the economy, but to concentrate on organizing human energy for the agricultural and light-industrial sectors without diverting material capital from heavy industry. Attention was paid to producing fertilizer, improving seeds, and developing irrigation and farm equipment.

But in opposition to some of the Chinese elite who argued for the ne-cessity of material incentives, Mao denounced capitalist tendencies that de-veloped among small producers as in agriculture. Ultimately, he sacrificed economic progress for the sake of his goal, which was the internationaliza-tion of Communist values through social education. He established the Cul-tural Revolution of 1966: He sent university students throughout China to spread his ideological doctrine, arresting capitalists and sending intellectuals out to work the fields. Pragmatist Deng Xiaoping, a former friend of Mao's in the leadership, was made a waiter.

Economic growth slowed in China and party unity was undermined as the political struggle between economic-growth-oriented technocrats and Maoist social revolutionaries polarized opinions in the society. Two years after Mao's death in 1976, following a period of understated "de-Maoification," Chinese leaders launched an ambitious investment program in industry and agriculture, depending upon imported technologies and loans from abroad.

The self-sufficient maintenance base of agriculture established by Mao became the launching pad for a series of market-oriented political and economic reforms that shook the socialist camp and impressed the industrialized West. China's annual average GNP growth rate went from 5.5 percent in the 1971–1975 period to 6.1 percent between 1976 and 1980, to top 9 percent throughout the 1980s.[38]

In the late 1970s, however, problems arose due to some of the consequences of the reforms: imbalances in industrial supplies, deterioration of consumption, higher state deficits, and inflation. In 1979 the Chinese took a step backward—called the policy of readjustment—in order to go ahead later with their major economic reform plans. Incentives in the farming sector were improved, permitting part of the farmland collectively owned by a state production team to be assigned to specific individuals, families, or groups. They, in turn, could keep the proceeds from any surplus production in excess of the contracted quota that went to the production team.

Gradually the distinction between "readjustment" and "reform" faded as more innovations were carefully introduced. Industrial firms were given more freedom in their production and marketing decisions and their managers became responsible for profits and losses. Bonuses and fringe benefits (such as company housing) could be used as incentives. And managers of such state-owned companies could sell or barter surplus products (after meeting their production quotas) and borrow funds from banks.

Beginning in 1981 small businesses were permitted to be opened in urban areas (if approved by government authorities) in fields like repairs, restaurants, or retailing. These entrepreneurs could hire one or two workers, or up to five apprentices in the case of skilled craftspeople. In 1984 a large private company was allowed to operate outside the state-planning system for the first time as a pilot experiment—the Minsheng Shipping Company.[39] As the largest Chinese conglomerate before the Revolution one has a sense here of the "restoration of an old maintenance base" to give it a better chance to succeed in an extremely competitive world economy—much as large German firms reemerged after a superficial effort at breaking them up after World War II or the Japanese *zaibatsu* (financial cliques) were reborn in their postwar reincarnation as *sogoshosha* or trading companies. *Political economic managers in times of structural stalemate attempt to breathe new life into their national economies by taking calculated entrepreneurial risks in support of the maintenance of old industrial champions from the past. Such maintenance-entrepreneurial strategy mixes are used as pilot experiments loaded toward recreating past success in new, competitive organizational forms.*

The collective learning strategy of the Chinese government before the 1989 rebellion was to call upon capitalists of former times to apply their skills to economic productivity. Thus the son of the founder of the Minsheng Shipping Company was put in charge of the company. Stockholders shared in profits and losses and paid taxes to the government on the company's profits. And the manager was free to hire and fire workers at will and to set business targets without interference by centralized planning. The experiment proved successful and was repeated in other regions, serving as a model.[40]

Similarly, in 1978 Zhao Ziyang, first secretary of the Communist Party in Sichuan Province, permitted six factories to keep a part of their profits for reinvestment in plant or distribution to the workers. Productive workers could be given bonuses and lazy ones punished. Within two years this pilot experiment spread to 6,600 enterprises, producing 45 percent of China's industrial output.[41] Such carefully planned and well-targeted pilot experiments in entrepreneurship could help to transform China into one of the world's great competitive nations in the twenty-first century.[42] Or, to paraphrase Mao, little sparks can set off forest fires. But fires have a way of suddenly springing out of control. . . .

To superimpose entrepreneurial market mechanisms on top of a Stalinesque centralized and control economy inevitably results in contradictions, confusion, and corruption. As permission to fire workers in China spread, state budget deficits escalated since the commitment to full employment must remain the top priority in a socialist state. Some entrepreneurs were obnoxiously successful, raising questions about the state's ability to keep the range of competitive inequalities in check. Workers soon learned to go after larger bonuses as a value rather than to produce or meet production targets as a social obligation above all others. Managers of refrigerator plants were subsidized with bonuses for producing a surplus much beyond the existing demand on the market, while less expensive items not as favorably targeted were underproduced although they were badly needed.

Such economic distortions and widespread reports of corruption on the part of selfish individuals led Chinese leaders to retrench and restore centralized planning where it had lapsed in the late 1980s. This retrenchment delayed plans to free prices of most goods and services, reimposed price controls that had been lifted, and cancelled construction projects and brought Beijing more actively back into managing the economy. While some feared that the retrenchment would slow down the initiative of restructuring in the Chinese economy, others thought the double-digit inflation rate, panic buying in anticipation of shortages, and reckless capital spending called for a reining in of the forces released by the decentralizing reforms.[43]

But typical of China's multiphase (as opposed to the West's polarized modes of either/or) policies, while some reforms were being pragmatically cut back, other forms of restructuring were being introduced, such as the transfer or ownership of homes from the state to private individuals. The pragmatism of China's reformist program is caught in the aphorism of the leader Deng Xiaoping: "It doesn't matter whether a cat is black or white; it matters only whether it can catch mice." And one new "mouse-trap" that China was experimenting with was the introduction of a more widespread stock market system. In 1988 the Communist party adopted a plan to turn state-owned companies into stock-issuing enterprises. And stock markets were set up in Beijing, Shenyang, and Shanghai, which mostly operated as do the Western bond markets, paying a fixed interest rate and not bringing ownership rights to shareholders. Initially, the stock system spread quite rapidly with between 7,000 and 10,000 firms having issued shares by 1989, one company on Hong Kong's border even trading stock to foreigners.[44] But then came the great democratic revolt and repression of 1989.

CAPITALIST REFORM MINUS DEMOCRACY EQUALS RAISED EXPECTATIONS AND REBELLION

In *The Old Regime and the French Revolution* (1856) Alexis de Tocqueville wrote that it is not always when things are going from bad to worse that revolutions break out, but rather when an oppressive rule over a long period without protest suddenly finds the government relaxing its pressure. So it was in the People's Republic of China where Deng thought capitalist reforms without political liberalization would modernize the Chinese state without difficulty. Even with economic growth and personal incomes expanding, the people found their raised expectations frustrated by inflation, political corruption, and the lack of freedom of speech. Resentment had also built up over market-oriented reforms near the coast by those in state-run firms inland.

In April of 1989, thousands of students, later joined by workers, marched through the capital of Beijing demanding more democracy and an end to government corruption. Defying a ban on public protests, they camped in Tiananmen Square, set up tents, and began a hunger strike. In the middle of this, Mikhail Gorbachev, on a state visit to China, arrived to formally reconcile the antagonism between the two Communist countries. Both the demonstrators and the government initially showed great restraint toward each other until a government split between hard-liners and those sympathetic with the students was resolved by the victory of the hard-liners. In early June, the hard-liners ordered troops from outlying parts of China who were unfamiliar with the meaning of the protests to come in and to take over the center of Beijing with force. Hundreds of people were killed or wounded by soldiers and tanks. Deng (fearing that another student cultural revolution would do him in again) and hard-liner Prime Minister Li Peng consolidated their power. Intellectuals and leaders of the democratic rebellion were imprisoned.

Initially, the government crackdown damaged the infrastructure in Chinese cities, raised great feelings of uncertainty among the Chinese people, and caused a mass exodus of foreigners. The American government, among others, halted weapons and technology transfer to China and was openly critical of human rights violations. But the Chinese regime ignored these criticisms and proceded with targeted economic reforms combined with political repression.

In 1990, the government permitted foreign development of land, the Shanghai stock exchange opened, and foreign banks began to resume lending to China. During the next two years, the government eliminated export subsidies, attempting to qualify for membership in the General Agreement on Tariffs and Trade (GATT). Tariffs were lowered on a number of goods and price controls were restricted to a handful of basic necessities. By 1993, the Chinese strategy appeared to have paid off as the Chinese economy grew at an inflation-adjusted rate of 12.8 percent and the Clinton administration renewed China's most-favored-nation trade status. (This was done on an annual basis, presumably pending "progress" on human rights.) While industrial output had increased six-fold compared to the late 1970s, the free market in China seemed almost out of control as acceptance of capitalism was often considered synonymous with corruption and crime rates rose as fast as economic growth.[45] The prices of property and stock skyrocketed and inflation at times appeared to be out of control. Deng praised moneymaking and made clear that government measures to curb corruption should not discourage enthusiasm for economic growth. The regime's strategy appeared to be to give the people the economic hope of becoming rich to distract them from the Western temptation of becoming liberated politically. It was a postliberal strategy of building a "socialist market economy" that seemed to result in short-term success, even though foreign observers worried about the Chinese economy "overheating." Foreigners fail to appreciate the existing stocks of **social capital,** the embedded community trust, norms and networks that facilitate collective learning, and the accurate targeting of local entrepreneurship.[46]

The Chinese are moving through the basic three stages of post-cold-war liberal economics we have identified: economic liberalization, macroeconomic stability, and privatization. But their development is distinguished by their unique culture and their geographic and demographic circumstances. The vast area of the country encouraged the Chinese government to target economic liberalization in certain "pilot areas," particularly regions near Hong Kong (such as Guangdong) and the coasts, where free-market behavior is most advanced. Macroeconomic stabilization has been extremely difficult since China has more of a society or civilization than a "state" in the Western sense.[47] This complicates the centralized control of the money supply by a "central bank." The risk of hyperinflation is thus built into the system, making it easier to stimulate economic growth than to slow down such stimulation when the economy threatens to become "too hot." In 1994, economic growth slowed sharply as inflation stayed high. Finally, privatization is being gradually introduced in targeting particular sectors and even specific "pilot companies." For example, the Shougang Corporation, a steel producer, has developed a unique "Shougang Contract System" personally approved by Deng Xiaoping, the general designer of China's economic reform.

The Shougang Contract System involves: the firm contracting with the state, defining the limits of privatization; internal contracts within the firm; salary increases tied to individual contributions; company policies decided upon democratically by workers and staff; and a share-holding system in which a certain percentage of the profits are remitted to the state. The hard negotiations in the system, not surprisingly, concern how much of the profits should be paid annually to the state. Such gradual privatization experiments in the large industrial sector permit the Chinese to maintain a sense of state control and "profit-sharing," while still providing autonomy and worker motivation. Shougang Corporation's productivity and profitability have increased significantly since the introduction of the contract system and the company has expanded from iron and steel to 17 other sectors including electronics, finance, shipbuilding, and tourism. By 1994, the Shougang Corporation was made up of 12 large companies with some 158 large- and medium-sized factories, 57 domestic affiliates, and 61 joint ventures with both Chinese and foreign partners.[48] About half of industrial output can be attributed to state enterprises. However, they usually lose money and tend to grow only with subsidies from Beijing.

LEARNING PRINCIPLES:
POSITIVE TRANSPARENCY AND AGENCY

In terms of collective learning, the Chinese elite observed the disintegration of the Soviet Union and its depressing economic consequences and decided to go their own way. Their strategy was based upon the assumption that economic liberalization could procede without significant political liberalization. That this strategy has largely succeeded despite the massive political repression of the democratic revolt of 1989 is due in large part to an astute policy of creating economic hope by praising the virtues of wealth and opening opportunities for entrepreneurship. This is a **policy of positive transparency:** *the reporting of facts in a context of hope that makes it imaginable that they can be changed, improved upon, and learned from in order to better the life chances of the people.*[49]

Contrast this Chinese policy, for a moment, with the inadvertent **policy of negative transparency** from which the communities in the former Soviet Union have suffered: suddenly, centralized barriers to information flow were stripped away, exposing overwhelming levels of hidden pollution, sickness, inflation, and social and economic underdevelopment. Overnight, the people in Russia, for example, were shocked to learn that birth defects among newborns were rising at almost the same sharp rate as the population growth was falling and that the number of mothers dying during pregnancy and childbirth was ten times higher in Russia than in developed countries. The same policy of negative transparency stunned the Russian people when they learned that the number of children born out of wedlock had risen to 15 percent. In the United States, the rate is above 25 percent and shocks no one![50]

The policy of negative transparency blocks collective learning with *future shock*—the sense of being overwhelmed with change, rather than stimulating positive collective action to adapt and to improve. Collective learning builds upon strength, not weakness. If the only news you hear is bad news, it is difficult to focus on your strength and to motivate others. Individuals overwhelmed with dismal facts presented in a negative context perceive themselves to be powerless. The incentives to learn are missing. The staggering environmental, social and economic problems of a society must be faced but in a context of positive transparency that gives them hope and a framework in which action can be seen to lead to concrete improvement. Collective learning that results in positive economic change depends upon a **sense of agency**—the belief that individual action makes a critical difference.

Psychologist M. Brewster Smith put it this way: "Some people more than others seem to be in charge of their lives—to be Agents or "Origins" of personal causation rather than Pawns. The unprecedented human situation with its headlong trends toward multiple disaster sets a high premium upon Agency, upon the rearing of people who will not passively take these trends for granted."[51]

A policy of positive transparency increases the sense of agency by giving dependent communities the self-confidence to become more independent and self-sufficient. The neoclassical recipes àla Jeffrey Sachs summed up here—economic liberalization, macroeconomic stability, and privatization—are keys to such independence in the post-cold-war world economy. But Sachs typically pushes all of these policies at the same time in a form of "shock therapy": controlling inflation, cutting subsidies to state industries, freeing up price controls so that prices follow the market, and so on. And some countries that have been "Sachsed," such as Poland and Russia (where government elites hired the Harvard economics professor as a key advisor) have discovered that despite positive initial economic results, a cultural and political reaction sets in, an understandable resistance to being shocked by so much change at once. Sachs's fast-fix tempo worked well when first tried in Bolivia, rapidly reducing the inflation rate of 24,000 percent per year in the mid-1980s. But the Polish and Russian resistance to radical neoclassical economic therapy was underestimated, leading the Polish to bring back hard-line Communists and the Russians to bring back right-wing nationalist extremists. U.S. Deputy Secretary of State Strobe Talbott, Clinton's key advisor on Russia, argued that Russia needed "less shock and more therapy," consolidating support for Yeltsin.[52] Too many people were thrown out of work and dislocated from social security and the traditional cultural context.

By 1994, Yeltsin's two-year proliberalism economic reform movement was over as his proreform cabinet ministers resigned under pressure from right-wing members of parliament. The reforms brought down the inflation rate from 2000 percent in 1992 to about 900 percent in 1993. The antireformist consolidation would serve to stabilize the Russian government in the short term but at the price of again increasing inflation as more rubles were printed and state-sponsored corruption spread. Sachs protested the idea that Russia had ever really had a "shock therapy" at all, given an inflation rate that never fell below 20 percent per month and the fact that only five privatized firms were declared bankrupt in 1993. And he accused the West of making the Russian problem worse by promising $28 billion in aid, while only putting $4 billion on the table.[53] Upon resigning as an advisor to Yeltsin in 1994, Sachs was sharply critical of the International Monetary Fund for pushing Russia to cut its deficit without providing any noninflationary means to finance part of it.[54]

The post-cold-war economic order has become a postliberal order in which each cultural unit first seeks the wealth and liberation promised by neoclassical economic recipes only to back off at some point in movements of resistance for the sake of political autonomy and cultural integrity. In this process, the world money system clearly plays a critical role, as illustrated in the next chapter.

THOUGHT QUESTIONS

1. Characterize the former Stalinist-Communist economic model by interrelating the following key terms:
   * allocation of resources
   * output goals
   * full ("overfull") employment
   * inflation
   * pricing system
   * marketing

   Why were managers inclined to "avoid new technology"? Why in general, was risk-reduction rewarded?

2. Describe the reform concept launched by Gorbachev using his own term and illustrating it in the framework of economic development in the post-Stalin era.

3. Explain the three stages of liberal economic reform identified by Jeffrey Sachs and their "Big Bang" implementation in Poland after January 1, 1990.

4. Show how Mao, Zhao Ziyang and Deng Xiaoping followed through on a multiphase economic policy, at times even taking "one step backward

in order to take two steps forward." What could have caused the rebellion of April-June 1990?

5. Evaluate the psychological elements expressed in the policies of positive/negative transparency in their effect on the success of economic reforms in the former USSR and in China. Give examples in your country of "the sense of agency."

NOTES

1. For a lucid example of the preoccupation of the industrialized countries of the North with themselves, see Lester Thurow, *Head to Head: The Coming Economic Battle Among Japan, Europe and America* (New York: William Morrow and Co., 1992).

2. See Wilhelm Hankel, *Die sieben Todsünden der Vereinigung: Wege aus dem Wirtschaftsdesaster* (Berlin: Siedler Verlag, 1993). For a more positive view, see W.R. Smyser, *The Economy of United Germany: Colossus at the Crossroads* (New York: St. Martin's Press, 1992).

3. See, for instance, Christopher Layne and Benjamin C. Schwarz, "The Perils of Stability," *The New York Times*, October 3, 1993, in which they suggest that "By linking America's prosperity to international economic interdependence and using our military commitments to secure that interdependence, U.S. strategy oddly conforms to the Marxist interpretation of American foreign policy."

4. See Samuel P. Huntington, "The Clash of Civilizations," *Foreign Affairs*, Summer, 1993, in which he argues that future conflicts in world politics will be dominated not by ideology or economics but by the clash of civilizations, and particularly Western civilization against the rest (which could, of course, be interpreted as an ideological viewpoint in itself).

5. V.I. Lenin, *Selected Works* (Moscow: Lenin Institute, 1963–1969), Vol. 2, p. 709. For a summary of Lenin's development, see "Lenin: Elites, Imperialism and Revolution," Chapter 2 in R. Isaak, *Individuals and World Politics*, 2nd edition (Belmont, CA: Duxbury Press of Wadsworth Publishing Co., 1981).

6. Ellen Comisso and Laura Tyson, "Preface" to special issue on "Power, Purpose and Collective Choice: Economic Strategy in Socialist States," *International Organization* Vol. 40, No. 2 (Spring 1986):189.

7. Franklyn D. Holzman and Robert Legvold, "The Economics and Politics of East–West Relations," in C. Fred Bergsten and Lawrence B. Krause, eds., *World Politics and International Economics* (Washington, DC: The Brookings Institution, 1975), p. 284. On "overfull" employment planning, see Franklyn D. Holzman, "Overfull Employment Planning, Input-Output, and The Soviet Economic Reforms," *Soviet Studies* 22 (October 1970):255–61.

8. See Ludwig von Mises, "Economic Calculation in the Socialist Commonwealth," in *Collectivist Economic Planning*, edited by F.A. Hayek (London: Routledge & Kegan Paul, Ltd., 1935), pp. 87–130.

9. Holzman and Legvold, "East–West Relations," pp. 285–286.

10. See János Kornai, *Economics of Shortage*, 2 vols (Amsterdam: North Holland, 1980), and Paul R. Gregory, "The Stalinist Command Economy," in *The Annals*, 507, January, 1990:18–25.

11. Holzman and Legvold, "East–West Relations," pp. 286–87.

12. Glen Alden Smith, *Soviet Foreign Trade* (New York: Praeger, 1973), pp. 81–83.

13. Edward Weisband, Robert Rosh, and Scott Rosenthal, "Dual Ghettos and Dependent Development: The Economic Consequences of Superpower Hegemony in Eastern Europe and Latin America," paper presented at the Annual Meeting of the International Studies Association, Atlanta, Georgia, March 27–30, 1984.

14. J. Wilcyznski, *The Economies of Socialism*, 4th edition (New York: George Allen and Unwin Press, 1982), p. 53.

15. Weisband et al., p. 17.

16. R.A. Isaak, "International Integration and Foreign Policy Decision-making," an unpublished doctoral dissertation (New York University, 1971), pp. 232–42.

17. See D.A. Loeber and A.P. Friedland, "Soviet Imports of Industrial Installations under Compensation Agreements: West Europe's Siberian Pipeline Revisited," *Columbia Journal of World Business* 18, No. 4 (Winter 1983):51–62. One observer has noted that the key rule operative in Cocom is that "In America everything is banned that is not expressly permitted, while in most of Europe the opposite is true." See Jürgen Klotz, "Not Everyone Believes Cocom Can Stop Technology Transfer to East Bloc," *The German Tribune*, No. 1289, September 1987, p. 7.

18. Frederick Kempe and Eduardo Lachica, "Cocom Feuds over Trade to East Bloc," *The Wall Street Journal*, July 17, 1984, p. 27.

19. See UNCTAD Secretariat, report of the Secretariat, *Towards the Technological Transformation of Developing Countries* (New York: United Nations, 1979) and Bruce R. Guile and Harvey Brooks, eds., *Technology and Global Industry: Companies and Nations in the World Economy* (Washington, DC: National Academy Press, 1987).

20. Statistics from the *CIA Handbook of Economic Statistics; International Institute for Strategic Studies: The Military Balance: 1988–1989; OECD Economic Outlook, December 1988* as reported in *The Wall Street Journal*, January 23, 1989.

21. Graham T. Allison, Jr., "Testing Gorbachev," *Foreign Affairs* 67, No. 1 (Fall 1988):20. For an analysis of the stalemated Soviet economy see Marshall I. Goldman, *U.S.S.R. in Crisis: The Failure of an Economic System* (New York: W.W. Norton, 1983).

22. Axel Lebahn, *Politische und wirtschaftliche Auswirkungen der Perestrojka auf die Sowjetunion sowie auf ihre Beziehungen zu Osteuropa und zum Westen, Aussenpolitik*, Jg. 39, No. II, 1988, p. 114.

23. Ibid., p. 109.

24. See Mikhail Gorbachev, *Perestroika: New Thinking for Our Country and the World* (New York: Harper & Row, 1987).

25. See, for example, Elisabeth Runfien, "Signs Grow of Cabinet Shake-Up, Retreat From Reforms in Russia: Postelection Decisions Are Counter to Austerity, Privatization Policies," *The Wall Street Journal*, Dec. 20, 1993, p. A8. And see "Institutes: Russian Economy Continues to Decline," *The Week in Germany* (New York: The German Information Center), May 13, 1994.

26. "Poll: Lack of Hard Currency Hinders German–Russian Business Deals," *The Week in Germany*, Nov. 26, 1993, p. 5.

27. For background on the Eastern European events, see Hoyt Gimlin, "Balkanization of Eastern Europe (Again)," *Congressional Quarterly Research Reports*, Vol. 2, No. 17, Nov. 3, 1989, pp. 618–630, and "East of Eden: A Survey of Eastern Europe," *The Economist*, Aug. 12, 1989, p. 11 and following.

28. The statistics above are from "Eastern Europe: Foreign Investment—A Harbinger of Economic Recovery," *Trends: Economy, Politics and Financial Markets* Frankfurt: Dresdner Bank, August 1993, pp. 13–17.

29. Ibid., pp. 14 and 17.

30. Gail E. Schares, "Eastern Europe Tries to Stoke up its Fire Sale," *Business Week,* October 21, 1991, p. 52.

31. Cited in Jeffrey Sachs, "The Economic Transformation of Eastern Europe: The Case of Poland," *The American Economist,* Vol. 36, No. 2 (Fall 1992), p. 4.

32. Sachs, p. 5 and following.

33. Ibid., p. 6. On the disappearance of aid to Poland, see Barry Newman, "Disappearing Act: West Pledged Billions of Aid to Poland—Where Did It All Go?", *The Wall Street Journal,* Feb. 23, 1994.

34. I am grateful to Alexander Keck of Pace University and the University of Heidelberg for this particular formulation of the dilemma. The following books and articles illustrate the growing literature on the trade-offs involved in the process of privatization: Raymond Vernon, *The Promise of Privatization* (New York: Council on Foreign Relations, 1988); John Vickers, *The Politics of Privatization in Western Europe* (London: Totowa, 1989); Dennis Gayle, *Privatization and Deregulation in Global Perspective* (New York: Quorum Books, 1990); Hans Blommestein, *Methodes de privatisation des grandes entreprises* (Paris: *Centre pour la cooperation avec les economies europeenes en transition,* 1993); Steve Hanke, ed., *Privatization and Development* (San Francisco, CA: The International Center for Economic Growth, 1987); Kevin R. McDonald, "Why Privatization Is Not Enough," *Harvard Business Review,* May–June 1993, pp. 49–59; Sandra Wilson, "The Private Sector and Local Authorities, *The OECD Observer,* October/November 1992, pp. 25–28; Ira Lieberman, "Why Is Privatization Currently A Major Issue?" *The Columbia Journal of World Business,* Spring 1993, pp. 9–17; "Why Jobs Come Last," *The Economist,* April 25, 1992, pp. 63–64; David Rudnick, "The Pains of Going Private," *Euromoney Supplement,* May 1993, pp. 21–23.

35. "Cracking the China Market," *The Wall Street Journal,* Dec. 10, 1993, R1.

36. See "Mao: Charisma, Limited Warfare and Modernization," Chapter 3 in Isaak, *Individuals and World Politics,* pp. 44–61.

37. Benjamin Schwartz, "China's Developmental Experience 1949–1972," in Michel Oksenberg, ed., *China's Developmental Experience* (New York: Praeger, 1973), p. 22. Also see Michel Oksenberg, "Policy Making under Mao Tse-tung 1949–1968," *Comparative Politics* 3, No. 3 (1971):323–60.

38. *The Wall Street Journal,* January 23, 1989, p. A8.

39. Haitani, "Market and Planning," pp. 359–60.

40. See Vigor Fung, "China Allows the Rebirth of Some Private Corporations," *The Wall Street Journal,* August 10, 1984, p. 22.

41. "China Walks the Edge of the Capitalist Road," *Business Week* October 18, 1982, pp. 80–86.

42. See Dwight H. Perkins, *China—Asia's Next Economic Giant.* Seattle: University of Washington Press, 1986; and N.J. Wang, *China's Modernization and Transnational Corporations* (Lexington, MA: D.C. Heath and Co., 1984).

43. Nicholas Kristof, "China's Big Lurch Backward Theory Is Now Seen as Study in Pragmatism," *The New York Times,* January 3, 1989.

44. Nicholas Kristof, "Selling China on a 'Public' Privatization," *The New York Times,* January 8, 1989. On events leading up to the 1989 policy reversal, see John P.

Burns, "China's Governance: Political Reform in a Turbulent Environment," *The China Quarterly* (Special Issue: The People's Republic of China after 40 Years), Sept. 1989, pp. 481–518.

45. "Cracking the China Market," R2 and following.

46. On social capital, see Robert D. Putnam, "The Prosperous Community: Social Capital and Economic Growth," *The American Prospect,* Spring 1993, pp. 35–42.

47. See, for example, Jonathan D. Spence, *The Search for Modern China* (New York: W.W. Norton, 1990), and Ezra Vogel, *One Step Ahead in China: Guangdong under Reform* (Cambridge, MA: Harvard University Press, 1989).

48. The data on the Shougang Contract System comes from Rong-pin Kang, "The Shougang Contract Management Responsibility System: Effects, Practices and Thoughts" (Beijing: Institute for International Business, Shougang Research and Development Co., 1993). Also see "China Economy Slows, Challenging Investors," *Wall St. Journal,* May 16, 1994.

49. R. Isaak, "Developing Country Recipes for Collective Learning, Economic Development & Global Environmental Responsibility," (p. 7), a paper first presented at the International Environmental Institutions Research Seminar at Harvard's Center for Science and International Affairs, December 11, 1992, revised for presentation at the 1993 annual International Studies Association Convention in Acapulco, March 27, 1993 and published as *Working Paper No. 116,* November 1993, by the Center for Applied Research, Pace University, 1 Pace Plaza, N.Y., N.Y. 10032.

50. Statistics from *The New York Times,* October 4, 1992.

51. M. Brewster Smith, "On Self-Actualization: A Transambivalent Examination of a Focal Theme in Maslow's Psychology," *Journal of Humanistic Psychology,* 13, No. 2 (1973), pp. 17–33.

52. Carla Anne Robbins, "Talbott's Abiding Passion for Russia Shapes His Career and Clinton Administration's Policy," *The Wall Street Journal,* January 7, 1994.

53. Interview with Jeffrey Sachs on the MacNeil-Lehrer Newshour, public television (Channel 13), New York City, January 21, 1994. Sachs forecast in this interview that Russia was moving towards incoherence, hyperinflation, huge budget deficits, and extensive corruption through black markets. He was pessimistic that Russia would be willing to adopt the necessary therapies of moving to print less money and to stop subsidies for firms.

54. Jeffrey Sachs, "The Reformers' Tragedy," *The New York Times,* Jan. 23, 1994, Op-Ed.

CHAPTER THREE

THE WORLD MONETARY SYSTEM

Money has a life of its own which it properly should not have.

Lionel Trilling

The status quo is no streetcar named desire.

Wilhelm Hankel

Money or currency (*Bargeld* in German) is a form of **liquidity** or lifeblood that keeps the pieces of the world economy moving. Like a motor without oil, an economic system without sufficient liquidity slows down until it reaches an ultimate break-point—entropy. But although money was once a commodity in former times like gold or potatoes, it has become a fiat object of desire—a mysterious subjective phenomenon: The value of one national form of money or currency relative to another is literally changing every minute. The key question of the world's monetary system is whose currency carries the most weight, why, and for how long relative to other currencies and reserve assets (that is, gold)?

The asymmetry between the rich and poor nations of the world is reflected in their currencies: The rich are usually **hard** (appreciation-tending) currency countries, the poor are normally **soft** or "weak" (depreciation-tending) currency countries. The richest of the rich—the United States—had the hardest of the hard currencies at its peak moment of hegemony following World War II. At this most sovereign moment of military and economic power, policymakers in the United States, in collaboration with those of the *pax Britannica* power structure whom they were replacing, symbolized the hardness of the dollar by guaranteeing that anyone who wanted to cash it in could do so for gold—at the 1934 rate of $35 an ounce. The dollar was declared as good as gold. It became the world's chief **reserve currency,** meaning that individuals and foreign governments were willing to hold dollars rather than to cash them in for gold held in the U.S. Treasury. As long as the emperor (or hegemon) was clothed in untouchable power and could maintain the legitimacy he had imposed in victory, the credibility of the paper dollar I.O.U.'s he printed remained intact.

Led by the United States, the hard-currency countries since World War II have pursued a maintenance strategy of preserving equilibrium among the world's currencies before all else. Generally, stability has been promoted over economic growth, and the containment of inflation over the creation of credit. It is as if Western managers were overawed by Lenin's declaration that the best way to destroy the capitalistic system was to debauch the currency.[1] The stability of the world's money system makes great sense to those who happen to have money—*hard* money. That this priority should have overwhelmed others in the economic settlement at Bretton Woods, in 1944 (as World War II was about to end) should come as little surprise in the conservative atmosphere inevitably generated by military chaos and its aftermath. The longing for peace and order included the desire for some fixed and stable source of value.

ORIGINS

The history of money is the story of an evolution from commodity money—shells and gold—to credit (or fiduciary) money—paper currency and credit cards. This evolution was marked by the increasing demystification of money through the secularization of culture. For example, in the West African monarchy of Dahomey, cowrie shell money was considered a sacred currency lending divinity to the king.* When Dahomey was conquered by the French, the franc replaced the cowrie shell in the African money market, and the shells lost their sacred aura with the secularization of the society.[2]

Financial innovation transformed barter transactions to paper credit transactions with the creation of letters of credit and, following the invention of the printing press, paper money. As credit money expanded, the status imbued in the possessor of money was democratized: Suddenly one could be rich without owning land, and entrepreneurs could start enterprises on credit, not having a penny of their own to put down on the project. As the

---

*In terms of etymology, the word *money* derives from the Latin words *monere* (admonish) and *moneta* (the mint in Rome: the temple of *Juno Moneta,* "the nagging Juno" who gave advice, warned, and admonished!).

technical means to create credit exploded—epitomized today by plastic credit cards and quiet ticks in computer banking systems—the inflationary effects undermining the class status of commodity ownership by the "old rich" nobility surfaced: The established naturally began to resist the inflationary financing and the taxing of old rich estates, thus creating large numbers of "new rich" competitors. By this time the new rich of the developed countries had accumulated assets of their own to protect against the loss of value, and a stability-over-growth savers' mentality became widespread.[3] This conservative maintenance preoccupation was further stimulated by the inflation following World War I and by the stock market crash and Great Depression that began in 1929. In the United States, between 1929 and 1933 the GNP dropped from $103 billion to $56 billion, resulting in hardship, bankruptcies, bank failures, and political unrest. Stability was sought over all else. And those framing the post–World War II settlement remembered this. From 1945 to 1950, the United States gave Western Europe $20 billion in grants and loans—the Marshall Plan (or "the First Redistribution"). Beyond this the Americans worked to stabilize postwar economic chaos with the Bretton Woods Exchange-Rate System, the International Monetary Fund, and the International Bank for Reconstruction and Development.

The Bretton Woods System

The **Bretton Woods system** refers to the charter negotiated in July 1944 at Bretton Woods, New Hampshire, which established the **International Monetary Fund (IMF)** as well as the fund's sister institution, the International Bank for Reconstruction and Development (IBRD), or **World Bank.** This monetary system was fundamentally aimed to avoid the competitive exchange rate devaluations and "beggar-thy-neighbor" policies that led to the breakdown of the international monetary system in the 1930s following the Great Depression. The system was thus preoccupied with equilibrium or system maintenance, deriving from Anglo-American hegemony, heavily weighted toward the American position.

American Secretary of State Cordell Hull had set the stage for American predominance in the negotiations with Britain by using the Lend-Lease Act of 1941 to break the back of the British financial empire. Desperate for war matériels with which to fight the Germans, the British agreed to the loan conditions, which Hull knew would put the British in a structural position of financial dependence after the war: an example *par excellence* of *positioning* as the critical activity of international political economy.

The U.S. plan for the postwar economic order originated, however, not in the State Department but in the Treasury Department, under the supervision of Harry Dexter White.[4] An ambitious man with foresight, White produced a plan for the postwar international monetary system that was to bear his name before the end of 1941. Initially, the White plan aimed to prevent the disruption of foreign exchanges and collapse of monetary and credit systems, to assure the restoration of foreign trade, and to supply the large volume of capital needed throughout the world for reconstruction, relief, and economic recovery. These tasks were to be performed by a stabilization institution (the IMF) and an international bank for reconstruction (the IBRD, or World Bank).

White's plan went boldly against the predominant American public opinion trends of isolation and financial orthodoxy. The Stabilization Fund was to be made up of at least $5 billion (from contributions of member countries in gold, local currency, and government securities). This money would be used to help member countries overcome short-term balance-of-payments difficulties. The World Bank was to have twice as much capital stock as the Stabilization Fund in order to provide the liquidity needed for reconstruction, relief, and economic recovery for the "united" nations. It was to do this by making long-term loans at very low interest rates. However, in 1942 White's group in the U.S. Treasury made the Stabilization Fund the priority, letting plans for the World Bank languish—a decisive preference that was stimulated by the emerging conservative political milieu in the United States.

The British were represented at Bretton Woods by economist John Maynard Keynes, for whom White had great respect. By late 1941 Keynes had developed a plan for an International Clearing Union based upon the centralization of exchange transactions through central banks in contrast to White's stress upon the restoration of competitive exchange markets with limited interventions by central markets to influence the exchange rate. The Keynes plan called for the creation of a new reserve asset, *bancor* (the forerunner of SDRs, or Special Drawing Rights, later adopted by the IMF), while White's design maintained the gold-exchange standard reinforced by a Stabilization Fund (the IMF). Keynes pushed for the symmetry in adjustment of exchange rate imbalances so that the creditor or surplus countries would share the burden with the debtor or deficit countries.

Anticipating a deflationary environment with a scarcity in demand after the war (a false prognosis as it turned out), the Keynes plan provided for overdraft rights of $26 billion, meaning that the potential U.S. liability could have amounted to as much as $23 billion—some $20 billion more than the final version of the White plan (calling for $5.2 billion with a U.S. contribution of $3.2 billion). And access to the credit under Keynes's plan was automatic, whereas White's plan called for strict lending conditions. Ultimately, the articles of the IMF reflected White's proposals rather than those of Keynes—a foregone conclusion given U.S. hegemony in 1944.

The Bretton Woods system, dominated as it was by the maintenance or stabilization bias of the IMF articles *a la* White, is perhaps most accurately seen as a system of macroeconomic management and microeconomic liberalism.[5] Paradoxically, this macromanagement, microliberalism mix was the intellectual position of Keynes preceding World War II—a position so influential that it had become the consensus epitomized by White at Bretton Woods.

Keynes, meanwhile, had gone on to more farsighted ideas of creating techniques of credit and liquidity that would assist the countries most devastated by the war with the least capability of helping themselves. This would be achieved by soft, long-term interest terms (or a heavy dose of "illiberalism" for the sake of the disadvantaged). Believing that U.S. policies would predominate over all others, Keynes successfully negotiated for a passive IMF role in economic adjustment against the American internationalist, interventionist position. This was consistent with the primacy of national sovereignty. It also squared with Keynes's interwar intellectual position (reflected in his *General Theory*) that exchange rates should be chosen with a view toward supporting domestic policy rather than using international exchange rates as a straitjacket to which domestic policy must conform (the position of some monetarists of the 1980s).

Keynes's position at Bretton Woods was not based merely on a short-term forecast of how he expected the world economy to go (into deflation). Rather, his economic perspective had an ethical base. Having studied the theory of probability under the influence of philosopher G.E. Moore's ethical system, Keynes was inspired by the obligation so to act as to produce by causal connection the most probable maximum amount of eventual good through the entire procession of future ages (as recorded in his *Two Memoirs*).[6] Keynes's long-term preoccupation was with the human suffering of unemployment. He was determined to fight for sufficient international liquidity to stimulate demand in critical situations in order to bring depressed countries back on their feet, providing work through economic growth. As Lord Keynes put it in an address to the House of Lords in which he sought to win British support for the Bretton Woods charter: "Sometimes almost alone, in popular articles in the press, in pamphlets, in dozens of letters to *The Times,* in text books, in enormous and obscure treatises I have spent my strength to persuade my countrymen and the world at large to change their traditional doctrines and, by taking better thought, to remove the curse of unemployment."[7] The IMF, Keynes claimed, would help check unemployment by supporting three key Keynesian principles:

1. Domestic policies should primarily determine the external value of a country's currency, not the other way around.
2. Domestic policy should have control over domestic rates of interest to keep them as low as suits the national purpose, without interference from the ebb and flow of international capital movements or flights of "hot money."
3. While countries should aim to prevent inflation at home, they should not accept deflation dictated by outside influences.

Naturally, Keynes argued these principles in terms of British national interests, the "dictates from outside" presumably being American influences. The United States opposed the larger amount of liquidity Keynes proposed. It wanted to limit its potential liability as the world's largest creditor nation in the postwar order and feared that unmanageable inflation would be generated. Similarly, the Americans did not want as much flexibility in exchange rates as the British sought. Finally, the United States lightened the potential sanction on surplus nations to get them to move toward balance-of-payments equilibrium, leaving the weight of the burden for adjustment heavily on the debtor nations. By limiting the amount of liquidity that could be lent by the IMF and by establishing strict conditions (or **conditionality**) for such loans, American diplomats sought to win over a skeptical, conservative U.S. Congress that must ultimately approve how government money is spent. In sum, the Americans succeeded in establishing a blueprint for noninflationary, economic growth aimed at full employment and restoring competitive exchange rates at Bretton Woods. The fatal flaw, which was later to bring down the system, was that everything was based on the assumption that the dollar could forever be converted freely into gold. This flaw was natural for a hegemonic power at its peak when both its dominance and legitimacy as reflected in the strength of its currency were taken for granted.

THE IMF.   The International Monetary Fund officially came into being when representatives of forty-four nations signed the Articles of Agreement stemming from the Anglo-American negotiations in July 1944 in Bretton Woods, New Hampshire.[8] By the end of 1945 the critical number of countries had ratified the agreement. The Board of Governors first met in March 1946, adopting by-laws and deciding to locate the IMF's headquarters in Washington, D.C. A year later the IMF began exchange operations. Its objectives were to secure international monetary cooperation, stabilize exchange rates, and expand international liquidity for the sake of international trade and full employment.

To achieve its aims, the IMF initially tried to maintain fixed exchange values of currencies (linked to the given dollar–gold rate) and to eliminate exchange controls. To ease the transition to the new system, a one-time adjustment of up to 10 percent in the initial value of each currency was permitted. However, once the designated *par value* of a currency had been established, a member country could only make major changes with the fund's approval. Such approval depended upon whether or not the country's balance of payments was in "fundamental disequilibrium." In other words, the key criterion of the IMF in terms of exchange rates is the *maintenance of stability,* or the recovery of stability or equilibrium in the case of countries with deficits. Such stability was assumed to be the prerequisite for the collective goals of economic growth and steady investment.

Upon joining the IMF, a country is assigned a quota depending upon its position* in the world economy, which governs the size of its cash sub-

---

*A member country's position is measured by its volume of international trade, national income, and international reserve holdings.

scriptions, its voting power, and its drawing rights. Each member nation pays a quarter of its quota in SDRs and the remainder in its own currency. When a member country runs into **balance-of-payments difficulties** (that is, if more payments by domestic residents have been paid out than received from foreigners), it can automatically buy foreign currencies equal in value to a quarter of its quota—the equivalent of its gold subscription. Beyond this limit, the country must receive specific approval from the fund based on significant policy changes aimed to solve the balance-of-payments problems. Typically this means striving to control domestic inflation. The IMF is uniquely positioned to influence national policies of countries threatened with balance-of-payments deficits, for much of the time a needy country will have to borrow more than the first "gold *tranche*" or quarter of its quota. Countries borrowing from the fund must repurchase their own currency (or repay the loan) within five years. *The IMF is geared to service short-term balance-of-payments adjustments, not long-term structural adjustments—the role of the World Bank.*

The head of the IMF is the managing director who leads the meetings and negotiations. At Bretton Woods the parties agreed that the head of the IMF should always be a European, whereas the head of the World Bank should be an American. Given the shift of world liquidity to Japan in the late twentieth century, it would not be surprising if eventually a Japanese was made head of the IMF.

Formally, the IMF is governed by two bodies: the Board of Governors and the Executive Board. The Board of Governors is made up of one governor for each nation with voting power proportional to subscription quotas. That is, each member is given 250 votes plus one vote for each $100,000 deposited, assuring that the major subscribers maintain a dominant role. Initially the dominant countries numbered ten: the United States, the United Kingdom, Canada, France, West Germany, Italy, the Netherlands, Belgium, Sweden, and Japan. Saudi Arabia later joined this group following the OPEC oil price hikes of the 1970s. The Board of Governors deals with changes in the Articles of Agreement, with the admission of new members, and with the election of the managing director.

The other body, the Executive Board, is comprised of appointed and elected directors. Those appointed are nominated by the five members with the largest quotas, while those elected are nominated by particular groups of member countries. The votes of these directors cannot be split and must be cast as a unit. The Executive Board is permanently in session and handles the everyday operations of the IMF.

The initial quotas assigned to member countries were found to be inadequate. They have been repeatedly increased to provide liquidity to cope with the increasing volume of transactions. A number of financial crises in the 1960s created a demand for additional reserves to be used in the settlement of international balances. The "management remedy" in 1969 was to introduce **Special Drawing Rights (SDRs)**—units of account that could be transferred between the IMF and national central banks to help resolve balance-of-payments problems. SDRs permit countries temporarily in deficit to draw supplies of foreign currencies according to predetermined quotas. The use of SDRs is not subject to negotiations or conditions, does not lead to repayment obligations if a member uses less than 70 percent of its SDR quota, and is accepted in final discharge of debts without being translated into any particular currency.

The first allocation of SDRs to IMF members in 1970 of $9.5 billion over three years represented the triumph of an American proliquidity policy over French resistance. American experts at the time argued that Keynes had been right after all at Bretton Woods: the initial IMF system did not provide enough international liquidity. During the era of dollar scarcity after World War II, the dollar had been forced into the role of key international reserve currency. The Americans moved to shift the international monetary system away from this overexposure by devising a new source of nonnational liquidity. Economist Robert Mundell later referred to the SDRs as "dollars in disguise." The French, on the other hand, wanted less than the $3 billion to $5 billion in SDR annual liquidity advocated by the Unites States. They demanded strict reconstitution obligations and that American deficits be put to an end before the SDR system went into operation. It was another instance of the recurrent classic debate in the history of the international monetary system of the need for expanded liquidity versus the need for IMF credibility and conditionality (that is, adjustments to IMF guidelines for non-inflationary economic growth by deficit countries seeking funds).

THE DECLINE OF BRETTON WOODS. The Bretton Woods system serviced economic growth throughout the world for two decades after its founding, less because of its design than because of the ability and willingness of the Americans to play the role of a world central bank, printing dollars to provide liquidity. The American balance-of-payments deficit allowed others to run surpluses, which was very convenient. As long as the Americans provided stable, responsible leadership in international economic policy and as long as the dollar was accepted abroad as a "legitimate" substitute for gold the system seemed to work. Yet Bretton Woods never functioned as Americans and the others had planned. After all, it was not the United States that was supposed to perform the role of a world bank but the International Monetary Fund and International Bank for Reconstruction and Development. This illusion had already dissolved by 1947 when the Americans realized how thoroughly World War II had destroyed the European economic system. The European system was based largely on trade that could not work with the sources of Europe's foreign earnings gone and with heavy European balance-of-payments deficits. So from 1947 until about 1960 the United States stepped in. The Americans assumed unilateral management of the international monetary system, appearing to use Bretton Woods as a veil of legitimacy for the liquidity provided by the outflow of American dollars.

However, the constant outflow of dollars from the United States undermined the very monetary system which it serviced.[9] In 1947 the United States held 70 percent of the world's official monetary gold stocks. Between the end of 1948 and the end of 1959 American gold holdings fell by 20 percent. In 1960 foreign dollar holdings exceeded American gold reserves for the first time. Many perceived the U.S. balance-of-payments deficit, which reached $3.7 billion in 1960, to be getting out of control. The weakness of the British pound and the speculative problems associated with European currency convertibility further weakened confidence in the world monetary system. From this point forward, it was no longer possible for the United States to manage the international management system alone. An informal multilateral form of international management emerged with the United States still predominant but with less clout.

As Europe and Japan recovered and prospered with American support, their bargaining power relative to the United States in international economic policy increased: They lost the war militarily to win the peace economically. For example, European Common Market countries became more independent. In 1958 only 29.6 percent of imports and 30.1 percent of exports by Common Market members came from other member nations. But by 1970, imports reached 48.4 percent and exports 48.9 percent.

In 1961 the most important finance ministers and their deputies in the IMF created the Group of Ten. This was a club within a club that served together with the central bankers in the Bank of International Settlements of Basel, Switzerland, to help manage the international monetary system throughout the 1960s. Working Party Three of the Organization for Economic Cooperation and Development also assisted in this *ad hoc*, multilateral form of crisis management that substituted for U.S. hegemony. As previously noted, Special Drawing Rights (SDRs), or artificial international reserve units to be used among central banks outside the control of the United States and managed by the Group of Ten, were created as a new form of liquidity in the 1960s. Because the Europeans had a veto power on the creation of new SDRs they came to represent a dilution of American financial power mirrored by the rise of European influence. American financial power was further diluted with the rise of the **Euromoney** or **offshore banking system,** which originated after 1917 when the Soviets wanted to protect their dollars from being seized by the United States and put them in "friendly" European banks. These offshore dollars started to grow in volume in the 1960s and multiplied immensely after the 1973 OPEC oil crisis, ultimately reaching into the trillions by the 1980s.

The greatest crisis in the confidence of the United States came in the late 1960s when President Lyndon Johnson decided to wage war on Vietnam abroad and war on poverty at home without raising taxes. This destabilizing, inflationary decision made the breakdown of the Bretton Woods framework imminent. This breakdown was indicated by three major currency turbulences—of the pound in late 1967, of the dollar in March 1968, and of the French franc and German mark in November 1968. French President Charles de Gaulle did what Frenchmen typically do in times of international crisis: buy gold. Already at his press conference of February 4, 1965, de Gaulle had argued passionately for "the supreme law, the golden rule": "Yes, gold, which does not change in nature, which can be made into bars, ingots, or coins, which has no nationality, which is considered in all places and at all times, the immutable and fiduciary value par excellence. Furthermore . . . it is a fact that even today no currency has any value except by direct or indirect relation to gold, real or supposed." So much for the French confidence in the dollar or acceptance of the legitimacy of American domination. The American government intervened, asking the German and British governments to buy up the dollars being sold off, temporarily stemming the crisis of confidence. But the Bretton Woods system based on a dollar fixed to gold (at $35 an ounce) was set up for self-destruction. It was only a matter of time.

From Gold to Floating

The shift from the fixed exchange-rate system, based on the dollar's convertibility to gold, to the floating exchange-rate system can be highlighted by tracing three permanent redistributions of wealth from Americans to others: the Marshall Plan of 1947, the OPEC oil price hike of 1973, and commercial bank lending in the late 1970s.

Because of the Marshall Plan (the first redistribution), American defense spending abroad, foreign aid, tourism, and foreign investment, a dollar scarcity following World War II was transformed into a dollar glut. Americans continued to spend more overseas than they earned from abroad. The United States shifted from being the world's principal short-term creditor to being its main short-term debtor. The willingness of the United States to run large deficits and thereby to provide the international money or liquidity to permit other countries to run surpluses undermined the discipline the Bretton Woods arrangement was supposed to instill, making the agreement increasingly irrelevant. As the United States functioned as a world central bank in promoting expansion by pumping up the world's money supply, developed Western countries were able to maintain currency convertibility without much domestic discipline, tight exchange controls, or protectionism. World trade and investment flourished. But the Achilles heel of the Bretton Woods system was the assumption that the dollar was convertible to gold.

For quite a while this weakness was successfully covered up. American experts advocated Special Drawing Rights—or "dollars in disguise"—as a new source of nonnational liquidity to supplement the dollar in its role as the key international reserve currency. Arguing that John Maynard Keynes had been right after all at the Bretton Woods Conference that the initial IMF system did not provide adequate sources of international liquidity, this shift by American advisors seemed to have an altruistic ring. But, in fact, it was consistent with the so-called *policy of benign neglect* (letting things go along as they are). This policy took politicians off the hook of having to decide whether to promote domestic recession on the one hand, or to restrict tourist, business, or military spending abroad on the other, so as to bring America's balance of payments back in line. *The dollar's position as the key reserve currency allowed the United States to run deficits to finance "global responsibilities" without having to cut back on private outflow.* Of course many American and European experts did honestly believe that SDRs could become the basis of a multilateral reserve system that might eventually replace the domination of the dollar. But the short-term effect was to provide another distraction from the problem of American deficits.

Observing that the United States had only a third enough gold in its coffers to cover the outstanding dollars and facing the certainty of another dollar devaluation, on August 15, 1971, President Richard Nixon did what perhaps any American president in that position might have been forced to do: Overnight he indefinitely suspended the dollar's official convertibility into either gold or foreign currencies. To put the best face possible on this move, Nixon called it his "New Economic Policy," simultaneously imposing a temporary surcharge of 10 percent on dutiable imports and freezing domestic wages, prices, and rents for ninety days, while cutting both federal taxes and expenditures. Using the outspoken Secretary of the Treasury, John Connally, as a lightning rod, Nixon managed to make the dollar's retreat appear to be an aggressive thrust to improve the U.S. trade balance. In an age when one person is considered to have almost no power, a single individual within twenty-four hours was able to shift the world economy from **fixed exchange rates** (the dollar fixed to the 1934 price of gold at $35 an ounce) to **floating exchange rates** (which officially emerged in 1973, signifying that any one country's currency is worth whatever people think it is worth at a particular moment). Characteristically, Nixon told no one of his intentions, including America's closest allies, thus deterring speculators and using the element of surprise to give drama to his decision. Much as Henry Kissinger, Nixon's national security advisor, used secret shuttle diplomacy to spring American–Chinese détente upon the world to distract public attention from American losses in Vietnam, so Nixon's New Economic Policy served as a red herring to shift attention away from the inherent weakness of the dollar. The very art of being a magician, after all, is to so dazzle the audience with the spectacle that the left hand is performing that no one notices the deceptive maneuvers of the right hand, which hide one's true intentions.

In the short transitional period between the fixed and flexible exchange rates in the early 1970s, Connally engaged in hard bargaining to assure that America's European allies and Japan would accept the change. An understanding was reached in the Azores, which resulted in the Smithsonian Agreement of the International Monetary Fund in December 1971.

However, the Europeans and the Japanese were "reluctant allies" at this point. As an émigré from Nazi Germany, Kissinger was wary of the Europeans and argued that they and the Japanese had become free-riders on the American security system, accepting the economic benefits of the postwar Western system without bearing their share of the burden. So Kissinger gave a cold shoulder to the Europeans, believing (probably correctly) that there was nothing to be gotten out of them. However, this "de Gaulle snubbing tactic" on Kissinger's part was to prove expensive later when the Americans found it increasingly difficult to obtain European cooperation for American objectives in the late 1970s. But perhaps what is most striking about the trilateral relationships of the early 1970s among the United States, Western Europe, and Japan are the similarities with some of the relationships existing in the 1980s: American policymakers, increasingly concerned with the U.S. trade deficit, desired to bring down the price of the overvalued dollar to increase the competitiveness of American exports abroad without losing American status in the process. They used hard bargaining tactics in trade and security negotiations with the Western Europeans and the Japanese, making use of the "free-ridership" argument and protectionist threats, and they shifted the flavor of American policy toward a nationalistic mercantilism with the predictable strains in American–Japanese and American–European relations. Tough, nationalist U.S. bargaining continued in the Clinton era.

Alas, in human affairs, throwing all of one's energies to win in one arena often guarantees losing in another. In their total preoccupation with the chess games going on in the strategic triangle (among the United States, Soviet Union, and People's Republic of China) and in the trilateral trade triangle (among the United States, Western Europe, and Japan), Nixon and Kissinger neglected the "North–South triangle" (among the oil-producing developing countries, the non-oil-producing developing countries, and the developed countries).[10] In fact, evidence suggests that Nixon and Kissinger were willing to sacrifice the North–South game for the sake of the trilateral trade and strategic games. In June 1972 at a meeting of the Organization of Petroleum Exporting Countries (OPEC), a top U.S. State Department official, James Akins, made a famous "impromptu speech" maintaining that oil prices could be "expected to go up sharply because of lack of short-term alternatives to Arab oil" and that higher oil prices were "an unavoidable trend." Conspiracy theorists use this speech to argue that the Nixon White House wanted to have OPEC raise oil prices in order to encourage domestic American production and to give the United States a competitive advantage over Europe and Japan, which were both more energy dependent upon OPEC oil than was the United States. At the very least, Nixon and Kissinger appeared to be blind to the consequences of the 1973 oil price hike, a blindness encouraged with their preoccupation with the strategic stakes in the Arab–Israeli war on the one hand, and with trilateral trade competition on the other. These "maintenance men" failed to appreciate the main fulcrum of historical change, so absorbed were they in the *ancien régime* mentality of shoring up the status quo.

THE RISE OF OPEC: THE SECOND REDISTRIBUTION. The quadrupling of oil prices by the OPEC oil cartel in 1973 was facilitated by the rise in the price of gold, gold reserves, and foreign-exchange holdings due to the shift to floating exchange rates. For under the floating system, which officially went into effect in 1973, no mechanism existed for the international control over the quantity of international reserves. The international monetary system floated around the dollar, but the dollar no longer possessed the discipline of gold convertibility. Countries could simply buy reserves if they wanted them, and there was no check on the inflationary production of liquidity in the system. Paper gold became "paper paper" and commodities in the ground and tangible goods appreciated steeply in value with the onslaught of widespread global inflation in the 1970s. The **Eurodollar** (dollars outside the United States) and credit markets—that "stateless money" which was the international banker's vehicle for expansion throughout the 1970s—financed national exchange rate and interest rate volatility after 1973 but at the cost of uncontrollable price rises.[11] Faced with this "inflation machine" and motivated to unite and act by the Arab–Israeli war, the oil-producing Arab nations used an oil embargo to jack up their prices.

Naturally, OPEC could only get away with its huge price hike by (correctly) assuming that United States would choose to do nothing about it. Given the American debacle in Vietnam and U.S. domestic political difficulties at home, it was accurately assessed that America's national will was lacking to support an invasion and occupation of Arab oil fields at the risk of a major confrontation with the USSR. The OPEC nations shrewdly guessed what price increase their rich customers would bear and launched what some called "the Arab decade." The Americans seemed collectively to have decided that their national power in the game of empires had peaked—at least for the moment. And history indicates that power vacuums are short-lived. Quite understandably, OPEC moved to fill the gap.

Leaders of OPEC preferred to view the oil price hikes of 1973 and 1979 as equitable "adjustments," not "revolution." They argued that up until 1973 the major oil companies largely dictated prices, even though oil was the critical developmental resource for many oil-producing countries. After 1973 governments as well as oil companies had a hand in the price-setting. From the viewpoint of oil producers, the first oil shock of 1973 was certainly a "revolution." From the viewpoint of consumers it was a crisis. And from the viewpoint of most developing nations in the world, the OPEC "coup" was a symbolic victory for Third-World unity, demonstrating that cartel power could lead to a redistribution of wealth from the rich to the poor countries and help to create a "New International Economic Order."[12]

The OPEC wealth redistribution through oil price escalation in 1973 and thereafter was to have revolutionary implications for the structure of national economies in the world system, implications that were slow to be fully appreciated. Many advanced Western economies, and particularly the United States, had built cheap energy assumptions into their economic and industrial calculations. When energy costs skyrocketed in the 1970s—complemented by the inflation stimulated by global food shortages, a flood of international liquidity, and increasing labor costs—many basic industries in advanced Western countries became increasingly less competitive on world markets. After the 1973 oil price rises, the major industrial nations of the West overreacted with deflationary policies, thus helping to prolong the recession of 1974/75. Old Western policymakers overreacted to international change with stop-go economic policies: putting on the monetary brakes too heavily all at once, rather like a nervous, elderly driver trying to descend a steep hill in an old car, only to speed up too quickly at the bottom out of fear of losing momentum. And citizens began to accept as inevitable the jerky ride caused by the quick shifts between the fear of inflationary booms and deflationary busts, whereas actually it was often a case of widespread, short-term-obsessed mismanagement. Western policymakers used deflationary policies, recycling the $30-billion deficit they acquired from the OPEC price rises to the poor, developing countries of the Third World. Then they expressed surprise in 1975 when these developing countries mobilized the "Group of 77" in the United Nations to demand economic justice.

THE DEBT TRAP: THE THIRD REDISTRIBUTION.   The global economic crisis in the 1980s shifted from the inflationary liquidity surplus of the 1970s to a deflationary liquidity shortage and global recession. Private, commercial multinational banks were the institutions of adjustment in the 1970s. They outbid each other to lend money to developing countries at high interest rates, believing that if worst came to worst they might not get back their principal but they could at least survive on the interest. There was little regulation of this international banking activity. The leaders of advanced industrial nations, which were themselves beset with economic and political problems, seemed relieved to have the private sector pick up the increasing burdens of international financial assistance. But both the developing debtor nations and the international banks falsely counted on the global inflation rate continuing at a level high enough to make the debts ever-cheaper from the perspective of the borrowers and to assure the repayment of the interest from the viewpoint of the banks. Conventional wisdom projected that oil prices would continue to rise, not fall.[*]

But in the early 1980s oil prices did fall. OPEC's share of the world market dropped below 40 percent and its cartel clout dissipated accordingly. Oil-producing developing countries suddenly found they could no longer pay

---

[*]Also see Chapter 6 under "The Debt Crisis" and "The Mexican Case."

back the interest on their debts. By January 1, 1983, the gross external debt of eight Latin American countries made up about 55 percent of the $550 billion that fifty developing countries owed to foreign creditors. And the debt of Argentina, Mexico, and Brazil alone amounted to more than $200 billion. The international banks and their Third-World clients discovered they had fallen into a debt trap: A third redistribution had taken place, not through a Marshall Plan or oil price hikes, but this time through indefinitely extended credit. Wealthy countries attempted to stem the crisis by increasing the resources of the IMF by almost 50 percent and by pressuring their major banks to continue lending to the deficit countries. But the world debt crisis, compounding the scarcity of liquidity so badly needed to stimulate a world economic recovery, appeared to be more than conventional government and private-sector strategies could cope with. It was not a time for the maintenance of the old as much as it was for reform and risk-taking to create new structures and strategies. The early 1980s tight-money, high-interest-rate policy of the U.S. Federal Reserve Bank—anti-inflation-over-everything-else— was part of the problem, driving up variable interest rates of foreign debts.

By 1987 the IMF had 151 member nations in its fold and was faced with a Third-World foreign debt of $1,080 billion. The 1987 increase in SDRs from $61 billion to $90 billion was not nearly enough to cope with the world debt problem. Given an American trade deficit of almost $160 billion, not to mention the large U.S. budget deficit, the U.S. Congress was in no mood to increase its funding to the IMF and World Bank significantly enough to have much effect. Rather, the American focus was upon persuading the key surplus trade countries (Japan with a positive balance of $106 billion and West Germany with one of about $62 billion) to stimulate domestic economic growth to foster imports in order to help correct the trade imbalance. That such domestic stimulation might lead to excessive inflation, thereby causing Germany and Japan to raise their interest rates at a time when the world economy (and especially the U.S.) needed lower rates to stimulate economic growth, was a possibility neglected by the Americans.

The Story of the European Monetary System

The economic recovery of Western Europe and Japan after World War II coincided with the decline in American hegemony, calling for a shift in the fulcrum of managing Western monetary affairs. The creation of the Common Market, or European Economic Community (EEC) in 1958, symbolized the rise of Western Europe as a trading bloc. But coordination of regional monetary matters did not really follow suit until the breakdown of the system of fixed exchange rates and Smithsonian Agreement in 1971. At the beginning of 1972, the six members of the EEC, soon joined by the United Kingdom, Ireland, Denmark, and Norway, created the "Snake"—an exchange-rate regime that obliged its members to keep their currencies within a relatively wide "tunnel." Each currency was assigned a bilateral central rate with every other currency involved and each member government was required to keep its currency within a 2.25 percent margin either way of this rate, thus limiting the range of exchange-rate fluctuation. While only reluctantly joining the Snake—for fear of the Bundesbank's loss of control over domestic economic stability—West Germany quickly came to dominate the Snake as the strongest or key currency. Indeed, some referred to the arrangement as the "DMZ"—not "demilitarized zone" but "Deutschmark zone." Weaker currencies—the pound, lira, and Norwegian krone—soon left the system, given speculation against the dollar and pound in the new floating exchange-rate system. By 1974 the French franc, too, pulled out of the Snake.

The mid-1970s proved a time of great uncertainty for those who would manage economic and political affairs. The dollar devaluations of 1971 and 1973, the quadrupling of oil prices, and the escalation of grain prices drained purchasing power from most nations in the world, resulting in a deflationary impact. Nevertheless, the advanced industrial countries reacted with anti-inflationary policies. Their leaders anticipated a global inflation fueled by the rise in oil prices, the expansion of world liquidity, and the absence of external restraint implied by the shift from fixed to floating exchange rates. This anti-inflation policy was based on an understanding among the United States, Japan, and West Germany, which broke down in the 1974/75 recession—partly the result of those deflationary policies. As the German mark rose 30 percent against the currencies of the Federal Republic's twenty-three major trading partners between 1972 and 1977, the pressure increased on the German authorities to permit the mark to be used as an international reserve currency. This pressure was strongly resisted, particularly by the Bundesbank, which feared losing control over domestic money markets. So while the Germans favored a moderately rising or revalued mark as a means to keep inflation out of Germany (provided that the mark did not rise too high and threaten the competitiveness of German exports), they were in the market for some external restraint or a system to take the pressure of adjustment from their shoulders.

Meanwhile, at EEC headquarters in Brussels, President Roy Jenkins of the European Commission perceived the European economies to be overwhelmed with global change, leading inevitably to disintegration in the European Community unless some way could be found to stem the crisis. His solution was to pick up the theory of European monetary union and to promote European unity as an "adventurous idea," which might help to make up for the threats posed by the expansion of the Common Market (enlarged in 1973 to include Britain, Ireland, and Denmark) and general economic uncertainty. In his Monnet Lecture at the European University Institute in Florence in October 1977, Jenkins spelled out five economic reasons for monetary union: (1) It would stimulate efficient rationalization of industry; (2)

provide the European Community with the advantages accruing to "the is-suer of a world currency" (buffering the Europeans somewhat against dollar instability); (3) contribute to the struggle against inflation; (4) help reduce unemployment; and (5) reinforce policies aimed at leveling out regional dif-ferences within the EEC.

Roy Jenkins, a professional politician of considerable skill, initiated his European monetary union strategy on two levels—at the "lower table" of public negotiations with others in the European Community bureaucracy and at the "higher table" of private talks with the leaders of key European currency countries—particularly West Germany, France, and Britain. At the lower table Jenkins, a British subject, had to confront his predecessor, F. X. Ortoli, a bureaucrat who had positioned himself well in the Central Bank Governors Committee with his typical strategy of small steps. Persuasion and cooptation were not in themselves sufficient means for Jenkins to sell his "wild idea" to Ortoli, who believed in achieving success by setting limited ob-jectives. So Jenkins turned to the "high table" in 1977 to persuade the leaders of Germany, France, and Britain to join in his monetary crusade for the sake of European unity.

While at first appearing reserved, world events and his own perceptions caused West Germany's Chancellor Helmut Schmidt to come out strongly for European monetary union in early 1978. Schmidt's dislike for both President Jimmy Carter and America's volatile economic policies (culminating in the dollar crisis of November and December 1977) led him to the conclusion that it was vital for Europe to have a grand design to counter or buffer the impact of U.S. economic inconsistency upon the economies of the European Community. Schmidt was particularly critical of the **locomotive theory** of the Americans, according to which the West Germans and Japanese were pres-sured to stimulate demand in their domestic economies, thus acting as loco-motives for world economic growth to counter the slowdown and stalemate of the U.S. economic situation.

Initially, French President Valéry Giscard d'Estaing stayed out of the controversial European monetary idea—until he safely steered his center-right coalition to election victory against a disunited left in the March 1978 French elections. Then Giscard D'Estaing, a former finance minister (as was his politically compatible friend, Helmut Schmidt), jumped on the German bandwagon, negotiating with Schmidt behind the scenes in order to an-nounce the European Monetary System as a joint German-French plan. The French president wanted to give the appearance that France was as strong, influential, and prestigious as West Germany, heading off domination of the European Common Market by one non-French country. The French were also concerned about monetary discipline and hoped that the European Monetary System (EMS) might provide an external restraint that could sub-stitute for a return to the system of fixed exchange rates.[13]

The West Germans and the French proposed the "parity grid" system of exchange rates, expanding the Snake in which each country was bound to every other currency. While elastic, the parity grid system allowed currencies to move only 2.25 percent either above or below the bilateral par value. Then the central banks of both the (over) high and (over) low currencies involved were required to act to bring their currencies back to the bandwidth permitted. The Germans liked this system, for the responsibility for exchange-rate adjustment fell equally upon both the strong currency (usually the mark) and weak currency involved. The weak-currency countries—particularly Britain and Italy—objected that it was unfair to put as much responsibility upon the weak as upon the strong.[14]

The weak-currency countries supported an alternative "basket system" based on a weighted average of all EEC currencies, called the European unit of account for central banks (ECU). The **ECU** is a reserve asset replacing part of the excessive dollar reserves. Elites in the European Union see in the ECU the potential for a European currency.

The debate between the parity grid and basket system proposals was resolved with a Belgian compromise that combined the two systems: The basket system would serve as an indicator of divergence ("the rattlesnake") *within* the parity grid system. It would signal central banks to start intervening at 75 percent of the 2.25 percent (× 1—the percent of national currency in the basket) limit of flexibility allowed on either side of the central rate. West Germany, France, Denmark, the Netherlands, Belgium, and Luxembourg agreed to this system in late 1978. The ECU was approved for settling accounts among European partners as well as a $35-billion financial cooperation fund for stabilizing currencies. Italy and Ireland joined the EMS agreement by the time it went into effect in 1979 after receiving informal financial concessions (including a 6 percent range of flexibility rather than the normal 2.5 percent). While Britain agreed to have the pound in the basket-indicator system, the English did not join the system given the high rate of the pound and domestic political opposition to further integration with Europe.

In the early years of the European Monetary System (EMS), when the dollar was on a steady uptrend or downtrend and inflation was the primary concern of the eight member nations, participants were more or less content to go along with West Germany's dominant role as disciplinarian and paymaster. The Socialist government of France even reversed its Keynesian policy of public spending pursued from 1981–83 to adjust to EMS discipline rather than quitting the EMS. But by 1987, when the dollar's rate had become volatile, European countries had become more concerned with slow growth and unemployment than with inflation. The anti-inflation austerity of the Bundesbank and its power to crimp the national sovereignty of the non-German members became unbearable. As Jean-Pierre Chevènement, a leader of the left wing of the French Socialist Party and presidential aspirant, put it: "We cannot accept forever that the EMS be no more than the camouflage of a mark zone." The non-German members received two concessions from the Germans: (1) West Germany would contribute more money earlier in necessary interventions for exchange-rate stability with fewer conditions and (2) West Germany would coordinate policies more frequently with other member nations (implying less autonomy for the German Bundesbank). In addition, the French pushed for Britain to enter the EMS to counter the power of West Germany in the system, but Prime Minister Margaret Thatcher held back, fearing for loss of national sovereignty over the British economy. Germany became discontented as the other members made their own economic policies while Germany footed most of the bill for exchange-rate adjustments. But, initially, the EMS provided for a tighter exchange rate system than the global one and a basis for the Common Market to work its way out of what political scientist Stanley Hoffmann called the European Community's "dark age" (1973 to 1984).

The success of the European Monetary System depended upon the predictability of the dollar, the world's key reserve currency, in the background. At first, the dollar was predictable in appreciating in the early 1980s as the U.S. tight-money, high-interest rate policy sought to lower the American rate of inflation. However, as the value of the dollar went up, so did the price of U.S. exports. Finally, the trade imbalance of imports over exports became so great that on September 22, 1985, the Americans called a meeting of the Group of Five major industrial nations' finance ministers at the Plaza Hotel in New York City. There the five (the U.S., Germany, Japan, France, and Britain) agreed to a plan for the "orderly appreciation" of the other currencies against the dollar to give American exports some relief. The Americans, in turn, promised to cut back on government spending. A little over a year later, the **Group of Seven (G-7)**—the Group of Five plus Canada and Italy—decided that the dollar had fallen far enough in value. At a meeting at the Louvre in Paris in February, 1987, they agreed to cooperate in order to stabilize it. The key players in this process were Germany, Japan, and the U.S. **(G-3)**, who agreed to set broad target zones of plus or minus 12 percent for the mark/dollar and yen/dollar exchange rates. This management system has since been called *The Plaza–Louvre Accords* or *regime*. The EMS thus operated smoothly as long as the G-7 managed the larger dollar problem. This was done largely through rare but concentrated interventions in the currency markets by the central banks of the G-3 countries (who bought up the dollar, for example, when it became too weak). Despite the flimsiness of the target zones, under the Plaza–Louvre regime they kept the dollar's exchange rates within narrower ranges from 1987 through 1992 than for the fourteen years from 1973–1987.[15]

However, the European Monetary System does not stay stable based upon "external" dollar management alone. The internal economic policies of the European Union countries determine the domestic inflation rates, interest rates, and ability of member nations to attract foreign investment. During 1992 the domestic economy of Great Britain slipped into such deep recession that on September 16 of that year, stock prices plummeted. Repeated efforts by Britain, and the central banks of Germany and France failed to stop the free fall of the British pound on the exchange markets. Britain was forced temporarily to pull out of the European Monetary System, resulting in chaos that forced weaker currencies, such as the Spanish peseta and Italian lira, to be devalued. A two-tier European monetary system emerged: strong currencies, such as the Dutch guilder, remained pegged to the German mark, while weaker currencies floated to their market levels. Through significant French domestic sacrifices and by heavy Germany intervention (buying up of francs), a run on the French franc was slowed down. In 1993 the European exchange rate mechanism (ERM) fell apart: the bands of fluctuation were expanded to 15 percent making them almost meaningless. The ongoing currency crisis was made more severe by industrial restructuring and rising unemployment. As a result, plans for developing a single European currency based upon the EMS by the year 2000 were indefinitely postponed.

INTERPRETATIONS

Adjustments in exchange rates due to balance-of-payments deficits are contemporary tips of old icebergs. They are but superficial indicators on the surface of the world monetary system representing the political and money constitutions of the nation-states underlying them. These adjustments can be interpreted differently depending upon whether the observer is from a rich country or a poor one, or is a classical economic liberal, a monetarist, a structuralist, a neorealist, or merely someone who seeks to maintain the stability of the status quo. By looking at the alternatives a nation has for solving a balance-of-payments problem from these different perspectives, one can get a sense of the complexity and political implications of the kaleidoscope called the world monetary system.

Balance-of-Payments Adjustments

When the sum of all economic transactions between a state's residents and foreigners is greater than all receipts coming into the state and its residents during a year, that country is running a **balance-of-payments deficit.** Should the amount coming in exceed that going out, that country enjoys a **balance-of-payments surplus.** The objective of conventional monetary theory calls for equilibrium rather than for a surplus or deficit. International management efforts in the world monetary system can often be most easily explained by a maintenance model, which aims toward stability over all else. While stability undoubtedly benefits both rich and poor nations, the adjustment required to recover or to maintain balance-of-payments equilibrium often falls most heavily upon those who are least well off in the status quo. This explains why conflicting perspectives emerge over the relative value of exchange-rate stability.

Three traditional methods exist for a country to cope with a balance-of-payments deficit:

1. *Internal economic policies:* typically deflationary policies to reduce the deficit such as a tighter budget or higher interest rates.
2. *External measures* to shift expenditures away from imports, securities, and other transactions that lead to payments to foreigners: typically involving import quotas, tariffs, or limiting the outflow of capital.
3. *Financing or raising liquidity:* typically cashing in gold or foreign-exchange reserves or borrowing through private markets or commercial banks.

In explaining these three adjustment choices to the U.S. Congress, Professor Richard Cooper of Yale used what has since become a classic diagram (see Figure 3–1).

Each point in the triangle in Figure 3–1 illustrates some mix of the three types of measures for managing an imbalance in the international payments of a country or region at a specific time under a fixed exchange-rate regime. Each one of the three vertices of the triangle symbolizes the exclusive use of one of the measures or policy approaches: The closer a point is to one of the vertices the more the policy solution represents that particular type of measure. Point G thus signifies a heavy focus on internal measures: domestic deflation to reduce a payments deficit or domestic expansion to re-

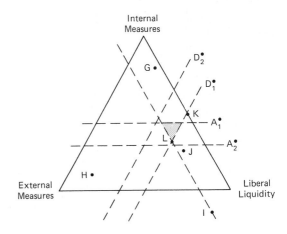

FIGURE 3–1
Classical Triangle Diagram

(*Source:* Richard N. Cooper, "Guidelines for International Monetary Reform," Hearings before the Subcommittee on International Exchange and Payments, Joint Econ. Comm., 89th Congress, 1st Session, Part 1: Hearings, July 29, 1965, pp. 109–113, 117, 119.)

Reprinted with permission from the publisher of Richard N. Cooper, *The Economics of Interdependence* (New York: McGraw-Hill, 1968), p. 18.

duce a payments surplus. Point H, on the other hand, stresses external measures: exchange controls and import quotas. Point K could be a state within the United States where external measures are ruled out.

Point J represents a country awash with gold or reserves that can finance its deficit—or that has the capacity to borrow such liquidity easily from someone else without having to make many internal or external adjustments. The pressures upon countries with balance-of-payments deficits are clearly greater than those with surpluses—which can finance those surpluses indefinitely. Thus, in Figure 3–1, Keynes's focus at Bretton Woods was upon the liberal liquidity vertice of the triangle for the sake of long-term adjustment of deficit countries, while the American position of Harry Dexter White was upon internal and (to a lesser extent) external measures as preconditions for receiving short-term liquidity from the IMF.

Classical Economic Liberalism

Any actual national policy involves some mix of internal, external, and financing measures in adjusting a country's balance of payments. But classical economic liberals stress avoiding policy trade-offs that utilize external measures, arguing that the free flow of capital, goods, and services between nations is essential to increase both economic growth at home and global economic prosperity. Secretary of State Cordell Hull under President Franklin Roosevelt before and during World War II epitomized the classical liberal position. He argued that free markets and free trade would lead to global economic prosperity, that the rising waters would lift all ships (or nations, weak or strong), and that global prosperity would assure world peace.[16] Harry Dexter White represented a more developed extension of this perspective: Balance-of-payments adjustments must focus on internal measures, getting one's own house in order, so as to benefit from and qualify for financing or liquidity provided by the IMF or commercial banks.

The Bretton Woods system was inspired from the American side by classical economic liberalism, which sought to deter obstructions to free trade and to head off competitive exchange-rate devaluations or external capital controls by providing a limited but reliable short-term source of liquidity to member states in need. However, the actual institutions of Bretton Woods represented a compromise, a manifestation that political scientist John Ruggie called "embedded liberalism." *Embedded liberalism* is the residue of power and social purpose still remaining in the institutions created by Bretton Woods despite the decline in hegemony or domination of the creator, the U.S., in the 1970s and 1980s.[17] At Bretton Woods, the Americans pushed for institutions that would move towards state self-sufficiency, economic growth, and free markets. The means were to be short-term loans to credible borrowers, which were to supplement adjustments towards free markets made by such states. The Americans wanted a detached, conservative, objective measure of "conditionality." They wanted a "thin" international monetary standard based upon momentary, short-term credit-worthiness to match their "thin" ethical notions of the self as a short-term interest maximizer (*a la* Adam Smith—see Chapter One). While the ideology of the IMF officially matched this American version of liberalism, institutionally the IMF evolved differently than the ideology.

Adam Smith, it will be recalled, thought that an "invisible hand" would steer private self-interest to the public good. The IMF did not become a surrogate "invisible hand," which would, indeed, have constituted a "thin" international monetary standard. Rather, the IMF developed into a collective, norm-governed balancing act between opening markets, on the one hand, and protecting the domestic stability of key states from having to bear undue costs of adjustment to world economic change, on the other. Late 20th-century Anglo-Saxon efforts to dislodge the original ideology of liberalism (that is, the praise for free markets and privatization) and to make it more pronounced—or, ethically speaking, to go back to a "thin" monetary system—may have destabilized the Bretton Woods system more than any overload of the regime due to domestic social objectives or protectionism in money and trade.[18]

Structuralism

From the perspective of the economic school called *structuralism,* Adam Smith's "invisible hand" is too invisible: Nations must use external measures in making balance-of-payments adjustments in a world where the flow of finance, liquidity, and trade is *structured* against them. It is the rich states, after all, who could afford to purchase the most shares in the IMF and who have the largest quotas when it comes time to borrow liquidity (the United States, for example, is one of the top borrowers from the IMF).

Structuralists argue that the world capitalist system must be tilted or restructured toward the interests of the least-advantaged nations. Nobel laureate Gunnar Myrdal, for instance, suggested that the U.S. redistribution to Europe in the form of the Marshall Plan went to the wrong countries. The "old rich" Europeans were capable of recovering on their own and the historical moment of American goodwill should have been targeted at the poorest countries in Asia or Africa without the training or tradition of economic recovery and development.[19]

Latin American economist Raul Prebisch argued that capital flows from poor countries to rich ones because the terms of trade are structured against the poor, who must live off the low price of commodities, while the rich countries benefit from the higher (and rising) prices of both manufactured goods and high-tech products and services.[20] The rich nations should therefore provide liberal liquidity for the poor countries and accept the external measures the developing countries require to protect their limited markets and resources. Keynesian liquidity creation and long-term soft loans would suit the structuralist perspective of reducing the inequities between the rich nations and the poor ones—not the liberal classical priority of putting one's own house in order first to qualify for short-term, highly conditional credit.

Marxism

From the Marxist perspective, the IMF provides a "debt trap" for the developing countries: it renders them forever dependent upon external financing by the rich industrialized nations.[21] The world capitalist system is eventually set to self-destruct, breaking down in the contradictions of social and international class conflicts according to neo-Marxists. In the meantime, several intermediate Marxist strategies are available for countries with balance-of-payments deficits to follow. One—the former Albanian and North Korean approach—is for such countries to isolate themselves from the world capitalist economy, creating import substitutes and attempting to become as self-sufficient as possible before once again opening the door to the outside world and to vulnerability. This is an extreme policy, one that emphasizes external measures over everything else.

Another strategy is that of the "Cambridge School." Many of the elites in the developing countries sent their children to study at Cambridge University in England. Partly as a result of this increasing influx of students from the developing world, a neo-Marxist economic wing developed at Cambridge, which Mexico called upon for advice in the late 1970s when Mexico was haunted by staggering balance-of-payments problems. Advisors influenced by Cambridge neo-Marxist thought persuaded Mexico to borrow as much as the Western commercial banks were willing to lend even though both sides knew the chances of paying back the principal on the loans were not good.* The Cambridge strategy was that even if the loans could never be paid back, Mexico would have the banks by their loans, a sort of reverse debt trap.

The banks, in turn, would have to continue to provide enough liquidity to Mexico to service the interest on the loans or risk a Western financial crisis by officially writing off the loans in reports to stockholders. And the banks ultimately had their governments by the debt. For if Citibank, for example, or one of the other nine largest banks in the United States threatened to go bankrupt and trigger a financial crisis, the U.S. government would have to step in to bail them out. Mexico, with the threat of proximity to the U.S. border and the ability to allow unemployed Mexicans to drift across, thus was

---

*Not all of these advisers were neo-Marxists. Carlos Tello, for example, a key Mexican figure behind the borrowing (under President Luis Echeverria) and behind the bank nationalization (under President López Portillo) was educated at Cambridge and influenced by neo-Marxist thinking but often supported neo-Keynesian economic policies for Mexico. Still, the influence of the eclectic neo-Marxist Cambridge School of thought should not be underestimated. See Chapter 6 for details of the Mexican case.

able to "restructure" global financial arrangements to create a permanent source of American liquidity. That David Rockefeller, chief executive officer of Chase Manhattan Bank, was one of the American elites strongly promoting this restructuring to make the Cambridge strategy successful is an historical paradox that Marxist theory alone might have a hard time explaining (not to mention the theory of classical economic liberalism!).

Monetarism

Monetarists, such as Nobel laureate Milton Friedman, argue that the money supply is the most important factor in a nation's economic policy and that only monetary policy can influence the course of the gross national product.[22] Monetarists usually assume that people tend to keep a fixed amount of money liquid, which they save (for example, the nonconsumed part of income held for convenience). Beyond this, if the nation's money supply provides citizens with easier access to money or credit, they will spend more. If, on the other hand, the nation's money supply is tightened the populace will consume and spend less. Moreover, if governments spend more, people or households will spend less since public spending presumably crowds out private and household spending. A nation with a balance-of-payments deficit, according to the monetarists, is probably living beyond its means and must focus upon internal (usually deflationary) measures to tighten up the money supply.

Monetarism is ultimately a free-market ideology advocating an anti-inflation policy above all else, and benefiting the most those who have something of value to lose from inflation—namely the wealthy. To the extent the IMF demands that countries reduce the money supply and adopt government austerity measures as prerequisites to IMF loans, it is adopting a monetarist policy.

Neorealism

Neorealism has its roots in the power precepts of Machiavelli and the nationalistic economic policies of mercantilism. The preoccupation with *power*—defined as control for the sake of the security, glory, and wealth of the imperial state—traces back to Thucydides in his *Peloponnesian War*. The modern tradition of realism is epitomized by the nine "elements of power" of Hans Morgenthau: geography, natural resources, industrial capacity, military preparedness, population, national character, national morale, quality of diplomacy, and quality of government.[23] The neorealists of the 1980s picked up Morgenthau's concern with calculations of power and national interest in the United States as a reaction against the demise of the nation-state forecast by the global idealists of the 1970s. The inability of nation-states to control or to manage turbulent change in the 1970s was not due to the demise of the nation-state, according to the neorealists, but to the power vacuum resulting from the decline of American hegemony following America's defeat in Vietnam.[24]

The neorealist interpretation of optimum balance-of-payments adjustments stresses maximizing the power and internal controls of the state. For nations enjoying a surplus, this means maintaining the surplus as a national security buffer or strong bargaining position and making only superficial compromises to the international community, striving not to weaken the maintenance base of power and wealth. Deficit nations must use their weakness strategically to seduce stronger nations, banks, and international organizations into granting them financing on soft terms. They must work to strengthen their power base at home, beginning, of course, with the power of the elites in charge. The maximization of national interest precedes international stability from the perspective of the neorealist: International agreements are nothing else than tough bargains struck between conflicting parties in which the strongest gets its way. Not to strive for hegemony is to lose the game.

IMPLICATIONS

Each of these interpretations or schools of thought has its own insights into how the world money system works. Each also has its drawbacks and blind spots. To use just one of these interpretations is like exploring a large, dark house with a flashlight: one sees only where one has shone the light at any given moment, leaving most of the structure in the dark. In the rapid transitions of the post-cold-war world economy, it may be even more important to utilize more than one perspective or school of thought in order to understand what is happening.

The world economy shifted in the late 1980s and early 1990s away from centralized, "command" economies typical of cold-war socialism towards decentralized market economies and privatization. Naturally, from the perspective of classical economic liberalism this shift was seen as a positive move towards tapping free-market potential for economic growth. But the liberal view, in its enthusiasm for chaotic growth, is usually blind to class-structured restrictions of opportunities for equal treatment: the newly industrializing countries of East Asia, for example, benefitted from free-market trends, whereas many developing countries went deeper into global recession and massive unemployment. Both structuralism and Marxism spotlight unequal distributions of the past that discriminate against poor nations in the present—resulting, for instance, in a net capital flow from the poor countries to the rich that still continues. However, these perspectives usually ignore emerging technological innovations that radically recast how money works and will be invested in the future. By focusing heavily upon the redistribution of the existing economic pie (or wealth), they fail to pay enough attention to how to make the economic pie grow in the future (or how to create new jobs through entrepreneurship).

Monetarists highlight money flows from the top of each national system downward and keep a close watch on existing liquidity or cash instruments (money, checks, credit). But they neglect existing fiscal and class structures that funnel cash in certain directions rather than others (towards high-tech and "supercar" industrial subsidies in Clinton's policy, for example).

For the neorealists, the more things change the more they stay the same. Politicians such as Senator Bob Dole, the Republican minority leader in the U.S. Senate, lack a positive vision for the future and underestimate those who act for altruistic motives or who seek international stability for its own sake. They are seduced by power and are often more interested in bringing opponents down than in building the country up. They are what sociologist C. Mills called "crackpot realists." They see the costs of programs and know where power lies. But rarely are they problem-solvers or visionaries. Like neoconservative novelist Ayn Rand, they are apt to be self-righteous defenders of "the virtue of selfishness."

The neorealists flourished during the cold-war era when power was more or less neatly divided into East and West blocs and national security issues were primary. But when the cold war was over, there was a shift from "high foreign policy issues" (national security and survival) to "low foreign policy issues" (foreign trade, investment, monetary, and financial issues).[25] The neorealists became mercantilists and shifted their "war-room games" to trade and money issues with very mixed success. For global money and trade games involve heavy interdependence and cooperation for stability and growth in future markets. A collective learning approach that integrates both conflict and cooperation within a global framework is more appropriate than the one-sided, short-term conflict-oriented perspective of neorealism. The United States, after all, can sell its domination more easily to the world if it is perceived as a moral force for the sake of human rights and global stability, rather than as merely a selfish, short-term maximizer of its own interest. It will be noted here that the perspectives of neorealism and classical American liberalism dovetail! But what is needed is a postliberal approach that systematically solves global maintenance or stability problems efficiently, while at the same time anticipating emerging trends and opportunities for innovation, growth, future redistribution, and job creation.

*   *   *

In any international exchange-rate system of N nations there are only N-1 exchange rates, rendering one currency redundant.[26] *If all N countries attempt actively to manipulate their exchange rates, the system is technically "overdetermined" and to that extent destabilized.* Since, in practice, the redundant currency tends to be the key international reserve currency—today's dollar—the clear implication is that key-currency country policymakers should maintain a more or less passive policy except when it is necessary to intervene to keep their currency stable on world markets. To do otherwise not only "overdetermines" the system theoretically but also politicizes the existing international exchange-rate regime unnecessarily, thus undermining its legitimacy.

Simultaneously, the authority of the key-currency country is undermined when others accuse it of mercantilistic currency manipulations for the sake of national interests. Thus American allies protested in the 1970s and late 1980s when the dollar was undervalued, stimulating American exports at their expense, and they complained in the early 1980s when the dollar was overvalued, sucking their capital into the United States as it chased the higher interest rates. In the late 1980s, American policy was to devalue the dollar and to persuade West Germany and Japan to stimulate demand (for imports) domestically in order to help balance the United States trade deficit. But by 1990, this short-term policy led to a jump in global interest rates as Japan and West Germany raised their interest rates to dampen the inflation caused by their stimulation of domestic demand. The higher global interest rates hit the U.S. exactly when it needed lower rates to encourage economic growth and head off a recession. Interest rate roulette played with the world's key currency is a precarious game. As a potential hegemon and superpower, the United States has the greatest stake in the stability of the existing dollar-dominated world monetary system and its more-or-less "apolitical" acceptance as *the* legitimate regime by other countries.

But the Americans mismanaged their position of privilege, overexposing their short-term national benefits and putting the very legitimacy of the monetary system in question. Erratic changes in economic policy under President Jimmy Carter undermined the system's stability and U.S. authority as the dollar fell 16 percent in value between the autumn of 1977 and the autumn of 1978. This mobilized the Europeans to create the European Monetary System—a joint float of European currencies intended to buffer European currencies from the dollar's instability.

In 1978 Carter appointed Paul Volcker as Chairman as the Board of Governors of the Federal Reserve System. Volcker applied the monetary brakes to bring down the U.S. inflation rate, which was about 13 percent. In so doing he "overdetermined" the international monetary system by refocusing Federal Reserve policy upon restricting the base of the entire U.S. money supply and not just upon interest rates. The Volcker policy of tightening the money and credit supply drove up U.S. interest rates to historically high levels and caused the dollar to be overvalued.

The high U.S. interest rates attracted capital from OECD and OPEC nations into American money funds and portfolio investment, draining the world market of liquidity where it was badly needed. American interest rates also helped to lock the United States into a structural trade deficit as the strong dollar made American exports less competitive on world markets. Since the Europeans and Japanese had planned on a strong American recovery to help their own domestic economies, not to mention the lesser-developed countries, the tight money policy of the Volcker regime had the effect of derailing yet another locomotive theory of economic growth. Late in the deep recession of 1981/82, Chairman Volcker then shifted to another extreme, loosening the money supply, ignoring M-1 (cash and checking account) fluctuations above his targets.

One reason for Volcker's "overmanagement" of the U.S. money supply was the creation of the *xeno* (foreign or "stateless") money and credit markets—usually known as the *Eurodollar* markets (any currency or dollar outside of its country of origin)—in the 1970s. The Eurodollar markets served to help recycle back into circulation the money flowing to OPEC for its oil. By the early 1980s the xeno or Eurodollar markets had expanded to *trillions* of U.S. dollars, none of which could be governed or controlled by the central banks of the key industrial countries. With their international control through currency monopoly and reserve requirements diluted, to have the slightest impact upon international money markets the central banks such as the Federal Reserve were tempted to overreact or to oversteer—extreme tightening or extreme loosening of the domestic money supply. And while this form of defensive management might make short-term policy sense domestically, it served to undermine the legitimacy of the monetary system dominated by the dollar in the long-run when the United States oversteered or overly-politicized the exchange-rate regime. For it soon became obvious that American policymakers were exploiting their "privileged position" in the world monetary system either to manipulate exchange rates so as to attract capital to cover U.S. balance-of-payments and federal deficits or to make U.S. exports more competitive to ease the U.S. trade deficit.

Managing the Crash of 1987

The dollar fell with the looser money supply and efforts of U.S. policymakers to turn their trade deficit around through competitive devaluation in the mid-1980s. Capital flowed out of lower, fixed-interest commitments into a speculative stock market, which was reaching record-level highs. Computer-programmed, futures-hedging systems—or "portfolio insurance"—ratcheted up (and later down) these massive speculative investments worldwide. This was done faster than those who would control the world monetary system could keep up with. The American policy of letting the dollar drop to help make U.S. exports more competitive failed to have any appreciable impact upon the U.S. trade deficit in 1987. As a result, the newly appointed head of the Federal Reserve System, Alan Greenspan, let interest rates rise to head off inflationary anticipations stemming from the lower dollar. Despite the

February 1987 Louvre agreement among the key Western industrial countries (the Group of Seven), U.S. policymakers again politicized the monetary
management system by publicly accusing the West Germans and Japanese of
not stimulating their domestic economies enough to help reverse U.S. trade
deficits and to act as locomotives of world economic growth.[*] Disenchantment with U.S. economic policy became widespread. It became clear that
Congress was making few significant steps to reduce the huge federal deficit
and that not enough internal restructuring measures were being taken in the
U.S. economy to reverse the large American trade deficit. Then, West Germany raised interest rates rather than lower them in accord with the wishes
of the Americans that the Germans stimulate demand. U.S. Treasury Secretary James A. Baker openly criticized the Germans on October 16, 1987, stimulating a drop in the prices of U.S. stocks to be followed on October 19 by
Black Monday—when the New York Stock Exchange saw its Dow-Jones average plummet 22 percent in a single day. The world's stock markets fell in tandem with the U.S. market, particularly given international, computerized
portfolio systems. Baker's clumsy criticism appeared to undermine the
Louvre agreement of industrialized countries to maintain exchange-rate stability. For an anonymous, highly placed American official implied that if the
West Germans did not lower their interest rates the Americans would push
the dollar down further as an intentional policy (undermining German exports). The threat was another symbol of U.S. politicization of the monetary
system for mercantilistic objectives. It epitomized massive disenchantment
abroad with a U.S. economic policy that drained the capital of other countries in order to plug up American federal and trade deficits, which the
Americans appeared unwilling or unable to do much about.

The residue of the Bretton Woods system—symbolized by the IMF-G-7
(or "Plaza-Louvre") regime—assured that October 19, 1987, would not be a
repeat of October 28, 1929 (Black Friday), even though in percentage terms
the stock market actually dropped more on Black Monday than on Black Friday. Late in the day on October 19 the U.S. Treasury Secretary, the West German Finance Minister, and the head of the German Bundesbank (central
bank) issued a joint statement from Europe assuring the financial markets
that the G-7 Louvre agreement was still operative and that they were doing
everything to cooperate. On the morning of October 20, Alan Greenspan,
head of the U.S. Federal Reserve System, publicly announced that the central
bank would provide all the liquidity necessary for the American banking system to stem the crisis. This loosening of U.S. monetary policy was the opposite from that of the Federal Reserve after the stock market crash of 1929,
when a tightening up of U.S. money policy led to an expansion of the stock

---

[*]Both the West Germans and the Japanese have been more concerned with keeping inflation low and their savings rate and export surplus high in the post–World War II period than
have the Americans.

market's fall to a run on the banks, thus helping to bring on the Great Depression. The fact that each individual bank account was insured for up to $100,000 (Federal Deposit Insurance) reassured the American public sufficiently in 1987 that they ran to U.S. banks to put money in this safe haven rather than taking all their savings out.

Once the stock slide started, computer-programmed trading increased the speed and volume of the fall to such an extent that the institutions of the stock exchange—much less federal government institutions—could not cope with what was happening. The managers of stock funds had protected themselves with dollar averaging: that is, as a stock declines, they sell in limited amounts at a time, and when it rises they buy in limited amounts. But this process was stimulated greatly by the difference in the margin requirements in the New York and Chicago exchanges, thus increasing the *arbitrage,* or speculation on the differences between the exchanges. The Chicago Mercantile Exchange, which possesses the largest stock index futures market, had only a 7 percent margin requirement, meaning a buyer has only to put up 7 percent of his or her own money. But the New York Stock Exchange had a 50 percent margin requirement, which stimulated margin buying (a parallel between the 1929 and 1987 crashes), even though in this case the margin buying was in derivative products, not the main market.

Additionally, this process was stimulated because of the fashion of big traders to take out "portfolio insurance," automatically buying futures contracts in Chicago to hedge against a decline in the New York market. Thus the computer trading programs tend to push the market in a single direction, faster than money or institutional managers can cope with the change.

All that managers can do to recover equilibrium is to try to slow things down in such a computerized market fall—what one could call a policy or strategy of retardation. John Phelan, chairman of the New York Stock Exchange, executed exactly this kind of strategy following Black Monday. He prohibited the use of the Big Board's order-distribution system on the New York Exchange for program trading, thus breaking the "financial meltdown" and stabilizing the market. He suspended trading on the ninety-one most volatile stocks, while approximately 1,500 kept trading. Yet his strategy showed moderation. He did not ban margin program trading entirely, but he took it off the computer system and told traders that they would have to do it by hand—a policy of retardation if there ever was one. Nor did Phelan close down the New York State Exchange (NYSE) for the day, only a couple of hours early on days of the heaviest trading. Hong Kong's more extreme policy of closing its exchange entirely helped to stimulate the 33-$\frac{1}{3}$ percent drop in its stocks the day it reopened. John Phelan also went to major member-dealer firms (as well as to the generous Federal Reserve Bank) to ask them to provide the NYSE with liquidity in case of need.

When it was all over, Phelan saw the need for a more structural embodiment of what has been called here a strategy of retardation. Phelan noted that the major lessons learned were (1) to give everyone a little time so that people with knowledge can assess what can be done; (2) to pump liquidity in "so everything just doesn't dry up;" and (3) to figure out a better way to plug the lender of last resort into the system.[27] The NYSE took these principles into account and changed its procedures to be able to cope more efficiently with the next such crisis. It came with the sharp drop in the American stock market on October 13, 1989 ("Friday the 13th"). But this time it was less the new management procedures of the NYSE exchange that slowed the effects of the fall than the cushioning by the globalization of stock markets. The self-confidence of the Japanese buffered the fall of the U.S. market as Japanese investors held onto their stocks. The more risk-shy Germans, in contrast, sold off their stocks and the German market fell 13 percent. Clearly, the power of any government to manage such a financial crisis alone is extremely limited given the globalization of financial markets, not to mention the inability to control the trillions of "stateless" Eurodollars offshore.

*   *   *

Retardation (or slowing things down) alone is ultimately a self-defeating form of crisis management. In addition, there must be international cooperation among the industrialized countries to reform the unstable, private-dollar-based world monetary system. Slowing down the entropy is not syntropy any more than slow death is resurrection.

Single-Key-Currency Anchors
versus G-3 Collective Learning

Much of the successful management of the world monetary system in the last half of the twentieth century was accidental and the good luck of being able to anchor the exchange rate system to a key currency. Such a key-anchor currency conveniently solved the problem of redundancy (that is, serving as the "redundant" currency or "standard" in a system with N-1 exchange rates).

First, the Marshall Plan of 1948 was meant to use American financial assistance to resore intra-European trade and financial stability. But it had the unintended effect of enthroning the dollar as the unit of account and as the basic means of settlement in the European exchange rate system (via the European Payments Union). The IMF faded quickly into the background in the 1950s as the U.S. Treasury became the world's surrogate central bank. The consumption-oriented U.S. economy served to provide the liquidity and import purchases that enabled all other countries to run export-oriented growth strategies. But eventually these neomercantilist strategies created a worldwide overcapacity in a deflationary environment.[28] A competitive struggle of downward adjustment ensued to match the low-cost competition. But this, too, reached a point of diminishing returns. Nevertheless, hard-currency countries such as West Germany and Japan often used currency revaluations (or upward floating—hardening their currency) to keep inflation out of their domestic economies, to keep costs down, and to keep their exports competitive. This amounted to an anti-inflationary policy in deflationary times, reinforced, in the German case, by the costs of reunification. Germany's desperate efforts to hold down the domestic inflation caused by deficit financing of former East Germany led to painfully high interest rates for the rest of Europe, which was mired in recession. Just as the dollar had become the accidental anchor currency in the fixed-exchange-rate system until that was no longer viable due to America's deficit spending, so, too did the German mark function as the key-anchor currency in the European Monetary System until German deficit spending made the European Exchange Rate System unviable. In both cases, the good luck of having a strong key currency available to serve the anchor function is not the same as the good management of an international exchange rate system. A more coordinated system of collective learning with limited targets is required.

The Plaza–Louvre regime, or G-3 system, that emerged in the 1980s holds more hope than any single anchor system since it is based on three anchor currencies rather than just one. The rules of this German–Japanese–U.S. system have been summed up by economist Ronald McKinnon as follows: (1) establish broad target zones of 12 percent of variation in both directions for mark/dollar and yen/dollar exchange rates, but keep agreed-on central rates secret; (2) change implicit central rates if fundamental disparities among the G-3 currencies emerge; (3) intervene rarely, but together, if needed to reverse short-run trends in the dollar that threaten to transgress the boundaries of the target zone; and signal G-3 intentions to intervene openly; (4) each of the G-3 should hold foreign exchange reserves symmetrically in each others' currencies; (5) "sterilize the immediate monetary impact of interventions by not adjusting short-term interest rates;" (6) aim to anchor each country's monetary policy to the national price level in tradable goods, indirectly stabilizing the world price level and keeping zones viable; and, (7) industrial countries other than the G-3 should support or at least not oppose G-3 interventions, buying dollars with their national currencies when the dollar is too weak and vice versa.[29] So far the G-3 system (underlying the annual G-7 economic summit meetings) has worked surprisingly well. But it, too, is apt to prove transitory as other currencies increasingly demonstrate their economic clout and call for political influence to match in the 21st century. The only principle to keep in mind is that too many cooks in the kitchen may spoil the meal.

THOUGHT QUESTIONS

1. Why does the author speak of a Bretton Woods system "*a la* White"? In contrast, what have been the propositions of the British economist J. M. Keynes? By enumerating important IMF principles, explain why "the IMF is uniquely positioned to influence national policies of countries threatened with balance-of-payment deficits."

2. Evaluate the assertion that "the constant outflow of dollars from the U.S. undermined the very monetary system which it serviced." How is the decline of Bretton Woods related to the subsequent rise of oil prices in the 1970s and the debt crisis of the beginning 1980s? Which "three redistributions" of world wealth does the author identify and why?

3. Describe the "parity grid" and the "basket" systems and how they combined into the "rattlesnake" of the European Monetary Union.

4. Compare and contrast the main ideas of liberalism, structuralism, Marxism, monetarism and neorealism in regard to the international monetary system.

5. Give examples of how the international monetary management system was politicized in the late 1970s and during the 1980s. Why does the author mention the "xeno dollars" or offshore currency when dealing with the "overmanagement" of the U.S. money supply? What are the "rules" of the G-3 system?

NOTES

1. John Maynard Keynes noted: "Lenin is said to have declared that the best way to destroy the capitalistic system was to debauch the currency." Keynes, *The Economic Consequences of The Peace* (London, 1920), p. 220.

2. Melville J. and Frances S. Herskovits, *Dahomean Narratives* (Evanston, IL: Northwestern University Press, 1958). Also see Paul Einzig, *Primitive Money* (Oxford: Pergamon Press, 1966).

3. See Wilhelm Hankel, "The Causes, History, and Illusions of Inflation," Part Two of W. Hankel and R. Isaak, *Modern Inflation: Its Economics and Its Politics* (Lanham, MD: University Press of America, 1983), pp. 25–90. Or, in the German edition: *Die moderne Inflation* (Köln: Bund-Verlag, 1981), pp. 31–114.

4. The best history of the founding of the Bretton Woods System from the conflicting perspectives of Harry Dexter White and John Maynard Keynes is Richard N. Gardner, *Sterling-Dollar Diplomacy in Current Perspective: The Origins and Prospects of Our International Economic Order* (New York: Columbia University Press, 1980).

5. See John Williamson, "Keynes and the International Economic Order," in Chris Milner, ed., *Political Economy and International Money: Selected Essays of John Williamson* (Brighton, Sussex: Wheatsheaf Books, 1987), pp. 37–59.

6. Joan Robinson, *Economic Philosophy* (New York: Penguin, 1981—orig. published 1962), p. 16.

7. John Maynard Keynes, May 23, 1944 address to the House of Lords, in Gerald M. Meier, *Problems of a World Monetary Order* (New York: Oxford University Press, 1974), p. 34.

8. The history of the IMF is reviewed in J. Keith Horsefield, ed., *The International Monetary Fund, 1945–1965: Twenty Years of International Monetary Cooperation* (Washington, D.C.: IMF, 1969). For earlier monetary systems, see Robert Triffin, *The Evolution of the International Monetary System: Historical Reappraisal and Future Perspectives* (Princeton, N.J.: International Finance Section, Department of Economics, Princeton University, 1964).

9. See David P. Calleo and Benjamin M. Rowland, *America and the World Political Economy* (Bloomington: Indiana University Press, 1973), Chapter 5, pp. 87–117.

10. See Stanley Hoffmann, "Choices," *Foreign Policy* 12 (Fall 1973): pp. 3–42.

11. See, for example, Eugène L. Versluysen, *The Political Economy of International Finance* (New York: St. Martin's Press, 1981).

12. See Karl P. Sauvant and Hajo Hasenflüg, eds., *The New International Economic Order: Confrontation or Cooperation between North and South?* (Boulder, CO: Westview Press, 1977).

13. See Peter Ludlow, *The Making of the European Monetary System* (London: Butterworth, 1982).

14. See Luigi Spaventa, "Italy Joins the EMS—A Political History," Occasional Paper No. 22, Research Institute, The Bologna Center, June 1980.

15. Ronald I. McKinnon, "The Rules of the Game: International Money in Historical Perspective," *Journal of Economic Literature,* Vol. XXXI (March 1993), p. 34.

16. See Cordell Hull, *Memoirs, Volumes I and II* (New York: Macmillan, 1948).

17. John G. Ruggie, "International Regimes, Transactions, and Change: Embedded Liberalism in the Postwar Economic Order," *International Organization* 36, No. 2, (Spring 1982).

18. *Ibid,* p. 413.

19. See, for example, Gunnar Myrdal, *Ökonomische Theorie und unterentwickelte Regionen: Weltproblem der Armut* (Frankfurt, 1974).

20. Raul Prebisch, *Towards a New Trade Policy for Development,* report by the Secretary-General of the United States Conference on Trade and Development, E/CONF 4613 (New York: United Nations, 1964).

21. See Cheryl Payer, "The Perpetuation of Dependence: The IMF and the Third World," *Monthly Review* 23, No. 4 (September 1971).

22. See, for example, Milton Friedman, *Tax Limitation, Inflation and the Role of Government* (Dallas: Fisher Institute, 1978). Also, Milton Friedman, ed., *Studies in the Quantity Theory of Money* (Chicago: University of Chicago Press, 1956).

23. See Hans Morgenthau, *Politics Among Nations,* 3rd ed. (New York: Knopf, 1960).

24. J. Martin Rochester, "The Rise and Fall of International Organization as a Field of Study," *International Organization* 40, No. 4 (Autumn 1986): 799. Prominent American "neorealists" include Kenneth N. Waltz (see his *Theory of International Politics:* Reading, MA: Addison-Wesley, 1979) and Robert G. Gilpin (see his *War and Change in World Politics,* Cambridge: Cambridge University Press, 1981). Also see Richard K. Ashley, "The Poverty of Neorealism," and Robert G. Gilpin,

"The Richness of the Tradition of Political Realism," both in *International Organization* 38 (Spring 1984).

25. C. Roe Goddard, "Seizing the Opportunity: International Political Economy and the End of the Cold War," *International Studies Notes* 18, No. 3 (Fall 1993): p. 17. The distinction between "high foreign policy" and "low foreign policy" was made by Richard N. Cooper in his "Trade Policy Is Foreign Policy," *Foreign Policy* No. 9 (Winter 1972–73) pp. 18–36.

26. The first part of this section was initially presented at The Research Institute of International Change at Columbia University, and an early version later appeared as R. Isaak, "The International Monetary Crisis and Economic Growth," *Working Papers in International Banking*, No. 4, Institute of International Banking, Pace University, New York, February 1983. For the basis of the "N-1" proposition see Robert A. Mundell, *Monetary Theory* (Pacific Palisades, CA: Goodyear, 1971).

27. George Melloan, "Stock Slide Makes Phelan a Prophet . . . ," *The Wall Street Journal,* October 28, 1987, Op. Ed Page.

28. See Winston Williams, "Waking Up to the Glut Economy," *The New York Times,* December 8, 1985; p. 1 of Business Section.

29. McKinnon, "The Rules of the Game," p. 32.

CHAPTER FOUR

THE WORLD
TRADE SYSTEM

Who can be blind today to the threat of a world gradually invaded by an identical culture, Anglo-Saxon culture, under the cover of economic liberalism?

Jacque Toubon, French Culture Minister (1993)

Current-account surplus can't be achieved by all countries simultaneously. Moreover, no country should seek to run its economy and society in such a way as to entrench a massive and permanent trade balance in its favor.

British Prime Minister Margaret Thatcher (1985)

Every man who lives by supplying any want dreads anything which tends either to dry up that want or to supply it more easily and abundantly. It is to his interest that scarcity should reign in the very thing which it is his function to make abundant, and that abundance should reign everywhere else.

Philip H. Wicksteed (1910)

International trade is trade with foreigners—an idea that takes getting used to. For people are brought up in sovereign nation-states where they are socialized to believe in the superiority, if not the self-sufficiency, of their own culture. **Ethnocentrism**—the belief in the primacy of one's own people or way of life—is the ultimate motive behind protectionism. Trade blocs create protective barriers separating "them" from "us" in order to assure one's own economic interests first. From the national perspective, if trade with foreigners is necessary for national prosperity then it seems natural to try to arrange it so that there is more money coming in than is going out. It is natural to try to create a trade surplus or buffer zone of wealth to protect one's people in case of a downturn in the turbulent world economy.

Of course there is more than one way to look at international trade. The British (followed by the Americans) came to look at a trade surplus as less important than a world system of free trade. In such a world, they could use their hegemonic power and their advanced economy to expand business worldwide for the sake of British prosperity at home. With the key international reserve currency backed by the British navy in the nineteenth century, they could run deficits without a short-run problem—unlike any other country. At its peak of power following World War II, the United States adopted the same classical liberal free-trade policy for many of the same reasons. Therefore, it was natural for the British and Americans to scold smaller nations (which saw trade surpluses as their only long-term security) for not aiming at an equilibrium in their trade balance. That up-and-coming economic powers did not always agree with this Anglo-Saxon free-trade position should come as no surprise.

The developing countries found that the price of their agricultural commodities, upon which their economies were based, did not keep up with the price of manufactured goods or financial services. This put them increasingly behind the developed countries in their terms of trade. From their perspective, the world trade system was structured against them, increasing the gap between their limited wealth and power and that of the rich nations. A banana republic with only bananas to export in exchange for everything else that it has to import can hardly be enthusiastic about a world system of free trade that permits wealthy, well-organized, multiresource nations to take advantage of vulnerable, single-commodity countries.

On the other hand, if borders shut down and each nation is forced to live off of what it has at home, the developed nations have most, the developing nations least. As uncertainty increases in the world economy, risk-shy, maintenance-oriented wealthy states are tempted to trade with other stable, well-to-do nations in their own image unless their governments or international organizations provide risk-insurance schemes to entice them to do business with less advantaged peoples. Financial crises, such as the stock crash of 1987, merely reinforce the natural conservative impulse and security consciousness of rich consumers, investors, and traders. Crises make protectionism and trade war more tempting unless world leaders cooperate politically to create counter-incentives in the world trading system.

ORIGINS

"Buy cheap and sell dear" is the motto of all business, including international business. Mass production is one way to make things cheaper—through "economies of scale." The ancient Greeks were the first to use mass production.

International trade is furthered by stable, routine relations among different peoples who can use a common currency in exchanges. The Romans provided such international laws and stability—laws that gave even non-Roman citizens certain rights. And the Roman dinarius was the first international currency. The hegemony of the Roman Empire (*particularly* in its period of slow decline) provided a predictable basis for international commerce. When the empire broke down through the invasion of the German tribes, international trade languished. The Western World entered the Dark Ages.

The next hegemonic order in the West was the Catholic Church. However, the spirit of the Church was not conducive to stimulating commercial activity or the accumulation of material wealth. Much of international trade was still done by the barter system or exchanging goods for other goods (a system that had shrunk to about 5 percent of total world trade by the end of the 1980s). During the feudal period, either the Church or ruling lord granted a charter to merchants in one section of the castle, called the *faubourg,* in which limited commercial activities and international trade could take place.[1] Located in most castles, abbeys, and cathedrals beginning in the late eleventh century, the *faubourg* merchant settlements led to charters being granted by lords to merchants for towns. These charters often gave permission for merchants to form guilds or cooperative associations. The guilds were forerunners of modern trade unions.

Initially towns were often granted the right to a guild, commercial court, and a low form of justice, but rarely the powers of self-government. This power deprivation later led the French and Italians to create *communes*—sworn alliances of groups of people associated for a stated purpose, often in revolt against the local lord. Commune movements ultimately permitted villages to win special rights of self-governance.

Champagne, France, became the meeting place for traders from both the north and the south. In the twelfth and early thirteenth centuries, the Champagne trade fairs became the most important trade centers in Western Europe. The counts of Champagne provided booths, money-changers, police, and judges for the merchants. Modern trade fairs, which still play an important part in European commerce, thus originated in Champagne—not to mention a celebratory form of effervescent liquidity (Champagne wines—with one of the most fiercely protected brand names in history).

From the guilds thus arose the towns and trade fairs that stimulated the modern system of international trade. The guilds had social and religious functions. They paid for the funerals of their members and took care of widows and children. *The weakness of the guild system, like that of the trade union system that grew out of it, was its inability to adjust to technological progress. The faubourg, guild, and contemporary trade union can all be seen as maintenance bases or traditional organizational buffers against the creative destruction of global capitalism. They seek to hold on to the rights of those already employed as members according to traditions of the past rather than to focus upon entrepreneurial adaptation to emerging technological and economic trends.*

The great Crusades of the feudal era served to prepare the way for world economic change. Military forces established major trade routes for the sake of ideological beliefs. Secularization was an inevitable trend as religious movements spent their legitimacy in bloody exhaustion.

The feudal order was displaced by national monarchic states at the close of the Middle Ages, customarily marked by the Treaty of Westphalia of 1648. **Mercantilism,** or the economic nationalism of states, flourished from the sixteenth through the nineteenth centuries. It was exemplified in the writings and policies of men such as Colbert, Burleigh, Cromwell, and Frederick the Great. Nation-states wanted to increase their power in the world and such national leaders viewed trade as a means to this end. They accumulated gold and silver to hire mercenaries and equip fleets of ships. Each state aimed to maximize its share of the world's limited gold supply. Exports were promoted and production costs were kept down so as to keep state competitiveness lean and mean in the trade struggle. A representative mercantilist pamphlet at the turn of the seventeenth century by Italian Antonio Serra was entitled *A Brief Treatise on the Causes Which Can Make Gold and Silver Plentiful in Kingdoms Where There Are No Mines.* Agriculture suffered hardships, for food prices were held down and luxury goods were considered taboo (enforced with heavy import duties). Foreigners were happily seen as customers, but not as suppliers.[2] It is little wonder that mercantilism often led to both military and trade conflicts.

If one flashes from mercantilism to the neo-mercantilism of the late twentieth century one notes great similarities in their aims: increase exports, reduce imports, and increase employment at home—regardless of the negative effects that these policies may have upon other nations. Indeed, these principles sound almost as if they could be the main platform planks in the electoral campaign in almost any contemporary democratic state. Export-oriented growth strategies are the panacea for the collective insecurity generated by turbulent world markets.

From Mercantilism to Classical Liberalism

In the eighteenth century a physician in the court of France's Louis XV, François Quesnay, propounded a school of economics called *Physiocracy,* even developing a *tableau économique*—a chart of economy. Insisting that wealth came not from gold and silver, Quesnay went against the tenets of mercantilism. He argued that wealth passed from person to person throughout the nation, replenishing the body politic like the circulation of blood. Quesnay's theory was not of much use for practical policy, however. For the production of "true wealth" was limited to the agricultural classes: The manufacturing and commercial classes were viewed as merely manipulating wealth in a sterile way.[3]

The French Physiocrats offered a doctrine based on free trade and competition to replace the nationalistic bias of mercantilism. Like certain late twentieth-century ecologists, they believed nature to be the only source of wealth; they (inaccurately) categorized manufacturers, artificers, and merchants as unproductive. Their list of proposals was topped by a call for a single tax on the net product of land—a list advising that industry and commerce be exempted from taxation. The phrase "Laissez faire, laissez passer" is attributed to an associate of Quesnay, Vincent de Gournany. The state was not to interfere with the authentic creators of natural wealth from whom society would ultimately benefit.

The **classical liberal school of economics,** was enunciated in Adam Smith's *Wealth of Nations,* published in 1776. Smith basically agreed with Quesnay and the physiocratic school apart from the doctrine that artificers, merchants, and manufacturers are unproductive. Gold and silver were asserted to be no more important than other commodities (in contrast to the mercantilist assumption), having their price like the others. Adam Smith was concerned with the natural laws of wealth. According to these laws of the market, the drive of individual self-interest in an environment of similarly motivated individuals would result in competition; competition, in turn, would provide society with wanted goods at acceptable prices. The market should be left alone: Its productivity would then spill over to the advantage of the public good as if by "an invisible hand." As long as a man does not violate "the laws of justice," he should be left perfectly free to pursue his own interest in his own way, bringing both his industry and capital into competition with those of any other men or order of men.

Smith's view was an optimistic, although realistic, economic philosophy: Increased competition would lead to increased productivity and increased wealth, making social progress through economic growth inevitable. It was, of course, a doctrine devised in a nation of small shopkeepers with limited factories in mind—not a world of giant multinational corporations, which Smith would probably have found abhorrent to the extent that they stifled competition. Nor did Smith foresee that his so-called "invisible hand" might indeed be totally invisible, leading to societies characterized by private wealth and public poverty (John Kenneth Galbraith's description of the United States in *The Affluent Society*).

The Politics of Comparative Advantage, or, Anglo-Saxon Ideology Applied

By the 1830s the Industrial Revolution had started to disrupt the comfortable mercantilism of the landed gentry in Great Britain, who found themselves at odds with the emerging industrialists. Economist David Ricardo, representing an industrial constituency in Parliament, proposed the theory of *comparative advantage* as a rationale for opposing the "Corn Law." The Corn

Law was designed to protect British grain from cheaper continental competitors—particularly imports from France. The industrialists wanted to keep down food prices so that they could keep wages low in England. Ricardo argued that differences between production costs on soil of maximum fertility and those on less fertile soil give rise to a differential income in favor of the owners of the more fertile soil.

According to Ricardo's **theory of comparative advantage,** even if one of two countries has an absolute advantage in producing two goods, it still pays for both to trade, with each specializing in that which each produces most efficiently. For example, assume that England had an absolute advantage in producing both woolen textiles and wine compared to Portugal. Let us say that the English needed only half the number of labor hours to produce the same amount of woolen products (two hours vs. four), but two-thirds the number of labor hours to produce wine compared to the Portuguese (two hours vs. three). In this case both countries would benefit more from trading if England specialized in producing textiles, at which the English were particularly efficient, and if the Portuguese specialized in producing wine, at which the Portuguese were comparatively more efficient than in making woolen products. The key is that the less efficient country, Portugal, was not equally less efficient in producing both wine and woolen products. The *cost ratio* (or *opportunity cost*) of producing the two products within the *same* country compared to the cost ratio in the second country is the decisive factor in determining whether or not a comparative advantage exists (i.e., England needing less labor time proportionately to produce textiles vs. wine in contrast with Portugal). The phrase **terms of trade,** in turn, refers to the exact exchange rate at a particular historical moment of one good or service in terms of another—such as of British woolen products in terms of Portugese wine.

For Ricardo, as pointed out in the first chapter of his *Principles of Political Economy* (1817), the value of a commodity depends on the relative quantity of labor necessary for its production. This is called the labor theory of value, which most modern economists, including many Marxists who favored it, have deserted as inadequate.[4] The terms-of-trade concept growing out of the theory of comparative advantage is critical for explaining the widening gap between the rich industrial nations and the poor agricultural countries in the nineteenth and twentieth centuries.

Perhaps the most persuasive explanation for the occurrence of the Industrial Revolution in Great Britain as opposed to any other country is that Great Britain was the country with the highest agricultural productivity at the end of the eighteenth century. As Nobel economist W. Arthur Lewis has shown, the Industrial Revolution did not create an industrial sector where none had been before. *Rather, the Industrial Revolution transformed an existing industrial sector by introducing new ways to make the same old things.* Thus, according to Lewis, the principal cause of poverty in the developing countries and of their poor factoral terms of trade is that about half of their labor force produces food at very low productivity levels, limiting the domestic market for manufactures and services. This keeps the propensity to import too high, reducing taxable capacity and savings, and bringing forth goods and services for export on unfavorable terms.[5] Even by the middle of the nineteenth century, Britain was the only country in the world where the agricultural population had fallen below 50 percent of the labor force. This signified a very slow industrial learning process even among developed countries. Throughout the world, landed classes well understood the benefits of cheap imports, whereas the advantages of displacing their own power with that of emerging new industrial classes were more mysterious. Resistance to industrial change was for the landed classes a rational politico-economic form of behavior.

In addition to resistance to industrialization from the top, another reason for the slow impact of the Industrial Revolution upon the volume of world trade was that the leading industrial countries—Britain, the United States, France, and Germany—were almost self-sufficient. Except for wool, these core countries had the raw materials they required for their industrialization—coal, iron ore, cotton, and wheat (for food). (So much for the theory that the Industrial Revolution depended upon raw materials from the Third World.) In short, *the mercantilist era provided* these *core developed countries with the maintenance base (typified by agricultural efficiency and relative self-sufficiency) that served as the take-off platform for their industrial development.* National trade patterns are shaped by relative self-sufficiency, the stage of agricultural development, and industrial capacity. These factors, in turn, determine the **absorptive capacity** of the nation—the extent to which a nation *can* absorb the products of another nation (either because of its own satiation in such products at home or because of a backward stage of development that limits the domestic market for industrial or technological products).

The spread of the Industrial Revolution and the resultant increase in the volume of world trade also depended upon the financing and developing of railroads and lines of communication. As these increased so did the volume of trade in the nineteenth century. London served as the chief source of financing for these "trade tracks" in North America as well as in Europe—part of the package of "invisible services" that made up for the British balance-of-payments deficit and kept British hegemony afloat.

The Heckscher-Ohlin-Samuelson (HOS) Theorem

The industrialization and trade patterns of the nineteenth century clearly divided the world into the developing agricultural states and the industrializing developed nations. It remained for economists in the twentieth century to refine Ricardo's theory of comparative advantage to try to explain emerging trade patterns within the context of classical economic liberalism. In 1919 Swedish economist Eli F. Heckscher argued that international trade altered *factor prices* (that is, the prices for land, labor, and capital) and therefore redistributed income within a country. Heckscher's student, Bertil Ohlin, went further in his 1924 thesis, *Interregional and International Trade*. Ohlin argued that certain countries were disproportionately favored with certain factors that led them to produce those commodities that were most to their advantage. Countries with lots of land produce lots of wheat, for example, or those with a great supply of labor might produce a great number of machines. Put another way, capital-abundant nations hold the comparative advantage when producing capital-intensive products for international trade, whereas labor-abundant countries hold export competitiveness in labor-intensive products. Countries, in short, should capitalize upon those factors in which they had a particular abundance in order to produce specialized products with a comparative advantage in world trade. American economist Paul Samuelson later extended the work of Heckscher and Ohlin to describe the conditions necessary for equalization of factor prices in international trade. Such equalization would presumably eliminate the need for migration from overpopulated to underpopulated countries.[6]

In sum, the classical theory of free trade assumes that national living standards are raised through the international specialization of production and international trade—even in a country rich in natural resources like the United States. From this viewpoint, **absolute advantage** refers to a situation when one country can produce an item better and more cheaply than another: coal production in the United States or sugar production in Puerto Rico, for example. *Comparative advantage is the principle that answers the following question: Supposing that a nation could produce everything more cheaply than any other nation, why should it buy anything from abroad? The answer is that the nation stands to benefit by specializing in those products in which its advantage is the greatest.* David Ricardo illustrated the principle of comparative advantage with a classical example:

> Two men can both make shoes and hats, and one is superior to the other in both employments; but in making hats he can only exceed his competitor by one-fifth, or 20 percent, and in making shoes he can excel him by one-third or 33-$\frac{1}{3}$ percent. Will it not be for the interest of both that the superior man should employ himself exclusively in making shoes, and the inferior man in making hats?[7]

To take another example, Babe Ruth began his career in baseball as a pitcher and was an excellent one. But he was even a greater hitter. Knowing that pitchers cannot play in every game, he gave up pitching to specialize in his greater comparative advantage in batting. Thus, it is the *ratio* between domestic advantages that counts.

If economic growth is the main value priority of a society, comparative advantage is a fairly persuasive theory. But how, exactly, did this "Anglo-Saxon ideology" come to be institutionalized in the world political economy?

GATT

The General Agreement on Tariffs and Trade (GATT) embodies the theory of comparative advantage with a tilt towards adjustment for domestic stability. That is, multilateral GATT negotiations have modified the doctrine of classical liberalism to take into account the need for political stability and domestic economic adjustments to tariff cuts. These economic adjustments come into play particularly in the case of mature, basic industries such as steel, textiles, shoes, and cars.

GATT is a voluntary commercial treaty that came to represent the third pillar of U.S.-British hegemony after World War II—the other two being the International Monetary Fund and the World Bank (or IBRD). This multinational organization monitors 90 percent of world merchandise trade and has stimulated industrial countries to reduce their tariffs more than 40 percent to an average of less than 5 percent since its founding.[8]

The origins of GATT must be traced back to the Stock Exchange crash of 1929 and the ensuing Great Depression. While nearly 45 percent of the world's production of manufactures was concentrated in the United States in 1929, and U.S. exports made up 20 percent of world exports, exports represented only 6 percent of the U.S. gross national product. The relative self-sufficiency of the American economy (backed by its unique natural resource base) encouraged Congress to enact the Smoot-Hawley Tariff Act of 1930, expanding the protection of the domestic market to cover an additional 900 items. This legislation set off a chain reaction of import restrictions in other countries, leading to a 40 percent decline in the volume of world trade in manufactures by 1933.[9]

Convinced that world peace depended upon the reduction of trade restrictions rather than upon their increase, U.S. Secretary of State Cordell Hull lobbied Congress to amend the Smoot-Hawley Act of 1930. The result was the passage of the Reciprocal Trade Agreements Act of 1934. Thus, the President was empowered for three years to initiate trade agreements based upon the reciprocal reductions of tariffs. This principle became known as "most favored nation" (MFN) treatment and led to reciprocal agreements with twenty-nine countries before World War II. These agreements had little overall impact on tariffs but had value as precedents for GATT rules.

The trade surplus of the United States with the rest of the world at the end of World War II made reciprocity a convenient policy for the U.S. hegemony. John Maynard Keynes argued before Bretton Woods for an International Clearing Union in which countries in surplus would disproportionately increase imports to ease the burden of those in deficit. But the American position ultimately adopted, which became the trade plank of *pax Americana,* was that strict reciprocity should be the basis for the GATT treaty with an American benefit in exports to other countries for each concession on reducing U.S. import restrictions, regardless of the significant advantages of the United States at the starting line. This principle contrasted with unilateral trade reductions made by the British under the *pax Britannica.*[10]

The development of trade agreements is particularly subject to domestic political pressures in the United States, for the President needs congressional approval for any trade accord. International monetary and financial issues tend to be left in the hands of the elite (that is, central bankers, finance ministers, and exchange rate experts). But trade issues are more broadly politicized and democratic, involving the livelihoods and pressure groups of the butcher, the baker, and the computer-maker. It is but a slight exaggeration to say that the world trading system that emerged after World War II was a product of the constitutional balance of power between the executive and legislative branches of the U.S. government. Congress, not the President, is granted the constitutional power to levy tariffs and regulate foreign commerce.

The executive branch at the close of World War II was dominated by Cordell Hull's liberal vision. This was reinforced by the willingness of American elites to use the economic surplus and security monopoly of the United States to establish a postwar commercial order based upon free trade. The liberal vision was articulated in the Havana Charter, the set of provisions to create an International Trade Organization (ITO), which was to be the trade equivalent of the IMF in the field of international monetary management.

The ITO was based upon an Anglo-American consensus as World War II drew to a close: Tariff reductions and the free flow of trade were essential to maintain high levels of domestic employment and income. Quantitative restrictions on trade must therefore be eliminated, and an automatic tariff-reducing formula should be found to assure "substantial" tariff reductions and the "elimination" of discriminatory treatment.[11] Based on these principles, in 1945 the United States proposed a plan for a multilateral commercial convention, providing for the ITO to oversee the trade system. However, the United States and Great Britain were not able to dominate in the international trade negotiations as easily as they had been able to in setting up the monetary system. European countries demanded safeguards for balance-of-payments problems. Even Britain insisted on maintaining its Imperial Preference System. The developing countries pressed for attention to economic development issues. Although the executive branch under both the Roosevelt and Truman administrations provided strong U.S. leadership for the ITO proposal, congressional opposition proved to be stronger. Protectionists opposed the arrangement for being too liberal, and liberals were against it for remaining too protectionist. In 1950 the Truman administration was forced to withdraw the proposal before it faced certain defeat in Congress. Without U.S. support the ITO was dead.

When the ITO failed to come into being, GATT took over its international trade function by default, even though GATT was designed as a commercial treaty between contracting parties rather than as an international organization that states join (such as the IMF). Negotiated by twenty-three countries in 1947, the General Agreement on Tariffs and Trade came into force in 1948 with a minimum of institutional arrangements. About once a year the Session of Contracting Parties is held, where decisions are generally taken by consensus rather than by vote. When voting does take place, each contracting party (or member country) has one vote—in contrast with the weighted voting system of the IMF. For most decisions a simple majority vote suffices. But for "waivers" or authorization to depart from specific contractual obligations a two-thirds vote of more than half the member countries is required (to approve an import surcharge, for example). Amendments to the key principles of GATT can only be made with unanimous agreement.

The first principle of GATT is that of **most favored nation (MFN) treatment**—committing all parties to conduct trade on the basis of nondiscrimination. Accordingly, all parties are bound to grant treatment to each other as favorable as they give to any other country in the application and administration of import and export duties. For example, if the United States reduces a tariff on machine tools from West Germany by 10 percent, it is then obligated to reduce the tariff on machine tools from all other GATT countries by the same amount. The MFN principle creates a *spill-over effect,* helping to make free trade contagious. It is based upon the assumption that no country within GATT should give special trading advantages to another country or to discriminate against another. All countries are in theory put on an equal basis, sharing in the benefits of any move toward lower trade barriers. The status of MFN is the motivator aimed to move nations from bilateral alliances to a cooperative multilateral system of world trade.

The second principle of GATT is **reciprocity.** Because GATT is a commercial treaty, nothing requires countries to reduce or abolish tariffs automatically. Tariffs are negotiable: Countries reduce tariffs in exchange for reciprocal reductions from other countries or trading partners. Without such an agreement, a contracting party is not obligated to make a reduction. Without reciprocity, examples of unrequested, unilateral tariff reductions are few in twentieth-century commercial history.[12]

The third GATT principle is **nondiscrimination.** Once foreign goods cross the border into another GATT country, they are to be treated as domestic goods in terms of equal rights of competition. According to Article III such "national treatment" means that foreign goods from other GATT members are not to be subject to discriminatory measures, such as higher taxes, compared to those produced domestically. It is the principle of nondiscrimination that was violated most often in the past several decades through "Voluntary Export Restrictions" (VERS), "Orderly Marketing Agreements" (OMAs), and other forms of discriminatory nontariff barriers (such as state subsidies and inspection regulations). State subsidies and obscure nontariff barriers are often difficult to detect, thus violating GATT's **principle of trans-**

parency: namely, that all producers and their governments should be aware of existing trade barriers.

The developing countries failed to achieve the inclusion of a separate chapter in the GATT treaty specifically devoted to problems of economic development (which they had sought in the Havana Charter). However, they did succeed in Article XVIII in addressing development needs in the context of post–World War II reconstruction. This article recognizes that special government aid may be needed to promote the establishment, development, or reconstruction of particular industries or branches of agriculture and that in "appropriate circumstances" granting such assistance through protective measures is justified. Later, developing countries assumed that Article XVIII "reflected the predominance of the import substitution approach to economic development."[13] **Import substitution** is the policy of systematically encouraging the domestic production of goods that used to be imported. The aim is economic self-sufficiency.

The major developed countries gradually restored the convertibility of their currencies after World War II. In step with this process, they used the principles of GATT to reduce restrictions on their trade. This was accomplished in the first eight rounds of multilateral trade negotiations in GATT: Geneva, 1947; Annecy, 1949; Torquay, 1950–51; Geneva, 1956; Dillon Round in Geneva, 1960–62; Kennedy Round, 1964; the Tokyo Round, 1973–74; and the Uruguay Round, 1986–93. The first five rounds represented renewals of the Reciprocal Trade Agreements Act of 1934. The Kennedy Round was the international counterpart of the Trade Expansion Act of 1962, while the Tokyo Round was made possible by the 1974 Trade Act. The passage of the North American Free Trade Agreement (NAFTA) paved the way for the conclusion of the Uruguay Round by a December 1993 deadline set by the U.S. Congress. *American hegemony is thus still alive, if not well, in GATT, which initially seems to be the international extension of U.S. tariff policy.*[14]

The first seven rounds of trade negotiations cut import tariffs for ninety-five countries from an average of over forty to 4 percent and served as a line of defense for governments against demands for protection from domestic interest groups.[15] As a result of the Tokyo Round alone, the weighted average (the average tariff measured against actual trade flows) on manufactured products in the world's nine major industrial markets declined from 7.0 to 4.7 percent—a 34 percent reduction in customs collection.

The Uruguay Round and U.S. Assertiveness

The eighth round of GATT trade negotiations, or Uruguay Round, was launched in 1986 and took seven frustrating years to conclude. The difficulty was partly the result of the U.S. attempt to use these talks to do what GATT had not done before—to extend trade reductions to agricultural subsidies and to financial services, as well as to protect intellectual property rights.

These talks also sought to shore up the shift from bilateral alliances to multi-lateral systems, which GATT represents. This is particularly true in the area of **nontariff trade barriers;** that is, quotas, customs, export subsidies, "voluntary" restraints, and domestic standards and rules. By 2000, some experts predict that tariffs will no longer be a serious obstacle to trade and that nontariff barriers will be the primary means of trade restriction.[16]

U.S. assertiveness in trade policy began with the free-market rhetoric of President Ronald Reagan. This was followed up with targeted hard-bargaining with European and Japanese allies by the administration of President George Bush. This raised little controversy since Bush was perceived as a strong supporter of GATT. But post-cold-war shifts culminated with President Bill Clinton, who linked trade policy with a new, aggressive U.S. **industrial policy** (state coordination with national business networks). For example, in February 1993, President Clinton publicly blamed the loss of jobs at Boeing, the U.S. aerospace giant, upon sales lost to Airbus Industrie, a European consortium, because of state subsidies going to Airbus. Later that year, Clinton came up with government subsidies for an energy-saving, new "supercar" to be produced jointly by the big three American auto manufacturers. The Clinton administration noted that between 1986 and 1990 the number of Americans who produced goods for exports increased from 5 to 7.2 million and that export-related jobs paid about $3,500 per year more than the average American job.[17] Trade issues rose to the top of the foreign-policy agenda.

As a member of the Clinton administration, Jeffery Garten, observed before going to Washington: "In abandoning the rhetoric of Adam Smith, President Clinton only recognized the reality that totally free markets are a myth. But without the kind of clear ideological direction that free-market theory provides, actions will often seem inconsistent and subject to the political winds of the moment."[18] Clinton advocated a get-tough "pragmatism" that initially focused attention on trade disputes and later upon trade blocs. But pragmatism, alone, may be hard to sell ideologically to the American public who long for the lost simplicity of liberalism in a postliberal world. And "pragmatism" at home may be perceived to be selfish nationalism or mercantilism abroad, undermining the GATT regime, which is an integral part of American hegemony.[19]

The French weighed in with the strongest reaction to the American position, led by French farmers who saw the threat of reduced subsidies as a threat to their way of life. French stubbornness on this and other issues paid off: the cuts in agricultural subsidies were reduced. Arguing for a "cultural exemption," the French also maintained their quota rule on films: 60 percent of their television programming must be produced within the European Community. The French Culture Minister Jacque Toubon argued that the world today is threatened by the gradual invasion of a dominant Anglo-Saxon culture under the cover of economic liberalism. Since movies are *cultural* products, nations should be permitted to create barriers to their entry for the sake of preserving their own cultural integrity.[20] The French won in this cultural resistance movement even given the strong protests by the American film industry, which gave major support to Clinton in the 1992 election.

The Uruguay round agreement will cut tariffs on manufactured products in most countries by one-third and ease barriers against grain imports. It also will gradually eliminate tariffs on textiles and clothing and make it harder for countries to impose new quantitative restrictions. Financial services were dropped from the negotiations in order to gain agreement among the 117 countries.

In the Uruguay round process, the developing countries mimicked the trade liberalization of the twenty-some developed countries of the **Organization for Economic Cooperation and Development (O.E.C.D.),** *which demonstrated such rapid economic growth in the 1950s and 1960s. It represents a proliberal, collective learning process of increasing market access and growth in exports, keeping inflation rates down, generating foreign exchange, acquiring technology, buying capital goods and supplies: learning by exporting.* This, in turn, results in global product specialization and divisions of labor following the principles of comparative and competitive advantage. As economist Sherman Robinson summed it up: "It's Adam Smith with a vengeance."[21]

INTERPRETATIONS

International trade is assumed to be important for economic development by most schools of economic thought. The decisive difference between perspectives is the degree to which trade should be "free" or be regulated by the state. A related issue is the extent to which the domestic economy should aim for self-sufficiency or autonomy. If autonomy becomes the top policy priority, this not only implies protectionism but can lead to temporary isolation from parts of the global trading system.

The masses in democratic states are usually willing to leave "estoric" issues of international money and exchange rates to elitist experts, at least in noncrisis situations. But this is not so with trade issues. For trade issues are politicized worldwide: first, by their dependence upon the whims of the U.S. Congress, European Union regulations and Japanese bureaucrats; and second, by the close tie of trade to jobs, to economic growth, and to the very survival of certain sectors and ways of life. Let us consider some different schools of thought concerning trade.

Neoclassical Theory

The neoclassical vision is liberalism modernized—from Adam Smith to David Ricardo to Heckscher, Ohlin, and Samuelson. Anglo-American hegemony after World War II focused ideas with the notion that each country should specialize in and export what it could produce more cheaply in exchange for goods and services produced comparatively more cheaply in other countries. International trade thus makes possible the division of labor and specialization upon which the productivity of global capitalism is based. Trade is the engine of economic growth as much as are investment and technological progress. Collective learning takes place as nations, locales, or producers discover which of the various advantageous products or services can be produced and exported with *most* advantage compared to others. Comparatively, this is where the optimum return lies, or the least "opportunity cost." **Opportunity cost** is the cost incurred by a company or nation as the result of foreclosing other sources of profit. Neoclassical theory suggests that, globally, costs will be cut and economic growth increased in a free-trade system without tariffs blocking the normal shift of production factors in the world market. According to Cordell Hull, economic growth, in turn, fosters global prosperity and increases the chances of world peace. Despite its compromises to permit domestic economic adaptation for the sake of political stability among its member states, GATT's liberalism is deeply embedded, tilting the organization toward the ideology of free trade and comparative advantage.

In the language of game theory, the neoclassical perspective interprets world trade generally as a positive-sum, cooperative game.[*] More precisely, it is a version in which everyone will be better off if all countries decide to maximize their long-term mutual interests by reducing tariffs and conforming to the rules of reciprocity and nondiscrimination set forth by GATT. Policymakers are constantly tempted to adopt programs of short-term expediency for the sake of national interest, setting the GATT rules aside. But this assures a better outcome only on the condition that everyone else (or at least almost everyone) continues to observe the rules. Otherwise, to use a metaphor, one person's advantage in standing on tiptoes in a crowd to better see the parade is canceled out as the whole crowd follows suit and stands on its tiptoes too. *Infractions of the rules, in short, set precedents. Precedents become models of collective learning for others, who are also then tempted to take shortcuts and break the rules, undermining the entire trading order of intricately specialized but coordinated activity.*

The thrust of the neoclassical vision of world trade is that if tariffs are dropped and the exchange of goods and services kept free among national borders, a more productive use of given resources (or "factor endowments") will result with gains in consumption, production, economies of scale, price

---

[*]The "variable-sum or positive-sum game" refers in economics to a situation in which two or more players have an option that permits them to cooperate for a greater mutual payoff (or the creation of additional "economic pie") than either would gain alone in making a choice that did not permit or involve cooperation. This contrasts with the "zero-sum game" (i.e., chess or checkers) in which cooperation is not "rational" since each choice with a positive payoff for one player has exactly the same negative payoff for the other player (thus summing to zero): The focus is upon the distribution of the existing pie (protectionism?) rather than upon the creation of new pie (free-trade capitalism?). (See John von Neumann and Oscar Morgenstern, *Theory of Games and Economic Behavior,* 2nd edition. (Princeton, NJ: Princeton University Press, 1947).

stability, competitiveness, economic growth, and employment.[22] The GATT rules serve as a code of behavior adding predictability and cooperative incentives for the long term to the anarchy of international markets.*

Nor is the neoclassical position unaware of the need for protection—*temporarily*—in certain circumstances, such as sheltering infant industries until they are strong enough to compete internationally. The infant-industry argument goes back to John Stuart Mill (in his *Principles of Political Economy*, [1848]) in which he maintains that the only case where protecting duties can be defensible is when they are imposed temporarily (particularly in a young and rising nation) in hope of "naturalizing a foreign industry" found to be suitable to the circumstances of the country. For, Mill continues, the superiority of one country over another in a sector of production often arises only from having begun it sooner, and it cannot be expected that individuals, risking almost certain loss, will introduce a new manufacturing product, bearing the burden until producers have refined their processes up to par with the competition.

The neoclassical school allows for temporary protection for certain infant industries for the sake of innovation, experimentation, or "vital economic interests" (such as protecting the nation's ability to become agriculturally self-sufficient). But there is an underlying assumption that all nations are potentially equals and can be brought quickly up to the standard of competitiveness in the world economy set by the leaders. A few short-term concessions in a few critical sectors should patch things up. Then all nations can become equally competent to participate in the free-for-all of the creative destruction of world capitalism.

On the one hand, the neoclassical school advocates a form of economic **Social Darwinism** for the sake of economic efficiency and technological progress (only the strong should survive in each economic sector, forcing the weak out of business until they find a niche in which they were meant to succeed given their natural, factor endowments). On the other hand, this perspective assumes that globally *everyone* will be better off if free markets and free trade prevail everywhere. The policymakers in a country like Honduras, which has sustained itself on two basic industries (bananas and rents received from U.S. military bases), must scratch their heads in wonder as to how the global prosperity promised by neoclassical economic theory is supposed to trickle down to them.

Structuralism

The collective learning through tariff reductions for the sake of free markets and world economic growth advocated by the neo-classical school was perceived to be blocked by many developing nations because of the way

---

*Significantly, the neoclassical vision does not dwell upon questions of distribution (i.e., gains in consumption and production *for whom?*).

they were structurally positioned in the global economy. In the 1950s two development economists proposed interpretations of world trade that became the basis of the "structuralist school" and reforms in the GATT—Raúl Prebisch, executive secretary for the Economic Commission for Latin America (ECLA), and Hans Singer.

Prebisch and Singer argued that the world economy was structured or tilted against those countries that depended upon the production of primary commodities for their economic survival (that is, structured against the interests of most developing countries). Rather than an equitable system of comparative advantage in which all countries benefited by maximizing production in those products most appropriate to their factor endowment, the structuralists found an asymmetrical or unequal system of trade. The demand for manufactured and industrial goods produced by **the center,** or developed countries, was much greater than the demand for the agricultural and basic mineral commodities in which **the periphery,** or developing countries, specialized. Therefore, *the terms of trade* were systematically structured against the position of the developing countries and in favor of the position of the developed industrialized countries.[23] This unequal structural position between the center and dependent periphery countries resulted in a **trade gap** between them (that is, a persistent disequilibrium in the trade balance of countries relying primarily upon prime commodities). The trade imbalance, in turn, meant that the periphery countries could not earn enough through exports to cover the cost of the imports they so badly needed for their development.[24]

Initially, the structuralists believed that industrialization was the key to development for the periphery. When it became clear that the center or developed countries would continue to trade predominantly among themselves and, therefore, limit the export earnings that the developing countries could expect from the developed world, Prebisch advocated that periphery countries create their own trading system or bloc until a certain "takeoff" point of modernization was reached. Perhaps eventually this would result in a regional or subregional common market made up of preferential agreements for dependent countries.[25] To achieve this takeoff position, the structuralists usually advocated a *strategy of import substitution* in order to reduce developing countries' dependence upon exports from the industrialized countries: Brazil's policy of producing automobile fuel from sugar cane to cut down on oil imports is a typical example. Both the neoclassical and structuralist schools assumed that international trade was an engine of growth. But whereas the neoclassical school stressed leaving things up to the markets alone, the structuralists advocated Keynesian controls, so convinced were they that unregulated markets would not change inequities among countries anymore than this economic philosophy solved inequities within them.[26]

The structuralist position was persuasive to the managers of developing economies since export earnings accounted for about three-fourths of their foreign-exchange resources. And primary products, in turn, accounted for about three-fourths of the exports from developing countries. Not only did the value of the primary products decline relative to the value of the manufactured products that dominated the trade of the developed countries, but productivity increases in advanced industrial states put a continual upward pressure on wages and other input costs, keeping prices constant or pushing them up. **Productivity** is the measure of how many inputs are required to produce how many outputs: for example, how many hours of work are needed to produce a car. To increase productivity means either to reduce the number of inputs (that is, to pay cheaper wages or to lower the number of working hours) or to increase outputs (produce more products while maintaining the same number of inputs).

However, Prebisch noted that in developing countries productivity increases do not translate into wage increases or constant prices given weak labor organizations and disguised unemployment. Rather, increases in productivity in the poor countries lead to the decline of prices—a savings passed on largely to consumers in the rich nations. Other factors put a downward pressure on the prices or demand for primary commodities as well. As income increases, the percentage spent on food declines, not to mention the percentage of primary products of the total factor inputs necessary to produce industrial goods. Furthermore, technological innovation provides synthetic substitutes at lower prices for many primary products.[27]

From the structuralist perspective, the game rules of GATT were tilted to the advantage of the multiresource, rich developed countries and to the disadvantage of the dependent developing countries: It was, in short, a "rich man's club"! The most favored nation principle (MFN) prevented rich nations from giving poor nations preferential treatment in importing their manufactured goods for the sake of fostering their development. Reciprocity sounds good in principle as long as there is a wide enough diversity of products to have something to exchange for concessions. But if bananas is all you have, you have nothing to negotiate with: You have to protect your bananas with all your might. The American principle of strict reciprocity meant that poor countries would have to make a concession to the United States for each tariff the United States agreed to lower: Clearly the rich countries had much more room for bargaining than did the poor countries when it came to making *quid pro quo* ("this-for-that") concessions. Thus, the initial GATT regime was a subtle maintenance system of preserving the asymmetrical structures of the status quo, giving most of the payoffs to the rich industrialized countries most able to take advantage of the GATT rules. (All boats might rise with the world economic growth stimulated by global trade but the big boats would stay big and the advantages of those most highly developed at the start of the voyage would be structurally consolidated, their relative position confirmed.)[28]

The **"principal supplier rule"** of GATT negotiations was also seen by the structuralists to discriminate against the developing countries. Briefly, according to this rule, negotiations begin bilaterally with requests (not offers) for tariff reductions on a particular product made only by the exporter of the largest volume of that product to the market of a second country. Most developing countries were not in this position and were, therefore, not able to request reductions. Their best hope was the "splashing effect" from the MFN clause allowing them to benefit from tariff reductions between developed countries that dealt with products of concern to them. But this "splashing effect" cut two ways: It also precluded developing countries from negotiating concessions just among themselves. The multilaterization process of GATT negotiations was dominated by the strongest trading countries, taking into account the competitiveness and capacity of these countries to overflow their home markets.[29] As the Indian representative noted in regard to the original GATT rules in 1955: "Equality of treatment is equitable only among equals."[30]

A key complaint concerning GATT by developing countries was that agriculture, one of the largest sectors of commodities, was excluded from the GATT and was, therefore, protected. The United States had received an exceptionally broad waiver for strategic, political, and social reasons.[31] And when the Treaty of Rome creating the European Common Market came into force, the Common Agricultural Policy of the Europeans was similarly protectionist. Later, with the expansion of these exclusions from the GATT to include textiles and footwear—products of particular importance to the developing countries—salt was added to the wound.

The acceptance of the Anglo-American hegemony of neoclassical assumptions behind the GATT was increasingly undermined when large numbers of colonies became politically independent in the 1950s and 1960s and sought economic independence as well. Provided that the colonizing power that had supervised them was a member of GATT, these nations were treated as *de facto* members and permitted to vote even though all the GATT regulations did not apply to them. In 1958 the Haberler Report by the well-known economists Gottfried Haberler, James Meade, Jan Tinbergen, and Roberto Campos provided a fulcrum for building pressures among the developing countries: it concluded that the dilemma of the developing countries was in large part due to the trade policies of the developed countries. Committee III of the GATT was set up as a result of this report to examine the obstacles faced by developing countries in getting their exports into developed countries. But nothing concrete came of the committee's recommendations.

Still, the Haberler Report and Committee III provided information and motivation for collective learning on the part of developing countries, stimulating the formation of a collective strategy. A year after the Haberler Report, fifteen developing countries got together to issue a *Note on the Expansion of International Trade* within GATT. They pointed out that developing countries were limited in their capacity to initiate negotiations and asked for negotiations on nontariff trade measures that discriminated against exports from developing countries.* In the early 1960s, some of the same fifteen nations combined with others to form a group of twenty-one, which proposed a *Programme of Action* calling for the unilateral reduction of tariffs and nontariff barriers affecting the exports from developing countries.† The stage was set for a major collective effort on the part of developing countries to pressure GATT for reform of existing rules and for enforcement of rules on the books of particular interest to the poorer nations.

UNCTAD

The structuralist perspective of Raúl Prebisch served as the ideological consensus behind the collective movement of developing countries to establish in 1964 the **United Nations Conference on Trade and Development (UNCTAD)** as an organ of the United Nations General Assembly. If GATT was "the rich man's club," UNCTAD was "the poor nations' pressure group" designed to change the GATT rules concerning trade and development for the sake of the developing countries and for a new international economic order.[32] A pressure group is just that, having no institutional power of its own. Indeed, some quipped that UNCTAD actually stood for "Under No Condition Take Any Decisions." But this understates the influence of an organization from which the well-known **"Group of 77"** (developing countries in the United Nations) emerged, not to mention GATT reforms such as the Generalized System of Preferences (GSP).

UNCTAD, in effect, is a series of conferences sponsored by the United Nations, which can make proposals or suggestions but which cannot force compliance. Prebisch, a dynamic Argentinian, was appointed the first secretary-general of UNCTAD, which he wanted to use to summon developed nations unilaterally to extend preferential treatment to less developed nations for their exports of manufactures and semimanufactures. However, the motivating force behind the initial creation of UNCTAD was not so much Prebisch as it was Wladek Malinowski, who was previously associated with the United Nations. Malinowski believed that the only hope for bettering the position of the developing countries in the world trading system was if they could unify under the prestigious umbrella of the United Nations. The enthusiasm of Malinowski for this strategy, combined with the intellectual leadership of Prebisch in the context of the proliferation of developing countries because of decolonialization, resulted in UNCTAD. Collective learning emerged from the influence of these spiritual and intellectual mod-

---

*These countries included Brazil, Burma, Cambodia, Chile, Cuba, Federation of Malaya, Federation of Rhodesia and Nyasaland, Ghana, Greece, India, Indonesia, Pakistan, Peru, and Uruguay.

†The twenty-one included Argentina, Brazil, Burma, Cambodia, Ceylon, Cuba, Chile, Nigeria, Federation of Malaya, Ghana, Haiti, India, Indonesia, Israel, Pakistan, Peru, United Arab Republic, Tanganyika, Tunisia, Uruguay, and Yugoslavia.

els. Nor should one neglect the influential role of Chile, whose delegate to GATT in the early 1960s, Federico Garcia Oldini, proposed that the developing countries be granted "concessions without compensation" and challenged the principal-supplier procedure.

The environmental context in which the "learning and positioning" by developing countries occurred was marked by a doubling in world trade from 1950 to 1960. But the leaders of developing countries noted that their share of world trade dropped from 41 percent in 1950 to 30 percent in 1960.[33] Diplomats from the East European countries and less developed nations joined forces at UNCTAD I in Geneva, which established UNCTAD as a permanent organ of the United Nations, and pressed for preferential trade agreements and special financial resources for developing countries from the advanced industrialized nations of GATT.

The founding of UNCTAD aimed to improve institutional arrangements and the machinery of the world economic order; to reduce or eliminate all barriers restricting exports from developing countries; to expand export markets for these countries; to create financial circumstances to more easily enable developing countries to increase imports, and to seek better coordination in world trade policies. From the UNCTAD perspective, the GATT market system was structured against the developing nations from the outset. It was buoyed by tariff barriers, protectionist policies, and discrimination on the part of the developed countries that worked to the detriment of their poor neighbors. The northern industrial countries were not only "the center" but were self-centered. And GATT was their greenhouse.

The UNCTAD conferences meet every two-to-four years at various developing country cities (New Delhi, Santiago, Nairobi, Cartageña de Indias, etc.), focusing on different but related issues: shipping, food problems, difficulties of land-locked countries, disarmament, duty-free entry, domestic production, technological capacity and technology transfer, the brain-drain from developing to developed countries, commodity stabilization, export earnings, and last but not least, environmental problems.

In the early 1970s, the developing countries succeeded in getting industrialized nations to adopt a **Generalized System of Preferences (GSP)** for ten years, which eliminated tariffs on manufactured and semimanufactured goods exported by developing countries. No tariff concessions were asked for in return, significantly modifying the reciprocity principle of GATT. The aim of the GSP was to promote industrialization in developing nations by stimulating their exports.

By 1974 the developing countries were able to use the impetus of UNCTAD to push for the *Integrated Program for Commodities* (IPC). The IPC sought to control price fluctuations and average prices of commodities negotiated on a case-by-case basis by exporters and importers. Its aim was to better the terms of trade structured against national economies dependent upon the export of primary commodities for the lion's share of export earnings in a world of falling commodity prices. Targeting ten of the eighteen agricultural and mineral commodities that made up three-fourths of the primary commodity exports of developing countries, the IPC called for stockpiling them to create a buffer zone against price instability. A $6 billion Common Fund was requested, which would be made up of contributions from exporters and importers to finance the scheme. However, Western countries, particularly the United States, were wary of any automatic, universal system of price control, such as that implied by the IPC. From their classical, liberal economic perspective, they feared losing flexibility and control and they were concerned that such a system would result in continual inflation. The Americans preferred case-by-case, market-oriented arrangements. Structuralism and neoclassical economic theory were at loggerheads. This blocked the fulfillment of the IPC proposal.

No doubt part of this diffusion of energies and disappointment in the results of UNCTAD conferences is attributable to the group system according to which UNCTAD is organized. For purposes of elections and voting, UNCTAD member states were classified into four groups: Group A: Afro-Asian states and Yugoslavia; Group B: developed market economies, or the West; Group C: Latin American states; Group D: states with a centrally planned economy, of the East European bloc. Cross-group alliances are rare except for the steady coalition of the countries of Groups A and C—the well-known "Group of 77."

Conventional wisdom holds that the UNCTAD conferences, which meet about every three years, have had but a minor impact on restructuring the world trade system to the advantage of the developing countries. But this misses the point: UNCTAD is but part of a long-term process of delegitimization of Anglo-American (and particularly American) hegemony in the world economy. Such a process does not have to sharply revise GATT decisions in the short-term to succeed. UNCTAD is but one form of strategic behavior illustrating a collective learning and Third-World positioning process in the world trade system in which great numbers (seventy-seven if not the absolute majority of the United Nations state membership) may lose through diffusion in the short run only to win by creating the groundswell or momentum for a global political economy sea change in the long run.

The Earth Summit and Sustainable Development

Such a sea change appeared to gather momentum at the "Earth Summit"—the United Nations conference on Environment and Development in Rio de Janeiro, Brazil in June 1992. UNCTAD helped to plan for this conference on linking issues such as hunger, poverty, illiteracy, and ill health with the ecological and economic consequences of ozone depletion, climate change, soil degradation, deforestation, declining biodiversity, and the increasing pollution of air, water, and land. New values of equity and environment were defined for the North-South agenda. A number of multilateral agreements resulted: 154 countries signed the climate protection convention, 156 signed the biodiversity protection convention and 178 agreed to Agenda 21—a mammoth (900-page) voluntary action plan.

Agenda 21 details strategies and integrated program measures to reverse the effects of environmental degradation and promote environmentally sound and sustainable development in all nations. Chapter 38 of Agenda 21 recommends that the U.N. General Assembly establish a permanent, high-level U.N. **Commission on Sustainable Development (CSD)** to implement Agenda 21 at the national, regional, and international levels. The question for the late 1990s is whether or not the CSD will become another "talk shop" with little impact, split by the conflict between the majority of developing countries holding the votes and the rich, developed nations with the cash, and stymied by the limits of national sovereignty that govern international law.[34]

The Bush administration already symbolized the resistance to be expected from those adhering to the doctrine of Anglo-Saxon liberalism: the American government dragged its feet to the point of being isolated at the Earth Summit, fearful that stringent environmental protection measures would force the U.S. to come up with a unified national energy policy that would cost Americans jobs. From this liberal view, environmental regulation and economic development are perceived to be in inevitable conflict and the threat of global warming is greatly overstated. In contrast, the Europeans and Japanese noted the long-term economic benefits that could be derived from environmental protection, the impact of climate change, and the importance of strengthening ties with the developing countries. The "postliberal" tilt of the Clinton-Gore administration strengthened U.S. commitment to the Agenda 21 program for sustainable development, although financial resources were severely limited given the administration's ambitious domestic agenda and the American budget deficit.

Trade Blocs: The EU, OPEC, NAFTA, and APEC

The archetype model of collective behavior of which UNCTAD is such a diffuse and imperfect example is the **trade bloc**—an organized group of nations of limited membership that attempts to create a buffer zone of import, export, and protectionist strategies to maximize the collective economic benefits of its members at the expense of those outside the bloc. *Given the increasing tempo of technological innovation, communication, and transnational exchanges in the "creative destruction" of the global capitalist system, it is a natural, human, and conservative impulse to band together with nearby friends to try to structure scarcity to mutual advantage and to protect one's own group from the competitive abundance of the production of others outside the group.*

The ultimate examples of the trade-bloc model of collective learning and positioning, which nations have tried to mimic in various forms in the post–World War II world trade system, are the European Economic Community (EEC), or European Common Market, and the Organization of Petroleum Exporting Countries (OPEC). By limiting the size of their membership to much less than the size of GATT or UNCTAD these organizations have reaped greater proportional rewards for their members and have at times demonstrated a bargaining cohesiveness that have surprised the rest of the international community. New trade blocs have formed to counter these successes: The North American Free Trade Association (NAFTA) and the Asian Pacific Economic Association (APEC).

THE EUROPEAN UNION (EU).   The European Union (formerly "The European Community") emerged from efforts of European businessmen and politicians to put the disintegration of World War II behind them, to cooperate in key economic sectors for their mutual advantage, and to protect themselves from future American and foreign competition. Specifically, a continuing Franco-German "axis" is the engine of the European integration movement in terms of trade and industrial cooperation.[35] Konrad Adenauer, the first chancellor of the German Federal Republic, viewed political and economic integration with the French as a strategy for reducing occupation restrictions upon Germany after its loss of the war and for creating a stable basis for future economic and strategic development. In 1950 French Foreign Minister Robert Schuman proposed the "Schuman Plan" for pooling German and French coal and steel production. Steel and coal are vital strategic industries. Schuman saw the advantages of controlling the rich resources of the Ruhr in northern Germany (which had serviced the German war machine in the past). And Adenauer perceived the Schuman Plan as a vehicle whereby the Germans might ease the French occupiers out of the Ruhr through future economic cooperation. The result was the founding of the **European Coal and Steel Community (ECSC)** in 1952, made up of six member states: West Germany, France, Italy, the Netherlands, Belgium, and Luxembourg.

The ECSC abolished customs duties, restrictions, duel pricing systems, and transport rates for coal, coke, iron ore, steel, and scrap for all community members and set production target and investment programs. To head off the dismantling and nationalization of German industries tainted by Nazi leadership, Adenauer promised the unions major participation in the running of private companies. As a result the workers in the ECSC coal and steel industries were allowed to elect 50 percent of the supervisory boards (the policy of *"co-determination"*) as compared to 33 percent in the rest of German industry. Moreover, the four institutions of the ECSC became the precursors of similar European Common Market (EEC) institutions: the High Authority (the EEC's Commission), the Council of Ministers (EEC's Council of Ministers), the Common Assembly (the EEC's European Parliament), and a Court of Justice (the EEC's Court of Justice).

The six original members of the ECSC founded the **European Common Market,** or **European Economic Community (EEC),** in the **Treaty of Rome** in 1957, led by the Franco-German dynamism and institutional framework of the ECSC. The Common Market, or EEC, succeeded in its basic objective of initially reducing all trade barriers among its members and then essentially eliminating them within twelve to fifteen years. Armed with a common customs tariff—the corollary of an internal customs union—the EEC greatly increased its external trade policy clout with its solidarity. Faced with this economic competition, in 1959 British paymaster-general Reginald Maulding led the way to create a second European bloc, the **European Free Trade Association (EFTA),** made up of "the Seven": Britain, Austria, Denmark, Norway, Portugal, Sweden, and Switzerland. This was the first clear example of collective learning from the EEC model for the sake of bettering the collective economic position of a group of allied countries. However, unlike the EEC, the EFTA did not aim to establish a common policy toward the outside world but merely to reduce and eventually abolish tariffs and other trade restrictions among EFTA members. Plagued by Britain's Commonwealth ties with former British colonies, EFTA was not nearly as successful as the EEC, and Britain soon applied for EEC membership.

The small Benelux countries—Belgium, the Netherlands, and Luxembourg—supported British membership in the EEC, calculating that Britain might offset the power of the Franco-German axis. The Germans also favored British entry, hoping it would end the division of Europe into competing trade blocs and knowing that Germany would stand to gain a great deal from trade with Britain and the Commonwealth. Indeed, West German trade with EFTA amounted to three times the sum of French trade with these countries. France, under the leadership of Charles de Gaulle, initially opposed British entry—which could dilute French power in the EEC and make decision making more difficult given Franco-British cultural differences (especially since England carried the baggage of the Commonwealth). De Gaulle also resented "special" British ties with the United States (that is, Anglo-Saxon hegemony). By holding out the longest against British membership, the French managed to tilt the European integration process toward the French position.

Nevertheless, in 1973 the United Kingdom, Ireland, and Denmark entered the European Common Market, following difficult negotiations. In the 1980s Greece, Spain, and Portugal followed suit, and "the Nine" became "the Twelve." By 1984, imports and exports of the Twelve (excluding trade among themselves) represented an average of 12.5 percent of their gross domestic product. This can be compared to 7.5 percent for the United States and 13.5 percent for Japan in 1984. According to GATT figures for that year, the EEC's share of world trade was 18 percent in contrast to 17 percent for the

United States and 9 percent for Japan. By 1985 the developing countries absorbed 34 percent of EEC exports.[36] Some 130 countries established diplomatic relations with the EEC as such, and the EEC received observer status in the United Nations and in some of its specialized agencies. Trade between EFTA and the Twelve makes up about a fifth of all EU trade (a little more than EU–U.S. trade). As of 1987, there were 322 million people living in the European Community, compared to 237 million in the United States and 275 million in the USSR. Between 1957 and 1986 trade among EEC countries increased sevenfold while EEC trade with the rest of the world tripled.

By 1985 the EEC was the largest trading bloc in the world in terms of exports and was barely surpassed by the United States in terms of imports. As a percentage of gross domestic product (GDP), the average external trade of the EEC in terms of both imports and exports was greater than that of either the United States or Japan.

In 1985, a second wave of EEC bloc dynamism was initiated when the European Council (made up of the heads of the twelve member states) agreed to constitute a single market by 1992. This initiative was aimed to break down national regulations within the bloc on things such as transportation, banking, copyrights, borders, industrial subsidies, professional certification and health requirements. A White Paper specified 300 areas for such deregulatory action complete with deadlines for EC* Commission proposals to deal with them. *In 1986, European Community members signed the Single European Act amending the Treaty of Rome by permitting decisions in most areas to be made by a qualified majority instead of unanimously* (although still leaving the European Council with the most authority). In principle, the unification of the market has been based upon (1) granting of "mutual recognition" of each others regulations and standards by members, and (2) home-country control, or the right of a company to operate throughout the community if licensed in one member country.

Such pragmatic principles eliminated the need for the commission to lose energy in "harmonizing" or adopting a single European standard or in pushing for "European companies." As political scientist Stanley Hoffmann noted: "There will be instead a kind of free market of competing national standards."[37] Nor do the member nation-states seem to "lose" what the European Community "gains" in power since governments and bureaucracies remain the chief players. *The European Union (EU) is best understood as a pooling of sovereignties.* Still, like de Gaulle before her, British Prime Minister Margaret Thatcher remained convinced that her nation's sovereignty was at stake and resisted any nibbling away of her authority, particularly when it came to issues such as the creation of a common central bank or one European cur-

---

*EC refers to "European Community"—all political, legal and economic institutions of the European Common Market (an updating of the more *economically* focused "EEC"). In 1993 the "EC" was renamed the "EU": "European Union."

rency. But in terms of collective learning, the persuasive power of Commission President Jacques Delors pushed through a new "European architecture" (see Figure 4–1), which became the basis of the **Maastricht Treaty.** This treaty, which proposed a single European currency, a single European central bank, and unified social and defense policies, was presented at the summit in Maastricht, Netherlands in December 1991.

Delors's vision of European architecture, which became the official view of the European Commission, was one of three concentric circles: the core circle representing 345 million people—members of the **European Union (EU)** made up of the single market, the European Monetary Union (EMU), and the European political union (of foreign, defense and immigrant policies, etc.); the second circle representing the 33 million people of the **European Economic Area (EEA),** confirmed in a treaty of May, 1992, including EFTA members presumably on the waiting list to join the EMU—Iceland, Norway, Sweden, Finland, Austria, Switzerland, and Lichtenstein; and the third circle representing the 123 million people of the **European Association Accords (EAA),** including the former East bloc countries of Central Europe wanting to join the EMU as well—*Poland, *Hungary, *The Czech Republic, *Slovakia, Romania, Bulgaria, Bosnia, Slovenia, etc. This European

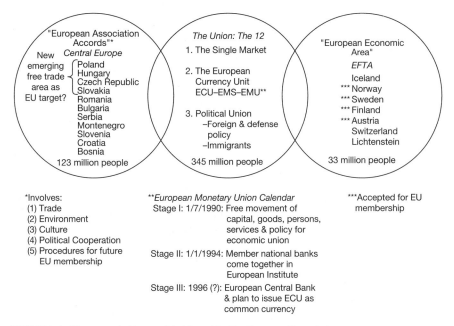

FIGURE 4–1 "European Architecture" As Viewed By The European Commission

*These four countries have been envisioned as an emerging free-trade area by some Eurocrats.

architecture finessed the post-cold-war dispute as to whether the European Union should *deepen* (integrate internally) before it *widens* (expands horizontally to take in new members to stabilize their fragile democracies and economies).[38] A more realistic assessment might be that this architecture legitimizes the exclusion of the EEA and EAA countries from membership in "the club," the European Union, until these would-be members become rich and stable enough to add more benefits than costs (such as Sweden, Finland, Norway and Austria, which were accepted into the EU in 1994—pending referendums by their home legislatures).

The deep recession in Europe in the early 1990s slowed down the ratification of the Maastricht Treaty until it finally was confirmed in diluted form in November 1993. The Danes initially rejected it until they received special conditions, Britain delayed deciding, and the French barely approved it. The EU bureaucracy at the headquarters in Brussels moved faster than the general populations of Europe. *The elite were slow to come down off their pinnacle to sell their vision to everyday citizens, who mistrusted the centralized "Eurocracy" and were concerned with preserving their sovereignty and cultural identities from further European integration and regulation. But no one should underestimate the importance of the regulations of the European Union nor of the European Institute in Frankfurt established by the Maastricht Treaty, which will become the European Central Bank designed to issue the ECU as a common currency.*

The recession of the early 1990s served to disguise the importance of the process of European integration and the long-term political significance of Maastricht. Economist Lester Thurow even declared the GATT-Bretton Woods system dead and claimed that the world's largest market, the European Union, has already informally written the new rules for the world's trading system.[39] Indeed, by the end of the 1980s the European Union was worth more than $4 trillion in purchasing power and investments from all over the world flowed in, as they did again as Europe began to recover from recession in 1994. Recall that the German unification process stimulated the French to push European integration faster, hoping to anchor Germany before her energies were distracted to the East. (This explains the aggressive European architecture of Delors and the push for the Maastricht treaty.) The percentage of total trade accounted for by intra-European Union trade rose from 35 percent in 1958 to 60 percent in 1990.[40] *One of the key trade rules the European Union has introduced is that in areas like banking and public procurement, foreign firms have full access to the EU market* if and only if *EU companies have similar open access to their home markets—reciprocity with a steel edge.*

The undisputed success of the EU as a regional trade bloc can be contrasted with other regional integration efforts—such as LAFTA—the Latin American Free Trade Association founded in 1960. The long history of European roots and regional trade traditions gives the EU a tremendous "learning by doing" advantage, based on the experience of centuries. (The first ideological proposal for a federated Europe was advanced by Pierre Dubois in

1306.) Moreover, when the highly developed Western European infrastructure was destroyed by World War II, the necessity for immediate reconstruction and modernization was clear. In addition, the cold war heightened the perception of the Soviet threat as seen from the American position, thus stimulating Marshall Plan aid for the sake of Western economic and military hegemony.

In contrast, the impulse for Latin American integration in LAFTA was strongest in times of world economic crisis when the Latin Americans adopted inward-looking policies. And while LAFTA countries also benefitted from "learning by doing" in diversifying their export products first in a regional context, as soon as world economic growth was resurrected, national interests in global markets displaced regional bloc preoccupations, weakening LAFTA's potential bargaining position immensely.[41] The only truly successful trading bloc among developing countries is OPEC.

ORGANIZATION OF PETROLEUM EXPORTING COUNTRIES (OPEC). While OPEC is often referred to as a commodity producer cartel rather than as a trading bloc, the effect in terms of the world economy is similar: A limited group of member nations strive to cooperate to increase their internal development benefits, shifting the costs to those outside the club wherever possible through joint pricing policies. The rationale for calling OPEC a trading bloc is increased when one notes that world economic data are usually broken down into "oil-producing" versus "non-oil-producing" developing countries, reflecting the continuing importance of the OPEC bloc.

Functionally, OPEC serves like the EU as a buffer zone against the creative destruction of turbulent change of global capitalism—an effort at cooperative management by individual states or organizations in order to cope with change to their mutual benefit. *Buffer zones such as trade blocs or commodity cartels can be seen as arenas of opportunity for collective learning and structural positioning, which succeed through solidarity and joint traditions of learning by doing and fail to the extent solidarity and such mutually beneficial learning traditions break down.*

After World War II the global economy was characterized by excess oil supply over demand, dominated by "the Seven Sisters"—the major multinational oil companies of the West: Exxon, Texaco, Mobil, Standard of California, Gulf, Shell, and British Petroleum. These seven companies controlled both production levels and prices throughout the 1950s and 1960s, more or less dictating management policies to the host developing countries whose oil provided the basic resource for the business. Given the surplus of supply over demand, oil prices were kept low, thus providing a cheap energy basis for the extraordinary economic growth rates of Western nations through the 1960s. In 1959, the Seven Sisters even went to the extreme of lowering oil prices, triggering the formation of OPEC by developing nations who defensively banded together in an initially impotent gesture in 1960 to try to hold the line on the price of the commodity upon which their economic survival seemed to depend.

OPEC was first made up of Iran, Iraq, Kuwait, Saudi Arabia, and Venezuela. Later, Indonesia, Algeria, Libya, Nigeria, Ecuador, Qatar, Abu Dhabi, Dubai, Sharjah, and Gabon joined them. Thus, one could say that OPEC was symbolically created from the threat imposed by a cartel of multinational corporations who overplayed their dominant hand to the point of making economic injustice patently blatant.

As the decade of the 1960s drew to a close, major shifts were occurring in the global oil industry. Independent oil companies—such as Occidental Petroleum—sprang up alongside the Seven Sisters, establishing their own sources of supply and diffusing the power of the major oil firms. High growth rates in the Western economies increased energy consumption to such an extent that the international oil market became tight as demand came in sight of matching supply. The dollar—the currency in which oil is priced—was devaluated, increasing the inflationary pressures already hitting the oil-producing developing countries hard. Col. Muammar el-Qaddafi, the unpredictable leader of Libya, correctly perceived an unusual bargaining opportunity in the changed world economy. He demanded a higher price from Occidental Petroleum for Libyan oil than the price asked in the Middle East, arguing that Occidental's transport costs for Libyan oil were cheaper and that the low sulfur content of Libyan crude gave it a special value to ecologically minded Western consumers with their rising environmental standards. Because Occidental Petroleum depended almost solely upon Libya as a source of supply, this independent company was eventually pressured to give into Qaddafi's demands despite counterpressures brought to bear by other oil companies.

Anticipating that Libya's success would lead to similar demands upon oil companies by other Middle Eastern states, which in turn would stimulate Qaddafi to raise Libyan prices even more—resulting in a vicious circle—the major oil companies got the oil-producing nations of the Middle East and North Africa to agree to the Teheran and Tripoli Agreements of 1971. These agreements were designed to manage world oil price increases in a stable structure of multinational cooperation. Alas, the major multinational companies had "learned" too late.

OPEC's breakthrough, largely inspired by Qaddafi, was based upon the willingness of major OPEC members to take concrete and concerted actions in the event that negotiations should fail.[42] Libya cut back its oil output to convince oil companies to lower their prices—at a moment when Libyan oil (supplying about a quarter of Western Europe's needs) was in great demand. When Occidental Petroleum agreed to Qaddafi's demands, other companies followed suit and that set the stage for the Teheran negotiations of February 1971, largely tilted in favor of the oil-producing countries.

However, global economic and political events quickly outstripped the Teheran and Tripoli Agreements—the 1971 and 1973 dollar devaluations, the outbreak of war in the Middle East in October 1973, and the resulting oil embargo by the Arab oil-producing states against the United States, the Netherlands, and Portugal for their support of Israel. Afraid that their vital oil-supply lines could be disrupted, Western nations bid up the price of oil. OPEC took advantage of this great uncertainty in the world oil markets to quadruple the price of petroleum. Given domestic political uncertainties in the United States (of which the Arabs were no doubt well aware), the Americans were in no position to follow political scientist Robert Tucker's risky advice to invade and occupy the Saudi Arabian oil fields until oil prices came down. OPEC's world energy "revolution" was thus a *fait accompli.*

From the perspective of the developed oil-importing countries, the quadrupling of oil prices in 1973 and the subsequent doubling of oil prices in 1979 following the revolution in Iran were seen as "crises." But from the perspective of the oil-producing states these price rises were perceived as "adjustments of imbalances" long overdue. As Dr. Fahil Al-Chalabi of Iraq, the second in command at the OPEC Secretariat in Vienna, noted in 1980, given the dollar devaluations and inflation of the 1970s, if the same quantities of oil continued to be pumped at the same low prices, the oil reserves would be depleted much sooner than anticipated. This would not give oil-producing developing countries the time to use their oil revenues to invest in infrastructure development and alternative industries to complement their lopsided oil economies.

Financially, the oil-producing countries would be better off to leave their oil in the ground than to deplete their lifeblood resources at low prices in an inflationary environment when developed Western countries were anxious to stockpile all the oil they could in case their supply should be cut off. Moreover, Al-Chalabi argued that a consistently rising price of this finite fuel was in the interest of Western economies, which desired to become less dependent upon OPEC oil and needed higher oil prices to stimulate the search and development of alternative sources of energy.[43]

OPEC's 1973 and 1979 price rises had a deflationary *rather than an inflationary impact on the world economy of the 1980s* for a complex set of reasons. Most of the OPEC oil-producing nations had an absolute preference for liquidity in their investment strategies, putting their petrodollars into short-term (usually off-shore) bank accounts where they could not be easily taxed or frozen by governmental authorities. This liquidity preference meant that the OPEC states served as a transformer of real investment capital into short-term liquidity, creating a worldwide liquidity surplus. Meanwhile, in the rich developed countries, inflationary fears led to anti-inflation policies and austerity measures, resulting in tight money policies and high interest rates. Inflation was subdued at significant social costs (for example, the severe U.S. recession of 1981–82). Conservation measures in the energy field and massive oil stockpiling by governments and companies led to an oil glut in the disinflationary environment of the mid-1980s. Paradoxically, this temporary situation of oil abundance diluted OPEC's power. By 1988 OPEC found it necessary to invite non-OPEC oil producers to their negotiations in order to consolidate the petroleum trading bloc and reduce production enough to keep prices rising. But these efforts were mixed given that OPEC members did not carry out all the promises made at the negotiations (that is, producing more oil than they were supposed to), particularly given the uncertainties of the war winding down between Iran and Iraq. And if OPEC members themselves refused to abide by their own agreements, compliance by non-OPEC oil producers was also undermined.

However, during the last three years of the 1980s the demand for oil steadily grew, along with the exports of crude oil by OPEC members. Moderates, such as Saudi Arabia's Oil Minister, Hirsham Nazer, saw to it that oil prices were kept stable and relatively low in order to take away the incentive for Western countries to develop their own new sources of energy. And to prevent other OPEC members from attempting to outposition Saudi dominance in the cartel, the Saudis threatened to pump oil freely if any other member tried to reduce its 25 percent share of total OPEC output. As the country with the largest proven untapped oil reserves, Saudi Arabia would like to extend the dependence of others upon its oil for as long as possible in order to have time to modernize and create non-oil sources of wealth. The Saudi fear of loss due to the threat of revolutionary change motivated the Saudi government to make its alliance with the U.S. explicit during the Gulf War of 1990–91.

Although the United States took only 10 percent of its oil from the Persian Gulf, while Japan and Europe depended upon oil from the region for more than half of their energy needs, the Bush administration saw an opportunity to manage the crisis caused by Iraq's invasion of Kuwait for both economic and strategic gains. By organizing the United Nations coalition of developed countries who could pay for the war, the United States subsidized its military risks and restored American hegemony. The compliance of the Arab states with the trade embargo against Iraq confirmed U.S. primacy and set the stage for not only restoring OPEC's ability to function after the war but for the wider Middle East peace agreements that emerged between Israel and her Arab neighbors in 1993. U.S. stability, in short, depends in part upon the moderate management of the OPEC cartel by the Saudis. This assumption of permanent dependence prevents the American government from having to bite the bullet of a painful reform of its energy policy. Twenty years after the 1973 Arab oil embargo, the U.S. continued to use approximately the same amount of oil. But in 1993 it imported 44.6 percent of its oil compared to 37.2 percent in 1973. And 11.6 percent of the oil in 1993 came from Arab members of OPEC as opposed to just 5.3 percent in 1973.[44]

As oil-producing Arab countries recover from the Gulf War, the impact is deflationary, supporting U.S. complacency in terms of its energy policy.

For example, by 1993 Kuwait was again producing almost as much oil as it had before the August 1990 Iraqi invasion—the third largest Arab producer after Saudi Arabia and Iran.[45] OPEC was confronted with how to share world oil markets without pushing down the prices of petroleum. The OPEC effort has been to try to impose quotas on the producers who have recovered from the war, but their motive is to make up for the revenues lost when they had no oil revenue and quotas are not apt to be effective. The result is apt to be continuous cheating within OPEC, increasing production beyond agreed upon targets, keeping oil prices down. This, in turn, will help keep inflation and gas prices down, encouraging Americans to continue their profligate uses of energy and their policy of increasing dependence upon foreign sources of oil. By 1994 crude oil prices hit a 5-year low and OPEC accounted for 37 percent of world oil production. OPEC's future success depends upon China and its Asian neighbors where demand is expected to grow by 5 million barrels a day by the year 2000. Western nations may come to regret stimulating the Chinese to trade in their bikes for gas-guzzling cars . . .

NAFTA and APEC: The New Blocs on the Block

While the Clinton administration was busy pushing for a new GATT agreement globally, it was simultaneously helping to support the **North Atlantic Free Trade Association (NAFTA)** and **Asian Pacific Economic Cooperation (APEC)** organization trade blocs to counter the European Union and to benefit from bloc privileges within the GATT. This two-tier strategy was the trade equivalent of the Clinton strategy of attempting to reduce nuclear arms proliferation globally, while supporting the rapid increase in all other kinds of weapons sales to the Third World (the U.S. share of arms sales in the Third World increased from less than 13 percent in 1987 to 57 percent in 1992).[46] The aim in both cases was to boost American economic growth and employment short-term in the post-cold-war era regardless of long-term negative consequences for the world community (i.e., potential trade bloc wars and conventional regional wars in other countries).

NAFTA negotiations began under the Bush administration in 1991. The aim was to counter the clout of the European Union by creating a free trading bloc of 364 million consumers in the U.S., Canada, and Mexico with a total output of $6 trillion (25 percent more than the EU). Since Canada's trade with Mexico was but 1 percent of its trade with the U.S., the controversy surrounding the final passage of NAFTA in the U.S. Congress in November 1993 centered on trade-offs between the U.S. and Mexico. In 1992 the U.S. had a $5 billion trade surplus with Mexico, in contrast, for example, to a $75 billion trade deficit with East Asia. About 70 percent of Mexico's imports came from the U.S.[47] President George Bush saw NAFTA as a way to support the open economic reforms and trade liberalization of Mexican President Carlos Salinas that were initiated in 1987. Moreover, without the international investor confidence generated by NAFTA it is hard to imagine how Mexico would have covered an unusually heavy external savings deficit (5–6 percent of its gross domestic product in 1993).[48] Proponents of NAFTA viewed the agreement as a natural evolution of an emerging architecture of North America that was happening anyway and as the first step toward a larger North American-South American bloc.[49]

Opponents to NAFTA argued that after the initial upsurge in exports of the three countries with tariffs removed, factories would be tempted to move from the U.S. (and eventually Canada) to Mexico, which would result in lower wages and looser environmental regulations. Although the Clinton administration included side agreements to help equalize environmental standards and enforce existing labor laws, skeptics noted that the money allocated for these activities was minimal—particularly in the case of labor law enforcement. Low-skill jobs are widely expected to shift to Mexico, hitting hardest those in the U.S. who need the work most. Americans have probably underestimated the existing training and skills of Mexicans who could fill higher-level jobs as well. Even if not, it is undoubtedly cheaper to train or retrain workers in Mexico than in the U.S. Another problem is that many Mexican corn farmers will be put out of work as the lowered tariffs let through a wave of highly competitive agricultural goods from the U.S. and Canada.[50] Larger companies, particularly financial services, benefit from NAFTA. And NAFTA may help to stem the tide of Mexicans seeking to emigrate to the U.S. The ultimate question is who will benefit the most from the redistribution of benefits, both short-term and long-term? Or will it be a positive-sum game of greater benefit to all?

As soon as NAFTA was passed in November 1993, President Clinton went to a meeting of the Asian Pacific Economic Cooperation (APEC) group in Seattle to counter the overselling of NAFTA as an exclusive North American trade bloc and to keep the U.S. from being excluded from an emerging Asian trade bloc. APEC was founded in 1989 as a consultative forum made up of Australia, Canada, Japan, the Republic of Korea, New Zealand, and the U.S. plus the **ASEAN** nations, Brunei, Indonesia, Malaysia, the Philippines, Singapore and Thailand. Soon the People's Republic of China, Hong Kong, and Taiwan (or "Chinese Taipei") joined the organization. It has an annual budget of $2 million and a small secretariat based in Singapore (paid for largely by the government of Singapore). High-level ministerial meetings are held once a year according to the APEC charter, aimed at trade liberalization and cooperating on issues such as investment regulations, technology transfer, telecommunications, and energy.[51]

Prime Minister Mahathir Mohamad of Malaysia boycotted the APEC meeting in Seattle, advocating an exclusive all-Asian grouping called the East Asian Economic Caucus he devised in 1990. He envisioned the caucus, which has failed to develop support, as a counterweight to the EU and NAFTA blocs.[52] More recently, Mahathir successfully organized a group of fifteen developing nations to block a U.S.-European move to link preferential access to their markets to workers' rights.

APEC's November 1994 meeting in Jakarta consolidates an investment code drafted by APEC subcommittees—common rules for investing in eighteen nations around the Pacific Rim. As a South Korean diplomat put it, abolishing protective laws is "a necessary evil" in order to expand the trade of East Asian countries. Although APEC is a thin, young, and fragile organization, it may assume growing importance as a trading group, particularly since more than 40 percent of U.S. trade is with the Pacific region. Given the commonality of the Chinese written language (upon which Japanese is based) in many of the APEC countries, it could easily be that a core Chinese-language-based trading bloc will emerge. This bloc would functionally exclude those countries incapable of adapting. In this regard, it is well to keep in mind that the major source of direct foreign investment in China is offshore Chinese in other countries. . . .[53]

IMPLICATIONS

Trade blocs may perhaps be best understood as buffer zones in the turbulent process of creative destruction that characterizes global capitalism. Such buffer zones provide time for politico-economic adjustment for member nations inside the zone and to coordinate policies in order to maximize the advantage of members in the economic competition with nations outside the bloc. The extraordinary successes of the European Union (EU) and the Organization for Petroleum Exporting Countries (OPEC) were preconditioned by unusual sets of fortunate historical circumstances. In the case of the EU, a long and deep educational, cultural, and technological infrastructure was not difficult to resurrect after World War II, particularly given Marshall Plan aid aimed to shore up Western Europe against the cold war threat from the Soviet Union. The Americans and British overlearned a lesson from the settlement of World War I—not to break the back of Germany economically, but to help the country reconstruct and be accepted in the family of nations. By giving grants in many cases rather than loans, the U.S. created the basis for a competitive economic bloc from which it could not ask for loan repayment when its own household went into deficit.

Similarly, the Americans could have intervened to prevent the formation of the OPEC cartel but decided against it. For the next two decades, the oil-dependent industrialized countries paid the price in higher energy bills and an increasingly dependent energy policy. By mismanaging their hegemony or domination of the world economy, the Americans created the opportunity for the formation of the European Union and OPEC trade blocs. Some have argued that the formation of these blocs actually helps the U.S. in the difficult task of steering the multilateral management of the world trade system. But the relative autonomy of decision-making by the EU and OPEC suggests that they signify the *decline* of American domination more than its extension. And if one considers all the dollars the U.S. had to print to bankroll European recovery and OPEC energy prices and the resulting U.S. deficit, the case becomes clear.

Thus the American efforts to create trade blocs through NAFTA and APEC can be seen as belated attempts to restore American domination. But the European Union was so far advanced structurally, institutionally, and strategically that its regulations may become the unofficial real rules that govern the GATT regime. The political and cultural differences between Mexico and the U.S. and Canada make NAFTA little more than a free-trade zone with limited potential compared to the EU. Mexico, after all, is still a one-party authoritarian state compared to the American and Canadian governmental systems (when it elects another party into power, then one might be able to argue otherwise).[54] APEC represents a fragile trading conference more than an institutionalized decision-making body. Even if it starts to take on more institutional status, the probability is that the Asians will operate as an informal pro-Asian trading bloc behind the scenes, perhaps based on the written Chinese language.

In sum, there has been a post-cold-war trade revolution to officially extend the free-trade regime of the GATT while informally using this framework as an umbrella to legitimate the creation of a world of competing trade blocs. *Anglo-Saxon liberalism has been ideologically extended to cover the reality of the rapid development of postliberal coalitions of regional trading regimes.* The freeing up of trade globally will help to stimulate economic growth in both the developed and developing countries. Meanwhile, the postliberal trading blocs will determine who benefits most from this growth and who gets which jobs. The rules of competitiveness that determine who gets what, when, and how are illustrated in the next chapter.

THOUGHT QUESTIONS

1. What is meant by this statement:

   "Export-oriented growth strategies are the panacea for the collective insecurity generated by turbulent world markets"? Why is such a strategy desirable?

2. To what degree should trade be "'free' or regulated" by the nation-state, and to what degree should a nation- state aim for self-sufficiency?

3. List and describe four important GATT principles. In what respect is the Smoot-Hawley Tariff Act responsible for an advantageous position of the U.S. at the "starting line" of trade talks?

4. Describe the structuralist perspective of world trade and its critical evaluation of the neoclassical assumptions and principles of GATT.

5. Trading blocs seem to be the wave of the future. Is it just a matter of time before trading blocs become political and economic unions (i.e., the direction of the EU)? Or will they disband after their purpose has been served? Can they remain constant indefinitely? What are the dynamic forces pushing for change within a trading bloc?

6. Which economic organizations most represent the developed countries and which the developing countries? Where does the U.N. Commission on Sustainable Development (CSD) fit in?

NOTES

1. Sidney Painter, *Mediaeval Society* (Ithaca, NY: Cornell University Press, 1951), pp. 72–73.

2. See, for example, Jan Penn, *A Primer on International Trade* (New York: Vintage Books, 1967), Chapter 1.

3. See Robert L. Heilbronner, *The Worldly Philosophers* (New York: Simon and Schuster, 1986), p. 49.

4. David Ricardo, *Principles of Political Economy* (London: Everyman's Library, 1911), Chapter 1.

5. W. Arthur Lewis, *The Evolution of the International Economic Order* (Princeton, NJ: Princeton University Press, 1978).

6. See Charles P. Kindleberger, "The 1977 Nobel Prize in Economics," *Science* 198 (November 25, 1977), pp. 813–14, 860.

7. Ricardo, *Political Economy*, p. 83.

8. Arthur Dunkel, Director General of the GATT, "GATT at 40: It's More Needed Than Ever," *International Herald Tribune*, October 30, 1987, Op-Ed page.

9. W. A. Lewis, *Economic Survey 1919–1939* (London: Allen & Unwin, 1949), p. 50.

10. See F. V. Meyer, *International Trade Policy* (London: Croom Helm, 1978).

11. See Richard N. Gardner, *Sterling-Dollar Diplomacy*, 2nd ed. (New York: McGraw-Hill, 1969), pp. 101–109.

12. See Diana Tussie, *The Less Developed Countries and the World Trading System: A Challenge to the GATT* (London: Francis Pinter, 1987), p. 19, fn. 4.

13. Kenneth Dam, *The GATT: Law and International Organization* (Chicago: University of Chicago Press, 1970), p. 227.

14. See Meyer, *International Trade Policy*, p. 126.

15. Arthur Dunkel, "To Put the Theory to Work: From Bilateral Alliances to Multilateral Systems," *Innovation* 11/12 (1987): 32.

16. See OECD, *Obstacles to Trade and Competition* (report by Janusz Ordover and Linda Goldberg) Paris: OECD, 1993.

17. Dan Goodgame, "Trade Warrior," *Time*, March 15, 1993, p. 51.

18. Jeffrey E. Garten, "Clinton's Emerging Trade Policy," *Foreign Affairs,* Summer, 1993, Vol. 72, No. 3, p. 185.

19. For a sampling of the growing literature on neomercantilist trade policies, see: Tim Jackson, *The Next Battleground: Japan, America and the New European Market* (New York: Houghton Mifflin, 1993); Laura D'Andrea Tyson, *Who's Bashing Whom? Trade Conflict in High Technology Industries* (Washington: Institute of International Economics, 1992); Daniel Burstein, *Turning the Tables: A Machiavellian Strategy for Dealing with Japan* (New York: Simon and Schuster, 1993); Charles Ferguson and Charles Morris, *Computer Wars: How the West Can Win in a Post-IBM World* (New York: Times Books, 1993); and Wayne Sandholtz *et al., The Highest Stakes: The Economic Foundations of the Next Security System* (New York: Oxford University Press, 1992).

20. See "The Culture War," *The Wall Street Journal,* Oct. 15, 1993. Also see John Rockwell, "The New Colossus: American Culture As Power Export," *The New York Times,* Jan. 30, 1994.

21. Sylvia Nasar, "GATT's Big Payoff for the U.S.," *The New York Times,* December 19, 1993.

22. See Richard Blackhurst, Nicolas Marian, and Jan Tumlir, *Trade Liberalization, Protectionism and Interdependence: GATT Studies in International Trade No. 5* (Geneva: General Agreement on Tariffs and Trade, 1977).

23. The first structuralist works of Raúl Prebisch: United Nations, *The Economic Development of Latin America,* E/CN. 12/89/Rev. 1, New York: U.N., 1950 (Spanish edition, 1949) and United Nations, *Economic Survey of Latin America,* 1949, E/CN.12/164/Rev. 1, New York: U.N. 1951. The seminal article of Hans W. Singer: "The Distribution of Gains between Investing and Borrowing Countries," *American Economic Review, Papers and Proceedings* II, No. 2 (1950).

24. See Tussie, *Less Developed Countries,* pp. 22–37.

25. Raúl Prebisch, "Five Stages in My Thinking on Development," (Washington, DC: World Bank, 1982) (mimeographed), p. 8.

26. Tussie, *Less Developed Countries,* p. 22.

27. Prebisch's viewpoint is summarized in Albert O. Hirschman, "Ideologies of Economic Development in Latin America," *Latin American Issues* (New York: Twentieth Century Fund, 1961), pp. 14–15.

28. See John W. Evans, "The General Agreement on Tariffs and Trade," in *The Global Partnership,* edited by R. Gardner and M. Millikan (New York: Praeger, 1968), pp. 92–93.

29. See S.B. Linder, "The Significance of GATT for Underdeveloped Countries," in Proceedings of the U.N. Conference on Trade and Development (New York: UNCTAD, 1964), p. 527.

30. As cited in Tussie, *Less Developed Countries,* p. 25.

31. See Dam, *The GATT,* p. 260.

32. See Joseph S. Nye, "UNCTAD: Poor Nations' Pressure Group," in Robert Cox and Harold Jacobsen, eds., *The Anatomy of Influence: Decision Making in International Organization* (New Haven, CT: Yale University Press, 1973), pp. 334–70.

33. Michael Zammit Cutajar, *UNCTAD and the North–South Dialogue, the First Twenty Years* (Oxford: Pergamon Press, 1985), p. 13.

34. See Kathyrn G. Sessions, *Institutionalizing the Earth Summit: The United Nations Commission on Sustainable Development* (New York: The United Nations Associa-

tion, 1992) and *The Global Partnership for Environment and Development: A Guide to Agenda 21* (Geneva: UNCED, 1992).

35. This Franco-German axis thesis as the basis of Common Market integration is demonstrated in "The Common Market: Organizing for Collective Bargaining Power," Chapter 6 of R. Isaak, *European Politics: Political Economy and Policy Making in Western Democracies* (New York: St. Martin's Press, 1980), pp. 151–85.

36. These statistics are from "The European Community in the World," *European File* 16/86 (October 1986), Brussels: Commission of the European Communities, pp. 3–4.

37. Stanley Hoffmann, "The European Community and 1992," *Foreign Affairs,* Fall 1989, Vol. 68, No. 4, p. 35.

38. Based on discussions with officials in the European Commission in Brussels in May 1992. For background leading up to Maastricht treaty, see *The Single Market in Action* (Brussels: Commission of the European Communities, 1992) and Robert O. Keohane and Stanley Hoffmann, eds., *The New European Community: Decisionmaking and Institutional Change* (Boulder, Colo.: Westview Press, 1991).

39. Lester Thurow, *Head to Head: The Coming Economic Battle Among Japan, Europe, and America* (New York: William Morrow and Co., 1992), p. 65. However, Thurow's "Europhoria" seems to overestimate the ability of the European Union to master its numerous socioeconomic problems and to underestimate NAFTA's potential, not to mention the impact of Japanese economic recovery and the East Asian boom. GATT, too, seems to be outliving Thurow's death sentence.

40. *The Single Market in Action,* p. 10.

41. See Tussie, *Less Developed Countries,* Chapter 5: "The Oscillations of Regional Economic Integration in Latin America: LAFTA-LAIA," pp. 104–35.

42. Karl P. Sauvant and Hajo Hasenpflug, *The New International Economic Order: Confrontation or Cooperation between North and South?* (Boulder, CO: Westview Press, 1977), p. 369.

43. Fahil Al-Chalabi, Deputy Secretary General of OPEC, "OPEC's View of the Second Oil Crisis," paper presented at the Johns Hopkins University, School of Advanced International Studies Center, Bologna, Italy, June 2, 1980.

44. Matthew L. Wald, "After 20 Years, America's Foot Is Still On the Gas," *The New York Times,* October 17, 1993.

45. James Tanner, "War-Ravaged Kuwait Rebounds Into Ranks of Major Oil Nations," *The Wall Street Journal,* June 7, 1993.

46. Jeff Cole and Sarah Lubman, "Weapons Merchants Are Going Great Guns in Post-Cold War Era," *The Wall Street Journal,* January 28, 1994.

47. David Hale, "The Trade Revolution," *The Wall Street Journal,* November 3, 1993.

48. *Ibid.*

49. See, for example, Stephen Blank, "The Emerging Architecture of North America," *The North-South Agenda,* Paper One, March 1993 (Coral Gables, Fl.: North-South Center, University of Miami).

50. See Timothy Koechlin and Mehrene Larudee, "The High Cost of NAFTA," *Challenge,* September-October, 1992, pp. 19–26. Also see Sheldon Friedman, "NAFTA as Social Dumping," in the same issue, pp. 27–32.

51. See Frank B. Gibney, "Creating a Pacific Community," *Foreign Affairs,* Nov./Dec. 1993, Vol. 72, no. 5, pp. 20–25.

52. Philip Shenon, "Boycott in Order, Malaysian Says," *The New York Times,* Nov. 21, 1993. And see "Malaysia's Mahathir: Leading A Crusade Against the West," *Business Week,* April 25, 1994.

53. Rong-pin Kang, "Technology Import Policy of China in 1990s", paper presented at International Symposium on Networking of Human Relations and Technology, at Tokyo Keizai University, Tokyo, October 25, 1993.

54. See, for example, Anthony DePalma, "Reform in Mexico: Now You See It, . . ." *The New York Times,* September 12, 1993.

CHAPTER FIVE

NORTH–NORTH COMPETITIVENESS

Like a once-flabby athlete, the U.S. has been working out at the health club for the past couple of years. And it has paid off. Germany and Japan have just finished a big lunch and are only now signing up at the local economic gym.

David Wessel, *Wall Street Journal* (1994)

To achieve competitive success, firms from the nation must possess a competitive advantage in the form of either lower costs or differentiated products that command premium prices . . . We must explain why a nation provides an environment in which firms improve and innovate and continue to do . . . The behavior required to create and . . . to sustain competitive advantage is an unnatural act in many companies . . .

Michael Porter, *The Competitive Advantage of Nations* (1990)

Looking backward, future historians will see the twentieth century as a century of niche competition and the twenty-first century as a century of head-to-head competition.

Lester Thurow, *Head to Head* (1992)

"The cold war is over and the Japanese won," stated former U.S. Senator Paul Tsongas in his 1992 presidential campaign. The cold war—focused on the Soviet threat—was the glue that held the German and Japanese allies in a position of permanent dependence in relation to the United States. It also served to drain American economic strength for the sake of preserving military predominance. When such overwhelming military strength suddenly appeared superfluous with the collapse of the U.S.S.R., the dependence of allies upon the American security umbrella waned as well. The Gulf War against Iraq in 1990–91 served more to underscore that America's security business was independent of European and Japanese concerns than anything else, despite the greater dependence of these allies upon foreign oil (witness Japan's slow response to joining the anti-Iraq coalition). The United States suddenly found itself specialized in an area with flawed comparative commercial advantages: military power. For to sell its high-tech weapons and planes in the short-term was to undermine American hegemony in the long-run (although this has not stopped the support of the Clinton administration for conventional arms sales abroad). With some desperation, the Americans began a massive building down of their armed forces and widespread industrial restructuring domestically, looking to Japanese and European commercial successes with wariness. Meanwhile, German and Japanese independence from the United States grew, epitomized by German reunification and the coining of a new Japanese term, *kenbei,* meaning dislike of the United States.[1]

From the perspective of collective learning, "the Big Three"—the U.S., Japan and Germany, have fallen into the habit of trying to learn most from each other. Or, put another way, they see each other as the major competitors whose standards they have to meet, if not to surpass. That this habit is probably a myopic one, which tends to blind the three major economic states of the industrialized North to breakthroughs in other nations will not, for the moment, concern us here. Rather, the focus will be upon the reasons for being so absorbed in trilateral competitiveness and the recipes of the Big Three for success. Each of these three countries is culturally complex enough to keep its two major opponents scratching their heads for years in trying to figure out what is really going on "over there." Indeed, these three major players in the world economy are so complicated to understand and to predict that it is no surprise that Northern industrialized countries become preoccupied with each other. They are often self-absorbed to the extent that they find little time left over to try to understand other cultures in depth— even though their long-term survival may depend upon it. Add in the complications of German unification and the interlocking of the German economy with the other members of the European Union (which the Germans themselves have a hard time sorting out) and it is not surprising that rich countries become bogged down trying to figure out the likely moves of their rich opponents.

ORIGINS

In considering the origins of the differences in American, Japanese, and German competitiveness, keep in mind that, in terms of being *a unified nation-
state*, the United States is the oldest (born in 1776). The centralized state of
modern Japan dates from 1868 and the first unification of Germany from
1871 (with the second unification still in progress). Political stability, therefore, gives the U.S. one kind of competitive edge. However, this very stability
is based upon preserving a chaos of individualism through federalism and
checks and balances that make any national reform or radical policy change
extremely difficult (except in wartime). The United States is a liberal state in
a postliberal era. Germany and Japan, on the other hand, have much longer
cultural histories than does the United States, which gives them a basis for
communitarianism or the cooperative group form of capitalism colored by
Gemeinschaft (community) in Germany or the spirit of *wa* (harmony) in
Japan. As Professor George Lodge of Harvard has noted, we are confronted
with a competition between the individualistic, Anglo-Saxon form of capitalism of the U.S. versus the communitarian capitalisms of Japan and Germany.[2]

The events that have taken place since World War II are well-known, so
we can make a long story short. The United States and Britain won the war
militarily and, therefore, were able to establish the Bretton Woods system—
the embodiment of Anglo-Saxon hegemony. However, by the late 20th century, it appeared to many that Germany and Japan had won the peace economically. By occupying West Germany and Japan and greatly restricting the
amount they could spend on the military, the United States forced its competitors to focus all of their efforts on applied economic success or commercial business. The Germans and Japanese, in short, were *forced* to free-ride
upon the American security system and the Bretton Woods dollar system.
They were also forced to rebuild their bombed-out factories and physical infrastructure totally, whereas the Americans and British made do with old
plants that had not been bombed. And just in case this modernization and
targeting did not do the trick to restore German and Japanese competitiveness, the Americans kicked in generous grants of economic aid (most no-
tably, the Marshall Fund). In their moment of glory at the top of the heap
militarily and economically, the Americans fell for the temptation of
hubris—the Greek concept of false pride in trying to do more than one can
(which leads ultimately to downfall). As noted previously, had the Americans
not given such great amounts of money away in the form of grants, the
United States could now recall the loans with interest and help to eliminate
its huge deficit problem. By 1990 the U.S. federal debt had climbed to 59
percent of Gross National Product (GNP), up from 34 percent in 1980. And
interest payments on the debt climbed to almost 15 percent of federal income (from 9 percent) in the same time period.

Perhaps the American dislike of **savings** (or postponed consumption) stems from the belief that the United States will always remain "Number One" in the world (hubris with a capital H). But, whatever the motivation, the Americans refuse to save compared to their Japanese and German competitors. If one takes the 1980–1988 period (up to the fall of the Berlin Wall), the net personal savings as a percent of disposable income was 5.5 percent for the Americans compared with 12.2 percent for the West Germans and 16.4 percent for the Japanese.[3] By 1993, the U.S. savings rate had fallen below 4 percent despite what initially was referred to as an anemic, jobless recovery from recession.

Why does savings matter? Savings provides the capital for investment in new equipment and plants—for new infrastructure creating new jobs. Their high savings rate permitted the Japanese to have factories constantly modernized, usually keeping them under seven years on average. In comparison, American plants are generally at least twelve years old. Old plants plus low savings rates adds up to a deep competitive disadvantage. In terms of private and public investment in plants and equipment, research and development, infrastructure, and skills, the U.S. invests only one-half of what the Japanese invest and two-thirds of what the Europeans invest.

A savings mentality, fostered in both the German and Japanese cultures, is a cheap way to productivity. *To increase productivity it is often cheaper and easier to reduce the inputs through savings than to increase the outputs with greater effort or technological innovation.* The Germans always think of savings first. They are brought up to be thrifty. As in the Japanese case, the experience of war fought on their soil taught them the meaning of scarcity and the necessity of savings. The Americans are at a competitive disadvantage with these opponents in not having had to fight a war on their own soil since the Civil War.[4] Wartime destruction and the scarcity of raw materials also taught the Japanese and Germans to rely upon their wits. *In developed economies, productivity increases stem from value added to existing production processes. Indeed, the trend is towards increasing productivity through innovation in production processes more than through creating new products.*[5]

The Japanese provide the clearest illustration here. After World War II they aimed to make the textile market more productive. But they gradually shifted to manufacturing, particularly to consumer electronics and automobiles. In all these cases, as an island economy the Japanese were obliged to import almost all of the raw materials (and often the technology) they required for production. So their competitiveness and productivity depended upon the value they added to these imported resources in terms of production and management processes, design, and adaptation to global markets. To put it more strongly: their economic survival depended upon adapting quickly to the outside global economy, collectively learning how to transform imported materials into manufactured goods that consumers wanted. Typically, they started at the low-price ends of the markets they targeted, aiming for increases in market share rather than short-term profitability. This strategy also shored up their full-employment objective. Once they had captured a large share of the market, their costs went down because of **economies of scale** (that is the lowering of production costs because of being able to operate on a large scale). This increased their competitiveness and made it difficult for others to meet their price. Then they increased the quality of the products and perfected the efficiency of their production processes, permitting them to go up-scale in product (for example, from small cars to luxury family automobiles). This had the virtue of permitting them to make more money on fewer products, so that external tariff penalties imposed by others (such as the U.S.) had little effect on the bottom line.

INDUSTRIAL POLICY AS A KEY TO COMPETITIVENESS

Japanese Targeting

It was no accident that the Japanese were able to target certain promising industries or markets for collective development at the exclusion of others, therefore reducing national "opportunity costs." *In common with the Germans and French and in contrast with the U.S., the Japanese have a feudal heritage, which accustoms them to accept the hierarchy of their society and the legitimacy of elite institutions.* After World War II, the Japanese were determined to catch up with the West economically, no matter what the short-term social and economic sacrifices might be for individual citizens or consumers. The bureaucratic governmental elite, which has much greater social status in Japan (and France) than in the United States, led this passionate battle for economic growth. It began with long-range plans for modernization in the 19th century. After World War II these efforts culminated in the cooperation between the prestigious Finance Ministry and *Ministry of International Trade and Industry (MITI), which aimed to create a Japanese environment conducive to the cultivation of world-class competitors among private companies in key economic sectors.*[6]

The divisions of MITI mimic the major trade associations and become the basis for sharing out quotas of business. These trade associations and major corporations, in turn, all belong to the *Keidandren*, the Federation of Economic Organizations, which is organized in a way that mirrors the divisions at MITI. Highly educated personnel go back and forth between these organizations much as they do between Pentagon posts and major defense industry management positions in the U.S.

There is a great thirst for knowledge and a social obligation to collect information in these bureaucracies—data on world market trends, the timing and nature of technological breakthroughs, and the reasons for the success of key industrial leaders. The purpose is to overlap sources of information so that industrial decision-makers are saturated with it. Together with the intelligence arms of the major **keiretsu** or cartel networks of companies (based on long-term, cross-shareholding among members), the entire Japanese economic system is like a global octopus with arms spread everywhere to pick up information of strategic economic significance. Companies are rarely subsidized directly by the government. Rather, the aim is to give companies the financial incentives to consolidate and become competitive enough that there are several key players in each field critical for national economic competitiveness. It is a matter of creating conditions under which such competitiveness can thrive and become effectively targeted. By obtaining extraordinarily high market shares of key economic sectors—electronic products, heavy equipment, steel, and transportation—Japan not only achieved economies of scale but greatly increased the entry costs of would-be new competitors.

None of these key industries were based on natural resources (which Japan had to import)—as opposed to the U.S., but were manufacturing sectors in which Japanese success depended upon high value added.[7] This, in turn, increased the payoffs of investing in research and development and in the practical application of innovations discovered by others. As was the case with Germany, Japan benefitted from having a large pool of trained engineers and a demanding educational structure that fostered applied, technological competitiveness (see the discussion of life chances in Chapter Seven). But while German scientists focused on basic research—inventing the fax machine in a Siemens AG lab, the Japanese stressed applied research—turning the fax into a marketable product.

Finally, Japanese elites have long-term vision. It is not unusual for Japanese companies to have a 200-year plan. The aim is to be strategically positioned for the long term in order to keep employment high, market share constant or expanding, and to reduce opportunity costs. Social harmony based on government-business-labor cooperation and a company commitment to lifetime employment for over 20 percent of the full-time work force reinforce this strategy as well as the Japanese work ethic. Financing of firms is typically done on a ten-year basis in which the local or regional bank has representatives on the board of directors. This permits long-term planning, since firms do not rely upon the annual support of stockholders for their financing—the system that forces managers of American companies to worry about how to return a profit *right now.*

These basic elements of the Japanese system remain intact despite the speculative financial run-up or "bubble" that grew from 1986–1991, only to collapse in deep recession in 1991–1993. In 1989, the central bank of Japan deliberately punctured the bubble of financial speculation at its peak by increasing discount rates to starve the money supply, thereby "normalizing" real estate prices.[8] And with this "non-Japanese" financial speculation and excessive consumption wrung out of the system, Japan can be expected to come back competitively stronger than ever in the late 1990s after its "cold shower." The corruption in the Liberal Democratic Party, which has governed since World War II, is also being attacked systematically. This is symbolized by the party's loss of domination in parliament and by the reforms pushed by a change-oriented Prime Minister, Morihiro Hosokawa. This Prime Minister briefly headed a fragile coalition government in the 1990s, but symbolized a social commitment to change. Large companies are downsizing and are even reducing commitments to lifetime employment. Japan, in short, is confronting global change head-on and is adapting its political economy accordingly to new realities of global competitiveness. This positioning is symbolized by one statistic, the annual percent of fixed investment as a percent of Gross Domestic Product (GDP) from 1988–1992: 32.7 percent in Japan compared to 21.3 percent in Europe (EU minus Luxembourg) and 15.1 percent in the U.S.[9]

Japan, in short, has come to represent the "entrepreneurial state," subsidizing key technology centers guided by MITI to bring together the "fusion technologies" of the future. Much of the funding is actually part of the proceeds from privatizing former Japanese government monopolies, which have gone into "industrial investment accounts" and from there to the technology centers. Germany, too, has funded technology centers: collective learning from each other's models has become critical for North-North competitiveness.

German Concentration and Follow-Through

The Japanese and Germans have a profound respect for each other's cultures despite significant differences in their industrial policies. Both cultures revere education. Both find waste distasteful, if not downright threatening to economic survival. Both have used order, efficiency, and collective learning to bring about post-World War II "economic miracles." Both benefit from taking a feudal, hierarchical past somewhat for granted as the basis of social stability from which to take calculated collective entrepreneurial risks. Both rely upon concentrations of big companies and financial institutions to lead the way in terms of global competitiveness. Neither culture likes to leave anything to chance. *Both Japan and Germany are "postliberal" and have always been postliberal.* As noted earlier, Germany and Japan have both benefitted often from free-riding upon the liberalism of the United States in terms of financial and military security. And both are coming out of their deepest recessions since World War II to challenge the U.S. in the late 1990s with a new, conservative, sober sense of the need to sharpen collective competitiveness.

Germany's collective conservatism goes back a long way. In a modern sense, it can be traced to Bismarck's Prussian "White Revolution," which united Germany in the 1870s by coopting working-class support through the establishment of worker disability and other forms of social security. This late industrialization gave the working class a greater political voice than in other nations because industrialization developed at the same time that the franchise (voting rights) expanded.[10] This was a "work-oriented" culture of strong unions, highly respected apprenticeship training (dating back to the feudal guilds), and an evolving system of **codetermination** in which management and workers cooperated to set long-term corporate policies in 50–50 percent participation schemes. In sum, Germany's is a **social market economy** in which the government assures the solidarity of the social contract through class-mitigating welfare measures (state-subsidized healthcare, pensions, unemployment and disability insurance, university tuition, labor advising and training, etc.), while leaving the private sector free to operate in the economic market. The social "maintenance base" is thus clearly separated from the freedom to take entrepreneurial risk. (See Chapter 8.) Government steering focuses upon economic process (i.e., tax subsidies for new housing), not upon economic results (i.e., rent control).[11] Political stability is furthered by a constitutional law limiting representation in the parliament to political parties which receive at least 5 percent of the vote.

Generally, German elites have been able to count on widespread social consensus on work-oriented policies, worker participation, and worker benefits at the bottom of society. This has permitted a consensus at the top of the society in the form of support for large firms or cartels in such key economic sectors as pharmaceuticals and banks. Just as the allies failed after World War II break up the essence of the *zaibatsu* financial cliques (which were merely reincarnated by *sogoshosha* trading companies and the *keiretsu*), so they failed to break up the domination of the German economy by major companies. The domination of I.G. Farben, for instance, was replaced with the hegemony of Bayer, Hoechst and BASF. And German financial markets are dominated by three large commercial banks—Deutsche Bank, Dresdner Bank, and Commerzbank. *State and economic tradition has assured Germany of the stability of industrial and financial concentration while a conservative, work-oriented culture and educational system have provided German business with predictable, systematic follow-through.*

Unlike Japan and the U.S., Germany's share of world exports has been higher than its share of the world economy represented by Gross National Product. It is a heavily export-dependent economy. Given high labor costs, due mainly to generous fringe benefits, Germany's competitiveness in exports has depended upon increasingly higher levels of **product differentiation**, that is, updating products with technology and sophistication in specialized market niches. Germany's problem in competitiveness in the 1980s, however, was that the business areas in which Germany had traditionally been most successful were the areas in which it had recently been losing market share. This included world exports such as transport, chemicals, power generation and distribution, office equipment, and semiconductors and computers.[12] In new areas, like microelectronics, German patents shrank between 1987 and 1992 by more than one third while rising by almost one third in Japan and doubling in the U.S. To shake up the complacency of the German system in order to make it hungry and competitive once more required a major crisis or historical change that would force it to restore its economic dynamism and to rethink its economic strategy: something like a second reunification, which, in fact, occurred in 1989.

German Unification: Bust or Bonanza?

The debate over whether the financial mismanagement of German unification will lead to a "bust" or whether the addition of East to West Germany will become an economic "bonanza" is misplaced. German unification is an historical process that transcends the political and economic and that represents a collective effort to integrate ethnically and culturally. It creates a new context for managing economic change that is apt to bring Germany a number of social, economic, and political problems in the short run followed by great political power and economic clout in the long run.

The political and economic reforms orchestrated by Gorbachev (see Chapter Two), which were to end the cold war and break apart the Soviet Union, provided a unique but narrow window of opportunity for Germany to reunify. In October 1989, Gorbachev visited orthodox Communist leader Erich Honecker for the fortieth celebration of the East German state. Just four months later, Gorbachev was asked to approve German reunification and accept a common German currency.

Specifically, Honecker fell soon after Gorbachev's visit given widespread protests the police were unable to contain. By November 1989, free travel was permitted for East German citizens and the Berlin Wall was opened. The Politburo had resigned and Communist reformist Hans Modrow headed a transitional government until free elections could be held in the spring of 1990. Chancellor Helmut Kohl of West Germany proposed a ten-point German federation plan for integrating the two Germanies. This political initiative mobilized all other political factions in West Germany to offer their own reunification ideas so as not to be outmaneuvered before the December 1990 West German election. Kohl's plan was soon countered with a proposal by Modrow (with Gorbachev's approval) for a neutral, demilitarized united Germany without ties to either the NATO or Warsaw Pact alliances (consistent with Soviet policy on the issue since Stalin ruled). Kohl and his Western allies turned down this proposal.

Meanwhile, over 2,000 East Germans per day were permanently migrating over the border to West Germany, leaving the East German economy (which already had a labor shortage before the exodus) in shambles. The East German currency fell like a rock. East German-made portable stereos in East Berlin, selling for twenty times the price of their better-made West German counterparts just a subway stop away, piled up on the shelves unsold.

Color T.V. sets in spacious East German apartments cost a hundred times as much as the monthly (subsidized) rent. By February, warnings seeped out of the West German capital of the imminent financial collapse of East Germany. Elections had been moved up from May to March 18, 1990. And in a political move without the Bundesbank's approval, Chancellor Kohl proposed to substitute the West German mark for the East German currency, hoping this symbolic gesture would give East Germans confidence and would stem the tide of people coming into his country and putting severe strains on a social system already suffering from unemployment and a housing shortage. Despite the warnings of Karl Otto Pöhl, president of the West German Bundesbank, that a rapid currency union would involve serious risks of rising inflation, higher interest rates, and deepening budget deficits, Chancellor Kohl's government went ahead with plans for monetary unification. Politics thus overwhelmed economics in the decision-making process.

Perhaps the key factor was the exchange rate used in the monetary reform. Rather than taking the exchange rate between West German and East German marks that the economic markets called for at that time—between 1:4 and 1:5—as the basis for currency unification, the Kohl government decided upon 1:1.8 (taking the average of active and passive money). If one compares this sudden hardening of the East German mark with the much slower hardening process of the West German mark in terms of its dollar exchange rate since the end of the Bretton Woods system in 1973, the contrast is staggering. In 1973, one dollar was worth 3.66 German marks (DM). In 1993 one dollar was worth about 1.60 DM. As German economist Wilhelm Hankel has pointed out, if one calculates the hardening—130 percent—and derives the annual average, one comes up with about 4.5 percent hardening per year. This gradual but consistent hardening of the DM permitted West Germany to keep inflation out of the domestic economy, but yet to keep its exports competitive in the global economy (keeping their rise in price typically just under the rise in the global inflation rate). But the West German-East German currency rate used had the effect of an overnight hardening of the East German mark of between 400 and 500 percent! Clearly the new price levels of East German goods (particularly given their lower quality) could not compete with the West German goods. As Hankel observed, overnight the real, manufacturing market of former East Germany was devastated by this overvalued currency and became merely a consumer market for goods produced in West Germany.[13] The whole economy of the East German states was declassed: the people felt entirely dependent upon the western states of Germany to which many self-respecting young, skilled people fled seeking truly productive jobs.

While relatively independent (and with an inflation-fighting priority, like the U.S. Federal Reserve Bank), the Bundesbank is forced by law to carry out West German government policy. Pöhl quickly adapted and became a leader in the monetary reform given certain prerequisites the West German government demanded: complete freedom of commercial activities, the recognition of private property, unlimited rights of investment and tax and price reforms, and last, but not least, East Germany's acceptance of the Federal Republic's Bundesbank as an autonomous institution for the securing of monetary stability.[14]

In the short term, higher inflation, higher interest rates, greater unemployment, larger public deficits and higher taxes were inevitable in West Germany as East and West German monetary and economic integration proceeded. However, as the world's largest exporter, with a record trade surplus of $81 billion in 1989 (exceeding Japan's for the first time since the 1970s), the booming West German economy was well-positioned to take on the responsibilities of subsidizing the East German economy and integration process. Many West German banks and industries, such as Siemens (electronics), Zeiss (optical equipment), Dresdner Bank, and Volkswagen had already revived ties with East German firms with the market openings made possible under *perestroika* and were ready to expand East German operations. And East Germany, after all, ranked second only to the Soviet Union among the East bloc's industrial powers. Given the common language, culture, and even educational structures—such as the apprenticeship system—the long-term prospects of a reunified Germany becoming an economic powerhouse (with a population of some 78 million) rivaling the United States and Japan appeared to become a self-fulfilling prophecy.

However, for some East Germans, such as novelist Christa Wolf, who were proud of the socialist cultural integrity of their own forty-year-old society and who believed that the creative destruction of capitalism would destroy this cultural integrity through the overbearing hegemony of West German business and government, these prospects were dark rather than bright. Social jealousy became pronounced as "the poor cousins" from the East experienced how far behind they were and as some of the established West Germans had second thoughts about overloaded social services, higher taxes, and increased competition for jobs and housing. The East Germans found it difficult to adjust to a social situation in which their apartments were not subsidized and in which work was not guaranteed as they had been used to under socialism.

Both the United States and the Soviet Union accepted the inevitability of German unification. Since the overwhelming majority of the East Germans polled supported reunification and both the Soviet Union and the U.S. had committed themselves to the "self-determination" of the East German people, they could do little but go along with the historical momentum. This momentum was, however, to some extent speeded up deliberately by Chancellor Helmut Kohl's foreign policy advisor, Horst Teltschik, who spoke of East Germany's imminent economic collapse in a press briefing before Kohl

went to Moscow for talks. This stoked alarmist fears that could only accelerate the pace of union.

The U.S. shifted towards an ambiguous policy about Germany's future
role in NATO in order to permit reunification to go through more easily. In
February 1990, the foreign ministers of the four major powers (the U.S.,
France, Britain, and the U.S.S.R) agreed with the foreign ministers of the two
Germanies at a meeting in Ottawa to a two-phase process of negotiating German unification. First, internal unification measures would be worked out by
the two Germanies after East German elections; and, second, external security measures would be negotiated with the four Allies. The fall, 1990 meeting of the 35-nation Conference on Security and Cooperation in Europe
then confirmed the conditions of the unification of the German state.

*German unification represents a form of "quick-study" collective learning—
using external change and opportunity (Gorbachev's "perestroika" policy) to restructure
an expanded maintenance base.*[15] The stimulus of German unification, in turn,
speeded up the process of European integration, led by the French who were
fearful of being declassed and pushed to the periphery as Germany again became the major Central European power. The influence of the United States
was set to decline in Europe as American troops were withdrawn and the cultural commonality of "Europe's Common House" found its own new integrity in differentiation from the American (and, to some extent, Anglo-
Saxon) culture. In his book *Perestroika* (1987), Gorbachev spoke of this threat
to European culture: "The threat emanates from an onslaught of 'mass culture' from across the Atlantic. . . . Indeed, one can only wonder that a deep,
profoundly intelligent and inherently humane European culture is retreat-
ing to the background before the primitive revelry of violence and pornogra-
phy and the flood of cheap feelings and low thoughts." French Eurocentric
film policy in the 1993 GATT talks confirmed this perception of the threat of
Anglo-Saxon (read "American") cultural hegemony (see Chapter 4). Similarly, in the 1990s, unemployed German youth in the East German states became mobilized in right-wing, ethnocentric group action against foreigners.
This movement was financed by (and spread to) right-wing groups in West
German states who feared being declassed by thousands of immigrants pour-
ing into Germany.

*Globally, Anglo-Saxon hegemony succeeded so well in creating prosperity that it
subsidized European and Pacific Rim countercultures which undermine some of its assumptions while pragmatically adopting others. Liberalism brings out postliberal reactions. Increasing global multipolarity in economic power breeds multicultural renais-
sance and the protectionism this implies in terms of preserving cultural identities from
the creative destruction of world capitalism.*[16]

In the post-unification era, Germany has discovered that increasing
productivity alone does not make for competitiveness if wage increases outstrip the growth in productivity. After Japan and Portugal, Germany posted
the biggest productivity gains (adjusted for inflation) between 1980 and

1993: 2.8 percent annually. In contrast, the U.S. and France were at the bottom of the list, and in Britain productivity actually declined. It is true that in most countries wages increased faster than productivity. But in the U.S. and Japan, wages and productivity have moved in unison.[17] By paying salaries in semiannual bonuses, Japan has been able to keep wage increases in line with what is going on in the real economy. **Wages**, which economist Lester Thurow defined as "bribes paid individuals to sacrifice an hour of leisure," reflect the German mark's external value. Both wages and real interest rates soared at the time of German unification. Export growth slumped. Imports poured in. These trends reflect the significant resources needed to modernize the eastern German states, leading to a large German current account deficit. This rebuilding of the eastern states will take years. When German interest rates go up faster than world market prices, the profit margins of German companies are squeezed. Since these companies rely upon domestic financing, their costs of capital go up. Therefore, although Germany was second only to the U.S. in terms of exports in 1992, the Germans will come under increasing pressure as domestic inflationary pressures and union militancy threaten to undermine German competitiveness.

The Industrial Policy Dilemma of the United States

Unlike Japan and Germany, the United States has no feudal heritage and no natural inclination to accept hierarchies of authority and status. Whether or not dogmatic liberalism is all that Americans know (as historian Louis Hartz argued), it *is* probably true that most Americans agree with the proposition that that government governs best which governs least.

Perhaps the greatest political and economic advantage of the United States is the stability of its constitutional framework. When things go wrong in the world, money and people flood into the United States—the last bastion of political stability, individual freedom, and government-protected capitalism. Private property is sacrosanct, the very extension of individual freedom as Americans understand it.

But the greatest advantage of the United States may, paradoxically, become at times the greatest obstacle to change in order to adapt collectively to new demands of the world economy. For if the stability of individual freedom and private property are sacred, everything else comes in a distant second— from social ethics to collective economic competitiveness to educational excellence to ecological survival. This is the dilemma of industrial policy in America.[18] Or, more specifically, it has been the particular dilemma of the administration of Bill Clinton.

The industrial policy debate has gone on in the United States since its founding. "Money is the vital principle of the body politic" said Alexander Hamilton, a founding father and the first secretary of the treasury. But Thomas Jefferson, founding father, author of the Declaration of Independence (1776), and the third American President, said "The care of human life and happiness, and not their destruction, is the first and only legitimate object of good government." Hamilton stood for a strong, centralized federal government steered by a financial aristocracy that strived for economic and financial power for the United States. In his "Report on Manufactures," Hamilton suggested the use of government subsidies and tariffs for industries in order to compete with the British. Jefferson, on the other hand, opposed the conservative, Federalist position of Hamilton and advocated a populist, decentralized form of agrarian democracy.

Although Jefferson initially appeared to win ideologically, ultimately Hamilton's ideas have prevailed. The competitive dynamism within the U.S. economy is in part due to the American refusal to decide clearly between these conceptions of Hamilton and Jefferson. While America avoided the mercantilism, represented at the time by countries such as Spain, as business historian Thomas McCraw noted "it did exhibit for 150 years after the Revolution a pronounced tendency towards protectionism, mostly through the device of the tariff." During the late 19th century, giant industrial monopolies emerged (see Chapter 9). These monopolies were later somewhat deterred by largely ineffective anti-trust legislation.

The major thrust of industrial policy, which often went unquestioned, was aimed to shore up national defense. From the Congressional approval to purchase muskets from inventor Eli Whitney at the end of the 18th century, to the tremendous subsidies for sophisticated technologies and weapons in World War II, to the skyrocketing defense budget of President Ronald Reagan (which helped to break the back of the Soviet empire), Americans have appeared to accept state subsidies for defense industries ("Pentagon Inc.") as part and parcel of becoming a powerful nation in the world. Hamilton would have smiled in agreement.

Adam Smith, on the other hand, would have had his doubts. Since World War II, myriads of American school children have been taught the virtues of free markets and economic processes in contrast to the statist economics of socialist systems. But the historical part about protectionism, subsidies, and cartels is usually touched on lightly, if at all. *Great industrial powers, such as Britain and the U.S., typically begin to propagate their classical economic liberalism* after *they establish an industrial base that is globally competitive.*[19] *After they establish an efficient maintenance base they benefit most from open markets around the world in which to launch their entrepreneurial expansion.*

The American government's problem in the post-cold-war era is how to get the public to back a centralized industrial policy that is not based on defense, or Pentagon, Inc. The solution of the Clinton administration was initially to focus on **managed trade**, or government intervention to steer trade relations with other countries towards the national interest, or at least to avoid unequal tariff trade-offs. The opposite of this philosophy is the laissez-faire liberal approach of Michael Boskin, Chairman of President George

Bush's Council of Economic Advisers, to whom is attributed the statement: "It does not make any difference whether a country makes computer chips or potato chips."[20] This assumes a world market in equilibrium where the costs of capital, labor, and physical plant are equal everywhere and workers are free to move from low-wage areas to higher ones to equalize things.

But in her book, *Who's Bashing Whom?: Trade Conflict in High Technology Industries*, Clinton's chairman of the Council of Economic Advisers, Laura D'Andrea Tyson, argues that it matters a great deal who is making what and where they are making it. Increasing returns from economies of scale, efficiencies from interacting learning curves, benefits from targeted external linkages, and technological spillovers "are not the stuff of perfect competition and market optimality." The key to competitiveness is for governments to help create "a virtuous cycle of economic growth, innovation, and learning by doing" (see Chapter 8). Big auto makers can pay high wages only due to great economies of scale. Productivity rises as new technology spills over from semiconductor machine tool makers to chip manufacturers. Lacking a strong machine-tool industry, the U.S. risks becoming dependent upon Japanese chip makers and the business groups that control them. While investments in research and development (R & D) typically bring returns of between 35 and 60 percent higher than those from investments in plants and equipment, companies alone are afraid to take the risk since it is uncertain who exactly will get the returns from R & D investment. Yet economies that tap into abnormally high returns from capital and labor will have higher incomes than those that do not (what Tyson refers to as the search and capture of "disequilibrium rents").

The shift from Bush to Clinton, in short, was a shift from an industrial policy that was officially laissez-faire liberal with implicit centralized industrial planning for defense to a policy of postliberal economic intervention that explicitly subsidizes technologies and training vital for U.S. competitiveness in high-tech industries, including defense. But this ideal focus on high-tech competitiveness and training was largely eclipsed by government interventions for universal healthcare, welfare reform, and criminal containment, not to mention legislative limits on spending in order to bring down the huge budget deficit.

In the decade-and-a-half following World War II, the U.S. had all the advantages: an unscathed industrial plant, a prosperous population, a backlog of large technological investments because of the war, a hunger to work, and a desire to restore peaceful harmony. American productivity overwhelmed that of other countries. However, by the late 1960s, trade gaps were emerging despite a falling dollar. Inflation was headed up. By the early 1970s, wage levels were stalemated or declining in real (inflation-adjusted) terms. Many of the fifty largest export firms depended upon natural resources (including agriculture), as opposed to the "value-added" manufacturing focus of the emerging Japanese and German economies.[21] The proportion of American-made goods subject to international competition leaped from 20 to 80 percent between 1972 and 1982! Semiconductor and computer firms slowly became complacent after a Pentagon, Inc. subsidized environment helped them to start up.

Perhaps the best example is the fall from competitiveness of IBM, which lost market share to the point it could no longer control the introduction of new innovations as it once could. By 1985 it had become clear that consumers had moved away from its mainframe computer business. Yet it took three years for IBM to shift gears and slowly to react.[22] Its downsizing and decentralization oriented towards customers in different markets is illustrative of America's transition from a manufacturing economy to a service and information economy and from complacency to aggressive, niche-specific competitiveness. As IBM's Robert Logan said in Brussels in 1992: "It used to be said that 'The big eat the small.' Today the motto has become 'The fast eat the slow.'" What is required is collective learning turned on high speed.[23]

A second case of complacency and decline in American competitiveness is the semiconductor industry. In the late 1970s, the semiconductor industry, based in Silicon Valley, California, represented all that people thought was ideal in American economic liberalism: fresh, innovative thinking, future-oriented entrepreneurship, long-term, risk-oriented companies not seeking government handouts but wealth and independence. At that time, 85 percent of the semiconductors in Japan came from America. But by 1983, with the help of government bureaucracies and financing, Japanese semiconductor companies were spending more on new facilities than were U.S. firms. Everything was downhill from there, epitomized by a MITI-steered shortage of 256-kilobyte DRAM chips in the late 1980s, thus jacking up the prices much as the OPEC cartel had done with oil. High-tech U.S. firms had become totally dependent upon the Japanese DRAMS. The 1986 Semiconductor Agreement between the U.S. and Japan, which gave the U.S. a 20 percent share of the domestic Japanese semiconductor market, underscored this trend.

Government policy shaped the microelectronics industry from the beginning— starting with the U.S. in World War II and the cold war with the Pentagon Inc. advantage, then shifting to the Japanese steered by MITI, and tilting in the 1990s to government-subsidized East Asian producers, particularly Korea.[24] American firms had cut down drastically in semiconductor production, since they could not make sufficient short-term profits, threatening to set up a situation of long-term American dependence. But then the pay-offs of the semiconductor agreement took hold and starting in 1992 the U.S. semiconductor industry rebounded sharply.

There is the clear danger that **downsizing** (reducing the number of employees and noncore related businesses) is but a one-shot booster of productivity. As Americans watched the slowdown in global economic growth in industrialized countries from 4.4 percent in 1988 to 3.3 percent in 1989 to 2.6 percent in 1990 to 0.9 percent in 1991 and 1.7 percent in 1992, it is little wonder that they went in for downsizing and radical restructuring.[25] But the side effects in the U.S. (as elsewhere in the world) included not only potential dependence on foreign producers but also rising joblessness, crime, ethnic hatred, religious extremism, and nationalism. American banks were reluctant to lend money even when interest rates fell. The infrastructure was falling apart and could not support the high-tech communications necessary for global competitiveness.[26] American teenagers scored near the bottom in math and science tests in comparison with other industrialized countries.[27] The very social fabric that underpinned the economy seemed to be coming apart. For example, in his 1994 State of the Union Address, President Bill Clinton spoke of the "stunning and simultaneous breakdown of community, family, and work—the heart and soul of civilized society." American companies merged with others for competitive strength and set up joint ventures with key competitors and suppliers abroad.[28] They became mean and lean and their manufacturing productivity rose.[29] Clinton's aim was to maintain this corporate competitiveness through managed trade in order to stimulate job creation at home, while simultaneously introducing legislation to buffer the domestic social costs—in healthcare, welfare, criminal activity and job training. And Congress and Ross Perot helped to persuade him to attack the American budget deficit as well, which amounted to $255 billion by 1994.

American liberalism seemed to have met its postliberal match. However, the diffusion of objectives on the part of the Clinton administration leaves one uncertain as to whether the payoffs from these many pursuits will ever catch up with the costs. This is illustrated by the lack of specific targeting in Vice-President Albert Gore's advocacy of government funding for an "information superhighway" throughout the U.S. This superhighway would provide two-way communication on multiple channels, thereby guaranteeing both rich and poor access to a service that does not yet exist and which they may or may not use.[30] The thrust of telecommunications mergers became to monopolize the structure of this market access before the "virtual reality" even came into being. *The new competitive trend is to reinvent social reality for markets of the future that do not yet exist.*[31]

THOUGHT QUESTIONS

1. ". . . the U.S., Japan and Germany . . . have fallen into the habit of trying to learn most from each other." Try to identify main characteristics that distinguish "the Big Three" from one another. Also pay close attention to historical and cultural issues as well as to their implications for economic behavior.

2. Why is "the entire Japanese economic system . . . like a global octopus with arms spread everywhere to pick up information"? How is this achieved?

3. Give a brief description of Germany's "collective conservatism" drawing parallels to Japanese culture wherever possible and considering explicitly the characteristics of Germany's social market economy.

4. Prove that "German unification represents a form of 'quick study' collective learning . . . using external change and opportunity . . . to restructure an expanded maintenance base" by summarizing the benchmarks of the reunification process.

5. Taking the industrial policies of Japan and Germany into consideration, why does the time seem to be ripe for the U.S. to follow a "centralized industrial policy that is not based on defense or Pentagon, Inc."? Evaluate Clinton's policy of "managed trade" as well as IBM's Robert Logan's motto "The fast eat the slow."

6. Can you think of some examples of "reinventing social reality for markets that do not yet exist"? How does this relate to (a) national levels of technological literacy, (b) the speed of business cycles and fashion changes, (c) "economies of scale"?

NOTES

1. See S. Ishihara, *The Japan that Can Say No* (New York: Simon and Schuster, 1991); see also, Kishore Mahbubani, "Japan Adrift," *Foreign Policy,* Fall 1992, No. 88, pp. 126–144.

2. George C. Lodge, *Perestroika for America* (Boston: Harvard Business School Press, 1991), pp. 15–16. Also see Charles Hampden-Turner and Alfons Trompenaars, *The Seven Cultures of Capitalism* (New York: Currency/Doubleday, 1993).

3. Nathaniel Nash, "Persuading Americans to Save," *The New York Times,* December 17, 1989. Notable is the continuous decline of U.S. personal savings from 1973, when it was 10 percent.

4. Economist Mancur Olson makes this case in, perhaps, the most extreme terms, arguing that the West German and Japanese "economic miracles" were largely due to the effects of totalitarian governments and foreign occupiers who broke up the old distributional coalitions in power and paved the way for growth as free and stable social systems were established. See Olson's *The Rise and Decline of Nations: Economic Growth, Stagflation, and Social Rigidities* (New Haven: Yale University Press, 1982), Chapter 4.

5. As economist Lester Thurow puts it: "In the twenty-first century sustainable competitive advantage will come much more out of newprocess technologies and much less out of newproduct technologies. Reverse engineering has become an art form . . . What used to be primary (inventing new products) becomes secondary, and what used to be secondary (inventing and perfecting new processes) becomes primary." Cf: L. Thurow, *Head to Head: The Coming Economic Battle Among Japan, Europe, and America* (New York: William Morrow and Co., 1992), p. 45.

6. See Chalmers Johnson, *MITI and the Japanese Miracle* (Stanford, CA: Stanford University Press, 1982); T. J. Pempel, *Policy and Politics in Japan: Creative Conservatism* (Philadelphia: Temple University Press, 1982); and Ezra Vogel, *Japan and Number One: Lessons for America* (Cambridge, MA: Harvard University Press, 1979). Vogel writes: "MITI's aim is not to reduce competition among Japanese companies but to create the strongest possible companies with the greatest competitive potential" (p. 72).

7. See Michael Porter, *The Competitive Advantage of Nations* (New York: The Free Press, 1990), pp. 384–421.

8. See Daniel Burstein, *Turning the Tables: A Machiavellian Strategy for Dealing with Japan* (New York: Simon and Schuster, 1993), p. 38.

9. Statistics from "The World Economy in Charts," *Fortune*, July 26, 1993, p. 92.

10. See R. Isaak, "Germany: Economic Powerhouse or Stalemate?" *Challenge*, September-October, 1992, pp. 41–46. Also see Thomas Janoski, *The Political Economy of Unemployment: Active Labor Market Policy in West Germany and the United States* (Berkeley, CA: University of California Press, 1990), pp. 9–33.

11. See "West Germany: A Social Market Economy," Chapter 2 in R. Isaak, *European Politics: Political Economy and Policy Making in Western Democracies* (New York: St. Martin's Press, 1980), pp. 27–62.

12. Porter, *The Competitive Advantage*, pp. 355–382.

13. Wilhelm Hankel, *Die sieben Todsünden der Vereinigigung* (Berlin: Siedler, 1993) pp. 22–23.

14. Ferdinand Protzman, "Bonn's Point Man on Currency," *The New York Times*, Feb. 12, 1990.

15. The growing literature on the process of German unification includes: W. R. Smyser, *The Economy of United Germany* (New York: St. Martin's Press, 1992); Konrad H. Jarausch, *The Rush to German Unity* (New York: Oxford University Press, 1993); Elizabeth Pond, *Beyond the Wall: Germany's Road to Unification* (Washington, D.C.: Brookings Institution/Twentieth Century Fund, 1993); and Peter H. Merkl, *German Unification in the European Context* (University Park, PA: Pennsylvania State University Press, 1993).

16. On cultural clashes resulting from this inevitable change, see Samuel Huntington, "The Clash of Civilizations?", *Foreign Affairs*, Summer, 1993 and Robert D. Kaplan, "The Coming Anarchy," *The Atlantic Monthly*, February, 1994, pp. 44–76.

17. Statistics above are from "Unification Has Weakened Germany's International Competitiveness," *Trends: Economy, Politics, Financial Markets* (Frankfurt: Dresdner Bank, August, 1993), pp. 3–7.

18. See "The Conservative Tradition of Liberalism," Introduction to R. Isaak, *American Political Thinking: Readings from the Origins to the 21st Century* (Fort Worth, TX: Harcourt, Brace, 1994).

19. See James Fallows, "How the World Works," *The Atlantic Monthly*, December, 1993, pp. 61–87.

20. The interpretation of this statement is indebted to Lester Thurow, "Free Market Fallacies," *Foreign Policy*, Fall, 1993, No. 92, pp. 187–191.

21. Porter, *The Competitive Advantage*, pp. 284–301.

22. See David Evans, "IBM Rediscovers Its Customers," *Canadian Business*, November, 1990, pp. 37–48.

23. On Pace University MBA International Field Study trip to IBM in Brussels, May 7, 1992.

24. Summary of a history of the semiconductor industry published in 1992 by the Semiconductor Industry Association as cited by James Fallows in "Looking at the Sun," *The Atlantic Monthly*, November, 1993, p. 90. The article by Fallows illustrates that the Japanese success in semiconductors and American failure cannot be explained by the economic rules of Anglo-American liberalism. But, by the same token, his logic may have a hard time explaining the strong recovery of the U.S. semiconductor industry since 1992.

25. Statistics are from Leonard Silk, "Dangers of Slow Growth," *Foreign Affairs*, Vol. 72, No. 1, 1992, pp. 167–182.

26. See Joan C. Szabo, "Our Crumbling Infrastructure," *Nation's Business*, August, 1989, pp. 16–24.

27. For example, the mathematics test scores of 13-year-olds in the U.S. in 1991 were lower than the students in many of the countries testing comprehensive education (only Spain, Slovenia, and Jordan had lower scores). International Assessment of Educational Progress: 1991 Statistics, National Center for Educational Studies, *Digest of Education*, 1993, Table 390, p. 415. Also see Kenneth J. Travers and Ian Westbury, "The IEA Study of Mathematics I: Analysis of Mathematics Curricula." Supplement (Urbana College of Education of Illinois University Study for International Association for the Evaluation of Educational Achievement, 1989), pp. 115 and 121; and "International Science Report Card" from the Second IEA Study (U.S. Teachers College, Columbia University, 1988), pp. 2–3. Also see David Kearns, "The Education Gap," *Institutional Investor*, December 1989.

28. See Lynn K. Mytelka, ed., *Strategic Partnerships and the World Economy* (Rutherford, N.J.: Fairleigh Dickinson University Press, 1991); and Martin Starr, *Global Corporate Alliances and the Competitive Edge* (Westport, Conn.: Quorum Books, 1991).

29. The U.S. productivity growth rate averaged 4 percent annually in manufacturing in the 1980s. But for Japan, the comparable productivity growth rate was 5.7 percent. Cf.: Keizai Koho Center, *Japan: A Comparison, 1991,* p. 70.

30. See "America's Information Highway: A Hitch-hiker's Guide," *The Economist*, Dec. 25, 1993–January 7, 1994, pp. 35–38.

31. See Tracy Goss, Richard Pascale, and Anthony Athos, "The Reinvention Roller Coaster: Risking the Present for a Powerful Future," *Harvard Business Review*, November–December, 1993, pp. 97–108; Ikujiro Nonaka, "The Knowledge-Creating Company," *Harvard Business Review*, November–December, 1991, especially, pp. 96–97, and William H. Davidow and Michael S. Malone, *The Virtual Corporation: Structuring and Revitalizing the Corporation for the 21st Century* (New York: HarperCollins, 1992).

CHAPTER SIX

NORTH–SOUTH STRUCTURES AND STRATEGY

The fastest-growing source of funds flowing to the developing world is private in-vestment capital, which seeks out the turnaround economies and avoids the back-sliders. . . . Poorer countries ignored by the multinationals and investors are left to rely on the aid mills in the industrial nations, which face new demands around the world and budget constraints at home. . . . What disturbs economists at the IMF and World Bank is that the Asian surge contradicts some of the stan-dard advice being pushed in the developing world: Open markets, pare the role of government and let the forces of competition govern the economy.

Tim Carrington, *Wall Street Journal* (9/27/93)

With respect to development, we should note that economic growth is not the only factor. There are countries, such as Venezuela and Brazil, which, in spite of strong economies, suffer from great instability because their economic growth does not translate into more options, better opportunities or higher living standards for the people. Economic growth that does not produce food, drinking water, housing and health and education represents a great security risk.

Oscar Arias Sanchez (1993)

The most poignant human focus of international political economy is the "North–South structure"—the asymmetrical or unequal relationship be-tween the developed and developing countries in the world economy. The shift toward a high technology/high information global economy has accelerated the widening of the gap in levels of development between rich and poor populations as money, technology, and skilled personnel flow to the secured, developed nations of the world. The poorest countries find themselves without the resources to even begin to catch up. The increasing speed of technological change works to the disproportionate benefit of the advantaged over the disadvantaged. Hence, movements on the part of lesser developed countries to slow the pace of technological transformations on their home ground should not be surprising: Their traditional way of life, the very cultural essence of their collective existence, becomes increasingly vulnerable to disruption if not eradication by foreign trends of modernity. From this perspective, resistance to technological change may be more rational than irrational as people desperately try to preserve the integrity of their own culture.

From the perspective of the rich nations of the "North"* the initial temptation is to maximize the self-interest of one's own people regardless of the consequences for the poorer developing nations of the "South." But this short-term viewpoint has become increasingly problematic in an interdependent world economy in which exports from the North can only be purchased by customers in the South if the North helps to provide the South with money or credit to make such purchases. Moreover, many regions of the so-called rich countries of the North are as poor in some ways as the poor developing countries of the South, which, in turn, are often studded with their own rich elites or minor metropoles. Hence the complex inequalities of the world economy are such that some analysts argue the North–South split is a myth—the figment of the polarizing logic of the Western imagination.

For instance, who is more "developed"—the man who dies at forty-five from a heart attack in a high-pressure, future-oriented, workaholic metropolitan center of the North or the man who dies at a similar age of a snake bite on a present-oriented, developing Pacific island of the South? The Northerner lives to work and has sacrificed his present for a future that never materializes. The Southerner lives each day to the hilt and dies as naturally as he lives—often with neither the promise nor the hazards of modern technology or drugs. Technology and drugs are making their way to the peripheries of the South, but will this really improve the quality of life and constitute a more meaningful level of human development?

Regardless of the meaning attributed to the process of Western modernization in the developing nations, one can identify dominant structures and strategies in North–South relations since World War II, highlighting Northern institutional efforts to "manage the economic problems of the

---

*"North" usually refers to developed, industrialized nations of the Northern Hemisphere, while "South" designates developing countries of the Southern Hemisphere; however, many countries and regions have a North–South economic split *within* them (such as southern Italy, the rural south of the U.S., the EU's southern members).

South" and attempts by the developing countries to change the game rules in their favor. One paradox is that Western industrial nations often assume that the leaders of developing countries are primarily after wealth whereas they may in fact be aiming first for control and less vulnerability. Conversely, the Southern developing countries often assume the industrial North is seeking imperialistic control as a primary motive whereas the rich countries may actually be in pursuit of more wealth.* From the perspective of collective learning, the management of North–South relations is a chaotic, politically charged adventure in which ideological blinders often obstruct long-term blueprints, tempting both sides to give up on each other or to insulate themselves from the other's problems. Meanwhile, the interdependent political economy of the world demands constant communication, negotiation, and adjustment on all sides to keep the global economy healthy. This is particularly true in a world in which the richest 20 percent of the world's people increased their share of global income from 70 percent in 1960 to 83 percent in 1989 (The ratio between the richest fifth and the poorest fifth thus grew from 30 to 1 to 59 to 1).

ORIGINS

While the origins of the relations between the developed and developing countries are deep and complex, some highlights are suggestive in terms of the collective learning approach used here and the notion of "modeling," which derives from it. Clearly the nation-states, which were first established in Europe—England and France, for example—had the advantages that all first arrivals enjoy. They had their choice of colonies, whereas nation-states united later—Italy and Germany—were forced to chose from leftovers. These late colonial efforts were perceived as illegitimate given the tides of late liberalism and parliamentary democracy that swept over Europe in the course of the nineteenth and early twentieth centuries. Even when France and England were eventually forced to give up their colonies in the course of the twentieth century, they left deeply rutted cultural and administrative traditions behind that would work in the favor of British and French trade: *The former colonies usually preferred to do business with "the bastards they knew the best."*

By the end of the nineteenth century, most of the prime global real estate was tied up one way or another by established interests, dominated by European nations. They had the advantages, in addition, of relatively unregulated flows of trade, capital, and labor, thus allowing them to profit as efficiently as the state of technology would allow from their colonial investments. Moreover, with minor exceptions, this colonial

---

*The pursuit of power and the pursuit of wealth, however, are often hard to distinguish from each other and may be flip sides of the same coin (as argued variously by political economists Jacob Viner, Robert Gilpin, and Stephen Krasner, and by historian Paul Kennedy).

business could be consolidated without any interruption from war. The colonial powers learned from each other how to set up colonies for power and business in such a way that benefits soon flowed to the home country.

Advocates of the Third World or developing country position argue that global economic opportunities have changed drastically since the nineteenth century. Goods and labor cannot move as freely over borders as they did for Europeans and Americans a century ago. Protective tariff barriers and strict immigration quotas block Third-World goods and labor from moving freely to the developed industrialized world, thus hindering modernization processes of the poorer countries. Dr. Mahbub ul Haq, former Director of Policy Planning and Program Review at the World Bank, maintains that the poor countries are not asking for a massive redistribution of wealth, even though three-fourths of the world's income, investment, and services and most of the world's research facilities are in the hands of one-fourth of its population. Rather, the developing nations want greater equality of opportunity, which is made impossible by existing economic imbalances and international structures skewed toward the rich nations.[1]

Whether speaking for the rich nations or the poor, no one denies the imbalance that exists between the economic structures of the developed and developing nations. The conflict of perspectives dwells not upon this basic fact of international political economy but upon whose fault it is and which means are most appropriate for improving the situation. The international institution emerging from the Bretton Woods settlement that has been caught with most of the practical long-term consequences of this North–South gap is the World Bank.

The World Bank

The perspective of the developed countries toward the South, or Third World, developing countries was initially set forth by the American-dominated Bretton Woods philosophy after World War II. As noted in Chapter 3, this philosophy initially represented a partial resurrection of classical economic liberalism according to which international credit should be given only to countries or projects that were "economically sound" (that is, "hard banker terms," not "soft loans"). The exception that proved the rule was the Marshall Plan program of outright grants for European reconstruction, to which we will later return. But the ruling constitution for managing the economic problems of the developing countries in the postwar era was the "embedded liberalism" of the Bretton Woods regime spearheaded by the International Monetary Fund (IMF) and the **World Bank,** or its formal name—the **International Bank for Reconstruction and Development (IBRD).**

While the IMF was founded to provide international liquidity and short-term credit to alleviate balance-of-payments problems of its member nations, the World Bank's major function has been to stimulate the flow of capital into long-term invest-

ment across national boundaries (although not always from the rich countries to the poor). At the time it came into being, on December 27, 1945, the International Bank for Reconstruction and Development was overshadowed by the IMF and was focused upon making loans to war-damaged countries in Western Europe, not to the underdeveloped countries where the credit risks were higher. As with the IMF, the site chosen for the headquarters of the World Bank was Washington, D.C. This upset John Maynard Keynes who preferred London or even New York but not a location "under the thumb of the U.S. government." Actually the IMF and World Bank headquarters are housed in the same building in Washington, sort of "Siamese twins" with representatives going to each other's meetings despite their different functions. The building could be considered a monument to U.S. hegemony in the Bretton Woods settlement. Membership in the World Bank has always been contingent upon membership in the IMF, and any nation expelled or withdrawing from the IMF automatically ceases to be a member of the World Bank.

With the adoption of the Marshall Plan or European Recovery Program (proposed in 1947 by U.S. General George Marshall), the World Bank was able to shift its priorities from reconstruction to development. However, the World Bank's role is not restricted to raising money in developed countries so it can lend to developing nations: The bank borrows from and makes loans to both groups. Loans are targeted for specific, viable economic projects—typically to build up the infrastructure of developing countries as a prerequisite to industrialization: highways, railroads, power and port facilities, irrigation and flood control (as contrasted with public health projects, schools, seeds, or houses). Normally loans by the World Bank cover only hard-currency import needs and have to be repaid in hard currency at long-term rates. Initially, the daily operations of the IBRD were steered by a group of executive directors, five appointed by the five member governments with the largest subscriptions to the bank, the rest elected biennially by the remaining members. A president was hired (and could be fired) by the executive directors, who, with their approval, could select a staff made up of as diverse a geographical representation as possible. Traditionally, the president of the World Bank has been American, and the president of the IMF a European. But this convention may change when a Japanese president is selected for one of these international bodies in an effort to draw Japan into more obligations in the management of a global economy from which the Japanese have benefitted most handsomely. Such an institutional development would be a natural outgrowth of the trilateralism that has emerged *de facto* in the management of the global economy.

In 1960 the **International Development Association (IDA)** was created as part of the World Bank Group in order to provide loans to developing countries on a more liberal basis than was permitted within normal IBRD guidelines—typically fifty-year, interest-free loans. Moreover, there is normally a ten-year grace period before loans must start to be repaid, and the repayment can be in local currency, provided that it is convertible. With resources of its own, the IDA loan projects go through the same World Bank evaluation process as do regular credit applications. The purpose is to provide liquidity on a more liberal, long-term basis to the poorest countries.

The post-cold-war world economy has put increased pressure on the **concessional financial assistance** (that is, either outright grants or soft loans) of the IDA. Because of the consequences of the war between Iran and Iraq, 1990 grants doubled to $29 billion, and rose again to $32 billion in 1991.[2] The former Soviet Union and eastern European governments were clearly not able to maintain the aid programs to which they contributed before 1989. Since 1991 at least eight new low-income member countries have been admitted to IDA membership. The "Tenth Replenishment" of funds for the IDA, which will not keep up with growing demand, extends from 1993–1996.

Another key organization within the World Bank Group is the **International Finance Corporation (IFC),** formed in 1956 to provide risk capital for productive private enterprises, to encourage the development of local capital markets, and to stimulate the international flow of capital. Loans by the IFC to private companies in developing countries are normally for seven- to twelve-year periods. Such loans can also be made for joint ventures between investors in developed and developing countries and cover a multitude of projects in such fields as mining, manufacturing, steel, textile production, food processing, machinery production, local development finance companies, and tourism.

Organizational "Modeling": Regional Development Banks

Collective learning is illustrated when one international organization is seen to have economic success and other countries or regions view it as a model to shape their own economic organizations. With the World Bank model in mind, regional development banks were created: the Inter-American Development Bank (IDB) in 1959 to provide World Bank-type services to countries in the Western Hemisphere (particularly the United States and Latin America); the African Development Bank (ADB), organized by a group of newly independent African countries in 1963 under United Nations auspices; and the Asian Development Bank, which set up headquarters in Manila in 1966. Nor do the offspring stop there. The World Bank has been instrumental in helping to found more than fifty development banks (mainly national banks) in member countries.

As an illustration of how the regional development banks work, consider the African Development Bank, which has become Africa's premier source of credit. With fifty African members and an additional twenty-five from the industrialized world, the ADB is structured like a mini-World Bank, financing projects in most African countries and granting soft, long-term loans to the poorest among them. By 1987 the ADB had approved about $10 billion in loans, including $4 billion interest-free through the African Development Fund (ADF)—the soft-loan window of the ADB modeled after the International Development Association. The money for ADF comes from the rich developed members of ADB, while the operating funds for the ADB come from all its members in addition to the loans raised on the international markets where the ADB has the same blue-chip rating as does the World Bank. With more than $19 billion in capital, the ADB worked towards doubling of its rate of lending to more than $10 billion from 1987 through 1991.[3] But what about the World Bank itself?

McNamara's Basic Human-Needs Orientation

When Robert McNamara became president of the World Bank in 1968, he shifted the bank's priorities away from focusing upon the modern sector of developing countries (usually cities) toward alleviating absolute poverty through direct action at the rural level. He defined **"absolute poverty"** as "conditions of deprivation that fall below any rational definition of human decency" in his speech at the Annual Meeting of the World Bank at Nairobi in 1973. In his first five-year term McNamara not only doubled the amount of lending by the World Bank (without losing its AAA-credit rating for never having anyone default on a loan). But he also changed bank policy, aiming to break the main constraints on development (such as population increase, malnutrition, and illiteracy) rather than limiting credit to conventional infrastructure projects. Thus, much more money went for agriculture, education, and the control of population growth (McNamara's original, controversial contribution to the mix) and to the poorest developing countries, particularly Africa. *The basic human-needs orientation (not original with McNamara) focuses upon alleviating the needs of the poorest individuals in the world as the appropriate orientation to the North–South dilemma.*

McNamara himself was somewhat of a Faustian figure as head of the World Bank. He had learned the cold, efficient techniques of managerial decision-making theory at Harvard, applying his cognitive skills later at Harvard as an accounting professor, at Ford Motor Company as chief executive officer, and then at the Pentagon as Secretary of Defense during the Vietnam War where efficiently maximizing "body counts" was the indicator of success rather than the reduction of absolute poverty. The legendary Faust, it will be recalled, sold his soul to the devil in exchange for knowledge, which he knew to be worldly power. By 1966 McNamara realized the Vietnam War was morally wrong. He stated in a speech in Montreal that peace and stability in the world depended less on building up armaments than on raising the living standards of the poorer two-thirds of mankind.

Given his academic brilliance, prodigious energy, and arrogant efficiency in applying powerful decision-making models, McNamara, who left the Pentagon for the World Bank, had discovered he was using technological means to the wrong ends. In his new job he set about to improve health care for the world's poor rather than to wage war against the Vietcong. There may be a moral in this tale that can be applied to the asymmetrical balance in world markets in terms of payoffs for arms and war versus support for health care and the alleviation of world poverty. The North knows its Faust well. . . .

While aware that four-fifths of the resources must come from the developing country itself, McNamara sought to use the other one-fifth to create a critical mass of financial and technical power through the World Bank so as to accelerate the process of development to a high but sustainable level. His purpose, using decision-theory methodology, was to maximize whatever small impact the World Bank funds had. He also expanded the research arm of the bank to make it one of the world's most authoritative centers for studies of key development problems and issues. Under McNamara's leadership the IDA portion of IBRD loans became even greater given the targeting of the poorest of the poor countries. While Nobel laureate and economist Arthur Lewis suggested separating the two organizations so that the IDA could focus solely upon development without the drag of banking orthodoxy, McNamara rejected this advice. Forced to choose between the two, he said he would select development over banking orthodoxy, but that this was a false choice that one did not have to make: By submitting all projects to the same procedures, development could be made more effective and the financial credibility of the World Bank preserved. McNamara pushed the IFC to select developmental projects benefiting the poor masses rather than more short-term profitable undertakings and to support local, home-grown enterprises instead of large multinational companies. Not surprisingly, the developed nations were split on their support of McNamara's policies. Several OECD nations observed that the IBRD poverty program was less than helpful in their export of capital goods.[4] But the Scandinavian countries and the Dutch strongly stood behind the new stress on poverty-oriented projects: It is no accident that these are generally nations that are known for contributing more than the average share of their GNP in foreign aid.

From OPEC to the New International Economic Order

As modeling goes, the most influential pro-Southern example in the world economy is OPEC, which other less successful would-be commodity cartels have tried to mimic. As documented in Chapter Four, OPEC's successes stem to a large extent from its oligopolistic roots in the oil industry, which has a history and structure different from the organization of other commodity businesses.[5] Of course the effectiveness of managerial structure cannot be separated from cyclic trends in the sectoral market: Since 1890, roughly every decade the dollar price of oil in real terms appears to go from trough to peak and then from peak to trough in the following decade. With a peak in oil prices in real terms reached in 1981 (a 225 percent increase over the previous decade), if the pattern is extended, a long price decline should bottom out in the 1990s.[6] After each trough in this twenty-year boom-and-bust pattern, the oil industry tends to reorganize. The collective learning and cooperation at this critical juncture set the stage for the relative efficacy of the cartel as demand again begins to outstrip supply. *Thus the efficiency of the maintenance learning base is prerequisite to the effectiveness of the collective, entrepreneurial bloc demand for certain prices and production quotas.* As the coordination or efficiency breaks down, OPEC's power is undermined.

The success of OPEC had great impact upon Third-World countries. Some attempted to form other commodity cartels—in copper and bananas, for example—without much success.[7] The OPEC situation was unique. Even given the development of other energy sources and oil discoveries in the world, by 1980 OPEC still accounted for two-thirds of the world's petroleum reserves and for over 40 percent of the world's petroleum production. *OPEC's success was contingent upon high demand, inelastic oil prices, tight supplies, a small number of producing countries, common political interests, a tradition of cooperation or "collective learning," and a sufficient supply of financial reserves.* The falling prices of other commodities and great number of alternative suppliers did not make them likely candidates for successful commodity cartels.

Nevertheless, the OPEC model inspired developing countries to band together to demand the establishment of a **New International Economic Order (NIEO)** at the United Nations' Sixth Special Session in 1974. Observing that between 1952 and 1972 per capita real income in developed market economies went up from about $2,000 to $4,000 (1973 prices) while in developing countries per capita income rose from $175 to $300, the developing countries concluded that the international economic system was skewed against them. Rather than catering only to the improvement of standards of living in the developed countries, the objective of the NIEO was to make the basic needs of developing countries a priority as well by restructuring the world economy to allow greater Third-World participation and effectiveness.[8]

The call for a New International Economic Order also pressured for a change in financial flows, beginning with a target of 0.7% of industrialized countries' GNP for aid to the developing countries. While the North resisted NIEO pressures, they served to change global consciousness on economic matters. U.S. Secretary of State Henry Kissinger reversed his policy of benign neglect in 1975 and the European Economic Community (EEC) signed the first **Lomé Convention** with forty-six developing countries from Africa, the Caribbean, and the Pacific to stabilize their export earnings and to make EEC capital and technical assistance available to them through a Center for Industrial Development. This was a major breakthrough in the Northern establishment for the sake of Southern interests.

The Lomé Strategy: A Model for North–South Economic Ties?

The world's largest regional agreement linking over 500 million people in industrialized European and developing countries was signed on February 28, 1975, as the result of hard bargaining inspired by the NIEO movement. The **African, Caribbean, and Pacific states (the ACP nations)** began from a maximal position in negotiations, demanding that export and import prices should be indexed in a stabilization system to guarantee the purchasing power of the developing countries based upon their major export products. The European Community (EC) opposed this indexation of export and import prices on two grounds: (1) such indexation could hurt some of the ACP states since trade took place not only between industrialized and developing states but also between developing states themselves; and (2) interference with the market mechanism could have negative, bottleneck effects such as the EC had experienced in the expensive subsidies for the EC's Common Agricultural Policy.[9] The European Commission did a study of the major ACP exports. It discovered that variations in quantities of key exports as well as price changes were responsible for the instability of ACP export earnings.[10] Partly because of this study, the EC agreed to stabilize export earnings instead of focusing upon prices, and it proposed a list of key exports from the ACP countries: groundnuts, cocoa, coffee, cotton, coconut products, and bananas. The ACP states responded with tough bargaining, which resulted in a list of twelve major products plus seventeen more derived from them. The twelve: groundnut products, cocoa products, coffee products, cotton products, coconut products, palm (palm nut and kernel) products, rawhides (skins and leather), wood products, fresh bananas, tea, raw sisal, and iron ore. With sugar, the stabilization guarantees go even further than with these dozen products. *Southern bloc unity at a propitious historical moment with a negotiating partner with long-term economic interests in the bloc were the main ingredients of the Lomé success.* The European Community, for its part, assured itself privileged access to the resources and markets of an important bloc of developing countries, which could become invaluable in the event of any future all out protectionist trade war in the global economy. Indeed, the potential power of the agreement could serve as a deterrent to exactly such a trade conflict.

By the mid-1980s, sixty-six ACP states had signed the Lomé Convention, which was renewed in 1979 and again in 1984. These include all the former French colonies, suggesting once again the shrewdness of French diplomacy within the European Community. The Lomé Convention frees ACP members from all customs duties on 99.5 percent of their exports to the EC with no reciprocal concessions required. Also, the EC grants the ACP countries technical and financial aid (including grants, loans, and low-interest agreements for risk-capital transactions). When the export earnings of the major ACP products listed above fall below the average of preceding years, the EC compensates them in repayable advances for the more prosperous ACP nations and in nonrepayable grants for the rest. An agreement was reached in 1979 to cover support for a certain level of production or export potential for key ACP minerals as well (called *Sysmin*). A 1985 agreement expanded cooperation in areas of rural development, energy, industry, fisheries, and social and cultural problems.[11]

The introduction of *programmed aid* under the Third Lomé Convention (1986–90) slowed down the allocation of aid due to the administration of the large-scale rural development programs involved. The *import programme* financing was dispersed more efficiently, however. And extra money was targeted for **structural adjustment** (basic institutional economic adaptation to world economic change) for the Fourth Lomé Convention (**Lomé IV**), covering 1991–1995, given the overload put on the Lomé's STABEX system.[12] STABEX is limited to *stabilizing the export earning* from products that affect employment and cause a deterioration in the overall terms of trade in ACP countries. By the early 1990s aid requests far exceeded available financial resources, particularly given the heavy indebtedness of many ACP nations. These nations were also worried about the erosion of their preferential access to the European markets because of the Single Market evolution of the European Union and the GATT Uruguay Round.

But *the positive model of the Lomé Convention broke beyond defensive, risk-shy maintenance strategies and stimulated collective learning—positive adaptation to world economic change targeting economic growth while supporting social equity and cultural integrity. In June 1992, non-European industrialized nations, including the U.S., agreed to the Lomé Convention in principle by supporting Chapter 33 of Agenda 21 at the Earth Summit or United Nations Conference on Environment and Development at Rio de Janeiro.*[13] *(See "Earth Summit," Chapter 4).*

Chapter 33 of Agenda 21, "Financial Resources and Mechanisms," proposes that since the 5-to-6 percent of Gross National Product (GNP) industrialized countries spend on defense is declining and 1-to-3 percent goes to environmental cleanup, it would be possible to shift levels of official development assistance from 0.35 percent to 1.0 percent of GNP, and call this the **Earth Increment.** The Earth Increment could add $150 billion to fund projects aimed to protect the ozone layer, biodiversity, and international waters. These funds could also be used to limit emissions of greenhouse gases, perhaps halving the debt of developing countries through such plans for sustainable development.

UNCTAD and UNIDO: Trade and Industrial Pressure Groups

The focus provided by the demand for a New International Economic Order in the 1970s motivated new efforts by existing international economic pressure groups for the developing countries, sponsored by the United Nations. As described in some detail in Chapter 4, **UNCTAD,** or the **United Nations Conference on Trade and Development,** had been organized to promote the interests of the countries disadvantaged by the asymmetrical or unequal world trading system. Recall the structuralist Raul Prebisch of Argentina, first head of UNCTAD, who argued that the Northern center of world trade was so structured as to keep the South on the periphery and to increase the North–South gap. Southern countries typically produce commodities and basic resources with prices that tend to fall, whereas developed countries specialize in finished manufactured goods with rising prices. Only by providing import substitutes for Northern goods could the South catch up. Prebisch concluded that the North was preoccupied with a maintenance strategy concerned with furthering the well-being of industrialized countries in the status quo. The concerns of the South were not even on the agenda of the North, which increasingly squeezed the poor countries out of the world trade system into poverty and despair. *GATT had become a* de facto *rich man's club—a commercial treaty organization that best served those who could afford its terms. UNCTAD, then, was the economic pressure group for the poor countries.*[14]

The NIEO helped to promote the implementation of UNCTAD's Integrated Program for commodities and the establishment of its Common Fund.[15]

On the industrial side, the **United Nations Industrial Development Organization (UNIDO)** was established in 1966 to help the developing countries in the private industrial sector. Headquartered in Vienna, UNIDO has set a target of at least 5 percent economic growth in gross domestic product for the developing countries, advocating that by the year 2000, 25 percent of all industrial output should be by the developing countries. Nations must come to UNIDO, which uses its Industrial and Technology Bank (established in 1976) to help them with marketing and capital financing strategies. In addition, there is a Special Industrial Services program (SIS) to provide specific project help in industrial development through, for example, a fellowship program for technological and managerial training for key personnel.

The Industrial Development Board, which governs UNIDO, is made up of forty-five seats elected from the General Assembly of the United Nations: fifteen seats for developed countries, eighteen seats for Africa, Asia, and Yugoslavia, seven seats for Latin America and the Caribbean, and five seats for socialist countries. Industrialization is not seen as an end in itself by UNIDO, but as a means to economic growth in developing nations. Projects are analyzed for visibility, cost-benefit ratios, and the promotion of financing. UNIDO encourages a focus initially upon agricultural and then other projects. At its 34th Conference in New Delhi in 1980, UNIDO proposed that a $300 billion fund be established by the year 2000 for industrial financing, which should become long term rather than short term in nature.

However, countries usually prefer short-term financing. *Conventional state development programs fail to reach the people who have the greatest need for fi-*

nancial services in the developing countries. This is particularly true for women. Large-scale, regulated subsidized programs fail to reach the poor. Successful alternative financial services rely, instead, upon reducing barriers to access to money such as high transaction costs for lenders and borrowers, high collateral requirements, and low levels of literacy and numeracy.[16]

Still, as a targeted organization for Southern economic unity, the collective learning potential of UNIDO shows promise of increasing flexibility and sophistication and should not be underestimated in the future. Such frail international economic organizations, however, were no match for the debt crisis of the 1980s and 1990s—a crisis "resolved" by commercial banks and private investors as substitutes for governments and international organizations, a role for which they were not designed.

The Debt Crisis

The seeds of the debt crisis in the world economy were planted with the quadrupling of oil prices in 1973: Transfer of wealth to the oil-producing Third-World countries amounted to a "tax" equivalent to 2–3 percent of the GNP (on average) of the industrialized countries. And this economic cost of some $30 billion was soon recycled from the North to the non-oil-producing South—those poorer countries that produced no oil and were least able to cope with the price increases.

Meanwhile, the OPEC nations, most of which were sparsely populated, found themselves with more wealth on their hands than they could absorb domestically. So they deposited their funds in "safe," short-term accounts in banks of the North—in Europe, the United States, and Japan. This game of "hot capital" (same rules as hot potato) was then continued by the commercial banks of the North who wanted so desperately to get rid of this abundance of cash that they hired hundreds of young graduates to fly around the world to sell loans to developing countries. And given that the economic growth rates in the oil-importing developing countries between 1973 and 1980 averaged 4.6 percent annually compared to a mere 2.5 percent in the industrialized countries, one can understand why the bankers were attracted.[17]

Citibank, the Bank of America, Chase Manhattan, the First National Bank of Chicago, the Bank of Tokyo, and other world-class banks (and some smaller ones who should not have been in the game at all) acted as turntables. They recycled the petrodollars deposited by OPEC to provide liquidity in the non-oil-developing countries who needed cash to pay for their higher oil bills. *Because some of these banks actually calculated that they probably would not get the principal back on the loans, planning to live a long time on high rates of interest, this massive commercial loan program has been referred to as "the third redistribution" (the first two redistributions from wealthy to disadvantaged nations being the Marshall Plan and OPEC's success in raising oil prices).* Since both industrialized governments and the international organizations they supported (the IMF, for instance) were under great financial pressures in the 1970s, they applauded the action of commercial banks without attempting to discern the long-term consequences. The outstanding debt of developing countries shot up from $161 billion in 1974 to $599 billion in 1982, and by 1982 debt-service payments claimed 24 percent of the export earnings of developing countries compared with 14 percent in the mid-1970s.[18]

Nevertheless, in the late 1970s the Marxist-oriented Cambridge School of economics in England sent advisors to Mexico who recommended that the Mexicans borrow all they could as long as North Americans were willing to lend. The loans would indirectly be insured by the U.S. government and even if the loans went bad, Mexico would have the Americans by their debt.

By 1982 some forty developing countries found themselves in a cash squeeze: Interest rates on their variable-rate loans were skyrocketing in tandem with the Paul Volcker tight-money, anti-inflation policy of the United States at the same time that their export earnings were falling because of a recession in the industrial world and because of plunging commodity prices. As economist John Maynard Keynes observed, if you owe your bank a hundred pounds, you have a problem; but if you owe your bank a million pounds the bank has a problem. And in a global economy, if a number of countries owe banks billions of pounds, everybody has a problem.

Poland, with $27 billion in debts, was the first casualty. Because of the imposition of martial law in Poland, the United States pushed for calling the loans in default, but was dissuaded from doing so by West European allies whose banks had large stakes in Poland.

In Latin America the debt stakes were even higher—$90 billion in Brazil, close to the same amount in Mexico, and $38 billion in Argentina. But it was not Poland but the Mexican debt crisis that shocked the financial markets severely in August 1982. The advice of the Cambridge School had come home to roost.

The Mexican Case, the Debt Trap and the Cover of Privatization

Commercial banks had been particularly anxious to lend money to developing countries where new oil had been discovered, as in Mexico, assuming that oil prices would continue to rise and back up the loans. And since the Mexican economy grew an average of 8 percent annually between 1978 and 1981, all looked well on the surface. But a structural crisis resulted when the oil price forecasts by the banks proved to be wrong. The demand and price for oil began to go down, not up.

Underlying this structural crisis we discover the hegemony of Anglo-Saxon economic theory at work (see the Introduction). Most policymakers from the developed world accept the assumptions of Keynesian economics that savings always equals investment, that whatever is not consumption is defined as savings, and that whatever is not consumption is defined as investment. While these assumptions might work in the economy of a closed domestic system (which does not exist in a global world economy), in an open economy imports and exports have to be worked into the definition of savings equalling investment. In the daily practice of balance-of-payments statistics, a **current account deficit** (or the total export of goods and services that is less than the total import of goods and services) goes down as a deficiency of domestic savings vis-à-vis investment. Since foreign savings (that is, foreign debt) can be tapped to supplement a shortfall in the domestic savings rate, according to this economic philosophy, the growth process for developing countries cannot help but be associated with foreign indebtedness. Current account deficits are perceived to be the normal way of life in this formulation. No great collective learning motivation exists for developing economies to concentrate upon suitable production for exports to balance foreign-exchange requirements. Initially Mexican President Luis Echeverria used foreign commercial bank loans in the early 1970s to back up state enterprises and public credit agencies for loans to small and medium-sized businesses. But the Mexican economy became overheated in the late 1970s and too dependent upon foreign sources of financing to repay both its old debt and to keep the hyped-up economic growth going.[19]

From the late 1970s onwards, Mexico's President José López Portillo pretended as if all was well until the election was won in July 1982. But in one week in August 1982, the peso lost half its value and the Mexican government declared it could not pay the $20 billion in principal repayments due on government debt through 1984. Mexico was broke and $10 billion was owed to the banks within a few months. The money borrowed by Portillo was to be used ostensibly for an ambitious industrial development program based on greatly expanded petroleum production. However, a large amount of the money lent—perhaps as much as half of it—was never invested in Mexico. The cash wound up in the Swiss bank accounts of corrupt government functionaries or was used by businessmen for secure investments and real estate purchases in the United States and Europe. Portillo's own assets and summer villas flourished. By August 1982 Mexico had only $200 million remaining in its central bank; it suspended commercial debt principal payments and requested a three-month moratorium on its debt. Mexico's decision to suspend payments on its foreign debts and to request $10 billion from the United States to bail itself out shocked the world and functioned as a model: Other Latin American countries followed suit in acknowledging their unserviceable debts publicly, igniting the world debt crisis.

Following an exhaustive weekend of negotiations, the United States agreed to purchase $1 billion of Mexican oil at $25 to $30 a barrel to go to the Strategic Petroleum Reserve and the Pentagon. The U.S. Federal Reserve was willing to put up $750 million for Mexico through the Bank for International Settlements if the Swiss, German, and British central banks would together put up the same amount. Nearly $4 billion was provided in emergency credit, almost $3 billion by the United States, and the rest by other central banks of the North. Another credit of about $4 billion was then granted by the IMF after negotiations with Mexico; the credit was contingent on stringent austerity measures that Mexico would enact.

A major Mexican problem was capital flight—Mexico was the largest of any debtor nation. Some $60 billion left the country between 1977 and 1984, and about $5 billion flowed out in the first half of 1985.[20] Such capital flight depleted foreign-exchange reserves, reduced the tax base, and eliminated investment resources, thus undermining economic growth. Traditionally the Mexicans tried to keep foreigners from acquiring a majority share of stock in a Mexican company. This deterred high-tech companies from investing a great deal or transferring technology to a situation that the companies could not control. The class structure of traditional wealthy Mexican families, who are jealous of foreign competition, reinforced this trend of cultural resistance.[21] This class structure appears to be compatible with the corruption of the Institutional Revolutionary Party, which has ruled Mexico for more than half a century.

However, the Mexican government made an exception to the rule for the *maquiladora* industrial plants just below the U.S. border, which assembled parts from abroad and exported the finished products. Between 1978 and 1988 the *maquiladoras* grew 14 percent annually, employing over 350,000 workers in some 1,500 plants. Under the protected economy of the early 1980s, the government used these plants to rent cheap workers to American firms to do piece work. But the new economic policies of President Carlos Salinas de Gortari, which *appeared* to tilt towards economic liberalism, converted the function of the *maquiladoras* to upgrade the skills of the workers in order to result in prize-winning quality production in the auto industry. By 1992, although the pay of the average Mexican worker was but one-sixth of that of his or her American counterpart, the level of Mexican productivity growth was double that of the U.S.[22] *The image of privatization projected by the policies of Salinas served to cover up the still existing heavy levels of Mexican debt in order to pull in foreign investment and bring about NAFTA approval. Behind the scenes Salinas fixed salaries through "el pacto," a business-labor agreement that keeps inflation and wages down while increasing productivity, employment, and worker training. But the poor Mayan Indians of Chiapas, who saw their minimum wage drop 24 percent (adjusted for inflation) since 1988, revolted after NAFTA was approved in 1993, focusing the 1994 elections on the postliberal issue of social justice.*[23]

Mexican debt, which seemed to fade from view, upstaged by all the liberal economic rhetoric and surface action of Mexican and American administrations, refused to go away. Already, by 1986, Mexico's total debt was $99 billion, with most of the $25 billion U.S. share held by the ten largest U.S. financial institutions.[24] In 1992, Mexico's ratio of total external debt to its

Gross National Product (GNP) or total annual economic output was still over 40 percent (outdoing Brazil's ratio, which was less than 25 percent, but better than Nigeria's disastrous 118 percent, not to mention the Ivory Coast, with an almost inconceivable 204 percent).[25] **External debt** is defined by the World Bank as the sum of portfolio investments and long-term capital inflows by nonresidents. It does not include foreign direct investment by nonresidents (the key category that causes the U.S. to be called the "world's largest debtor nation").

*   *   *

Brazil and Argentina mimicked Mexico's behavior in seeking aid from the IMF and a rescheduling of their debts. By 1982 the Third World and Eastern European countries combined had foreign debts totaling $626 billion—three times as much as in 1976.[26] The key international economic organizations that the North used to attempt to manage or analyze the world economy—the OECD and World Bank—both initially underplayed the debt crisis. These organizations focused upon the largest debtor country problems, hoping to prevent a general loss of confidence in the Western financial markets. For if the commercial loans could not be rescheduled and were officially declared in default and written off as losses, the stocks of the large banks involved could plummet, risking a run on the banks or, at the least, a great crisis in confidence in the stability of world finance. A comment made in 1982 attributed to Arthur Burns, former Chairman of the Federal Reserve Board, summed up the situation: "The international banks have made many foolish loans and now we can only pray they will make some more of them."

However, to receive IMF-sponsored loans, which permit developing countries to reschedule their debts with lower interest rates spread out over a longer time period, the debtor governments usually were forced to agree to austerity conditions that initially cut economic growth and caused unemployment, lower living standards, and domestic political unrest. Mexico, for example, had to agree to cut government subsidies and employment, curb imports and inflation, and permit the peso to float against the dollar. Between 1982 and 1987 real income in Mexico fell 40 percent and annual inflation reached 160 percent. Thousands of workers lost their jobs.

The following year, preceding the national election of Salinas the government's six-year-old austerity plan finally slowed the inflation rate and foreign trade surpluses doubled to $8.4 billion. Mexico also followed the advice of Ronald Reagan's Treasury Secretary, James Baker, to start selling state enterprises, reduce tariffs, ease restrictions on foreign investment, and encourage non-oil exports. To make the economy look good before the election, the government negotiated the wage-and-price pact with workers and manufacturers and increased the availability of consumer goods. But the successful political strategy, which barely gave the incoming president over 50 percent of the vote in a contested election, caused chaos in Mexico's balance of payments, already suffering from a drop in oil prices. Capital flew the coop for safer havens abroad.

Mexico illustrates the "debt trap" situation of debtor developing countries caused by economic policies of the Reagan administration: A nation can either aim for an external balance-of-payments policy or it can try to meet the population's demand for a higher quality life—but not both. Most of the resources needed to service Mexico's external debts come out of domestic investment. Between 1982 and 1988 the investment rate within Mexico fell 6 percent and Mexico's GNP shrank even though the population grew by 13 percent.[27] About 4 percent of Mexican GNP went to foreigners for debt servicing. So the $3.5 billion loan given to Mexico by the United States in 1988 paradoxically sank Mexico deeper into the debt trap.[28] Nor did the landmark deal completed in 1990 with American bankers under the Brady plan, under which most banks reduced the value of Mexico's debt by 35 percent (by lowering the principal on existing loans or accepting lower interest payments) change this structure of dependence. It remains to be seen if the passage of the North American Free Trade Agreement in 1993 will do the trick. . . .

INTERPRETATIONS

In contemplating the past three decades, one cannot help but note that the tempo of global economic change and technological innovation has speeded up. This has put increased psychosocial and financial pressures upon rich and poor alike. The rich have the resources to create more buffer zones between themselves and socioeconomic change, if they choose to do so. Nevertheless, Swedish economist Staffan Linder has argued in *The Harried Leisure Class* that the higher one is on the class scale, the more harried one's "leisure" time becomes as the goods and opportunities to be consumed grow geometrically while the time one has in the day is still finite—24 hours for the rich as well as for the poor. Or, as poet Antonio Machado put it: "Speed kills the soul."

Whether this increase in speed has increased the gap between the rich and poor nations is less often asked than this question: How great has the gap become and how fast is it increasing? Still, among economists based in the classical liberal school, such as W.W. Rostow, it has appeared that the poor have gotten richer while the rich have slowed down.[29] Growth rates among the developing countries, particularly those in the newly industrializing category (the NICs), have often exceeded those of the developed countries.

On the other hand, developing countries start with much less so there is more room for growth (or the numbers are easier to double). From the reformist liberal perspective, world capitalism can be made to work for the poor if it is better targeted for economic growth in the less developed regions—as in the case of Michael J. Camdessus's growth-before-austerity policy at the IMF.[30] The basic human needs perspective represented by the philosophy of Robert McNamara at the World Bank focuses upon helping the poorest of the poor individually.[31] Such a target seems unrealistic to the realist school: The power, security, control, and vulnerability of the nation-state make up the dominant reality for these analysts.[32]

The interdependence school stresses the increasing global dependency of rich and poor nations upon each other.[33] Finally, the neo-Marxists perceive global capitalism as a system headed for self-destruction.[34] A brief look at how such perspectives conflict in their interpretation of foreign aid as a means to lessen the gap between rich and poor nations may serve as a useful illustration of the main theme of international political economy: the positioning for power and wealth among rich and poor nations.

Foreign Aid: Partial Solution, Drug, or Panacea?

The success of OPEC and demands for the New International Economic Order set the stage for an expansion of multinational financial aid for the developing countries in the 1970s. Bilateral foreign aid,* which dominated the discussion concerning economic relations between developed and developing countries in the 1950s and 1960s, came to be viewed with skepticism by not only the poor nations but also by the mass publics of the industrialized world. The widely read book *The Ugly American* told the tale of the United States donating thousands of sacks of wheat to malnourished countries only to have Soviet agents stamp the sacks upon arrival as gifts from the USSR. The American share of total Western financial aid fell from 59 percent in 1961 to 27 percent in 1980, when the United States ranked only thirteenth among the top seventeen Western aid donors in terms of percentage of aid relative to GNP.[35] In terms of absolute quantity, Japan in 1989 surpassed the United States as the number-one giver of foreign aid. Given the pressures in the 1990s for budget reductions in U.S. domestic programs, foreign aid bills have had a difficult time getting through Congress.

The "postliberal" nations of Scandinavia and the Netherlands, on the other hand, have continued to support foreign aid strongly, leading the world in 1992 in terms of aid as a percent of GDP. So have Japan and West Germany, beginning in the 1970s after their postwar reconstruction and economic successes were assured. In 1989 Japan targeted $65 billion for recycling to indebted countries from 1990–1993. China more or less stopped its

---

*Defined as official financial assistance, excluding military aid, private philanthropy, and private investment.

foreign-aid program in the late 1970s, while aid from Russia and Eastern bloc countries declined to insignificance in the post-cold-war economy.

Although foreign aid or economic assistance typically makes up only 10 percent of the cash received by developing countries (compared with some 70 percent for export receipts), this 10 percent can be more easily targeted by governments for specific projects than can commercial money, giving foreign aid more influence on national economic development than its percentage weight might suggest. Clearly, foreign aid cannot be more than a partial solution to the North–South economic imbalance, but as Robert McNamara was well aware, aid can be carefully targeted as a strategic tool to greatly influence national policies.

While McNamara used foreign aid via the World Bank to target the poorest individuals in the poorest countries, others have found this nonstructural approach too diffuse to have anything but a short-term effect. McNamara's focus on individuals is a typical example of the humanism of Western culture. Taking more the viewpoint of the power realists, the Soviet Union and Eastern European countries targeted long-term strategic states for aid—Cuba, North Korea, and Vietnam—as did OPEC in targeting Islamic states—Syria, Jordan, and Egypt—and the United States in shoring up Middle Eastern allies—Israel and Egypt. *According to the realist perspective, foreign economic assistance becomes a form of political war fought by means other than force.* For the realist the national security of the nation and its allies becomes the criterion for granting aid—a criterion that may better serve the interests of one-party, authoritarian economies than of multiparty, factional democracies.[36] The cold war motivation of Marshall Plan reconstruction of Western Europe, for example, served as a defense against Soviet influence only in the short-term, while at the same time building up the economies of future competitors in the world economy. Opposing the dispensing of foreign aid as a gift (except when the beneficiary is a developing country with deep structural problems) as unnecessary, unnatural, and unwise, structuralist economist Gunnar Myrdal noted in 1970: "The whole international exchange situation would have been more wholesome now and in the past decade if the United States could have called for repayments of loans from West European governments—gradually and with due considerations."[37] Myrdal noted that aid policies cannot be morally neutral: From a realist's state-centered focus, the Swedish government's criterion for aid is to promote political democracy and social equality, not to preserve anti-progressive social structures (too often the case in the use of shortsighted cold war realism as an aid criterion).

As a structuralist (see Chapter 4), Myrdal agreed with the reformist school of liberalism to the extent that he suggested the capitalist world economy can be fixed to be more human and less asymmetrical. And while somewhat belonging to a category all of his own, Myrdal has much in common with what has been called the *"interdependence school": the stress upon the mutual dependency of developed and developing countries.* This school of thought grew out of the momentum of the NIEO movement and the growing consensus that the decision-making framework of international organizations gave more bargaining leverage to developing countries in **multilateral** aid negotiations where norms and rules are more clear than they would in **bilateral** negotiations (between two states) preferred by the realists, where asymmetry of inequality is likely to be the dominant perception.[38]

The interdependence school rejects the realist's state-centered focus of international political economy in the late twentieth century, arguing that this form of analysis cannot capture the reality of many transnational flows that have little to do with the nation-state—the transactions of multinational companies, for instance. State sovereignty, in short, has become as leaky as a sieve. The global political economy can only be understood in terms of a network of domestic, business, cultural, political, and economic linkages that perforate the pretentious control of the nation-state. Technology and financial flows are cited as evidence of the need for an interdependence perspective.

Perhaps the ultimate example of the interdependence perspective is the initial report of the Independent Commission for International Economic Cooperation chaired by Willy Brandt of West Germany—the well-known *Brandt Report* of 1980.[39] Using a vision of global Keynesianism, the Brandt Commission argued that the Third World must carry the main share of its own burden but cannot be left alone to the world markets or haphazard nature of the liberal or basic-human-needs perspectives. Rather, aid must be shifted from bilateral to multilateral forms and focus, for the sake of the South, upon an automatic international tax on armaments, the trade of luxury goods, the use of the global commons (that is, the international seabed), and so forth. Without general increases in aid levels based on these and other policies, economic forces left to themselves tend to produce growing inequalities.

From the radical or neo-Marxist perspective, foreign aid is a tool for imperialism and social control, aiming to undermine the independence of developing countries.[40] In *The Debt Trap*, Cheryl Payer, for example, implies that the solution to this dilemma of becoming dependent upon the debt trap cultivated by foreign-aid donors from the industrialized world and the growth-dampening austerity measures of the IMF is to try going it alone as much as possible. The North Korean constitution is cited as a model.[41] In the postwar period Albania tried this strategy only to face ever-greater poverty until reluctantly the Albanians rejoined the world economy.

On the other hand, the People's Republic of China successfully modernized its agricultural base largely in isolation, joining the world economy officially as it was becoming a net exporter of food, thus giving the country a less dependent bargaining position. From the contemporary radical perspective, models of the ideal socialist society must be established to be ready to take over when global capitalism breaks apart from its own contradictions.

Marxism and Dependency Theory

Marx himself, however, believed that the role of capitalist or bourgeois imperialism was revolutionary and would transform all traditional societies until they used the same mode of commodity production. In his *Communist Manifesto* of 1848, Marx wrote: "It compels all nations, on pain of extinction, to adopt the bourgeois mode of production . . . compels them to introduce what it calls civilization into their midst, . . . creates a world after its own image." But in going beyond the Continent, Marx discovered that his European theory of development did not seem to apply. In Asia and the Middle East, precapitalist stages did not appear to exist. These societies were stuck in what Marx termed the "Asiatic mode of production," based on the unity and autarchy of agriculture and manufacturing at the village level and an autonomous, parasitic state split from the rest of society at the top. Since nothing existed internally to change such a conservative social structure, Marx thought the external force of Western imperialism would be the agent of change.[42] Thus, nineteenth-century-England's role in India was both the destruction of the old Asian society and the laying of the groundwork for the material basis of Western society in Asia. Lenin extended this thinking to conclude that the inherent contradiction of capitalism was that it developed, not underdeveloped, the world, spreading its technology and industry to lesser-developed nations, thus undermining its position, preparing the competitive basis for its own destruction.[43]

Picking up Marx's theory of capitalist imperialism and Marx's concern for the domestic distribution of wealth, dependency theory arose in the mid-1960s, adding a strong dose of economic nationalism to its recipe. Disenchanted with the inadequacy of the structuralists' strategy of import substitution as a means to wealth for the developing countries, dependency theorists were convinced that the failure lay in the inability of this strategy to change the traditional social and economic conditions of peripheral states. *Whereas the Marxist-Leninist thesis of capitalist imperialism suggests the necessity of foreign aid as part of the process of inevitable capitalist development, dependency theory argues that dependency causes underdevelopment and is apt to be critical of aid.*

According to Brazilian scholar Theotonio Dos Santos, **dependence** is "a situation in which the economy of certain countries is conditioned by the development and expansion of another economy to which the former is subjected."[44] Whereas liberals perceive underdevelopment as a *condition* of countries that have not kept up with the leaders in the world economy, dependency theorists view it as a *process* inherent in an asymmetrical system that continually restructures developing countries into underdeveloped positions compared to developed countries.[45] Rather than the liberal vision of developing countries as split between modern sectors well integrated into the national and international economies and backward sectors that have not yet adapted, the dependency school sees the developing countries locked into a backward position on the periphery of an integrated global economy. This position of "negative self-fulfilling prophecy" is characterized typically by an overdependence upon raw materials with unsteady prices; inequitably distributed national income catering to the tastes of the elite and not targeted toward the needs of the masses; distorting investments by multinational companies that stymie local entrepreneurship and technological innovation as profits are recycled abroad; an undermining of the local labor market as foreign firms pay higher salaries, creating structural unemployment; and dependence upon foreign capital that fosters authoritarian governments, which provide multinational companies with the stability they require.[46] The underdevelopment of dependent countries is caused, according to dependency theorists, by transnational class linkages between the metropolitan international centers of world capitalism and parasitic, feudal clientele class dominating the political system of the country at the periphery. True nationalists must rise up against this international class hegemony and pursue the welfare of the entire society, not just of the class in which they find themselves. The aim is to create an autonomous, industrialized state characterized by equality, not parasitic dependence. As this goal is achieved, foreign aid presumably becomes less and less necessary.

While dependency theory describes certain cases of poor, exploited, commodity-producing states—such as the Philippines of Ferdinand Marcos—it cannot account for the higher growth rate characterizing lesser-developed countries as a group over that of the developed countries in the recent past.[47] Rather than systematically underdeveloping the developing countries, the global economy appears inadvertently to have helped many of them, although in a sporadic way that has worked to help the least advantaged nations the least (such as those of sub-Sahara Africa). Thus, the 40 percent of the developing countries that are the richest get about twice as much aid per head as the poorest 40 percent. Other theories, such as the *world-system* perspective, fault dependence theory for neglecting the implication of the *global* division of labor.

The World-System Perspective

From the viewpoint of sociologist Immanuel Wallerstein's world-system perspective, foreign aid is no more than a transitory epiphenomenon, distracting one from the essential structural transformations, macro-cycles and trends of global capitalism. In his book *The Modern World System II* (1980), Wallerstein argues that the modern world system emerged from the transformation of European feudalism and mercantilism into a capitalist world economy colored by Europe's particular redistributive or tributary mode of production. This transformation originated in the economic expansion of the sixteenth century (phase A) and subsequent contraction, depression, or "crisis" in the seventeenth century (phase B). Ever since then, the capitalist world economy has expanded to cover the entire globe, manifesting a cyclical pattern of economic expansion and contraction (phases A and B) with shifting geographic locations of economic roles (the rise and fall of hegemonies and hierarchical displacements of particular core, peripheral, and semi-peripheral zones). It has continued to undergo a process of secular transformation (that is, of technological advance, industrialization, proletarianization, and of the emergence of structural resistance to the system itself).

According to Wallerstein, the French Revolution and its Napoleonic continuation catalyzed the ideological transformation of the capitalist world economy *as a world system,* creating three new sets of cultural institutions central to this system: the ideologies (conservatism, liberalism, and Marxism), the social sciences, and the social movements.* The antisystemic national and social movements are created by growing economic constraints at those cyclical moments when world economic production is in excess of world demand, precipitating stagnation (or phase B—contraction). Labor unions, socialist parties, and other kinds of workers' organizations are examples of social movements, emphasizing the growing polarity between successful bourgeois groups and the proletariat caught in the economic squeeze. Paradoxically, according to Wallerstein, these worker movements turn to the state to maximize their collective interests, further strengthening the governmental structural supports of the bourgeois classes against whom they feel the sting of increasing inequality.

While in the nineteenth century the process of the social movement spread from core to periphery in the world economy, the national movement went from periphery to core. But in the late twentieth century, Wallerstein argues, they are no longer ideological rivals: "Today there is scarcely a social movement which is not nationalist, and there are few national movements which are not socialist."[48] This questionable supposition (given national conservative movements in the United States and Great Britain, as well as in France, West Germany and Eastern Europe) permits Wallerstein to project that we are living in a global transition from capitalism to socialism that may take more than a century to complete given capitalism's tendency to reemerge in cyclic ways. Such a transformation would presumably bring more equity to a world system now flawed by the absence of an overarching international political authority to match the global scope of the world economy.

* * *

---

*Wallerstein argues that the French Revolution did not change France very much but did change the world system very much: Immanuel Wallerstein, "The French Revolution as a World Historical Event," *Social Research* 56, No. 1 (Spring 1989): 33–52.

Curiously, there appears to be a meeting of the minds in the rejection of foreign aid on the part of the extreme, socialist perspective to the left and the extreme capitalist viewpoint on the orthodox, liberal right. Orthodox liberal economists Peter T. Bauer and Basil S. Yamey argue that foreign aid serves to magnify and politicize the state in a developing country, giving power to corrupt leaders who have their own personal and political interests in mind rather than the interests of the poorest people in their nation. Thus Dr. Julius K. Nyerere of Tanzania used aid to force millions of people to move from their homes into socialist villages, devastating food production. And President Mobutu of Zaire, who received a great deal of aid, expelled traders, bringing the society back to subsistence production and widespread deprivation. Aid, according to this perspective, lowers international competitiveness of a developing country by permitting governments to disguise the worst aspects of their economic policies—such as creating or maintaining overvalued exchange rates or increasing the domestic money supply, often leading to inflation, a lack of confidence, and a flight of capital.[49] Indeed, economists Bauer and Yamey observe: "The concept of the Third World and the policy of official aid are inseparable. Without foreign aid there is no Third World."[50] In other words, foreign aid is similar to a drug that corrupts the economic competitiveness of a country, rendering it dependent upon the aid-giving North as long as the drug is consumed. Economic growth has been negligible in many of the countries that receive the most aid and have the highest levels of capital investment. While aid made up more than 5% of the GNP of some 47 countries in 1988 (particularly in sub-Saharan Africa), where GDP per head has been flat for twenty-five years.[51]

The Environmental Perspective

If aid is a drug, there is always the chance of taking it to the point that a nation goes crazy in stimulating short-term economic growth no matter what the consequences are for the environment long-term. Thus the primary rain forest of Sierra Leone, which covered about 60 percent of the country when it achieved independence in 1961, had shrunk to 6 percent by 1994 due to harvesting for economic survival. The rain forest in the Ivory Coast has been reduced from 38 percent to 8 percent. While the coastal areas of China have boomed economically, the quality of the vast expanses of land in the interior have declined rapidly due to deforestation, loss of topsoil, and salinization. Water supplies have been lost or contaminated, population growth climbs (projected to be 1.54 billion by 2025), and crime and corruption are rampant.[52] Environmental theorist Thomas Fraser Homer-Dixon projects that future civil violence, war, and floods of refugees will often be caused by scarcities in resources such as water, cropland, forests, and fish. The countries most threatened by such resource scarcities will be most likely to turn to "hard regimes" of concentrated authoritarian military power.[53] Such developments are stimulated by existing foreign aid priorities: big military spenders get about twice as much aid per head as do the less belligerent.

Environmental journalist Robert D. Kaplan projects that West Africa symbolizes the future for much of the developing world: deforested, hungry, waterless areas with massive population riddled with disease—malaria and AIDS, crime and anarchy. As he sums it up: "Part of the globe is inhabited by Hegel's and Fukuyama's Last Man, healthy, well fed, and pampered by technology. The other, large, part is inhabited by Hobbes's First Man, condemned to a life that is "poor, nasty, brutish, and short." Although both parts will be threatened by environmental stress, the Last Man will be able to master it; the First Man will not."[54]

Another school of environmental thought accepts this analysis and proceeds to argue that the management of global environmental change must be linked to definable processes of social and collective learning if improvement is to be expected.[55] Aid policies must be targeted to convert nations suffering from **policies of negative transparency,** in which they are overwhelmed with news of pollution, sickness, crime, inflation, and underdevelopment to **policies of positive transparency,** which place hard facts in a context of hope with a concrete plan for sustained local economic development. *Collective learning, in short, must be made a tool of concrete, targeted recipes for "green-growth consciousness" and self-help to create increasingly self-sufficient communities of environmentally sustainable access to work, food, water, and community self-confidence. The principle is to go from powerlessness to a **sense of agency** or positive self-determination by keeping money and jobs at home, adding value to existing resources and products, doing surveys to determine local and regional needs, upgrading the community aesthetically, refurbishing local cultural traditions, and involving everyone with enthusiasm in the project.*[56]

IMPLICATIONS

From a collective learning perspective, foreign aid or financial assistance must be structured and targeted for the economic interests of the countries involved according to a model that links short-term help to long-term rewards and mutual benefits. Leaving the world markets alone to run their own course—an orthodox liberal policy—amounts to a *de facto* maintenance strategy that leaves existing inequalities between the North and South in place. This causes the gap between rich and poor to widen as the high technology and information revolutions speed up economic transactions, leaving the underequipped or less informed further and further behind.

The North–South gap widened in the past decade because of the debt crisis, which discouraged commercial banks from lending any new money to debtor nations (a negative trend reinforced by new banking regulations).

Money was granted for interest repayments on outstanding loans. But this caused increasing political unrest in Latin American democracies, which saw such a large share of their scarce export earnings going to pay interest on debt rather than being reinvested in their own economies to stimulate economic growth and employment.

By 1989, Latin American governments had paid $160 billion in interest on their $420 billion foreign debt, and to avoid default many of them cut back essential imports, reduced government spending, and watched economic growth and political support evaporate.[57] The largest Latin American debtors saw themselves as caught in a vicious circle or debt trap in which the banks just granted them enough money to tide them over until the next payment was due to avoid having to formally write off the loans and cause a crisis in world financial markets: This sense of running in place and never catching up with their collective economic problems led to a widespread political and economic malaise throughout Latin America.[58] Thus, in terms of change in per capita gross domestic product from 1981 to 1989: Mexico: –9.2, Venezuela: –24.9, Colombia: 13.9, Brazil: –0.4, Ecuador: –1.1, Peru: –24.7, Bolivia: –26.6, Chile: 9.6; and Argentina: –23.5.

In the 1990s Chile and Bolivia benefitted from tough austerity and free market measures taken (although at significant social cost—particularly for the poor). The younger generation of the old established elite classes made a killing on privatization. Most people were not so fortunate, however, and poverty deepened.[59]

The 1985 plan of U.S. Treasury Secretary James Baker—to encourage more World Bank and commercial lending to debtor countries in return for privatization and opening up of their economies to foreigners—did not work. Nevertheless, as Baker was appointed Secretary of State under President George Bush, the ideology behind the Baker Plan continued, broken down on a case-by-case basis as a reformist liberal tried to head off political and economic crises in key countries (starting with Mexico) in terms of U.S. national interests on a cost-effective basis. Since the United States had itself run up debts amounting to nearly four times that of the greatest Latin American debtor (Brazil) by the end of the 1980s, there were financial constraints on how far the United States could go on its own to help alleviate Third-World debt. Europe and Japan became increasingly involved, whether they liked it or not. Indeed, the Lomé Convention provided one model that worked quite well in targeting aid to a large number of developing countries—sector-specific support of benefit to donors and recipients alike in the long-run. Rather than its typical short-term, put-out-the-fire crisis management, the U.S. government might do well to create its own form of Lomé Convention, building on the NAFTA agreement. The Japanese could do the same for their region. Both could do this by following through with their voluntary agreement to Agenda 21 of the Earth Summit, targeting 1 percent of GNP for the "Earth Increment" in their own regional areas.

In the decade of the 1980s official development assistance from all sources ran about $55 billion annually, 90 percent of this coming from the industrialized countries of the OECD.[60] The difficulty with the assumption of defense spending declines in the Earth Summit post-cold-war financing calculations is that defense spending appeared to start to rise again in 1994. Even the presumably liberal President Bill Clinton submitted a $1.5 trillion budget in 1994 with a $3.2 billion defense spending increase over 1993 (although Clinton's budget projects defense spending to fall again from 1995–1997).[61] But this initial defense spending increase reflected post-cold-war philosophy: no money for new fighter planes or tanks, but more money for environmental clean-up and U.N. peacekeeping operations. Clinton's budget had to fight the big deficits inherited from the Reagan and Bush administrations and follow strict spending caps legislated by Congress, leaving him little room for increasing items without much domestic support, such as foreign aid. As a result, the odds of the U.S. leading the way on the "Earth Increment" seem slim indeed.

To move beyond what sociologist C. Wright Mills called "crack-pot realism," industrialized nations need to look beyond short-term economic and power interests to long-term regional and global strategies that integrate idealism and realism in mutual benefit packages. From Myrdal and the Swedes one learns not only that foreign aid is not morally neutral but that it can also further national ideological objectives to the extent these are long term and exportable. The key prerequisite here for successful long-term support and success is not to mix kinds of aid just to get one bill through a parliament or Congress but to clearly distinguish humanitarian aid, development or modernization aid, and military assistance for national security from each other; and, as one moves from the humanitarian to the military, also shift from multilateral to bilateral organization for financing.[62] It is unrealistic to expect governments of developed countries to give foreign aid without targeting it to be consistent with their national interest. But those nation-states with long-term visions of global strategy and a *positive,* community-oriented rationale for foreign aid will reap the benefits of solidarity with allies, while those with short-term, defensive, national security Band-Aid policies will find themselves lining the pockets of corrupt authoritarian leaders, who in turn, generate more animosity toward the donor than good-will.[63] Collective models of equality of economic opportunity should be cultivated as the rule in targeting aid, not the exception. Apart from aid, developing countries look to Newly Industrialized Countries (NICs) for models of successful *internal* development—longing for more independence.

In the post-cold-war economy, the International Labor Organization (ILO) reported in 1994 that some 30 percent of the world's labor force was unemployed or underemployed, more than ever before. By the end of that year, the ILO forecast that unemployment would reach 8.6 percent in the industrialized nations alone—the highest level of joblessness since the Depression of the 1930s. In the developing world, unemployment is growing in all regions except Southeast Asia and East Asia.[64] These exceptions to the rule, the East Asian **Newly Industrialized Countries (NICs),** provide models of successful *internal development* that give other developing countries the hope of finding recipes that will get them beyond aid to economic independence.

East Asian "Miracles": Postliberal Models

From 1965 through 1990, eight East Asian economies achieved annual increases in income per head of 5.5 percent (compared to less than 3 percent for OECD countries and less than 2 percent for Latin America). The eight "miracle" countries were led by Japan and followed by South Korea, Taiwan, Singapore, Hong Kong, and finally by Indonesia, Malaysia, and Thailand. Not only did these countries set an historical record for growing economically so fast for so long, but the wealth generated was spread through the broad population and was not concentrated in a narrow elite (as happens in Latin America). For example, in South Korea the income of the richest fifth of the population is eight times that of the poorest fifth. Compare this with Mexico and Brazil, where the richest fifth receive an income some twenty times greater than the poorest fifth.[65] Finally, success leads to more success: in the early 1990s there was an investment boom as private investors in the rich industrialized countries poured money into East Asian stockmarkets.

However, since the East Asian miracles involved economic recipes that included state intervention and other elements that were not part of the orthodoxy of the neoclassical economic liberalism of the policies of the World Bank and the International Monetary Fund, these two Bretton Woods institutions became concerned that other developing countries might be tempted to follow these "postliberal" models. To head off such collective learning, which would be awkward to justify from the "free market" perspective, the World Bank published a massive study, "The East Asian Miracle," in 1993. While hedging carefully between the "liberal" and "postliberal" or "revisionist" schools of thought, the World Bank stressed that the miracle countries maintained relatively low rates of inflation (averaging 8 percent annually over thirty years compared to 18 percent for other developing countries), sound fiscal policies, high domestic savings rates, heavy investment in primary and secondary education, and kept their economies more open to foreign technologies than did other countries. However, the World Bank did point out that almost all the governments of East Asia intervened in their economies, particularly in Japan (see Chapter Five) and South Korea. The most successful government intervention recipes were identified as **export promotion** (subsidies and attractive access to foreign borrowing and foreign exchange), **directed credit** (easier money access for targeted industries), and **interest rate manipulation** (keeping interest rates low to reduce the cost of capital for firms). But the World Bank noted that such policies might not work in the 1990s since the capital controls that permitted Japan, South Korea, and Taiwan to hold down interest rates and boost investment are much looser in the present integrated global capital markets. And efforts to subsidize exporters in key trading sectors are more apt to hit resistance and retaliation from industrialized countries in the GATT if such policies go against GATT rules.

But regardless of the implicit "warnings" of the World Bank, it pays at least to scratch the surface of the history of these economic "miracles" to see what elements were involved.

While there is a significant cultural background of Confucianism in the East Asian countries, which predisposes them to accept the wisdom of older elites and to learn continually for the sake of learning, the breakdown of traditional Confucian regimes by Japanese occupation is at least as important in their success. Japan destroyed the old conservative political order through colonial conquest—in Hong Kong, Korea, Taiwan, and Singapore. The new governments were able to develop "strong states" that were relatively isolated from local elites.[66] One is reminded of the same phenomenon, which occurred after World War II. At that time, the U.S. and its allies broke up the hold of the conservative elites (or "distributive coalitions") in Japan and Germany, thereby making way for their economic miracles.[67]

In addition to the destruction of the old order, Asian scholar Ezra Vogel identifies a number of other factors in the economic success of East Asia: (1) massive aid from the U.S. and international organizations; (2) a sense of political and economic urgency aiding in the mobilization of local support for industrial development; (3) an eager and plentiful labor force; (4) the nearby example of the Japanese model of development, technology, and investment; (5) the acceptance of a meritocratic elite—"industrial neo-Confucianism"; (6) rigorous university entrance exam systems; and (7) the importance of the group over the individual stemming from the Confucian tradition.[68]

The role of the Japanese model in the collective learning process cannot be overestimated. The American occupier and Bretton Woods institutions both forced the Japanese to become entrepreneurs and to free-ride on the security base provided by the allies, while financing Japanese development. (See Chapter 5.) By targeting the electronics and machine industries, Japan guaranteed itself both a natural process of technology transfer and an expanding opportunity for employment of its workers. When the G-5 forced Japan to revalue or increase the value of the yen in 1985, this forced Japan to further globalize and set up direct manufacturing facilities in other East Asian countries, transferring management know-how, technology, and jobs to provide the basis for their economic boom. And they had already become top competitors in certain industries causing the Japanese to update their own processes.[69] *A mutually reinforcing collective learning network, based upon taken-for-granted neo-Confucian assumptions and positioning to ride the waves of global economic expansion, was the critical platform for the East Asian economic take-off.*

In short, it is too simplistic to assume *either* that the East Asian NICs are models of classical liberal economic efficiency *or* that they can easily serve as models for other cultures. While Karl Marx appears to have been wrong in his negative prognosis for the "Asian mode of production," both he and Lenin were correct that state managers of developing countries would succeed only if they used capitalist tools and adapted to the technological change diffused by dominant capitalist states. And while the dependency school is onto something when they discuss the need for developing countries to create distinctive forms of economic nationalism, the argument goes too far in advocating an objective of autonomy from the world economy: witness the disastrous economic examples of Albania, Cuba, and Rumania, all of whom used a variant of this strategy.

If one avoids the macro-abstraction and determinism implicit in world-systems theory, one can learn from this perspective the importance of positioning one's state carefully in the international division of labor in order to put unique, national factor endowments in a competitive mix that is effective in global capitalism. Last, but not least, environmental schools of thought suggest that natural security policy and environmental policy may well become one in the 21st century. Those who learn to grow ecologically responsible industries may, indeed, refine a competitive edge that differentiates them from their opponents in an increasingly sophisticated global market.

The true message of the East Asian miracles is that effective models of collective competitiveness are most apt to be postliberal: not simply nuances of promarket, neoclassical liberalism, but complex mixes of market forces, public policies, and "velvet-gloved" government intervention by highly educated, well-paid technocrats who form flexible bureaucracies with status and staying power. The East Asian NICS have demonstrated that successful development can grow out of import substitution and export promotion policies that work together consistently.[70] The old Western polarization of thought between promarket (liberalism) and pro-state (nationalism) does not work any more to explain what is going on either in the industrializing NICs or in the industrialized OECD economies. Collective learning and positioning theory is more useful than others in distinguishing between *maintenance efficiency* and *entrepreneurial effectiveness:* between the *"stabilization"* policies critical for an *efficient maintenance base* (i.e., government-corporate-labor pacts that keep inflation in control, reasonable ratios between highest and lowest incomes of workers, equality of opportunity in a well-funded educational meritocracy, high savings rates, etc.) and the *effectiveness of targeted entrepreneurial risk-taking* from this base (i.e., through targeted export subsidies, directed credit, timely interest rate manipulation, freedom for entrepreneurship).

Let us consider a few examples. (For others, see the discussion of state strategies in Chapter 8.) South Korea shifted from a general export drive in the 1960s to a successful selective promotion of heavy industry in the 1970s. This success can only be explained by the extensive subsidies on capital use—at least 10 percent of annual GNP (assuring maintenance base stability) combined with targeting export growth for highly capital-intensive goods (the entrepreneurial side of the strategy mix).[71] In the 1980s, state managers shifted the strategy mix again to focus on developing technology (entrepreneurial effectiveness) and restructuring weak industries (more efficient maintenance base). South Korea illustrated collecting learning by mimicking Japanese organizations from the Finance Ministry to the Ministry of Trade and Industry down to the overseas trade association to promote foreign trade!

Taiwan used import substitution (maintenance) to accompany, not merely precede, export promotion (entrepreneurship). In this collective learning process, the government selectively managed the volume and composition of imports and fiscal incentives for new export sectors.[72] As late as 1980, for example, more than 40 percent of imports into Taiwan were tagged with various tariffs amounting to over 31 percent.[73]

One of the most market-driven of the East Asian NICs (after Hong Kong), Singapore, relied heavily on private enterprise for its development. Nevertheless, some analysts have found that the targeted structuring of the maintenance base was the most important factor behind Singapore's success. The state provided middle-range (five- to ten-year) tax relief for specified pioneer industries, heavy tax deduction incentives for new fixed investment in plant, machinery and factory buildings (up to 50 percent), and tax incentives and long-term, low-interest loans for research and development in the manufacturing sector.[74] There was a similar set of gradual maintenance-base targeted incentives and lifting of constraints in the financial sector of Singapore.[75]

Using the high growth 1960s as a staging ground and Japan as an inspiration and model for outward or export-oriented development in the 1970s (in contrast to the inward-oriented Latin American development strategies), the East Asian NICs provide examples of successful postliberal strategies combining state and market forces consistently for targeted growth—*provided* that the global environment remains benign, if not positive. Without such a positive global background, developing countries will have to continue to rely upon external aid to get export-oriented growth started.

THOUGHT QUESTIONS

1. What characterizes the relationship between the South and the North in terms of attitudes towards one another, trade, and ways of living?

2. Briefly summarize the borrowing policies of the World Bank. What changes were induced by McNamara taking over the presidency?

3. What are the key achievements of the Lomé Convention and why can OPEC be said to have inspired the push for a New International Economic Order (NIEO)?

4. Outline the mechanisms that led from the quadrupling of oil prices to the debt crisis. Illustrate a "debt trap" situation by briefly discussing the case of Mexico. Why weren't the loans officially declared in default and written off as losses?

5. Evaluate the concept of foreign aid for the developing countries after considering the different schools of thought and facts mentioned in the text. Dedicate some deliberation to the dependency thesis, the Brandt Report and the environmental perspective. Without foreign aid, is there really no Third World? (Bauer/Yamey)

6. Compare the cases of Hong Kong, Singapore, Taiwan, and South Korea in order to show the successful mix of "state" and "market" forces.

7. "Modeling" (countries patterning their economic systems after other countries' successes) is a major effect of collective learning. Be prepared to discuss several "models" that are currently in use as discussed in the text.

NOTES

1. Mahbub ul Haq, "The New International Economic Order," paper presented at the Faculty Seminar on International Political Economy at Columbia University, December 17, 1975. See Haq's *The Poverty Curtain: Choices for the Third World* (New York: Columbia University Press, 1976).

2. *World Economic Survey 1992* (New York: United Nations, 1992), p. 74.

3. Fiametta Rocco, "ADB Becomes Premier Source of Credit," *International Herald Tribune,* September 28, 1987, p. 10.

4. William Clark, "Robert McNamara at the World Bank," *Foreign Affairs* (Fall 1981): 171–74.

5. See Stephen D. Krasner, "Oil Is the Exception," *Foreign Policy* 14 (Spring 1974): 68–84.

6. Edward L. Morse, "After the Fall: The Politics of Oil," *Foreign Affairs* 64, No. 4 (Spring 1986): 793.

7. On prerequisites for successful producer cartels, see C. Fred Bergsten, "The Threat from the Third World," *Foreign Policy* (Summer 1973): 102–24; and Benson Varon and Kenji Takenchi, "Developing Countries and Non-Fuel Minerals," *Foreign Affairs* 52 (1974): 497–510.

8. See Karl P. Sauvant and Hajo Hasenpflug, eds., *The New International Economic Order: Confrontation or Cooperation between North and South?* (Boulder, CO: Westview Press, 1977).

9. Ibid., pp. 165–66.

10. Commission of the European Communities, "The Lomé Convention: The Stabilization of Export Earnings," *Information Development and Cooperation* No. 94 (1975): 2–3.

11. "The European Community in the World," *European File,* Commission of the European Communities (Brussels, Belgium, October 1986), pp. 9–10.

12. Adrianus Koetsenruijter, "A Review of Financial Cooperation under the Lomé Convention," *The ACP-EEC Courier,* No. 132, March–April 1992 (Brussels: Commission of the European Communities), pp. 4–9.

13. See *The Global Partnership for Environment and Development: A Guide to Agenda 21* (Geneva: UNCED, 1992).

14. Michael Zammit Cutjar, *UNCTAD and the North–South Dialogue: The First Twenty Years* (Oxford: Pergamon Press, 1985).

15. See Donald J. Puchala, ed., *Issues Before the 35th General Assembly of the United Nations 1980–1981* (New York: United Nations Association of the United States, 1980), pp. 73–104.

16. Sharon L. Holt and Helena Ribe, *"Developing Financial Institutions for the Poor and Reducing Barriers to Access for Women,"* (Washington, D.C.: The World Bank, 1991).

17. Christopher A. Kojm, ed., *The Problem of International Debt* (New York: H. W. Wilson Co., 1984), p. 14. See also Philip A. Wellons, *Passing the Buck: Governments and the Third World Debt* (Cambridge, MA: Harvard Business School Press, 1987); Miles Kahler, "Politics and International Debt: Explaining the Crisis," *International Organization* 39, No. 3 (Summer 1985): 357–82; and Michael Palmer and Kenneth R. Gordon, "External Indebtedness and Debt Servicing Problems of Developing Countries," *Columbia Journal of World Business* (Spring 1985): 37–43.

18. C. Bogdanowicz-Bindert, "Financial Crisis of 1982: A Debtor's Perspective," in *International Banking and Global Financing,* edited by S.K. Kaushik (New York: Pace University, 1983), pp. 203–204.

19. Luis Catan, "The Future of Debtor Countries in Latin America," in *The Debt Crisis and Financial Stability,* edited by S.K. Kaushik (New York: Pace University, 1985), pp. 17–31. Also see Jorge I. Dominquez, *Mexico's Political Economy* (London: Sage Publications, 1982) and C.W. Reynolds and C. Tello, *U.S.–Mexico Relations* (Stanford, CA: Stanford University Press, 1983). On money going into Swiss accounts, see Curtis Skinner, "The Next Earthquake," *Commonweal* (July 11, 1986), p. 397.

20. Ibid., p. 398.

21. Brian O'Reilly, "Doing Business on Mexico's Volcano," *Fortune* (August 29, 1988), p. 74.

22. "The Mexican Worker," *Business Week* (April 19, 1993), pp. 85–92.

23. Paul B. Carroll and Craig Torres, "As Elections Approach, the Uprising in Mexico Is Shaking Up Politics," *The Wall Street Journal,* February 7, 1994.

24. House of Representatives, Committee on Foreign Affairs, "Global Debt Crisis: Mexican Debt Situation" (Washington, DC: U.S. Congress, July 30, 1986), p. 58. See also "U.S. Senate Committee on Finance, Subcommittee on International Debt, Hearings on Third World Debt," April 6, 1987, 100th Congress, 1st session, U.S. Superintendent of Public Documents, 1987.

25. *World Debt Tables 1991–92.* (Washington, D.C.: The World Bank, 1992), p. 25.

26. Kojm, *Problem of International Debt,* p. 38.

27. Karin Lissakers, "More Funds for Mexico, More Debt Trap," *The New York Times,* November 8, 1988. For alternative views, see Benjamin J. Cohen, "International Debt and U.S. Policy," *International Organization* 39, No. 4 (Autumn 1985): 699–727, and Henry S. Bienen and Mark Gersovitz, "Economic Stabilization, Conditionality, and Political Stability," pp. 729–754 in the same issue.

28. For a neo-Marxist interpretation of the debt trap, see Cheryl Payer, *The Debt Trap: The IMF and the Third World* (New York: Monthly Review Press, 1974).

29. W.W. Rostow, *Why the Poor Get Richer and the Rich Slow Down* (Austin: The University of Texas Press, 1980).

30. For an example of the reformist liberal perspective, see Albert Fishlow, "A New International Economic Order: What Kind?," in A. Fishlow et al., *Rich and Poor Nations in the World Economy* (New York: McGraw-Hill, 1978). Also see Robert E. Wood, *From Marshall Plan to Debt Crisis: Foreign Aid and Development Choices in the World Economy* (Berkeley: University of California Press, 1986).

31. See Robert S. McNamara, *Address to the Board of Governors,* International Bank for Reconstruction and Development, October 2, 1979 (Washington, DC: IBRD) and R. McNamara, "The Population Problem," *Foreign Affairs* 62 (Summer 1984).

32. See Hedley Bull, *The Anarchical Society* (New York: Columbia University Press, 1977); Robert W. Tucker, *The Inequality of Nations* (New York: Basic Books, 1977); and Stephen D. Krasner, *Structural Conflict: The Third World Against Global Liberalism* (Berkeley: University of California Press, 1985).

33. Robert Keohane and Joseph Nye, *Power and Interdependence* (Boston: Little, Brown, 1977).

34. See, for example, André Gunder Frank, *Latin America: Underdevelopment or Revolution:* (New York: Monthly Review Press, 1969); Arghiri Emmanuel, *Unequal Exchange: A Study of the Imperialism of Trade* (New York: Monthly Review Press, 1972); and Samire Amin, *Accumulation on a World Scale: A Critique of the Theory of Development,* 2 vols. (New York: Monthly Review Press, 1974).

35. Organization for Economic Cooperation and Development, *Development Cooperation 1980 Review* (Paris: OECD, 1980), p. 99.

36. See Robert S. Walters, *American and Soviet Aid: A Comparative Analysis* (Pittsburgh: University of Pittsburgh Press, 1970), p. 240.

37. Gunnar Myrdal, *The Challenge of World Poverty: A World Anti-Poverty Program in Outline* (New York: Random House, 1970), p. 338.

38. See Leon Gordenker, *International Aid and National Decisions* (Princeton, NJ: Princeton University Press, 1976), pp. 57–58, 67.

39. Willy Brandt and Anthony Sampson, eds., *North–South: A Program for Survival* (Cambridge, MA: MIT Press, 1980).

40. See, for example, Steven Weisman, ed., *The Trojan Horse: A Radical Look at Foreign Aid* (San Francisco: Ramparts Press, 1974) and Teresa Hayter, *Aid as Imperialism* (Middlesex, England: Penguin, 1971).

41. Payer, *The Debt Trap.*

42. See Shlomo Avineri, ed., *Karl Marx on Colonialism and Modernization* (Garden City, NY: Anchor Books, 1969).

43. V.I. Lenin, *Imperialism: The Highest Stage of Capitalism* (New York: International Publishers, 1917, 1939), p. 65.

44. Theotonio Dos Santos, "The Structure of Dependence," *American Economic Review* 60 (May, 1970): 231.

45. Robert Gilpin, "The Issue of Dependency and Economic Development," Chapter 7 in *The Political Economy of International Relations* (Princeton, NJ: Princeton University Press, 1987), p. 282.

46. Ibid, pp. 285–86. See, for example, Peter Evens, *Dependent Development: The Alliance of Multinational, State and Local Capital in Brazil* (Princeton, NJ: Princeton University Press, 1979).

47. Krasner, *Structural Conflict,* pp. 97–101.

48. Immanuel Wallerstein, "The Future of the World-Economy," in Charles Kegley and Eugene Wittkopf, eds., *The Global Agenda* (New York: Random House, 1984), p. 279. For a critical view of Wallerstein, see Theda Skocpol, "Wallerstein's World Capitalist System: A Theoretical and Historical Critique," *American Journal of Sociology* 82 (March, 1977): 1075–90.

49. See Hans O. Schmitt, "Development Assistance: A View from Bretton Woods," *Public Policy* (Fall 1973).

50. Peter T. Bauer and Basil S. Yamey, "Foreign Aid: What Is at Stake?," in W. Scott Thompson, ed., *The Third World: Premises of U.S. Policy* (San Francisco: Institute of Contemporary Studies, 1983), p. 117.

51. "Foreign Aid: The Kindness of Strangers," *The Economist,* May 7, 1994, p. 20.

52. The statistics above are from Robert D. Kaplan, "The Coming Anarchy," *The Atlantic Monthly,* Vol. 273, No. 2, Feb. 1994, pp. 48 and 60. Also see Paul Kennedy, *Preparing for the Twenty-First Century* (New York: Random House, 1993).

53. Thomas Fraser Homer-Dixon, "On the Threshold: Environmental Changes as Causes of Acute Conflict," *International Security,* Fall, 1991.

54. Kaplan, "The Coming Anarchy," p. 60.

55. See, for example, E. Parson and W. Clark, "Learning to Manage Global Environmental Change: A Review of Relevant Theory," Discussion Paper 91–13 of The Center for Science and International Affairs, (Boston: John F. Kennedy School of Government, 1991). Also see Hilary French, "Rebuilding the World Bank," in Lester Brown et al., *The State of the World 1994* (New York: W.W. Norton: 1994), pp. 156–176.

56. First presented in R. Isaak, "Developing Country Recipes for Collective Learning, Economic Development and Global Environmental Responsibility," a paper given at the International Environmental Institutions Research Seminar at Harvard's Center for Science and International Affairs, Dec. 11, 1992. Revised version presented at the International Studies Association Convention in Acapulco, Mexico, March 27, 1993. Published as *Working Paper* No. 116, Nov. 1993, The Center for Applied Research, The Lubin School, Pace University, Pace Plaza, N.Y., N.Y. 10038.

57. Alan Riding, "Latins Want Bush to Help on Debts," *The New York Times,* November 29, 1988.

58. Sarah Bartlett, "A Vicious Circle Keeps Latin America in Debt," *The New York Times,* January 15, 1989.

59. Henry Veltmeyer's analysis of Latin America, which illustrates deepening and broadening poverty as the social cost of privatization: Panel on "Neoliberal Programs of Adjustment," International Studies Association Convention, Acapulco, Mexico, March 26, 1993.

60. See *Development Cooperation,* Paris: Organization of Economic Cooperation and Development, Dec. 1991, p. 172.

61. See "The Clinton Budget," *The Wall Street Journal,* Feb. 8, 1994, p. A12.

62. See "Public Opinion, Foreign Policy Making and Foreign Aid," Chapter 6 of R. Isaak, *American Democracy and World Power* (New York: St. Martin's Press, 1977).

63. Or, as economist Barbara Ward put it: "In all this welter of Western insistence upon self-interest and self-defense, one looks in vain for any consistent exposition of a *positive* policy of foreign aid, some general political philosophy to match the Communist confidence in world brotherhood based on Socialist production, some framework of solidarity between givers and takers of aid, some aspect of human concern beyond the narrow limits of common fear." In B. Ward's "For a New Foreign Aid Concept," in Robert A. Goldwin and Harry M. Clor, eds., *Readings in American Foreign Policy* (New York: Oxford University Press, 1970), p. 582.

64. ILO statistics and projections as cited in "The Labor Letter," *The Wall Street Journal*, Feb. 8, 1994.

65. See "Riddle of East Asia's Success: Economic Miracle or Myth?" *The Economist*, Oct. 2, 1993, pp. 41–42. *The Economist* editorializes in its interpretation with a proliberal defensiveness that is less muted than that of the World Bank in "Message in a Miracle," *The Economist*, Oct. 2, 1993, pp. 18 and 20.

66. See Stephen Haggard, *Pathways from the Periphery: The Politics of Growth in the Newly Industrializing Countries* (Ithaca, NY: Cornell University Press, 1990).

67. See Mancur Olson, *The Rise and Decline of Nations* (New Haven, CT: Yale University Press, 1982), Ch. 4.

68. Ezra Vogel, *The Four Little Dragons: The Spread of Industrialization in East Asia* (Cambridge, MA: Harvard University Press, 1991), pp. 83–112.

69. Hisao Kanamori, "Economic Development in East Asia and the Role of Surrounding Countries," Keynote speech at International Symposium on "Networking of Human Relations and Technology," Tokyo Keizai University, Tokyo, October 25, 1993.

70. Colin I. Bradford, "East Asian 'Models': Myths and Lessons," in John P. Lewis and Valeriana Kallab, eds., *Development Strategies Reconsidered* (Overseas Development Council Publication) New Brunswick, NJ: Transaction Books, 1986, pp. 115–28. And see: Robert Wade, "What Can Economics Learn from East Asian Success?," in *The Annals*, 505, Sept., 1989, pp. 68–79.

71. Wontack Hong, "Export Oriented Growth and Trade Patterns of Korea," in Colin I. Bradford and William H. Branson, eds., *Trade and Structural Change in Pacific Asia* (Chicago: University of Chicago Press, forthcoming).

72. See Robert Wade, "Dirigisme Taiwan-Style," in Robert Wade and Gorden White, eds., *Development State in East Asia: Capitalist and Socialist, IDS Bulletin*, Vol. 5, No. 2 (Sussex, U.K.: Institute of Development Studies, 1984) and Chi Schive, *A Measure of Secondary Import Substitution in Taiwan* (Cambridge, MA: Harvard-Yenching Institute, 1985).

73. "Riddle of East Asia's Success," p. 42.

74. Chung M. Wong, "Trends and Patterns of Singapore's Trade in Manufacturers," in Bradford and Branson, *Trade and Structural Change*.

75. Ralph C. Bryant, "Financial Structure and International Banking in Singapore," *Brookings Discussion Papers in International Economics*, Washington, DC, May 1985.

CHAPTER SEVEN

LIFE CHANCES, CLASS, AND EDUCATION

In general, women in developing countries with seven or more years of education (and presumably from the better-off classes?) marry approximately four years later than those without education, have higher rates of contraceptive use, and enjoy lower maternal and child mortality rates—so both they and their offspring have better chances in life.

Paul Kennedy, *Preparing for the Twenty-first Century* (1993)

Crisis, the Greek term that has designated "choice" or "turning point" in all modern languages, now means "driver, step on the gas" . . . understood in this way, crisis is always good for executives and commissars, especially those scavengers who live on the side effects of yesterday's growth: educators who live on society's alienation, doctors who prosper on the work and leisure that have destroyed health, politicians who thrive on the distribution of welfare which in the first instance was financed by those assisted.

Ivan Illich, "Useful Unemployment and Its Professional Enemies" (1987)

No human being can choose where or when to be born. Each individual represents a collective throwing of dice at this starting position, a cluster of probabilities thrust into a particular culture, family, and historical set of circumstances. Life chances are first born, then made. Those born rich naturally try to maintain their position: They can never really understand those in poverty without experiencing poverty themselves. Thus, the human condition is inherently tragic: Individuals are arbitrarily thrown into cultures, classes, languages, and historical conditions that are exceedingly difficult to transcend if they are to understand those born otherwise. Collective learning for the sake of a national or global community involves a lifetime of unlearning parochial habits, languages, and ways of seeing with which one is inevitably born.

By 1987 there were 5 billion people on the planet—double the population of 1950 and a billion more than in 1974. If all 5 billion stood shoulder to shoulder they could fit into Hong Kong: It is more the relative distribution of people upon the earth's surface that determines their life chances than the absolute quantity of people. Globally, the population is growing too rapidly in the wrong places, creating dense pockets of poverty and deprivation.

By 1994, the world population had reached 5.5 billion, doubling over the past 50 years.[1] One out of four human beings was absolutely poor in terms of living in conditions of malnutrition, illiteracy, disease, high infant mortality, and low life expectancy. More than half of these poor were small farmers, while 20–25 percent were landless laborers. Eighty percent of poor workers in these categories live in India, Pakistan, and Bangladesh.[2] In the developing countries, only 20 percent of the 300 million people above age 60 have any form of income security; 17 million people die annually from infectious and parasitic diseases; 800 million people do not get enough food; two-thirds of the illiterates are women; 850 million people live in areas of desertification; tropical forests are being destroyed at the rate of the equivalent of one soccer field per second; and these nations are home to 80 percent of the 12–13 million people infected with the HIV virus.[3]

Some scholars—all living in the rich, developed countries—have argued that the world's poor are materially better off in the late twentieth century than they were in earlier times.[4] The majority of the world's population no longer earns its living from agriculture, for example.[5] But what if I as a human being believe that I am worse off in a situation where I am no longer able to live off the land as a self-sufficient farmer? The industrial process of modernization works to homogenize life chances worldwide, rendering people impotent to satisfy their own basic needs independently.[6] Global industrialization makes the masses of the world population increasingly dependent upon ever-accelerating *global* market processes—creative destruction turned on high speed.[7]

An overabundant global food supply is mismanaged and maldistributed: As with any domestic economy, the global economy cannot depend alone upon the "invisible hand" of surplus production automatically to spill over and satisfy public needs. Life chances are indeed chancy for most people if left merely to laissez-faire markets. Poor nations provide few opportunities for those with talent to develop. Of course, the argument that the world economy in no way approaches a total laissez-faire free-market system is also valid. Still, the collective management implied by the doctrine of global Keynesianism seems more hopeful to the disadvantaged of the earth than the winner-take-all premise of Adam Smith's laissez-faire capitalism. The creative destruction of global capitalism is more of a threat to those down the class scale without the resources to buffer themselves from the uncertainties of change than it is to the wealthy minority, who may well perceive change to be more of an opportunity than a threat. Sociologists have noted that those in the underclass tend to perceive life chances merely as a matter of "luck," whereas those up the class scale have the resources and educational tools to give them the self-confidence that their life chances can, at least in part, be "managed."[8]

ORIGINS

The notion of "life chances" can be traced back at least to Aristotle's conception of the human being as a political animal inclined to live in cities or states and who often wants more than he or she needs, but is constrained by existing social and economic conditions and the competition of others. Early in the twentieth century, sociologist Max Weber used the concept of **life chances** to imply a competitive struggle for survival among individuals or types of people.[9] In the late twentieth century, sociologist Ralf Dahrendorf interpreted life chances as the odds of fulfilling the full range of human possibilities given the individual's social ties and options.[10] Weber's vision has a pessimistic tone of Social Darwinism, stemming in part from the social struggle for the survival of the fittest in the wake of the Industrial Revolution. Dahrendorf's more positive view of life chances, on the other hand, grew out of socioeconomic conditions created by the abnormally high economic growth rates in advanced developed countries in the 1950s and 1960s. Then it was sometimes assumed that affluence could be taken for granted—along with lower-level material needs. By the last decade of the twentieth century this assumption did not seem to hold except for a wealthy minority of the world's population.

Life chances, in short, is the concept that allows one to locate an individual in the class structure or stratification system of his or her society at a particular historical moment. From a materialistic point of view, **class** refers to how much you have got of what your society considers it important to get. **Status** is how much others *think* you have got or the degree of deference others give to you based on how you got the goods or go about getting them. *Social class constrains or supports an individual's life chances. If you are born rich, you usually sense social support for your efforts to maximize your life chances, whereas if you are born poor, your daily experience is more apt to be one of constant constraints.* Of course if the capitalist society into which you are born has a socialist revolution, you may find the rules of the game reversed, leading to social discrimination against the rich. Ever since the French Revolution, the importance of equality as a social value in Western democratic countries has become ingrained in public consciousness. Often the rich find it more comfortable to understate their wealth and social standing in order to reduce envy and potential social and political animosity from the majority down the class scale. The French Revolution served to delegitimize the aristocratic upper classes of the *ancien régime* once and for all. We are still experiencing its social effects.

Class position depends upon how many people are living together on how much space under which economic conditions. Before the Industrial Revolution, life for the majority of people was more often than not, as philosopher Thomas Hobbes described it, "nasty, brutish and short." The Industrial Revolution of the eighteenth century introduced technologies that were soon to lift the life standards of the masses way beyond the expectations of pessimists such as Karl Marx, who projected (wrongly) that the poor would become increasingly worse off. Indeed, despite the pockets of poverty and deprivation still remaining, by the 1970s much of the population of the United States lived as well as did the wealthy of the colonial era.[11] Such technology did little to sweeten the fate of those born in Bangladesh rather than the United States, however: In Bangladesh some 110 million people survive on one of the smaller gross national products per capita in the world, and two-thirds of the country was flooded in 1988, causing rampant medical and malnutrition problems. *Numbers, space, and natural resources (or disasters) are all determinants of class position in the world economy, not to mention the level of technological and educational development.*

The impact of numbers on personal welfare is notable in the differences in the sizes of generations *within* countries as well. The coming of mass production in industrialized countries did serve to diminish the importance of being born high or low on the class scale. But in the period between the world wars, industrial society brought on a new form of economic uncertainty: periodic recessions (or depressions) brought mass unemployment that could undermine an individual's life chances overnight. Fortunately, since that time unemployment insurance has been provided in most developed countries (such as the 1946 Employment Act in the United States). Nevertheless, *if one is lucky enough to be born in a generation when the birthrates are low, one will find oneself to be relatively much better off than a generation in the same country born when birthrates were high.* Thus, between the end of World War II and 1960, individuals born in the low-birth rate 1930s found their services in high demand given labor shortages (aggravated by losses of manpower during the war): They prospered and tended to have large families. They were the baby-boom generation of the 1950s, who, in turn, found the competition keen, their standard of living under financial pressure, and the temptation to limit the size of the family they intended to have an accepted social reality.

Baby-bust generations tend to bring baby-boom generations into the world, and vice versa, creating an economic cycle of life chances unforeseen a century ago.[12]

Social Class and Educational Level

While it is true that the higher the social class, the higher the educational level for most people, there are increasingly important economic and political implications in an emerging high-technology, high-information global economy. *Nam et ipsa scientia potestas est*—"Knowledge is power," wrote Francis Bacon in 1597. Today this has been reduced to "information is power" in an age of uncertainty when people are distrustful that such a thing as objective knowledge truly exists. Hence, *Kenneth Boulding's definition of knowledge as the systematic loss of information makes modern sense of Bacon's proposition in a postmodern world. The key question in terms of social class is: Which kind of information is an individual from the lower class most apt to "lose"—or, more important, to keep and cling to—compared to someone from the upper class? And what is the difference in lower-class and upper-class time horizons?*

The short answer to these questions from psychologists and political sociologists is that people from lower classes tend to lose the abstract and to cling to the concrete, focusing upon the present at the expense of thoughts about the past or the future.

Low-status or working-class individuals are typically characterized as lacking an adequate frame of reference or general perspective—or of possessing a fixed, rigid one. Such a mind-set opens them to suggestibility in terms of participation in extremist movements.[13] Lack of education of lower-class individuals means that they do not have a sophisticated worldview nor the ability to form abstractions from concrete experience. They demonstrate an absence of imaginative flexibility. They lack a prolonged time perspective, without an historical sense of continuing tradition reaching toward the past and without a cultivated ability to make imaginative, strategic plans to shape their own future. Typically, they react immediately to the present, absorbed by its daily routine business.[14] They feel driven to adjust to the outside world rather than to cultivate their own impulses by fantasy and introspection, according to studies of lower-class children.[15] Working-class people are not as apt as middle-class people to see the *structure* of an object, but are characterized in their perception by an action-oriented behavior in reaction to an object's *content*.[16] American attitude surveys over time show that *elites are interested in abstract values such as freedom and stability in foreign affairs, whereas the masses focus upon simple, concrete values such as improving their own income, housing, and schools.[18]*

The correlation between social class and educational level extends from the national to the international level. A direct relationship is apparent between high national economic status or economic growth and levels of primary and secondary school enrollment and national literacy. For example, the ten nations with the highest percentage of children aged between six and seventeen enrolled in primary and secondary schools in the mid-1980s— Denmark, France, New Zealand, Finland, the United States, Norway, Canada, Spain, the Netherlands, and Japan—were all among the top fifty countries in the world in terms of GNP. Six of the ten with highest enrollment percentages were among the top fourteen nations in terms of GNP.[18] A comparison of country literacy rates in Europe in the mid-nineteenth century reveals a strong correlation with rates of economic development in the same countries a century later.[19] Emmanuel Todd's 1970 data on literacy rates in various areas of civilization ranked those areas highest in literacy from which a number of the most dynamic newly industrialized countries emerged in the late twentieth century: (1) *Buddhist and Confucian Asia* (Taiwan, China, Vietnam, and Korea): 83 percent average literacy; (2) *"Indian" America* (Peru, Ecuador, Bolivia, Paraguay, Mexico, Venezuela, Colombia, El Salvador, Honduras, Guatemala, Nicaragua, and Panama): 70 percent literacy; (3) *"Small Vehicle" Buddhist Asia* (Sri Lanka, Thailand, Burma, Laos, and Cambodia): 63 percent literacy; (4) *South India* (States of Kerala, Tamil Nadu, Karnataka, Orissa, Andhra Pradesh, and Maharashtra): 37 percent, (5) *Central and Western Moslem World* (Syria, Tunisia, Egypt, Algeria, Iraq, Morocco, Sudan, Iran, Afghanistan, Pakistan, and Bangladesh): 35 percent; and (6) *Northern India* (Indo-European) (Gujarat, Punjab, Uttar Pradesh, Rajasthan, Bihar, Madhya Pradesh, and West Bengal; Nepal): 26 percent.[20]

Studies done of individual countries, such as France, reveal that only half of the economy's post–World War II growth rate can be accounted for by changes in capital and labor: The other half is ascribed to "residual" factors, the most important of which is education.[21] Powerful group learning potential is enhanced in countries like China, Japan, Korea, and overseas Chinese communities where the common Confucian culture represents a dynamic force in the receptivity to learning and in the collective capacity for cultural and economic development.[22] In Japan, for instance, neo-Confucian respect for knowledge and teachers extends basic learning throughout the life-cycle; information gathering becomes focused and "takes on a special campaign-like intensity when an organization recognizes an issue as preeminently important."[23]

The United States has demonstrated a heavy correlation between high levels of education and high lifetime earnings: The average eighteen-year-old male graduating from college was projected to earn more than $250,000 compared to $170,000 for those graduating only from high school, or $120,000 for those not completing high school. Education, of course, provides only a potential power basis or springboard for socioeconomic clout. The richest Americans explain their wealth overwhelmingly in terms of entrepreneurship, to a much smaller extent in terms of inheritance, with financial acumen and invention being even less weighty factors.[24]

National competitiveness—the transformation of an efficient maintenance base into dynamic, export-oriented entrepreneurship—is a function
not merely of the level of education and literacy in the country, but of the
degree to which this education is entrepreneurial (pro-economic growth and
technology) in orientation and group-consensus building in terms of social
equity and cultural values. There are conflicting interpretations of this "effi-
ciency-equity trade off" that can lead to such ideological polarization that the
political economy can make little headway toward either more economic
growth or toward greater social fairness.

INTERPRETATIONS

Societies, and Western societies in particular, develop cultural splits or polarizations that undermine economic effectiveness and are rooted in the educational and class structure. *Knowledge itself has no edge to it: It is infinite, overwhelming, diffusing, forgiving, and unforgiving. The individual—guided by class
and culture—must give knowledge an arbitrary edge—a slant or niche to render it useful for specific purposes.*

The Gentleman versus the Craftsman
or Tradesman

Within the industrial society—particularly in its British manifestation,
which served as the model for so many countries*—the archetype of educational success is the gentleman. According to economist Thorstein Veblen in
his classic *The Theory of the Leisure Class* (1899), this role model of leisure-class
life was characterized by a conspicuous exemption from all useful employment. Typically the occupations chosen by "gentlemen" symbolizing this
characteristic are government, war, sports, and devout observances.[25] Clearly
Veblen did not have a high opinion of the ability of these occupations to
contribute to a society's economy. The solution, as he saw it, was to resurrect
the status of the craftsman and technician (or engineer), demoting "proper"
or "useless" occupations to their appropriately low rank of contribution to
productive enterprise. In the process the "invidious distinctions" created by
the leisure class to shore up their status—their pecuniary trophies of material
success and ownership and conspicuous consumption of unnecessary luxuries—would be shown up for the decadence they symbolized.

The decline of the British economy in the twentieth century is often attributed to the gentleman's narrow, invidious distinctions, which are the soul
of elitist British education. The essence of British elitist education is marked

---

*Another example of the worldwide influence of Anglo-Saxon ideology capped with Eng-
lish as the global language of business.

by the values of exhibition, symbolization, self-expression, sociability, and consumption—as opposed to spectatorship, the management of things, social utility, task, and production. *This being-before-doing culture of sociability and polite behavior looks down upon entrepreneurship and mere money-making. The gentleman looks down on the mere tradesman, and in the process the basis of the British economy is slowly undermined as the hard-working producers are discriminated against socially.*[26] This class-based snobbism is epitomized by a story told by British journalist Claude Cockburn about his father, who had a first-class upbringing, following World War II. "A friend said there was a position available as chief of an interallied financial mission to oversee the finances of Hungary. My father replied that he knew almost nothing about Hungary and absolutely nothing about finance. Would this not be a disadvantage? The friend said that this missed the point: They had a man doing this job who knew all about Hungary and a lot about finance, but he had been seen picking his teeth with a tram-ticket in the lounge at the Hungaria Hotel and was regarded as socially impossible. My father said that if such were the situation he would be prepared to take over the job."[27]

The British model of elitist education has had more than its share of influence as elites in the developing countries have sent their children to Oxford and Cambridge to study and "ape the British gentleman" before coming home to manage their own societies. By socially discriminating against pragmatic, mundane, "hands-on" models of the mind, the traditional British priorities undermined the will to self-sufficiency so important for the autonomous development of the developing countries. As British writer C.P. Snow noted, literary intellectuals are often "natural Luddites"—a reference to a band of workers in the early nineteenth century who tried to prevent the use of laborsaving machinery by destroying it and burning down factories. As Snow observed:

> Industrialisation is the only hope of the poor. I use the word "hope" in a crude prosaic sense. I have not much use for the moral sensibility of anyone who is too refined to use it so. It is all very well for us, sitting pretty, to think that material standards of living don't matter all that much. It is all very well for one, as a personal choice, to reject industrialisation—do a modern Walden, if you like, and if you go without much food, see most of your children die in infancy, despise the comforts of literacy, accept twenty years off your own life, then I respect you for the strength of your aesthetic revulsion. But I don't respect you in the slightest if, even passively, you try to impose the same choice on others who are not free to choose.[28]

The Two Cultures
and Educational Consequences

The passage above is from C.P. Snow's influential 1959 Rede lectures, published as *The Two Cultures and the Scientific Revolution.* Deploring that academia was divided into two mutually incomprehensible intellectual camps—the literary intellectuals versus the scientist/technologists—Snow argued that this cultural divide split societies and helped to explain why the Soviet Union was training so many more engineers than were being trained in the West. The higher status of literary intellectual studies in traditional British centers of elitist institutions of education drew many highly qualified minds away from careers in science and engineering, diminishing the technological power base of Great Britain compared to the USSR. Critics accurately noted that Snow's thesis applied particularly to Anglo-Saxon cultures and was not as universal as Snow implied. Yet given the domination of the British Empire followed by American hegemony and the residual status of British and American universities as educational models, the consequences of the cultural split between the humanities and scientific technology should not be underestimated.

During the 1980s and 1990s, the United States continued to graduate many more lawyers and liberal arts graduates than required for existing job positions in the information-processing, technological economy, and too few electrical engineers and computer scientists for existing slots—particularly on university faculties. Already by the late 1970s, Japan was graduating 21,090 electrical engineers annually, compared with 14,085 for the United States, 6,649 for West Germany, and 1,749 for France.* Computers and electronics represented 4.3 percent of the gross domestic product in Japan, compared to 2.7 percent of the U.S. GDP, 2.1 percent for West Germany, and 2.3 percent for France.[29] This educational mismatch with the job market presumably signified a lack of competitiveness in the United States compared to Japan. *The major educational debate for the twenty-first century is to what extent high-technology developments will further aggravate structural unemployment and underemployment and what the training policy implications are for the sake of international competitiveness and social well-being.*

The U.S. economy shifted away from manufacturing (about 25 percent of workers employed) toward the service sector (75 percent of workers). Many information-processing jobs in the service sector may not require high-tech skills. Yet if American educational institutions aim merely to satisfy the needs of the existing low-skill job market with vocational, pragmatic curricula to boost their enrollments in the short term, the long-term needs in terms of theoretical and experimental research and development will be short-changed. The United States will pay the price in global competitiveness with the Japanese and other rivals. What is at stake here is not just a college "major" nor a professional goals portfolio but the education *structure* of the entire society: Short-term entrepreneurship does not always result in long-term economic competitiveness nor necessarily in social respect for the work required for such competitiveness.

---

*There are trade-offs for democratic freedom of course: The Japanese administrative bureaucracy allows only 2 percent of applicants to pass the bar exam each year, reducing the number of lawyers compared to the United States.

At the secondary, high school, and university levels, educators were initially deeply polarized about the extent to which curricula should be radically retooled with computers for the high-tech future. During the 1980s, for example, at Vassar College in Poughkeepsie, New York, the debate turned on whether computer facilities should be expanded to attract more students in a declining market, or whether limited resources should rather be used for other objectives—such as the hiring of new faculty. At the same time a nationwide debate raged in West Germany as to whether it was desirable for every student to learn how to use computers at school. While computer science was first introduced in 1972 in German high schools, there was controversy about "computer illiterates" who may have mastered reading, writing, and arithmetic but not this fourth "basic" skill. In the West German educational system, the computer market pressure (and opportunities) grew immensely by the 1990s. And there was a shortage of trained teachers as well as computers in all countries of the world. Student frustration with the existing educational system in West Germany extended to the point that the share of *Abitur* (the high school passport to the almost totally subsidized university system) graduates planning to go to the university dropped from 90 percent in 1972 to 62 percent in 1983 according to the German Federal Bureau of Statistics. Instead, by 1984 nearly a fourth of the *Abitur* graduates opted for job-training programs in an apprenticeship system that brings the workers in Germany to the highest technological level in the world. Economic competitiveness depends upon how a society treats and trains its *non-college bound* population.

With one of the highest percentages worldwide of high school graduates going on to study at the university level, the United States inadvertently declasses the value of high school education and those in American society who perform low-skill jobs not requiring academic qualifications. High school is thus seen as a mere transition to a higher-level education and is often not taken seriously. Those individuals (with or without high school degrees) desperately needed to perform blue-collar and low-skill, white-collar jobs do not receive sufficient respect in American society, making their job functions socially unattractive. This class discrimination effect exists also in West Germany, but not to the extreme that it does in the United States, largely because of the apprenticeship system that receives high respect from most people in German society. Ranging from glass-blowing to high-tech robotics to training to become a bank teller, the apprenticeship system in West Germany permits students of about age 16 to divide their time for 2–3 years between on-the-job training and theoretical studies (regulated by the state but paid for by firms including training salaries for students).* The *structure*

---

*By 1990, these dual German training programs had been "exported" to sixteen other countries, including a two-year applied international banking studies program in New York City sponsored by eight German and Swiss banks for local American B.A. students. For the origins, see Stephen F. Hamilton, "Apprenticeship as a Tradition to Adulthood in West Germany," *American Journal of Education,* Vol. 95, No. 2, February 1987.

of the German society allows respect for blue-collar and low-skill white-collar workers and for those who have no university education—the majority. The system structures everyone "in" and almost no one "out" in terms of social respect. One senses this in meeting people socially where it may be months or years before one person finds out what another does for a living, whereas in the United States one usually finds out within ten minutes. Social respect, in short, is accorded to the *human being per se* first and to his or her status in a job hierarchy only in retrospect. While the West Germans have a well-articulated social class structure, basic social politeness calls for understatement concerning one's job status and for sensitivity in asking what could be embarrassing questions of another in terms of how he or she earns a living. *Politeness implies that social solidarity or equal human dignity overshadows social competitiveness or divisive class discrimination—at least formally. And social consensus is indispensable for an efficient national maintenance base that provides a reliable take-off platform for effective global export-oriented entrepreneurship.*

Equality and Efficiency?: The Swedish Model

The commonplace Western assumption is that an inverse relationship exists between equality or solidarity and efficiency or economic competitiveness. According to this premise, the Western society with the highest taxes and greatest percent of government spending compared to gross domestic product (that is, welfare spending for the sake of solidarity) should not be an efficient or economically competitive society. But, in fact, this society—Sweden—has been often remarkably efficient and competitive given its expensive welfare system.

The Swedish model assumes that whether equality is compatible with efficiency or not is a question of organization. *If the society is overwhelmingly committed to full employment, equality, and democracy as basic values,* work *can be used as a proxy for efficiency instead of profit or money.* In other words, if efficiency is defined as the optimal use of resources, a maximum amount of work performed in a competitive market economy approximates an efficient situation (that is, a situation when the benefit or value of production cannot increase anymore).[30] Sweden's commitment to full employment resulted in an unemployment rate of less than 2 percent in the late 1980s—a period in which most Western economies had an unemployment rate six to eight times higher. In a country characterized by a strong labor and Social Democratic movement (typical for Scandinavian countries), the apparently dispassionate Swedes seem to have a passion for work, which they believe is vital for individual welfare. *Work brings self-esteem, a sense of a significant social role, a means to create social prosperity and self-respect.* The work ethic in Sweden appears to be almost universal, transcending the motive for profit maximization and permitting the society to limit the income gaps between people (that is, equality for the sake of solidarity). The cultural schemata is one of *social* individualism.

In Sweden, the life chances of all citizens are given higher priority than extraordinary salaries for competent superstars. Sweden developed the highest labor force participation rate among Western industrialized countries—82 percent (compared with 76 percent in the United States, 73 percent in Great Britain, 65 percent in France and 64 percent in West Germany).[31] This high participation rate may partly be a result of more than 80 percent of Swedish blue-collar workers belonging to unions, and even more telling—70 percent of white-collar workers. Swedish unions assume that even a small amount of unemployment signifies great losses in potential production and wealth, thus undermining the welfare state as it is forced to distribute money for unproductive unemployment benefits.

The inequality of family income is lower in Sweden than in other industrialized countries. In order of least inequality in family income are: Sweden, Norway, United Kingdom, Canada, West Germany, and the United States (with the most market-oriented wage structures having the greatest extremes). The Scandinavian welfare system is universal, giving all children (not only the poor) an equal right to good, free education and all people (not only the poor) access to free medical care—the best available. The aim was to restructure society toward becoming a classless society by organizing the public sector for everyone. The most needy stages of the life cycle—those of children, families, and the aged—are supported, while the most prosperous phases—those of the young adult and middle-aged—are tapped for progressively greater contributions.

But what does all of this cost?

Lots! The Swedes achieved a world record in terms of public expenditure as a percent of GDP—70 percent under the Social Democratic government. And the volume of Sweden's GDP increased 35 percent between 1970 and 1986, compared to an average of 47 percent for European OECD countries and 59 percent for all OECD (developed) countries. During the 1980s, inflation in Sweden was higher than the overall OECD average and higher than in European OECD countries (averaging 9 percent compared to 3.5 percent in West Germany, one of Sweden's most important competitors). And tax rates in Sweden were also among the highest in the world. The average full professor earned $32,000 in gross income and $17,000 net income after tax, for example. But given Sweden's generous welfare system, the professor had more disposable income than this indicates and did not need as much income as a professor in a country with a greater market orientation, such as the United States.[32]

What is striking in the Swedish equation is that, until the economic crises of the 1990s, despite the high costs in taxes and government spending, the Swedish economy remained competitive, the unions remained responsible, and the system delivered a GDP per capita that was higher than that of

West Germany, Denmark, Finland, France, the Netherlands, Belgium, and the United Kingdom (and is just behind Japan, Norway, and the United States)—all with close to full employment! Even unemployment among Swedish youth was down to 6 percent in the 1980s—substantially below the corresponding figure for the OECD countries as a whole.* So while Sweden did not deliver the highest abstract growth rates in the world and spread taxes as thick as peanut butter, hardly anyone was out of a job, education was free, health and pension benefits were among the best in the world, the average wealth level was significant, and the companies maintained high liquidity. During the 1980s, the Swedish stock market outperformed that of almost all other industrial countries. Exporting 40 percent of its manufactured goods, Sweden is the most 'international' economy of all except for "island economies" like Hong Kong and Singapore.

This stable, work-oriented welfare state formed the basis of an unusual program for the handicapped as well. In 1980 the Swedish government centralized employment for the handicapped under the Samhall Group—an amalgamation of all sheltered workshops and industrial relief work facilities in the country that were owned by the government. Based on the principle that meaningful work is more important than meaningful products, twenty hours of work were demanded per week in this group of twenty-four companies made up of 350 factories. But no one was fired for absenteeism or low productivity. Of the 34,000 workers in the Samhall Group, 29,000 were handicapped. The centralization provided more equality for the handicapped all over the country, more equal competitiveness, and a more equal cost structure, lowering the support necessary from society. Beginning with a 70 percent level of government support in 1980, by 1988 the Samhall Group lowered the subsidy level to 50 percent, making up more than a half billion dollars in savings for the government. The Samhall Group became the biggest producer of Swedish furniture and a large producer of textiles, with 20 percent of their products exported. The 1980 centralization resulted in 7,000 more people obtaining jobs by 1988 at less expense per employee (despite a 12 percent rate of employees leaving the group each year). Thus, a universal commitment to full employment and equality of opportunity in Swedish society provided a framework for self-respect and economic competitiveness for even the most disadvantaged groups in the population.[33]

For the 1945–1990 period, the Swedish case demonstrated that equality and efficiency need not be mutually exclusive *in a growing, supportive, international economy.* But "hedging" all equality risks can lead to bureaucratic stalemate, motivational malaise, and social instability.[34] And this extreme form of social insurance made the Swedish economy less competitive than other "leaner" nations in the global recession of the early 1990s. In 1991, the

---

*While the unemployment rate was still 6 percent (and rising) in 1993, if all those in worker retraining programs were counted it would be double this rate.

Swedes voted the Social Democrats out in favor of a center-right coalition government on a platform of drastic cutbacks in the welfare system to restore national competitiveness. In 1992, a $9 billion package of cuts was pushed through parliament. In 1993, another $2 billion in cuts was proposed, most of which were passed. In total, the combined cuts amounted to more than 6 percent of the gross domestic product (GDP)—a proportion that would wipe out the entire federal budget deficit in the U.S.![35] From the state with the world's heaviest tax burden (over 57 percent of GDP in 1990 compared to 30 percent in the U.S. or the 38 percent average for industrialized nations), Sweden managed to cut the top tax rate from 50 percent in 1986 to 20 percent in 1993 (compared to U.S. cuts of 50 percent to 31 percent).[36] The *social capital* or widespread consensus that enabled Sweden to establish a generous welfare state permitted the Swedes to cut back sharply when necessary for the sake of solvency, competitiveness, and a more private-oriented vision of their still-sacred collective work ethic.

Collective Learning as Unlearning in Kenya

Equality versus efficiency is not the only polarity that must somehow be brought into synthesis in the process of collective learning. "Work smarts" versus "school smarts" is another such split to be overcome, particularly in developing countries like Kenya, which is undergoing rapid modernization. In the case of Kokwet, a rural farming community in Kenya, the natives found themselves having to unlearn traditional models of childrearing. They needed to refocus educational development upon training children to work in the home economy at a tender age for the sake of adapting to compulsory schooling introduced with the modernization process. Whether the loss of traditional cultural values is worth the sacrifice for the sake of Western modernization goals is an open question.

Given the differences in physical settings, Kokwet babies sleep less than their American counterparts: Americans have more rooms and Kokwet children sleep with their mothers, not in separate places. By the time the Kokwet child is seven years old, half of its time is spent in work activities in the household economy—processing food, cooking, tending the fire, taking care of animals and siblings. In contrast to the emphasis upon play in the development of the middle-class Western child, work is considered the main task of the traditional Kokwet childhood.[37] Language development for the natives of Kokwet is minimal, stressing commands and socialization for obedience and responsibility in contrast to the focus upon expressive verbal individuality in the American culture.[38] A traditional concept, *ng'om*, translated as intelligence, implied responsibility to group obligations. But after compulsory schooling was introduced, which meant that work time had to be sacrificed to homework and test preparation, this concept had to be "unlearned" or differentiated into *ng' om en ga* ("intelligent at home") and *nq' om en sukul* ("intelligent at school"). Moreover, these two kinds of "intelligence" are generally agreed to be uncorrelated.[39] Whether such language differentiation, which is absolutely necessary for modernization toward the Western industrial model, makes the individual human being "more whole" than the old traditional model (or a better citizen, for that matter) is clearly a question worth pondering.

IMPLICATIONS

Each society has its relevant fictions or utopias, which guide its educational system, structure its class system, and condition the life chances of its citizens.[40] In Sweden, equality through full employment was the predominant "postliberal" vision. In the United States, individual freedom through various checks and balances of prevailing governmental powers is the ideology. The market dominates the United States, and extreme disparities of income mark its socioeconomic structure. The state is the largest actor in the Swedish system, and organizations within it usually tend to work to lower disparities of income as much as they can for the sake of equality, while still striving for competitiveness. Swedish individualism is social individualism.

Game theorist Anatole Rapoport did a comparative study of values in the United States and in Denmark (which is similar to Sweden in its tilt toward equality) using the famous "Prisoners' Dilemma" as a tool. The Prisoners' Dilemma gives two people, who cannot communicate, the option of maximizing their own interest at the heavy expense of the other person or the choice of settling for a more moderate payoff, which would be better for both people and maintain the basis for long-term cooperation. Two-thirds of the American students in Rapoport's experiment opted for maximizing their own interests (the tilt toward freedom whatever the social costs), whereas the Danes overwhelmingly selected the more moderate reward for the sake of cooperation (respecting equality despite the individual cost to themselves). Value frameworks or structures are passed on as if by osmosis in each society, predisposing individuals to behave in one way rather than another and to strive for socially acceptable goals. In Kokwet, Kenya, as we have seen, "work intelligence" shifted to "school intelligence." *Collective learning begins with individual adaptation to specific social norms, whether or not these norms are the best for the society as a whole or are helpful in national adaptation for the sake of competitiveness in the world economy. These norms become* **schemata** *or prototypes for learning.*

As a society is industrialized, knowledge is organized for the sake of certain human interests over others.[41] In Great Britain, the values of the gentleman have traditionally been ranked above those of the craftsman or merchant, and the most prestigious universities have cultivated a certain disdain for the mere man of affairs. This ideology was a contributing factor in the decline of the British economy in the late twentieth century.

In contrast, the strong work ethic in Sweden helped to keep that country competitive economically despite its heavy government spending and tax burdens. The freedom *not* to work was favored in old England; the equal opportunity *to* work was the guiding motivation of the Swedish economy. And a shift away from work responsibility in the household characterized modernization in rural Kenya.

The Collective Work Ethic and a Sense of Calling

The collective work ethic waned in Great Britain and waxed in Sweden, resulting in Sweden's greater relative success in the 1980s in producing sufficient economic development to service its welfare state while maintaining its competitiveness in the world economy. This interpretation is based on German sociologist Max Weber's *The Protestant Ethic and the Spirit of Capitalism.* In this classic work, Weber argues that the Industrial Revolution occurred first in Western Europe (and then America) not because of accident but because the asceticism of the spirit of Protestantism had prepared European society psychologically for this form of economic development. *Weber derived the spirit of capitalism from the development of rationalism as a whole: Capitalism is a special form of rationalism in which the individual is dominated with acquisition and action in rational pursuit of more acquisition as the ultimate purpose in life.* Idle pleasure and spontaneous enjoyment are not "rationally" part of this Protestant asceticism in which both uncontrolled consumption and spending are regarded as sinful; acquisition and profit-making become a **calling** or vocation, causing the capitalist to be a constant innovator in order to be better positioned for new acquisition and material achievement.

According to Weber, "The most important opponent with which the spirit of capitalism . . . has had to struggle was that type of attitude and reaction to new situations which we may designate as traditionalism."[42] Innovative action in pursuit of profits and acquisition regardless of the impact upon the status quo is the calling of the capitalist. The future-oriented, business entrepreneur is set into conflict with historical traditions or mere maintenance thinking. If a whole society is socialized and taught in this tradition, a collective capitalism can emerge based upon an ethos of "workaholics" who define collective economic growth, efficiency, and international competitiveness to be the main sources of their international pride (as in the case of post–World War II Japan). *A nation sets people up for certain kinds of collective learning, which may or may not encourage the calling of "ascetic, accumulative entrepreneurship" over the callings of roles that maintain existing traditions of the past. But if certain nations become tightly integrated "hit teams" of efficiency, information-gathering and competitiveness regardless of the social consequences at home or abroad they can set the tone of international competition in the world economy,* setting the standards to which other nations must adapt or else pay the price: The threat of Japanese displacement of American economic power in the late twentieth century is a case in point.

The significance of Weber's distinction between entrepreneurial capitalism based on the work ethic and the maintenance of traditions of the past in terms of economic development must be separated from Protestantism. Critics have pointed out that the spirit of capitalism was not the creator of capitalism as much as the emerging class of businessmen, and that people need not be "called" to riches to devote themselves fully to their pursuit without stopping to enjoy them.[43] In fact, the capitalist spirit appears to have existed long before the Reformation. Protestantism was more of a product of intellectual, social, and cultural changes toward a more secular, rational world-view than it was a father of this secular shift. Indeed, although the economic development of the Netherlands, England, France, and Germany, as well as other European countries, can be correlated with Protestantism, it could well be that prosperity leads to Protestantism rather than the other way around.[44]

One must avoid throwing the baby out with the bathwater, however. Weber's contribution was to stress the *psycho-cultural* bases or prerequisites involved in dynamic industrial development and to focus upon the importance of the cultural milieu in preconditioning individuals' selections of one "calling" and educational path over other possible options.

For Weber, a *social event* was an empirical or existential occurrence *plus* the significance with which it was imbued. One must go beyond Marx and the proposition that existence precedes and determines consciousness to recognize that certain ideological, religious and value constructs precondition occupational and economic choices. One is, in other words, not just "called" *from* but "called" *to*. Cultural schemata legitimate particular career paths. Certain societies are more apt to raise the status of the calling to become an electrical engineer or technician than others and these will reap collective economic benefits in the high-tech global economy of the twenty-first century. The West German apprenticeship system is a case in point. Research has demonstrated that crafts or occupations create their own states of consciousness (or what Thorstein Veblen termed "habits of mind") that are independent from other bases of knowledge such as an individual's social origins, the market position of a person's occupation, or even someone's own economic interests.[45] The logics and schemata of an individual's cultural milieu are becoming increasingly differentiated in the world economy. Family, class, occupation, craft habits, tax incentives, religious and ideological affiliations all can play independent roles in influencing economic behavior. *To maintain national competitiveness, the state must "call" individuals into certain fields over others in order to become collectively more effective in targeted niches of the increasingly differentiated world economy. Otherwise, the mismatch between traditional educational paths and emerging economic and technological opportunities will grow worse rather than better.*

In looking at the emerging needs of the world economy, Dr. Nancy J. Needham, president of the Institute for Corporate and Government Strategy, Inc., identified five technological trends related to training needs:

1. *Trends of reversal*—no longer beginning with the material and then asking what can be done with it, but beginning with a need and going back to the lab to perfect a material to address that need.
2. *Specificity*—sharpening the ability to pinpoint on an ever-more minute level.
3. *Explosion and implosion in terms of scale*—things are being done on an ever-smaller (microelectronics) *and* an ever-larger scale, thus increasing the number of projects that cannot be handled by a single company, institution, or government.
4. *Acceleration*—high tech has increased the speed at which things are done.
5. *Growing recognition of the need for cooperation*—this despite our ability to specialize and to be specific.[46]

Emerging "technotrends" can even be broken down into "new rules." Five of thirty such "rules" identified in 1993 by technology forecaster Daniel Burrus include: 1. "if it works, it's obsolete"; 2. "past success is your worst enemy"; 3. "learn to fail fast"; 4. "think ten years out and plan back to the present"; and 5. "find out what the other guy is doing and do something else."[47]

Equality of opportunity must be combined with a collective sense of competitiveness targeted at such emerging trends and structured into occupational niches that make sense in terms of a country's comparative advantage if a nation is to experience efficient collective learning. It may help to explore briefly the typical phases of national economic development and to identify viable strategies at each stage in order to better understand how one can differentiate educational structures for the sake of optimum life chances for the citizens of a nation. This will be the focus of the following chapter.

THOUGHT QUESTIONS

1. How does social class determine or influence life chances within a society? Compare life chances in one developed and one developing country.
2. Account for the relationship between education, social consensus, and effective global entrepreneurship by briefly describing and comparing the relevant particularities of the educational systems of the U.S. and Germany.

How does Sweden overcome the seeming inverse relationship between equality and economic efficiency?

3. Suppose a nation-state wanted to choose between the "culture of the literary intellectuals" and the "culture of the scientists/technologists" as the path for its society. Follow each course to the extreme as a hypothetical exercise and describe the characteristics of a society on its chosen course. (Remember, not both in the same society at the same time.)

4. Name a specific example for each of the five technological trends listed at the end of the chapter. Can you identify one or more trends that were left out? In terms of the five "new rules" then listed, explain what "Learn to fail fast" might mean, giving specific examples.

NOTES

1. Edward O. Wilson, "Is Humanity Suicidal?," *The New York Times Magazine*, May 30, 1993, p. 24.

2. *The New Book of World Rankings* (New York: Facts on File, 1991), p. 74.

3. United Nations Development Program (UNDP), *Human Development Report* (New York: Oxford University Press, 1993), p. 12.

4. See, for example, Raymond Vernon, "Global Interdependence in a Historical Perspective," in *Interdependence and Co-operation in Tomorrow's World* (Paris: OECD, 1987), pp. 22–35. Also, Jonathan Power, "Population: Don't Be Frightened by the Numbers," *International Herald Tribune*, April 27, 1987.

5. Karl Deutsch dwelled on this point in a lecture at the University of Mannheim, Germany, June 7, 1988.

6. See Ivan Illich, *Toward a History of Needs* (New York: Pantheon Books, 1978).

7. See Theodore Levitt, "The Globalization of Markets," *Harvard Business Review* 61, No. 3 (May–June 1983).

8. See, for example, Frank Parkin, *Class Inequality and Political Order: Social Stratification in Capitalist and Communist Societies* (New York: Praeger, 1975), pp. 76–77.

9. See Max Weber, *Wirtschaft und Gesellschaft* (Tübingen, 1956), p. 20.

10. Ralf Dahrendorf, *Lebenschancen* (Frankfurt: Suhrkamp, 1979), pp. 48–50.

11. Lance E. Davis et al., *American Economic Growth: An Economist's History of the United States* (New York: Harper & Row, 1972), p. 84.

12. See Richard A. Easterlin, *Birth and Fortune: The Impact of Numbers on Personal Welfare* (New York: Basic Books, 1980).

13. Hadley Cantril, *The Psychology of Social Movements* (New York: Wiley, 1941), Chapters 8 and 9, and Seymour Martin Lipset, *Political Man: The Social Bases of Politics* (New York: Doubleday-Anchor, 1963), Chapter 4.

14. Richard Hoggart, *The Uses of Literacy* (London: Chatto and Windus, 1957), pp. 158–59. For the American case, see E.D. Hirsch, *Cultural Literacy* (Boston: Houghton Mifflin Co., 1987).

15. B.M. Spinley, *The Deprived and the Privileged* (London: Routledge & Kegan Paul,

1953), pp. 115–16. Also see W.T. Grant, "The Forgotten Half; Non College Youth in America," *Phi Delta Kappan*, Vol. 69:408–14, February 1988.

16. B. Bernstein, "Some Sociological Determinants of Perception," *The British Journal of Sociology*, 9(1958): 160. Also see: Harry C. Triandis, *Variations in Black and White Perceptions of the Social Environment* (Urbana: University of Illinois Press, 1976); and Christine Oppong, ed., *Female and Male in West Africa* (London: George Allen and Unwin), 1983, esp. pp. 10–5 and 223–235.

17. Philip E. Converse, "The Nature of Belief Systems in Mass Publics," in *Ideology and Discontent*, edited by David E. Apter (New York: Free Press, 1964), pp. 206–61.

18. "School Enrollment Ratio, 1984," in *The World Bank Atlas 1987* (for 184 countries and territories) (Washington, DC: The World Bank, 1987), pp. 24–25.

19. C.M. Cipolla, *Literacy and Development in the West* (London: Penguin, 1969), p. 115.

20. Emmanuel Todd, *L'enfance du monde*, as cited in Jean Boissonnat, "World Economic Development: Some Observations," in *Interdependence and Co-operation in Tomorrow's World* (Paris: OECD, 1987), p. 38.

21. Boissonnat, "World Economic Development," p. 36.

22. William Theodore de Bary and John W. Chaffee, eds., *Neo-Confucian Education: The Formative Stage* (Berkeley: University of California Press, 1989).

23. Ezra A. Vogel, *Japan as Number One: Lessons for America* (New York: Harper and Row, 1979), p. 31.

24. Michael Cieply, "Mutiny in the Galley," *Forbes*, Sept. 12, 1983, pp. 126–137.

25. Thorstein Veblen, *The Theory of the Leisure Class* (New York: The New American Library, orig. 1899, 1953 Mentor ed.), p. 44.

26. See Charles Hampden-Turner, *Gentlemen and Tradesmen: The Values of Economic Catastrophe* (London: Routledge & Kegan Paul, 1983, especially Chapter 2).

27. *The Autobiography of Claude Cockburn* (Harmondsworth, Middlesex: Penguin, 1967), pp. 37–38. Also see R. Isaak, "Great Britain: A Socialized Economy in Crisis," Chapter 4 of *European Politics: Political Economy and Policy Making in Western Democracies* (New York: St. Martin's Press, 1980), pp. 99–125.

28. C.P. Snow, *The Two Cultures* (London: Cambridge University Press, 1969), pp. 25–26.

29. James Botkin, Dan Dimancescu, and Ray Strata, *Global Stakes: The Future of High Technology in America* (Cambridge, MA: Ballinger, 1982), p. 13. Also: R. Isaak, "Mismatches Between Jobs and Education: Collective Learning Across Cultures," a paper presented at the International Studies Association meeting April 12, 1990 in Washington, D.C.

30. Anna Hedborg (Director of Swedish Association of Local Authorities), "The Swedish Model—A Happy Marriage between Efficiency and Equality," paper presented at the "Sweden: Equality and Efficiency?" Conference at Indiana University, Bloomington, September 30–October 1, 1988. This section draws heavily upon insights derived from this conference organized by Professor Tim Tilton of Indiana University.

31. Ibid., p. 4. Statistics from 1987.

32. The above statistics (except for the 70 percent public expenditure as percentage of GDP figure, which is from the OECD) are from "The Swedish Economy: Facts and Figures 1988," published by the Swedish Institute of Stockholm. For Sweden's role as one of the most international economies in the

world, see Michael Maccoby, ed. (*Sweden at the Edge*, Philadelphia: University of Pennsylvania Press, 1991).

33. Based on a personal interview with President of the Samhall Group, Gerhard Larsson, on October 1, 1988, in Bloomington, Indiana.

34. See Hugh Heclo and Henrik Madsen, *Policy and Politics in Sweden* (Philadelphia: Temple University Press, 1987). But also see "Sweden's Social Individualism: Between Raging Horses," Chapter 10 in Charles Hampden-Turner and Alfons Trompenaars, *The Seven Cultures of Capitalism* (NY: Doubleday, 1993), pp. 233–260.

35. Richard W. Stevenson, "Swedes Facing Rigors of Welfare Cuts," *The New York Times*, March 14, 1993.

36. Stevenson, "Swedes . . ."; and "Tax Deform," *The Wall Street Journal*, February 3, 1993.

37. Sara Harkness and Charles M. Super, "The Cultural Structuring of Children's Play in a Rural African Community," in K. Blanchard, ed., *The Many Faces of Play* (Champaign, IL: Human Kinetics, 1986), pp. 96–103.

38. S. Harkness and C.M. Super, "Why African Children Are So Hard to Test," in L.L. Adler, ed., *Cross-Cultural Research at Issue* (New York: Academic Press, 1982), pp. 145–52.

39. Charles M. Super and Sara Harkness, "The Developmental Niche: A Conceptualization at the Interface of Child and Culture," *International Journal of Behavioral Development* (North Holland: Elsevier Science Pub.; Dec. 1986), Vol. 9, No. 4, pp. 545–69. Also see R.H. Munroe, R.L. Munroe, and B.B. Whiting, eds., *Handbook of Cross-Cultural Human Development* (New York: Garland, 1981), particularly pp. 181–270.

40. See Karl Mannheim, *Ideology and Utopia: An Introduction to the Sociology of Knowledge* (New York: Harcourt, Brace and World, Inc., 1936).

41. For an analysis of the victory of positivism in this process of development, see Jürgen Habermas, *Knowledge and Human Interests* (Boston: Beacon Press, 1972).

42. Max Weber, *The Protestant Ethic and the Spirit of Capitalism*, translated by Talcott Parsons (New York: Scribner's, 1958), pp. 58–59.

43. See H.M. Robertson, *Aspects of the Rise of Economic Individualism: A Criticism of Max Weber and His School* (London: Cambridge University Press, 1933).

44. See Kurt Samuelsson, *Religion and Economic Action*, translated from the Swedish by E. Geoffrey French, ed. by D.C. Coleman (New York: Basic Books, 1961).

45. See Joseph Bensman and Robert Lilienfeld, *Craft and Consciousness: Occupational Technique and the Development of World Images* (New York: Wiley, 1973).

46. Paper presented at the "Training for a High Technology Future" Conference of the German American Institute of Pace University, New York City, April 19, 1985. See "Quality and Competitiveness" and "Where to Target Training," in *The German American Trends Letter* II, No. 1 (Winter 1985):1–2, in R. Isaak, *German American Trends: 1984–1989.* Published by The German American Institute, Pace University, Pleasantville, NY 10570.

47. See Daniel Burrus, *Technotrends* (New York: Harper Collins, 1993), pp. 353–354.

CHAPTER EIGHT

STATE STRATEGIES
AND STAGES
OF DEVELOPMENT

But where do the moral values that drive wealth creation come from? They origi-nate in culture—*the word actually means "to work upon," as in* agriculture, *which means "to work upon soil or ground."* . . . *In any culture, a deep structure of beliefs is the invisible hand that regulates economic activity."*

Charles Hampden-Turner and Alfons Trompenaars,
The Seven Cultures of Capitalism (1993)

From the global perspective, the striking success stories in the world econ-omy in the late twentieth century appear to be Japan and the newly industri-alizing "dragons" of Asia, namely Taiwan, South Korea, Hong Kong, and Sin-gapore. These are tight ships in a storm of economic turbulence, which set the standards for manufacturing competitiveness in many key areas. Other looser, more democratic communities may enjoy more freedom individually at home only to find that their individualism has a high economic opportu-nity cost in the form of trade conflicts with other nations. Japan was permit-ted by others to rise quickly economically following World War II, using pro-tectionism to cultivate many "infant industries" until the Japanese could compete as equals on the world market. This opportunity was available par-tially because it was the only newly industrializing country systematically using these strategies at the time. Had Japan and the four dragons risen si-multaneously, they might well have been slowed down, if not stopped, by the key countries in the world economic community. Japan benefitted by a strategy out of sync with most other states.

The Japanese example of turning a situation of wartime defeat and dependence into one of economic competitiveness and independence shone through the world economy like a lantern in the dark. The Japanese mastered the principles of the world economy, organized themselves collectively to be effective in it by targeting their efforts, and converted weakness into strength, poverty into wealth. It was not a matter just of strategies but of structures—educational structures for setting up the most effective systems in which collective learning could take place; industrial structures of close government-business cooperation; financial structures of long-term local financing for firms; job structures of lifetime employment and commitment for that portion of the working population employed in key sectors of manufacturing competitiveness; and value structures of group solidarity and community loyalty, which encouraged short-term savings and sacrifice for the sake of long-term collective gains and security. (See Chapter Five.)

Theories of international political economy are usually abstract; the astonishing Japanese results are concrete. This chapter will attempt to relate the theoretical abstraction to comparative concreteness in state strategies at various phases of economic development. In the process, polarizations of Western thought—capitalism versus socialism, short-term versus long-term, homogeneity versus duality—seem to collapse.

As striking as the successes of the Japanese and Far Eastern "dragon" economies is the unraveling of industrial economies in processes of deindustrialization, deregulation, and cutbacks in welfare-state development. The linear Western assumption of progress has been turned on its head with regressive taxes replacing progressive taxes, disintegration replacing integration, illiteracy replacing literacy, and economic dualisms of various sorts replacing any single homogeneous standard of national economic development in so-called developed countries. The "postindustrial" society has been shown to be a misnomer: The competitiveness of the "service economy" depends upon the efficacy of its manufacturing base much as the competitiveness of industrial development depends upon the efficiency of the agricultural sector. The deindustrialization of both Great Britain and the United States in the second half of the twentieth century demonstrates that imperial economic designs have points of diminishing returns—as the Soviet economy demonstrated in the Eastern bloc with its desperate *perestroika* program. In 1989, *perestroika* released grass-roots democratic revolutions from below throughout Eastern Europe—from Poland and Hungary to East Germany and Rumania—making a shell of the one-party Communist state, which broke up as mass movements demanded political freedom and market-oriented reforms. But efforts of socialist states to move toward market incentives were not always one-way streets: In the late 1980s the People's Republic of China rolled back its free-market strategies after price increases outstripped wage increases and a 50 percent inflation rate and economic corruption caused disenchantment among the masses of the Chinese population. National student demonstrations for reforms were crushed with the massacre at Tiananmen Square in Beijing June 3, 1989. Liberal economic "shock therapies" were countered with postliberal reactions in Poland and Russia in the 1990s. (See Chapter Two.)

Despite the discontinuities stemming from the linear, progressive sequence of development posited by Western theorists, it is useful to summarize briefly the origins of these assumptions as a point of departure. To the extent that the dynamic of the late twentieth-century world economy is capitalism, competitive strategies of "state capitalism" are vital to understand.

ORIGINS

Conventional Western theories of national economic development assume a universal process of modernization, rationalization, secularization, and democratization. This focus is Eurocentric. Most of the social theorists came from the European tradition (and its American extension). The conventional modernization paradigm is the story of how the agrarian, feudal societies of Europe were transformed by the Industrial Revolution and the applied techniques of capitalism into modern, industrial societies of expanding markets, secular values, and institutions of democratic pluralism. The universality of this paradigm was taken for granted by Westerners. It was just a matter of time until other fortunate parts of the world would undergo European modernization, flavored with the egalitarian ideals of the French Revolution and the worldly aims of export-oriented, economic growth using the manufacturing sector as the engine and trade as the means. That everyone would be better off for this transformation was also taken for granted as the prosperity of free markets supported and stimulated the growth of democratic political institutions, thus increasing individual rights and autonomy.

Modernization and Purposive Rationality

Modernization as understood in the Western tradition is a process of disenchantment in which reason, science, and technology systematically undermine traditional belief systems, mythologies, and spontaneous ways of doing things. *Knowledge itself involves a process of disenchantment: The knower tests hypotheses against empirical experience, learning what the truth is as false assumptions are displaced in the process. Western modernization, however, turns this scientific testing process into a systematic ideology of applied reason or purposive rationality.*

Modernization involves a certain cooling-off process in collective learning as people learn to detach themselves from their traditional habits and opinions and to test their behaviors for efficacy in the real world. To be modern is to be cool. Science and technology reign; superstition and emotion are edited out. Armed with reason—or technology, which is but reason applied—the individual becomes more autonomous and free of traditional social bonds. The state bureaucracy, in turn, becomes more powerful and centralized in order to keep individuals from spinning out into chaos or violence against the law. But how does this process of modernization get going and take off?

In 1861 Sir Henry Maine suggested that progress entailed a shift from a "status" society to a "contract" society. An individual in a status society is accorded rights and duties on the basis of family and kinship ties, whereas a contract society relies upon contractual relationships between individuals, grounded upon territorial ties and enforced by the acceptance of a universally defined code of ethics.[1] In 1887 Ferdinand Toennies elaborated upon Maine's distinction, contrasting *Gemeinschaft* (community) with *Gesellschaft* (society). *Gemeinschaft* is characterized by human association based on affective, nonrational, emotional ties of kinship, community, and neighborly spirit. *Gesellschaft*, in contrast, is marked by neutral human relations of rational, calculating individuals whose relationships are distinguished by contractual arrangements aimed at maximizing an individual's strategic goals. Belongingness was displaced by cool, contractual exchange as a society was modernized by the Industrial Revolution.[2]

In his *De la Division du travail social* of 1893, sociologist Emile Durkheim stressed the positive advantages of modern society (which he termed "organic") in terms of its potential for individual development. This contrasts with the repressive and "mechanical" nature of traditional society. Rather than seeing the danger of class conflict in greater role differentiation in a modern society, Durkheim perceived greater individual opportunities and a social solidarity based upon diverse but authentic interests in contrast to the more authoritarian form of solidarity imposed by traditional societies.[3]

At least three distinct phases of modernization can be identified—the traditional, the legal-rational, and the technological. After creation, a society hardens into routines and traditions—the *traditional* phase. The **traditional society** is based on affective or prerational community relationships (blood ties), diffuse role structures (jack-of-all-trades), and ascriptive notions of social and political authority (that is, deference for being the son of the king or a witch doctor). Eventually, the traditional society becomes so encumbered with routines and rites that people are obstructed from satisfying their needs—the original purpose of the society. At this point, sociologist Max Weber notes that a social crisis usually occurs: Political authority flows away from traditional roles (such as the king) to a charismatic leader who symbolizes the solution to the crisis. For Weber, the key to modernization was the shift in authority patterns from the traditional to the legal-rational, with the charismatic performing the function of transition.[4]

A **legal-rational society** is one made up of contractual community relations (work prescribed by legal contracts), specific role structures (specialization rather than jack-of-all-trades), and achievement-oriented modes of social and political authority (deference given on the basis of accomplishment rather than blood ties to the king or the witch doctor). Of course legal-rational societies retain some of their traditional aspects, for no pure legal-rational societies exist anywhere in the world. The "traditional," "legal-rational," and "charismatic" are what Max Weber called **ideal types** of authority patterns—abstract theoretical constructs that represent or typify certain kinds of social realities.

Traditional societies become modern when their cultural norms of legitimacy are undermined and overwhelmed by the forces of rationalization and bureaucratization. Social thinker Jürgen Habermas defined this Western process of rationalization as the proliferation of *subsystems of purposive-rational action*. And far from being "value-free" or neutral, Habermas stressed the ideological nature of the uses of science and technology in this process of modernization.[5] Such forces of rationalization are marked by new bureaucratic reorganizations in legal-rational societies and by the dominance of applied scientific technology in technological societies.

In **technological societies** technologically exploitable knowledge undermines both traditional cultural norms and the social cooperation made possible by the legal-rational framework. Traditions are overwhelmed by scientific techniques, monarchs are replaced by technological maintenance professionals, roles dominate personalities, conditioning steers socialization: Humans as traditionally cultured beings are overwhelmed and dominated by the so-called apolitics of scientific technique and expertise. When Habermas in the late 1960s first pointed to purposive-rational action as being destructive of existing social bonds and community ties, the counterculture student rebellion (which latched on to his work) prevented him from being taken too seriously. But considering the displacement of foreign-language requirements (the study of at least one other traditional, cultural world) with computer science "literacy" in American high schools and colleges in the 1970s and 1980s, Habermas' insights have become almost conventional wisdom. Technological societies tend not toward technological limits but toward technological satiation as an ever-greater percentage of the population clamors to get on board.

The ideological nature of purposive-rational action or the transformation into a technological society is manifest in the unwillingness to see social reality in any *other* way without identifying this alternative as "old-fashioned" or "archaic." For example, some of the world's greatest poets (perhaps the least economically motivated of people) insist on writing first in longhand rather than composing on a typewriter. Similarly, they may keep to an old typewriter rather than switch to a modern computer. Each of these technological innovations speeds up the writing process, but the poet wants to slow down the process for the sake of quality and tone; some of the best poems require as much as ten years of quiet incubation! But modern technological society pays no one to slow down; quite the contrary—even when it may be in society's best interest. I recall being annoyed when first arriving in Bologna, Italy, from Manhattan to discover that the mail was not picked up each day (much less several times each day as I was used to) at the Johns Hopkins University Center where I worked. For six months I lambasted this lack of efficiency, this hopeless lack of modernization as my letters sat for three days before they were taken out. By the end of my three-year stay I found that I either withdrew or changed one-third of my letters, increasing their quality. Back in the United States, I miss the slower pace and opportunity to retrieve my flawed work before it officially becomes "an anonymous product." Similarly, in Spain I was amazed to see a plumber use the palm of his hand in a pumping fashion to unclog a bathtub drain. Without the modern technology of a "plumber's helper" nearby I'd forgotten many of the original uses of the hand. It may be that the failures of the technological society will eventually teach us to slow down and to become more human. Technology is ideology insofar as it becomes a way of life, displacing other ways that may be more humanly satisfying.

In sum, *the modernization process from the agricultural, traditional society to the industrial, legal-rational society and finally to the technological, high-information society presupposes a process of systematic rationalization and a cooling down of values—sometimes in abstract, dehumanized forms. That there is often cultural resistance to this linear assumption of economic development or "progress" is hardly surprising and may, indeed, be wholesome.* There is something in human collectivities that demands a balance between the "hot" (emotional belief) and the "cool" (rationalization and industrialization). To neglect this need for balance is to invite another Iranian Revolution—a case in which a Westernized, technocratic Shah attempted to modernize his people too quickly on the Western model and was insensitive to the resistance on the part of the traditional segments of Iranian culture until fundamentalist leaders struck back with a vengeance from which the world still reverberates.

INTERPRETATIONS

Although the origins of the Western sequence of modernization are not difficult to sketch, the multitude of interpretations of the process of state economic development and effective strategies involves an immense literature. The best one can do is to highlight a few basic themes as they relate to the fundamental thesis of the book—that there are universal patterns of collective learning which go a long way toward explaining the economic positioning of both the developed and developing nations in the global economy. "Universal" here clearly transcends "Western": Japan and the four dragons have illustrated that it is more apt to be an astute blend of Western and Eastern techniques that makes for extraordinary collective competitiveness than it is the contribution of any one region or culture. "Universal" has the scientific promise of getting beyond any particular culture or ideology in terms of effectively managing collective change.

Neoclassical versus Transformational Schools

Perhaps the main "civil war" between schools of thought on economic development since World War II has been the debate between the neoclassical and transformational schools. Derived from Adam Smith, neoclassical models stress the linearity of economic growth with collective learning most effectively triggered by market mechanisms (as opposed to being imposed by state intervention). In contrast, the transformational school argues that the neoclassical argument is far too simplistic and that successful modern capitalist societies involve major restructuring of sectors, social relations of production, investment targets, and institutional frameworks conducive to entrepreneurial risk and innovation. Indeed, Charles Lindblom's *Politics and Markets* could be seen as a response to this debate in which Lindblom suggests that the most useful political economy question is: How much state and how much market? This either/or framework, however, leads him to a rather typical American liberal stress on the antagonism between the state and the business sector, with the nontypical surprise ending: Big companies have won the struggle in the American economy by out-positioning every other potentially threatening interest group.[6] However, the oversimplifying abstraction—state versus market—underestimates the subtleties of mixed economies in the late twentieth century.

Rather than asking "How much state and how much market?" it may be more compelling to ask "How much capitalism is necessary for modernization?" And "How much modernization is possible without undermining cultural integrity?" In the late twentieth century many developing countries headed by governments publicly "anticapitalist" privately sought financial and technological support from developed capitalist nations. Ideological compromises were made to achieve the "takeoff" from agricultural to industrial stages of economic development—as in the de-Maofication of China and the early 1980s' emphasis there upon private economic incentives and "zones."[7] The intelligence of Mao Zedong permitted him to see that "purposive rational action" was overwhelming his socialist agenda, thus causing him to try to turn back the clock with his Cultural Revolution (against the intellectuals and technocrats) in the late 1960s. But it was too late. Once the forces of technological society have been released from the bottle, no magician can wish them back into it again by merely waving an ideological wand. Nevertheless, the leaders of the People's Republic of China reversed themselves again in 1988, fearing that entrepreneurial individualism, soaring inflation, and economic corruption were getting out of hand in Chinese society.[8] As we know from Chapter Two, their question must have been: "How much capitalism is really necessary for the modernization of China?" In Eastern Europe the question was reversed after the revolutions of 1989: "How much socialism can we afford to keep if we are to become autonomous and competitive nations in the postmodern world economy?"

Capitalist Incentives and Economic Growth

The historical evidence since World War II suggests that "the inevitability of capitalism" is less of a passing phase of modern development than either Marx or Lenin supposed. On the one hand, socialist economies were forced to introduce capitalist or private-market incentives to stimulate economic growth and industrial production. On the other hand, the postindustrial phase has proved to be elusive for developed Western economies, which have resorted to fiscal austerity and tax-cutting measures to rekindle falling growth rates in productivity and to raise stalemated national growth rates and national competitiveness in world markets.[9]

Economic growth depends upon the effective collective motivation of human activity—ultimately on a large scale. But human motives start small.[10] *Economic motives necessarily address the self-interest of the individual. Noneconomic, social, or ideological motives may spark unusual individual initiative at certain critical, charismatic phases of historical development and revolutionary transformation, but as passions abate so does the influence of this "selfless" collective form of motivation in the economy.*[11] *The stick replaces the ideological carrot and when the stick no longer works, the private market incentives of Adam Smith are (re)introduced through the back door.* Consider the private garden plots promoted to reverse agricultural stalemate in the Soviet Union, or the capitalist economic zones set up in the People's Republic of China to attract foreign investment and technology.

STAGES OF ECONOMIC GROWTH: A CAPITALIST MANIFESTO.   Perhaps the best-known summary of the vision of inevitable capitalist stages of economic development in the modern state is W.W. Rostow's influential book *The Stages of Economic Growth: A Non-Communist Manifesto* (1960). Rostow, an economic historian, describes states as interacting organisms whose development is marked by social, political, and economic motivations. *According to Rostow, all modern societies since about 1700 can be located within one of five categories in terms of their economic dimensions: the traditional society; the preconditions for takeoff; the takeoff; the drive to maturity; and the age of high mass-consumption.*

While not static, the initial traditional phase is limited in attainable output per head by "pre-Newtonian science and technology and pre-Newtonian attitudes toward the physical world." Given this limitation on productivity, traditional societies generally devote a high proportion of their resources to agriculture. This, in turn, involves an hierarchical social structure with relatively narrow scope for vertical mobility.

Rostow compares the second stage, "preconditions for takeoff," to the process of building up compound interest in a savings account by leaving in interest to compound with principal. That is, growth normally proceeds by geometric progression, and this requires a transition involving education, increased receptivity to modern science, and the assumption of the necessity of growth; increased investment in transportation, communications, and raw materials; and the emergence of entrepreneurs in the private sector and in government willing to mobilize savings and to take risks in pursuit of profit or modernization. The scope of commerce expands as modern manufacturing evolves using new methods. Still, the socioeconomic pace remains traditionally slow with low-productivity methods predominating. A decisive feature at this stage is the political development of an effective, centralized state. This state brings forth a new nationalism, creating coalitions in opposition to traditional landed regional interests and colonial power.

The third stage of economic growth, the "takeoff phase," is the watershed of modernity. Growth becomes the society's normal condition as old ways and resistances are overcome: "Compound interest becomes built, as it were, into its habits and institutional structure."[12]

In the terms of *this* book, a collective learning or adaptation process has taken place and becomes part of the infrastructure of social institutions and the motivational milieu of the citizenry. Rostow maintains that the main stimulus for takeoff in the Anglo-Saxon countries (Britain, the United States, and Canada) was technological. Not only is there a buildup of social overhead capital and technological development in agriculture and industry, but also a group comes to political power determined to make economic modernization a high priority on the government's agenda. Typically, the rate of effective investment and savings doubles and new industries expand rapidly, plowing back a large share of their profits into new plant and equipment. The new class of entrepreneurs expands, channeling investment funds into the private sector. Agriculture as well as industry are marked by new production techniques, particularly given that revolutionary changes in agricultural productivity are a precondition for takeoff. Within a decade or two the political, economic, and social structures are so transformed that self-sustaining growth can continue.

The fourth stage of economic growth, the drive to maturity, involves a 10 percent to 20 percent investment of the national income. This allows output to keep ahead of population increases and stimulates the spread of technology throughout the nation's economy. Fluctuations in progress and ceaseless shifting in economic sectors lead the society to discover its role in the world economy. About sixty years after the beginning of the takeoff phase, maturity is usually attained, involving refined and technologically complex economic processes. At this point the economy demonstrates the capacity to move beyond the key industries that powered its takeoff to apply modern technology and efficiency to managing the resources throughout the nation. The society shows that it has the technology and entrepreneurial skills to produce whatever it decides to produce (although it may lack the resources or preconditions to provide everything).

Finally, the economy moves into the fifth and final stage of economic growth, the age of high mass-consumption, which stresses durable consumer goods and services. Basic needs have been met. A high percentage of the population works in offices or in skilled factory positions. In this "postmaturity" phase, the further extension of technology is no longer accepted as an overriding objective. Social welfare and security emerge as primary areas of state spending in the society where consumer sovereignty reigns. Beyond this mass-consumption phase, Rostow envisioned the possibility of a value shift, subsequently termed "postindustrialism," in which basic material satisfactions could be taken for granted and most people would seek higher-level satisfactions.[13]

Rostow called this hypothetical future "the pattern of Buddenbrooks dynamics" after the novel by Thomas Mann that traces several generations of the Buddenbrook family: the first seeking money; the second taking money for granted and desiring social and civic position; and the third, born of both comfort and family prestige, looking toward music for satisfaction. The "Buddenbrooks behavioral dynamics" epitomized the changing aspirations of succeeding generations as they give low value to that which they take for granted while seeking newer sources of satisfaction.

As the late twentieth-century world economy shifted back towards pro-market, pro-capitalist models, Rostow's influential stage-model appears somewhat prophetic, which is why his theory is detailed here. Yet one must be wary of its oversimplification, pretense of universality, and Eurocentric (if not Anglo-Saxon) bias. The experience of Latin American industrialization illustrates that takeoff stages were never really reached. Takeoff was blocked by production bottlenecks, the saturation of domestic markets for consumer nondurables, and the difficulty that countries discovered in graduating to the manufacturing of consumer durables without foreign corporate ownership of such manufacturing enterprises. As a recipe grounded in various interlocking forms of collective learning, Rostow's sequence is more attractive as a blueprint than as a forecast. But it pinpoints key factors in the collective coordination of economic growth that cannot be ignored.

SOCIAL COSTS OF CAPITALIST GROWTH.   Every recipe has its opportunity costs: One may not like the taste of the meal that results, no matter how abundant it may be. Capitalist growth has social and environmental costs. Most of the negative social effects of capitalism are well known. Indeed, they are too often taken for granted by those in the "capitalist habit of mind" and too often underestimated by developing societies that hunger for the material luxuries of advanced Western nations. The free pursuit of individual self-interest creates a society of winners and losers. Moreover, capitalism appeals to those with a winner's instinct; socialism to those with a loser's. Assuming he or she will win, the capitalist wants the greatest share of the economic product that he or she had a hand in producing, paying as little as possible to the government umpire in the form of taxes. However, assuming one will sooner or later lose leads one to desire social insurance and security provided by the state even if the cost in taxes of this risk-reducing insurance keeps going up. Thus, *the priority of economic growth accentuates the distance between the winning and losing social groups, constantly redirecting resources to the winners in order to make them self-fulfilling prophecies and "locomotives" for the economy. To the extent capitalist incentives are inevitable, so are manifestations of social inequality.*[14]

Karl Marx, of course, took this as his point of departure, saying that the winners in capitalism were few and the losers many: Eventually he anticipated a point in economic development and polarization in which quantity would be transformed into quality as the many rejected a system in which they, as the absolute majority, were structured to be the losers. However, rather than the many becoming increasingly impoverished, they have become at least marginally better off in capitalist societies, undoing the collective motivation that Marx believed would lead to revolution. And, when interviewed, even those who are not better off in capitalist society are against turning over the system, for they seem to be confident that their children or grandchildren will be better off: They want a better shake and a larger share rather than a revolutionary transformation. Perhaps these attitudes can be explained by the findings in the previous chapter on education and class, which demonstrated those down the class scale are more likely to focus on concrete values today rather than upon abstract ideological convictions: mass consumerism *ad absurdum.*

Thus the classical liberal ideology of maximizing national economic growth over all other values is inherently unlimited. The increase of anything is equal to the additions minus the subtractions: More additions mean growth. Growth tends to expand until its ecological niche is filled—and the niche is ever-changing. The concept of equilibrium is thus a fiction—it is a mere temporary state when an ecological niche has momentarily been filled. Even the earth is an open system of disequilibrium in that when fossil fuels are exhausted, solar energy from outside the terrestrial sphere provides an alternative. Because everything is either in growth or decline—in a normal state of *dis*equilibrium—the natural, democratic political appeal has to be for more growth (not decline). *The crucial question of political economy is: Whose growth is it or who will it belong to? And further, At what social and ecological cost will this growth take place? The natural tendency is for each nation to run an export-oriented growth policy in order to maximize domestic wealth even at every other nation's expense, using the rest of the world in free-rider fashion as a dumping ground for industrial waste, unemployment, inflation, wars, and so on. Because there is no international police force, there is nothing to prevent the most powerful nation from maximiz-*

ing its own growth at everyone else's expense and distributing the benefits of this growth to a small minority of its people. In a world economy that has become a global village, any one nation's growth has social and ecological implications for every other nation.

However, even the successful state operated like an economic growth machine needs to keep its legitimacy going to maintain itself. *The key question for the legitimacy of the state is whether or not the marginal inequality necessary for economic growth incentives is based upon an "open" meritocracy or upon a "closed" concentration of resources.* The development of democratic institutions fosters openness. Even if one does not go as far as to accept Marxian class analysis, which argues that the appropriation of surplus labor in the form of surplus value by the upper classes will undermine legitimacy, a process of "delegitimization" appears to accompany the progressive "rationalization" of society as scientific and technical development is institutionalized. Sociologist Jürgen Habermas observed that the technical and organizational conditions under which social wealth is produced by industrially advanced capitalism make it increasingly difficult to assign status in an even subjectively convincing manner through the mechanism for evaluating individual achievement.[15] In other words, as the "rational" status-hierarchy of achievement of the industrial stage of development is undermined by technological advances in the "casino capitalism" of the high-tech, high-information economy, profit and social status often seem less associated with greater productivity than with successful speculation. Take corporate takeover efforts or computer stock arbitrage, for example. As the old industrial class system is undermined, individuals shuffle between social categories more loosely in society— particularly in the United States where status, not class, is the measure of social significance and the cash nexus in the 1980s became the driving force behind the achievement of status.[16]

The classical liberal ideology of growth assumes that capitalism will generate enough opportunities so that the disadvantaged can pick themselves up by their own bootstraps, thus eliminating the need for extensive redistributions of wealth by the state. *The bootstrap theory of growth as a substitute for redistribution has failed exactly to the extent that most existing capitalist societies shortchange open meritocracy or opportunity for the sake of established concentrations of resources and interest groups.*[17] Democratic institutions have become too abstractly representative and technocratic, if not oligarchical.

Greater economic production pulls up the entire society and provides for employment, but usually at the social cost of creating greater gaps between the rich and the poor and of sharpening the competition for access to meaningful jobs.[18] If the gap between the high earners and low earners becomes too great for the legitimacy of the social system to bear, a political shift to the left for the sake of fairer redistribution is a probable result. If, on the other hand, the pendulum swings too far to the other end of the spectrum in providing and redistributing more social services than the economy can bear, a deficit-cutting austerity policy and shift to the political right tends to result.[19]

Such pendular extremes in societies heavily reliant upon capitalist incentives have helped to lead some to conclude that capitalism has a tendency to create a social context in which it "self-destructs."[20] According to this interpretation, capitalist growth results in such a level of affluence that an overdose of leisure time and overeducated citizens are spawned—forces that undermine the bureaucratic rationality of industrial efficiency with counterculture lifestyles and socialist attacks by intellectuals. Antigrowth, antibusiness, antitechnology constituencies emerge in this "destructive" Buddenbrooks behavior scenario, undermining the legitimacy of the economic growth as the highest priority in society.

The challenge confronting postmodern managers is to find a way to structure the inevitable capitalist incentives and inequalities necessary for economic growth in a socially acceptable framework of meritocracy and opportunity so that both social equity and prosperity are furthered, thus making legitimacy self-sustaining as well as growth. Full employment is not possible without economic growth, but economic growth is quite feasible without full-employment. And as if it were not difficult enough to find out how to establish social limits for the sake of legitimacy without killing the goose that lays the golden egg, different rates of economic growth in different sectors of the economy complicate the problem.

Dual Economies and Engines of Creative Destruction

Capitalism is a philosophy of winners who become self-fulfilling prophecies of success. Winners consolidate their positions and attract resources sometimes to the point of monopoly. Successful centers of development thus tend to draw off resources from peripheral areas where they may be more badly needed. Dual economies operate at many levels during all phases of a nation's economic development. Indeed, to the extent that the world economy is driven by capitalist incentives and technological progress is permitted to drive out the old with the new at an ever-increasing tempo, any existing economic sector in any society could be considered "dual": what exists will soon inevitably become obsolete and be displaced by a more dynamic and adaptive development. State strategies may be most effective in assuming themselves to be obsolete upon birth. By permitting national institutions to cushion their infancy and to pay back their "opportunity costs," they plough themselves under with their own self-spawned technological replacements. But if effectiveness is the only social criterion, vast regions of the country may be left temporarily unemployed, in the dark, as it were, as the limelight shifts to the newest technological development. Few are in the economic sunshine at any one moment, while the majority exist in some kind of shadow economy.

The reality of dualism and discontinuity in even the most developed technological economies shatters the myth that one homogeneous national economy can be managed with supply-and-demand tools from a centralized cockpit and that macroeconomic trends can be projected only "from the top." While some centralization and use of supply-and-demand tools are necessary, they are not sufficient to explain, control, or project national economic trends. "The system" is a composite of systems.

Dualism and discontinuity are most obvious in developing countries predominated by small domestic markets and industries that produce low output over time. The emerging modern sector in these countries produces high output over time, composed of enclave economies directed toward large **metropoles** (metropolitan centers of large, developed economies) or toward the world market. And given the larger sizes of these developed or extensive markets, the modern sector tends to consist of large, capital-intensive enterprises. Dualism in both developing and developed economies results from factors relating to the market, the division of labor, and productivity. But the specific causes of dualism are usually different in the two cases. In the case of the lesser-developed country, dualism usually emerges because of industries of different sizes. In the developed country, on the other hand, dualism most often stems from the varying degrees of the stability of markets within the same industries.[21]

In *Modern Capitalism,* John Cornwall demonstrates that *the dual-economy model can be a powerful mode of explaining growth-rate differences in the more advanced OECD (developed) market economies* in the period since World War II. Cornwall stresses the importance of entrepreneurship and investment in manufacturing technologies as catalysts in bringing about qualitative changes or structural transformations.[22] *The key is the importance of demand and of the opportunity of absorbing less productive workers in a traditional sector (say agriculture) into a more productive manufacturing sector without unduly raising their wages.* The beginning of the development process entails the enlargement of the advanced sector (usually but not necessarily the industrial). At this stage there is no emphasis upon wages, for the backward sector has a backlog of underemployed workers who can be released for the advanced sector—workers who demand only slightly higher salaries due to their marginal productivity. Thus the industrial sector can be widened without the deepening of capital through hefty wage increases and expanding employment. At a certain point the backward sector becomes so small that stable wages cannot be maintained and intense structural change results.

Virtuous versus Vicious Circles and Learning by Doing

Cornwall's explanation takes **Engel's law** into account: that at different levels of income people have an elasticity of demand that differs (for example, in becoming richer at a certain point you cannot continue to buy more steak instead of chicken for dinner and shift your money somewhere else). Accordingly, various sectors of the economy grow at a different pace. In the process of structural change, technology gaps emerge in different areas in different countries. But the manufacturing sector is "the engine of growth." And following Verdoorn's law (the "learning-by-doing approach," roughly speaking), *there are numerous advantages that are derived from a fast-growing manufacturing sector due to learning-by-doing as workers go through new technological steps.*

The learning-by-doing approach depends upon a distinction between *static* and *dynamic economies of scale* in the manufacturing sector. A **static economy of scale** refers to a reduction of unit costs (and a rise in average productivity) as output over a given production period goes up. Typically, static economies of scale come from increases in plant, firm, or industry size. Longer production runs in the same production time reduce unit costs since production does not have to be stopped and started up again, less inventory has to be kept, and there is less loss of downtime to make adjustments for running through different models. *The Deming principle of increasing quality by reducing variation* seems to be at work here.* In contrast, **dynamic economies of scale** are "learning economies" since they involve continuous reductions in unit costs and increases in productivity attributable to continuous increases in output of a corporation, industry, or economy over time. The key of **Verdoorn's law** is the stress on the growth of output in determining the rate of growth of productivity rather than the level of output determining the average level of productivity.[23] Productivity growth results from a learning process, particularly in the capital goods industry, a process that can be maintained only by constant new investment.[24] The industrialization of Japan and the de-industrialization of Great Britain since World War II provide two illustrations of learning-by-doing in the context of economic dualism.[25]

Thus, *the manufacturing sector acts as an engine of economic growth* (or creative destruction) *in having not only backward but also forward linkages as it propels the dynamic-learning economy in a virtuous economic circle and demonstrates positive learning reactions. The strategic nature of manufacturing output becomes clear in the links between domestic economic conditions and external export and monetary results.*

The dual-economy structure sets the state up for either vicious or virtuous circles, which are critical for international competitiveness. In the

---

*W. Edwards Deming's essential fourteen points for managers aim to create constancy of purpose toward improvement of product and service by ceasing dependence on inspection to achieve quality by eliminating the need for inspection on a mass basis by building quality into the product in the first place, moving to minimize total costs by awarding business on the basis of price tag, and moving toward a single supplier with long-term trust and commitment. See Bruce Serlen, "W. Edwards Deming: The Man Who Made Japan Famous—For Quality," *New York Univerity Business* (Fall 1987/Winter 1988): 18. Or: Andrea Gabor, *The Man Who Discovered Quality* (N.Y.: Penguin Books, 1990).

post–World War II period, Britain, for example, often slipped into a **vicious circle** of sluggish productivity, which led to difficulties in exports, problems in the balance of payments, lower productivity growth, excessive wage increases, and a decline in competitiveness in world markets. *Typically, a vicious-circle strategy involves devaluing the currency in order to stimulate export sales in the short term by making them cheaper; but this has the effect of increasing inflation at home, thus causing workers to demand higher wages to match rising living costs, driving up the costs of production, and making exports less competitive until the government intervenes with another devaluation to start the circle anew.* An economy in a *virtuous circle* such as West Germany after World War II, on the other hand, *shows a steady or improving level of productivity at home, leading to competitiveness abroad with export growth resulting in opportunities for employment and investment, which, in turn, help to stimulate productivity, revalue the currency upwards to head off inflation, maintain competitiveness, and lead to an avoidance of balance-of-payments problems.*

Neo-corporatism

Neo-corporatism is another interpretation of successful capitalist economies since World War II that stresses not the underlying economic factors of production, labor cost, inflation, investment, and learning-by-doing but *the institutional relationships among major business, labor, and governmental interest groups, which are conducive to harmonious collective management and equity in representation by various levels of workers in society.* The original notion of *corporatism,* or "state corporatism," stems from a belief in political representation through functional, occupation-related institutions, not geographically defined electoral units. State corporatism is embodied in the right-wing Fascist regimes of Mussolini in Italy and Franco in Spain. The "new" or "neo" or "liberal" corporatism is used to describe post-1945 Western economies that still guarantee certain functional labor, management, and employee interest groups more or less a monopoly right to represent their part of society in government negotiations but without the coercive aspects of state corporatism negatively associated with the Fascist governments.[26] Free elections, democratic rights, and the ability to withdraw from negotiations voluntarily as an interest group are political characteristics of neo-corporatism, as contrasted with corporatism. Yet neo-corporatism still maintains integrated, functional "peak" organizations as the chief labor-management bargainers in the government—labor organizations for workers, business federations for employers, agricultural organizations for farmers, and so forth. Each worker or employer is automatically a member of the organization relevant to that economic sector in government policy-making. Neo-corporatist states can be contrasted with non-corporatist states with fragmented economic interest groups without such widespread membership that are only intermittently consulted by the government and where such interest groups rarely carry out administrative duties on behalf of the state.[27]

Neo-corporatist states tend to have large working-class movements, a heavily unionized labor force, and a social democratic tradition. The neo-corporatist states of Norway, Sweden, and Austria, for instance, have a unionized labor force making up more than 80 percent of the work force. The Social Democratic Party has also done well in these countries, particularly in Sweden, where it has dominated the government for half a century until the 1990 austerity program freezing wages, prices, rents, local taxes and stock dividends plus a two-year ban on strikes undermined the Social Democratic party, leading to electoral defeat. And in West Germany, often identified as having many neo-corporatist characteristics, unionized labor plays a strong role in labor-management-government relations, and the Social Democratic Party is one of the two major parties. A country with strong corporatist traditions is one in which the trade union leadership and employers' associations are committed to an ideology of social partnership and where the trade unions, employers, and the state cooperate in some economic policy areas. Usually the number of labor strikes is low in such states and "authoritarian" income policies are not imposed by the state. Switzerland is sometimes interpreted as a liberal form of corporatism—with comparatively low state involvement.[28] And Japan is sometimes described as "corporatism without labor" or "private corporatism." The Japanese represent a consortium of big business and government with labor largely coopted in unions organized *within* specific firms that often promise lifetime employment.

The countries with corporatist modes of policy coordination, whether of the liberal (meaning less state) or more heavily social democratic versions—Austria, Japan, Norway, Sweden, and Switzerland—managed to maintain relatively low levels of unemployment from 1974 into the 1980s compared to the mass unemployment that plagued all other OECD countries during this period.[29] So if full employment is the number-one policy priority, corporatist or neo-corporatist modes of policy coordination appear to be useful, if not necessary, preconditions for successful anti-unemployment strategies. The consensus on social cooperation reinforces the stability of the maintenance base of these welfare states. The key question raised is: To what extent can these societies afford the trade-off costs in terms of economic growth and entrepreneurial innovation implied by state-centered as opposed to more pluralistic market-oriented economies? Or could it be that this whole notion of "trade-off" is a short-term, polarized Western black-and-white interpretation of phenomena that can be subtly integrated into a tight state strategy that provides both high levels of employment and high levels of economic growth and entrepreneurship (Japan?)? Perhaps it is useful to identify the dominant types of state strategies that emerged in the 1970s and 1980s in order to determine which mixes of these types are most fruitful in terms of maximizing both the objectives of full employment and dynamic economic growth.

A Typology of State Strategies

An empirical examination of the strategies of both hard and soft currency states undertaken in the 1970s in order to discover which strategies were most effective in coping with inflation resulted in the derivation of four ideal typical strategies at the individual, corporate, and state levels.[30] Each strategy was broken down into risk orientation, time orientation, guiding motive, consumption pattern, and characteristic policy or portfolio mix. The four types are the modes of conduct of the Defeatist, the Free-rider, the Maintenance Man, and the Entrepreneur—"pure" (Weberian) types of strategies that in any concrete situation are usually mixed. Table 8–1 summarizes them.

Rather than starting with preconceptions, these types were derived by observing the various reactions to the global inflation of the 1970s. These reactions then were sorted into their common characteristics, with four categories emerging as predominant. **Defeatist strategies** are past-oriented and defensive, designed to take as few risks as possible, while seeking out bargains. Defeatist policies typically focus on security and passive attempts to head off the worst possible outcomes. Total ideological rigidity or total compromise out of fear of loss are not uncommon to this type.

Free-rider strategies, in contrast, are present-oriented with a more active than passive set of policies aimed at high risk as long as someone else is paying or the cost is low. Free-rider policies aim to export domestic costs to others, to take on debt, to postpone repayment of debt, to devalue currency for short-term export growth (postponing the costs of the "vicious circle" until tomorrow), to subsidize lame-duck industries, to index wages of existing workers to inflation increases, and to use selected protectionism when advantageous.

Maintenance strategies are grounded in present-to-middle-range-future time perspective, strive for limited risks at moderate cost, and try just to keep up with the economic or business cycle. Maintenance policies stress co-opting change to keep costs and benefits in balance for the sake of stability or equilibrium: co-determination between unions and management, for example. The thrust of the maintenance strategy is to manage the status quo efficiently, anticipating change in order to adjust the political economy in time to maintain its stability.

Entrepreneurial strategies, in contrast, are future-oriented, aimed at taking high risks even at high costs in order to put most of one's chips in the avant-garde, high-growth sectors that will permit one to come out significantly ahead of the short-term business cycle or economic average. The focus is upon outwitting the future with extraordinary achievement, creative high-

TABLE 8-1

Ideal Types of State Strategies	Time Perspective	Risk Orientation	Characteristic Policies
DEFEATIST	Past-oriented	As few risks as possible: fear of loss and bargain-hunting	*Focus* on security and defending past policies and values Passive and defensive policies to head off worst outcomes Rigid adherence to past ideologies or total compromise Aid requests at lowest interest rates for decaying infrastructure and to meet daily food and energy needs
FREE-RIDER	Present-oriented	High risks at low cost	*Focus* on exporting domestic costs to others, on loans, postponing payments, on exploiting the international arena for short-term benefits (i.e., devaluations) Indexation; agricultural subsidies Government subsidies for lame-duck industries Periodically tapping IMF and others for loans Wage and price controls when necessary Selected protectionism when advantageous
MAINTENANCE	Present-middle-range future	Limited risks at moderate cost	*Focus* on coopting change to keep costs and benefits in balance for stability Use of voluntary wage and price guidelines Tight monetary and fiscal policies as needed Preservation of steady exchange rate Stress on bringing federal budget more into balance Simultaneous cuts in taxes and government spending Elimination of excessive imported labor, immigration limits Co-determination policy with unions and management
ENTREPRENEURIAL	Future-oriented	High risks even at high costs	*Focus* on outwitting the future with extraordinary achievement, productivity, innovation Elimination of indexation Elimination of subsidies for lame-duck industries, farms, agriculture Payoffs to stimulate productivity and export-oriented growth (through tax cuts, stimuli, etc.) Eliminate double-tax on corporate gains, encourage long-term capital investment and research and development Support accelerated depreciation based on replacement cost State subsidies for long-range technological breakthroughs Antitrust legislation and seed money for startling small businesses

risk investment for boosting productivity, and effective innovation for the sake of competitiveness. This involves shifting support from declining, or sunset, industries to sunrise, or emerging, high-tech and high-information sectors, creating payoffs for research and development, and stimulating both productivity and export-oriented growth. Targeted state subsidies for long-range technological breakthroughs are an example, while subsidies for lame-duck industries, agriculture, and declining sectors are apt to be cut.

The next step in theory-building using this approach is to hypothesize into which priority the types are most apt to fall in the typical strategic mix or constellation at different stages of state development. Such clusters of hypothetical priorities are illustrated in Table 8–2.

Strategy clusters or portfolios articulate the choice menus available to state managers at different phases of economic development. Typically lesser-developed states find themselves locked into defeatist and free-rider strategies without the financial or technological resources to break out and to modernize. The precondition for this takeoff is an entrepreneurial strategy applied initially to increasing agricultural productivity and efficiency and secondarily to uncovering manufacturing niches in which the lesser-developed country has significant potential comparative advantages. Modernization away from the traditional, agricultural economy is therefore measurable in terms of the extent to which entrepreneurial strategies displace defeatist and free-rider strategies targeted toward agricultural self-sufficiency and the emergence of industrial competitiveness.

When India and the People's Republic of China became self-sufficient in food, their next step was to use targeted entrepreneurial strategies aimed at the global economy both in terms of agricultural and manufactured products. India, for example, targeted machine tools in niches of the U.S. market, which had become too small to interest large American manufacturers any longer. But in addition to these openings led by entrepreneurial strategies, both China and India were heavily preoccupied with maintenance strategies aimed to increase the efficiency of their domestic economies, to ensure domestic political stability, and to create an atmosphere attractive to future foreign investment and technology transfers. Nor were these countries beyond using free-rider strategies in efforts to secure development loans from abroad—whether from the World Bank, commercial banks, or foreign gov-

TABLE 8–2   Hypothetical Priorities Among Strategies at Different Stages of State Development

Agricultural	Newly Industrializing	Industrial– Super-industrial	Postindustrial or Postmodern
1. Defeatist	1. Entrepreneurial	1. Maintenance	1. Free-rider
2. Free-rider	2. Maintenance	2. Entrepreneurial	2. Maintenance
3. Entrepreneurial	3. Free-rider	3. Free-rider	3. Defeatist/Entrepreneurial

ernments interested in better diplomatic relations. Indeed, there is usually a free-rider component to entrepreneurship—spending someone else's money.

In the case of China, the maintenance base is a centrally steered economy within which entrepreneurial free-market islands are targeted to make the political economy more flexible and to increase individual initiative (see Chapter 2). Outside China, international organizations and the experiences of smaller newly industrialized Asian countries are used as free-rider opportunities of surrogate experience and potential sources for hard currency and technological innovation—what some have called the **"Greater China" strategy** of letting other Asian countries be the pilot tests for China's long-term positioning. The Chinese maintenance base remains as a vertical, centralized structure, not comparable with the horizontally structured market economies of the West—what the Chinese see as "institutionalized chaos."[31]

As we move to the industrial–super-industrial* phase of development, efficient maintenance strategies become the dominant preoccupation supplemented by entrepreneurial export-oriented growth and stimulation for innovation, research, and development at home. Free-rider strategies are used as icing on the cake whenever opportunities arise to reduce costs at home or to exploit unusual exchange-rate and financing opportunities abroad. Japan is the clearest example of this combination of industrial–super-industrial strategies, which might be summed up as **maintenpreneurial:** the overwhelming efficiency concentration at the maintenance base providing the opportunities for entrepreneurial effectiveness at home and abroad, or, using the maintenance base as a launching pad for entrepreneurial risk. This strategy synthesis is probably the optimum strategic structure for the "learning economy" or "learning state" in the world economy: always reducing costs and increasing efficiency at home and using the resources this frees up to take growth-oriented, market-share expanding, targeted risks for the long term. The sophistication of the Japanese maintenance base takes years of study to understand fully. (See Chapter 5.) An extremely hierarchical educational and social structure with Confucian value elements of humility, respect for knowledge and one's elders provides the basis for a society that smothers problems with targeted information, uses group decision-making processes to increase motivation, cuts costs and reduces errors, and relies upon a neo-corporatist interrelationship between government ministries and big business to give priority to collective learning and economic adaptation.[32] From an economic and competitive business viewpoint, Japan's learning culture is formidable in no small part because it integrates simplistic Western polarities (centralization and decentralization), prefers the pragmatic and concrete to

---

*"Super-industrial" refers to the large size and scale of modern enterprise and its social and environmental impact. See Herman Kahn and J.B. Phelps, "The Economic Future," in F. Feather, ed., *Through the '80s* (Washington, DC: World Future Society, 1980), pp. 202–09.

the intellectually abstract, and focuses upon improving existing innovations by cutting costs and increasing quality rather than aiming to discover something new under the sun.[33]

Another, more maintenance-oriented maintenpreneurial strategy is represented by Germany with its **social market economy,** which presupposes a delicate but dynamic balance between social stability and free-market entrepreneurship.[34] (See Chapter 5). Social stability results from widespread consensus on a maintenance base of fundamental social rights and duties protected by the government. Recent efforts to decode the meaning of "social" in the social market economy resulted in conceiving social as the collective efforts within a market economy to create a situation where ideally everyone in the society is involved in the market forces and is thereby guaranteed a direct share of the product of the market economy.[35] From this maintenance base of social consensus, corporate teams of aggressive entrepreneurs are given the freedom to operate worldwide, knowing in advance their range of domestic responsibility. The stable, "apolitical" social base, in short, provides the predictability that makes long-term economic planning and investment possible on the part of the private sector. The social market economy is grounded on the German distinctions between *economic order* (the state-stabilized structure or maintenance base) and *economic process* (free-market entrepreneurship) and between state intervention (*Marktbeeinflussungen*) and state *control* of the market. For instance, if the policy objective is to lower the cost of housing for the poor, the payment of a housing allowance is consistent with a free market in housing (and free-market assumption of social economy), whereas rent control is not.

Since 1973, the emergence of the floating exchange-rate regime, the volatility of oil prices, and the policy-linked distortions of the value of the dollar warped the context of global economic development and severely limited the strategy options available to all nation-states, rich or poor. Still, the hard-currency maintenpreneurial countries had much more flexibility than did the majority of the world's soft-currency nations whether the fashionable policies were inflationary or (more commonly) anti-inflationary. Able to take their maintenance domestic frameworks for granted, these hard-currency countries were able to pursue entrepreneurial strategies using the Eurodollar markets as free-riders to reduce the cost of imported inflation. The successful West German strategy in the "floating game," for example, was to appreciate the value of the mark to push down imported inflation, but not to the level of global inflation, thus preserving West German export markets.[36] Hooking their own currency to the value of the West German mark, the Austrians maintained a hard-currency policy, using foreign-exchange-rate subsidized capital imports to finance domestic restructuring and development.[37] Both in the industrial–super-industrial category of development, West Germany and Austria used the priority of stable maintenance strategies as a base for secondary entrepreneurial and free-rider strategies in order to protect themselves from inflation and to maintain their international competitiveness.

The Swiss had another effective brand of maintenpreneurial strategy. They used monetary policy to neutralize foreign inflows through a wide range of controls. And they used their effective federal Export Risk Insurance scheme to protect Swiss exporters from all sorts of risks stemming from transfer, bad debts, production, politics, and particularly the threat to their prices and profits resulting from the appreciation of the Swiss franc.[38]

The strategies of weak-currency countries in the agricultural development category, on the other hand, aimed for mere maintenance as a goal. They used depreciation to improve their balance of current accounts and to substitute for imported depression or unemployment. Taking economic advice from the Cambridge School, developing countries in Latin America, such as Mexico, took all the credit they could get from private commercial banks (the OPEC-dollar recycling agents of the 1970s)—a consummate free-rider/defeatist strategy blend. But such vicious-circle strategies are expensive in terms of stimulating world inflation and creating burdens for future domestic development when the foreign debt mortgages must be repaid. Carefully timed, one-shot free-rider strategies (suspending payments on international debts) combined with short-term, anti-inflation shock treatment (deep cuts in wages and state spending) may work to break states out of vicious, inflationary cycles if democratic populations are patient enough—as in Bolivia in 1985 and in Poland in 1990.[39] (See Chapter 2.)

Another weak-currency-country strategy variation is the free-rider indexation scheme used by nations whose credit is good because of their strategic importance, such as Israel and Iceland. **Indexation** refers to automatic, indexed hikes in industrial wages linked to inflation or rises in consumer prices. But the Italians discovered that the unarguable benefits of redistribution to those down the class scale resulting from such indexation schemes can reach a point of diminishing returns: To attempt to restore international competitiveness and to break free of vicious circles, the Italians began in the 1980s to dismantle their system of indexation. After all, the free-rider has to know when to get off since the status quo is no streetcar named desire.

The United States used yet another version of a complex free-rider strategy, manipulating dollar exchange rates and high U.S. interest rates in order to keep international money flowing into the United States to offset the crowding out of U.S. private investment by government borrowing that was feared due to the large federal deficit. The shift in the mid-1980s to use a falling dollar to make American exports cheaper and to improve the large U.S. trade deficit appeared to many critics to be another free ride on the world economy—a potentially vicious-circle-strategy of devaluation that permitted the Americans to postpone inevitable internal (budget cuts or tax increases) and external (protectionist tariffs to match competitors subsidy for subsidy) adjustments that are politically unpopular at home. Such free-rider preoccupations threaten to move the United States precipitously from the super-industrial to postmodern or post-industrial phase in which a nation hangs onto maintenance by burden-sharing or attempting to shift more of the costs to other states (as Clinton tried to do in "managed trade" talks with Japan).

IMPLICATIONS

In a global capitalist economy, rational choice for the individual citizen is apt to be maximized in a free-wheeling, deregulated domestic market like that of the United States. But as a consequence, a small minority of individuals in the national community—the professional speculators—are positioned to make the most rational use of available choices given the information overload of a system in which the set of available choices is the greatest in the world.

A political economy maximizing laissez-faire entrepreneurship pays off in terms of the great range of freedom or the range of choice in professional work, investments, and so forth. By the same token, the overwhelming majority of citizens at any one historical moment are structurally in a position where they will most probably make less than rationally optimal decisions or even make irrational decisions, thus increasing the gap between their own life chances and those of the rational few (a sort of "reverse Donald Trump effect"). Such nonadaptive, ill-informed decision making, in turn, risks undermining the basis of the large middle class, which Aristotle believed to be the prerequisite to his ideal form of balanced, democratic-aristocratic state—the **politea.**

As a contrast, the trade-off of neo-corporatist political economies is to give citizens a more limited range of freedom of choice for the sake of greater social stability and coverage of the risk of social failure (falling to the bottom, "down-and-out"). Governmental bureaucracies tend to make routine decisions concerning health, old-age pension, unemployment insurance benefits, and educational structures, leaving citizens with less routine decisions (and less decision stress), thus freeing time for the kinds of decision making they most enjoy.

In *The Overworked American* (1992) economist Juliet Schor demonstrated that although the level of productivity of the U.S. worker more than doubled between 1948 and 1990, none of this increase went into more leisure time. American workers could have used this productivity increase to take every other year off *with pay*. On the contrary, however, the average American owns and consumes more than twice what he or she did in 1948 but has less free time. Americans are trapped in an insidious cycle of work-and-spend.[40]

Sociologist Philip Slater, in *The Pursuit of Loneliness*, argued that Americans have to make more decisions than do people in any other culture in the world.[41] The opportunity cost of this freedom is to be overwhelmed as an individual and having to make more decisions than one wants to in any one day, eating up time with "busyness" and leaving the individual autonomous but lonely as he or she has to sort out everything individually. The neoconservative solution of Alan Bloom in *The Closing of The American Mind* is to reduce this "openness" for the sake of cultural calculability.[42] Or, in W. Edwards Deming's terms, by reducing the amount of variation, the quality of any process can be increased. The problem, of course, is whether in an anti-state liberal society such as that of the United States the majority of citizens would tolerate the arbitrary closing down of options or openness by the state for the sake of increased predictability collectively desired. The evolving U.S. health care reform may suggest the answer.

Americans, for example, typically want improvements in public services, but no increases in taxes to pay for such improvements—a free-rider strategy of improving the maintenance base grounded on borrowing from others, a policy that may not be able to last indefinitely. Indeed, by 1990 national opinion polls suggested a shift toward tolerating a marginal tax increase if the money were spent to fight drugs and to improve the environment.

The problem, as we have seen, lies not just in getting the majority of people in a nation to choose differently at any one moment, but in restructuring the society so that all individual choices are perceived as social choices, and that the individual and community learn to work in harmony for the sake of long-term social adaptation and economic competitiveness. Structure, in short, seems to precede strategy rather than the other way around. In the United States, individual freedom has been structured as primary in the social system no matter what the cost in social or economic distance between individuals or groups.[43] In the neo-corporatist economies, autonomy for the "peak" interest groups of labor, management, and government bureaucracies is structured to predominate over individual choice, limiting individual freedom somewhat but increasing social harmony and decreasing social distance between individuals and groups.

Still, we have seen that at certain transitional phases of economic development, nations collectively appear to have strategic choices between strategy mixes that can restructure their economies toward more industrial competitiveness or not (see Chapters 2 and 5). One concrete measure of the existing political economy strategy mix in a society is the amount of the nation's economic product devoted to government spending.

State Spending as a Measure
of Political Economy Constitutions

To compare how different national political economies are structured, the nature and amount of government spending is the best point of departure. The OECD publishes these data annually under the title "Total Outlays of General Government" in which government outlays include goods, services, public investments, interest payments on debts, and the cost of social (welfare) transfer payments. These comparative data show how limited the room for political flexibility since 1960 has become. The state most heavily burdened with government spending (note the correlation with *social democratic neo-corporatism*) have been Sweden, the Netherlands, Denmark, Belgium, and Luxembourg. Between 1960 and 1985, government outlays as a percentage of the annual total GNP rose for Sweden from 31 percent to 65 percent (the government outlay as a percentage of the GNP is called the **state quota**). Similarly, the state quota for the Netherlands and Denmark rose to 60 percent in the same period. West Germany's state quota—somewhat representative of the average for Europe—rose from 32 percent in 1960 to 48 percent in 1985. In contrast, *liberal neo-corporatist* states such as Japan and Switzerland had much lower state quotas—about 30 percent in 1985. And the state quota of the most liberal of nations, the United States, rose only from 27 percent to 36 percent between 1960 and 1985.

By 1991, the state quota of Sweden fell to 44 percent, that of the Netherlands to 53 percent, and that of Denmark to 42 percent in reaction to global competitive pressures. During 1991 the state quota of the U.S. was 25 percent, that of Germany 33 percent, and that of Japan 16 percent.[44]

The key questions in terms of strategic choices available for restructuring of a political economy are (1) Why are the differences between the state quotas so different—from 30 percent to 60 percent, and (2) What are the consequences of a large or small state quota for international competitiveness and social welfare? One way of explaining these differences is the "openness-of-the-economy hypothesis." Political scientist David Cameron of Yale University demonstrated that political economies that were more strongly integrated in the world economy in terms of international trade have higher state quotas, whereas nations with a small portion of their GNP made up of foreign trade have much smaller state quotas.[45] Thus, European countries that are heavily integrated into the world economy have high state quotas, whereas the United States and Japan, which are heavily oriented domestically in terms of their political economies (foreign trade making up some 15 percent of the U.S. economy and 20 percent of the Japanese), have low state quotas.

The second well-grounded hypothesis explaining the differences in state quotas is the "power-and-party-division hypothesis." Political scientist Manfred Schmidt of the University of Heidelberg has shown that since 1960 the countries with the smallest state quotas—the United States, Japan and Switzerland—have been dominated by bourgeois right-wing parties, whereas Denmark and Sweden, with high state quotas, have been dominated by Social Democratic parties. This Social Democratic tradition has seeped into the cultures of Denmark and Sweden to the point where politicians take social democracy for granted, while in the United States and Switzerland the state plays a more restrained role. In strategic terms, one could say that *political economies with high state quotas are more maintenance-bound, whereas those with the more liberal, less Social Democratic tradition are more entrepreneurial in orientation (self-help versus state-security).*

As to the second question—the consequences of high state quotas for international competitiveness—the empirical findings are less conclusive and dependent upon changing global economic conditions. In his book *Sozialdemokratische Krisenpolitik,* political economist Fritz Scharpf showed that Sweden, Austria, West Germany, and Great Britain developed successful Keynesian recipes for coping with the word economy dilemmas of the late 1970s: There was a consensus among their unions not to push for wage hikes to match the rising inflation rates. This enabled their governments to carry on state-deficit economic politics with low interest rates. Austria had full employment with a low inflation rate. Sweden maintained full employment as unemployment declined. West Germany held the world record for fighting inflation, but lost jobs in the process. And for two years Great Britain slowed down unemployment and inflation only to have the government lose control over the unions, which raised their demands.

However, in the 1980s these successful Keynesian recipes no longer worked. The high real dollar interest rates transformed the international capital market, which had become globally integrated. Money flowed toward the highest real return wherever that happened to be in the world. Consequently the incomes of taxpayers stagnated while the profits of investors soared. Given the high interest rates and loss of domestic capital, governments had to pay more money to cover their budget debts and thereby nearly lost the flexibility to use the Keynesian instrument of intervention in the domestic economy.[46] Thus *the high-real-interest-rate strategy of the United States to attract the money needed to service its deficits skewed the world economy toward the American position—a policy perceived by Europeans as a free-rider tactic on the part of the United States. This delayed the inevitable long-term economic adjustment domestically in America at the cost of making mere maintenance in European economies more expensive.*

By 1994 the long-delayed American economic adjustment began to kick in, however slowly. Clinton's proposed $1.5 trillion budget preserved the strict spending limits imposed in the 1993 deficit-reduction law and reduced the deficit for the third consecutive year. In the 1990s, though, it will continue to be difficult to reduce the federal budget. Clinton's defense budget actually went up $3.2 billion from 1993–1994 (although small reductions are projected in the future).[47] The American commitment to human service programs will expand, particularly given the health and welfare reforms, crime prevention, and job retraining programs. Largely stagnant American incomes mean that taxes will be difficult to raise. And Americans do not see themselves as getting the services for their taxes that Europeans do, thereby magnifying the problem. Postliberal consciousness has been raised in the U.S. given the excesses of the conservative liberalism of Reagan and Bush, particularly in terms of defense spending. But the follow-through to restructure America's maintenance base to make it more efficient and communitarian is unlikely to come soon given the conservatism of the American liberal tradition and voter resistance to state intervention and taxes.

THOUGHT QUESTIONS

1. Describe briefly the three different phases of modernization. What is the usefulness of the term "purposive rationality" within this context?
2. Characterize as precisely as possible Rostow's five stages of economic growth in key terms. Give examples of countries in the different stages.
3. Why does capitalist growth seem to be inevitably related to social inequality? Consider as well the cases of export-oriented growth, "casino capitalism" and oligarchism. If efficacy is the only social criterion, why is there a high probability of a "dual economy"?
4. A dynamic, i.e., "learning," dual economy easily sets the state up for either a virtuous or a vicious economic circle. Describe both in the form of a circular graph. Then use the graph to explain the examples of Germany and Great Britain. Instead of stressing economic factors, what do neo-corporatist states like Sweden and Austria focus on?
5. Identify countries that fall into the state strategy categories of *defeatist, free-rider, maintenance* and *entrepreneur*. Consider explicitly the general economic behavior of countries like Germany and Japan that successfully blend maintenance and entrepreneurship.
6. Discuss the trade-off between individual freedom and social stability. Compare relevant situations in the U.S. and in Sweden. What is your personal preference?

NOTES

1. Henry Maine, *Ancient Law: Its Connection with the Early History of Society and Its Relation to Modern Ideas* (London: Lardon J. Murray, 1861).
2. Ferdinand Toennies, *Gemeinschaft und Gesellschaft* (1887), translated by Charles P. Loomis, *Fundamental Concepts of Sociology* (New York: American Book Co., 1940).
3. Emile Durkheim, *De la Division du travail social* (1893), translated by George Simpson, *The Division of Labor in Society* (Glencoe: The Free Press, 1949).
4. See Max Weber, *The Theory of Social and Economic Organization,* translated by A.M. Henderson and Talcott Parsons (Glencoe: The Free Press, 1947).
5. Jürgen Habermas, *Toward a Rational Society* (Boston: Beacon Press, 1970).
6. Charles Lindblom, *Politics and Markets: The World's Political-Economic Systems* (New York: Basic Books, 1977).

7. See, for example, Christopher S. Wren, "China's Courtship of Capitalism," in *The New York Times,* December 25, 1983; and C. Wren, "China Turning Back to Its Educated for Help," *The New York Times,* March 4, 1984.

8. See, for example, Edward A. Gargan, "China Explains Policy Shift Retightening Economic Grip," *The New York Times,* October 28, 1988.

9. See Sylvia Ostry, "The World Economy in 1983: Marking Time," *Foreign Affairs,* "America and the World," Vol. 62, No. 3, pp. 553–60.

10. According to an MIT survey of 5.6 million firms between 1968 and 1976, 80 percent of the jobs in the United States were created by companies that were four years old or less and employed 100 or fewer workers. See David L. Birch, "Who Creates Jobs?" *The Public Interest* 65 (Fall 1981). On the theory of motivation in the welfare state, see Kenneth E. Boulding, *The Economy of Love and Fear* (Belmont, CA: Wadsworth Publishing Co., 1973), and Thomas C. Schelling, *Micromotives and Macrobehavior* (New York: W.W. Norton, 1978).

11. Economist Albert Hirschman has identified alternating cycles of public involvement and return to private interest maximization: see A.O. Hirschman, *Shifting Involvements: Private Interests and Public Action* (Princeton, NJ: Princeton University Press, 1982).

12. W.W. Rostow, *The Stages of Economic Growth: A Non-Communist Manifesto* (London: Cambridge University Press, 1960), p. 7.

13. For other interpretations of "postindustrial" values, see Ronald Inglehart, "The Silent Revolution in Europe: Intergenerational Change in Postindustrial Societies," *American Political Science Review,* 65 (December 1971); Fred Hirsch, *The Social Limits to Growth* (London: Routledge & Kegan Paul, 1978), and Daniel Bell, *The Coming of Post-Industrial Society* (New York: Basic Books, 1973) and Daniel Bell, *The Cultural Contradictions of Capitalism* (New York: Basic Books, 1976).

14. See, for example, Frank Parkin, *Class Inequality and Political Order: Social Stratification in Capitalist and Communist Societies* (New York: Praeger, 1975); and "Social Liberalism: A New Political Economy," Chapter 11 in R. Isaak, *American Democracy and World Power* (New York: St. Martin's Press, 1977), pp. 172–86.

15. Habermas, *Rational Society,* p. 122. For a Marxian class analysis, see Stephen Resnik, John Sinisi, and Richard Wolff, "Class Analysis of International Relations," in *An International Political Economy,* International Political Economy Yearbook, Vol. I, ed. by W. Ladd Hollis and F. LaMond Tullis (Boulder, CO: Westview Press, 1985), pp. 87–123.

16. See Part III: "The Loose Individual" of Robert Nisbet, *The Present Age: Progress and Anarchy in Modern America* (New York: Harper & Row, 1988), especially pp. 122–25.

17. See Charles S. Maier, "The Politics of Inflation in the Twentieth Century," in *The Political Economy of Inflation,* edited by Fred Hirsch and John H. Goldthorpe (Cambridge, MA: Harvard University Press, 1978).

18. See Hirsch, *The Social Limits of Growth* and Staffan B. Linder, *The Harried Leisure Class* (New York: Columbia University Press, 1970).

19. See R. Isaak, *European Politics: Political Economy and Policy Making in Western Democracies* (New York: St. Martin's Press, 1980).

20. See Daniel Bell, *The Cultural Contradictions of Capitalism,* Joseph Schumpeter, *Capitalism, Socialism and Democracy,* and Fred Hirsch, "The Ideological Underlay of Inflation," in Hirsch and Goldthorpe, *Political Economy of Inflation,* pp. 263–84.

21. See Suzanne Berger and Michael Piore, *Dualism and Discontinuity in Industrial Societies* (New York: Cambridge University Press, 1980), p. 69 ff.

22. See Ingar Svennilson, *Growth and Stagnation in the European Economy* (Geneva: Economic Commission for Europe, 1954); Joseph Schumpeter, *The Theory of Economic Development* (New York: Oxford University Press, 1961); and John Cornwall, *Modern Capitalism: Its Growth and Transformation* (Oxford: Martin, Robertson and Co., 1977).

    Certain important qualifications apply to Cornwall's model at certain stages of development: In less developed nations the key emphasis which Cornwall gives the manufacturing sector as a means to achieve the take-off stage to industrialization can also result in growing unemployment and a failure in agricultural and domestic market development. Cornwall also neglects an important exogenous variable, namely the country's effort to borrow or develop technology, which is not insignificant in a theory driven by technical progress.

23. See N. Kaldor, *Strategic Factors in Economic Development* (Ithaca, NY: Cornell University Press, 1967) and N. Kaldor, "Economic Growth and the Verdoorn Law: A Comment of Mr. Rowthorn's Article," *Economic Journal* (December 1975).

24. Kenneth Arrow, "The Economic Implications of Learning by Doing," *Review of Economic Studies* (June 1962).

25. See Cornwall, pp. 152 ff. and R. Minami, *The Turning Point in Economic Development: Japan's Experience* (Tokyo, 1973).

26. See Philippe Schmitter, "Interest Intermediation and Regime Governability in Western Europe and North America," in Suzanne Berger, ed., *Organizing Interests in Western Europe: Pluralism and the Transformation of Politics* (Cambridge, England: Cambridge University Press, 1981); P. Schmitter, "Still the Century of Corporatism," *Review of Politics* 36 (January 1974): 85–131; and Gerhard Lehmbruch, "Consociational Democracy, Class Conflict and the New Corporatism," in Philippe Schmitter and Gerhard Lehmbruch, eds., *Trends toward Corporatist Intermediation* (London: Sage, 1979), pp. 53–62.

27. See Chapter 7, "The Neo-corporatist Nations" of Graham K. Wilson, *Business and Politics* (Chatham, NJ: Chatham House Publishers, Inc., 1985), pp. 103–13.

28. See, for example, Peter J. Katzenstein, "Capitalism in One Country? Switzerland in the International Economy," *International Organization* 35 (Autumn 1980): 507–40. And, for a contrast of Switzerland as a form of "liberal corporatism" and Austria as an example of "social democratic corporatism," see P. Katzenstein, *Small States in World Markets: Industrial Policy in Europe* (Ithaca, NY: Cornell University Press, 1985).

29. See Manfred G. Schmidt, "The Politics of Labour Market Policy: Structural and Political Determinants of Rates of Unemployment in Industrial Nations," in *Managing Mixed Economies* edited by Francis G. Castles, Franz Lehner, and Manfred G. Schmidt (Volume 3 of *The Future of Party Government,* edited by Rudolf Wildenmann) (Berlin/New York: Walter De Gruyter, 1988), p. 6.

30. See R. Isaak, "Modern Reactions to Inflation: Private and Public Strategies," in Part II of Wilhelm Hankel and R. Isaak, *Modern Inflation: Its Economics and Its Politics* (Lanham, MD: University Press of America, 1983); in German: *Die moderne Inflation* (Cologne: Bund-Verlag, 1981). The initial version of the application of the typology to stages of development was presented as a paper, "State Strategies and Stages of Development: Shards of a Theory," at the 25th Annual Convention of the International Studies Association at Atlanta, Georgia, March 27–31, 1984. When first presented at a conference at the Johns Hopkins Uni-

versity SAIS Center in Bologna, Italy in 1981, Professor Karl Deutsch summarized the methodology used to derive the typology as follows: "He observed what certain individuals did to try to cope with the inflation of the 1970s and organized the results in four categories. Then he examined the behavior of corporations and states during the same period in black-box fashion, without concerning himself with their inner structures, to determine what kind of similarities the input-output behavior of these units had with the four categories of individual behavior. Larger systems can be exactly as aggressive in their behavior as the individuals are who lead them. Hitler's Germany is a perfect example. Both the behavior of the individual and the state he governed were nasty and aggressive. Such a distribution of psychological types that can be applied at different levels may take us methodologically beyond the complicated theories of Erik Erikson, enabling social scientists to do a kind of market research analysis: for example, a state or corporation might be in the market for a maintenance man in a certain historical phase—supported by people who, themselves, may not be conservative." (Karl Deutsch's conference commentary in taped transcript, *Modern Inflation,* pp. 198–199.)

31. Guy Kirsch and Klaus Mackscheidt, "Western Ideas about China's Economic Direction Are Mostly Wrong," *The German Tribune,* No. 1266, March 15, 1987, p. 8.

32. See Ezra F. Vogel, *Japan as Number 1* (Cambridge, MA: Harvard University Press, 1979); Chalmers Johnson, *MITI and the Japanese Miracle, The Growth of Industrial Policy 1925–75* (Stanford, CA: Stanford University Press, 1982); and T.J. Pempel and Keiich Tsunekawa, "Corporatism without Labour," in Schmitter and Lehmbruch, eds., *Corporatist Intermediation,* pp. 231–70.

33. See R.G.H. Siu, *The Tao of Science* (Cambridge, MA: MIT Press, 1957), T.S. Lebra, *Japanese Patterns of Behavior* (Honolulu: University Press of Hawaii, 1976), and Richard Tanner Pascale and Anthony G. Athos, *The Art of Japanese Management* (New York: Warner Books, 1981).

34. See R. Isaak, "The West German Industrial Model Under Seige," *Adherent* (Spring 1983); Graham Hallett, *The Social Market Economy of West Germany* (New York: Macmillan, 1973), pp. 19–20; and "West Germany: A Social-market Economy," Chapter 2 in *European Politics,* pp. 27–62.

35. See Klaus Peter Krause, "In Search of the Meaning of 'Social' in a Social Market Economy" (originally in German in the *Frankfurter Allgemeine Zeitung,* October 8, 1988), *The German Tribune,* No. 1344, October 23, 1988, p. 7.

36. See Part II of *Modern Inflation.* Also see Wilhelm Hankel, "Germany: Economic Nationalism in the International Economy," in Wilfred Kohl and Giorgio Basevi, eds., *West Germany: A European and Global Power* (Lexington, MA: D.C. Health, 1980), pp. 21–43.

37. See W. Hankel, *Prosperity Amidst Crisis: Austria's Economic Policy and the Energy Crunch* (Boulder, CO: Westview Press, 1980), p. 149. Originally published as *Prosperität in der Krise* (Vienna: Molden, 1979).

38. Katzenstein, "Capitalism in One Country?," p. 511.

39. Robert E. Norton, "The American Out to Save Poland," *Fortune,* Vol. 121, No. 3, Jan. 29, 1990, pp. 129–134.

40. Juliet B. Schor, *The Overworked American: The Unexpected Decline of Leisure* (New York: Basic Books, 1992).

41. Philip Slater, *The Pursuit of Loneliness* (Boston: Beacon Press, 1976).

42. Alan Bloom, *The Closing of the American Mind* (New York: Simon & Schuster, 1987).

43. See R. Isaak, "The Conservative Tradition of American Liberalism," *American Political Thinking: Readings from the Origins to the 21st Century* (Fort Worth: Harcourt, Brace, 1994), pp. 1–13.

44. World Bank, *World Development Report 1993* (Washington, D.C.: World Bank, 1993), Table 11, p. 259.

45. David Cameron, "The Expansion of the Public Economy: A Comparative Analysis: *The American Political Science Review* 72, (December 1978): 1243–61.

46. Lecture by Fritz Scharpf on *Sozialdemokratische Krisenpolitik in Europa* at the University of Heidelberg, June 9, 1988.

47. "The Clinton Budget," *The Wall Street Journal,* Feb. 8, 1994., p. A12.

CHAPTER NINE

MULTINATIONAL STRATEGIES, ECONOMIC CYCLES, AND DIRECT INVESTMENT

An alliance is a device to reduce costs by creating the opportunity to access or develop different cognitive frames, work arrangements and cultures so that the firm is able to look at both itself and the environment . . . in a fundamentally different way, smashing old frames and overcoming organizational inertia.

Claudio Ciborra, "Alliances as Learning Experiments" (1991)

Giant organizations are nothing new in international trade. They were a characteristic form of the mercantilist period when large joint-stock companies, e.g., The Hudson's Bay Company, the Royal African Company, The East India Company, to name the major English merchant firms, organized long-distance trade with America, Africa and Asia. But neither these firms, nor the large mining and plantation enterprises in the production sector, were the forerunners of the multinational corporation. They were like dinosaurs, large in bulk, but small in brain, feeding on the lush vegetation of the new worlds (the planters and miners in America were literally Tyrannosaurus rex).

Stephen Hymer, *The Multinational Corporation
and the Law of Uneven Development* (1972)

The nation-state often appears to be an antique, if not obsolete, structure from the perspective of global economic change: To shore up its overloaded maintenance base, national leaders seek to use multinational corporations as the vanguards of economic growth, development, and employment. The locus of economic dynamism has shifted from the state to the global company, which offers more flexibility and higher salaries to its managers than does any government. Given normal geographical fixity, the world of nation-states often seems like an ice-cube tray with global liquidity flowing over it or not depending upon the capriciousness of external trends.

While multinational companies can invest or disinvest, merge with others or go it alone, rise from nothing or disappear in bankruptcy, the state seems stodgy and stuck in comparison. The state is glued more or less to one piece of territory, fighting off entropy and budget crises, the national community usually assessing the latest foreign attacks upon a condition of declining competitiveness and the vulnerability in its domestic markets. Thus, it is beneficial to examine briefly the sources of dynamism behind the strategies of multinational companies and the ways in which these strategies are targeted to take advantage of shifts in economic or business cycles.

The changing nature of multinational corporations and direct investment in a global era of high technology and instant information flows makes it ever more important to understand the nature of economic cycles and the strategies available for coping with them. For no small part of the inequality between rich and poor nations is due to the collective learning capacity of multinational companies based in different countries in terms of responding effectively to shifting business cycles. While national resources, state structures, and access to foreign capital are significant constraints, the collective learning ability of the private sector in cooperation with public-sector support may well be the cutting edge in turning a political economy around from a dependent, deficit-ridden condition to a more self-sufficient, surplus-bound situation where efficient maintenance strategies are not a dream but a daily habit. This suggests that the factors contributing to the bargaining power of the multinational corporation (versus that of both the home and host governments) are the essential elements of competitiveness in international political economy. Also vital is the extent to which the economic fruits of this competitiveness are reinvested in long-term infrastructure (industrial plant and equipment) for the sake of employment and social prosperity, or are diffused in short-term accumulation strategies of private investors.

ORIGINS

Generally a **"multinational" corporation** in a strict sense refers to a company owned by stockholders in several countries that is also based in two countries—Royal-Dutch Shell and Unilever (in Britain and the Netherlands), for example. But these are the exceptions, not the rule. Usually multinational corporations are based and owned in one country with manufacturing facilities in two or more other countries that repatriate profits that are not reinvested. Such firms based in one country are sometimes called "transnational" corporations to distinguish them from the purer, two-country-based companies. But everyday usage suggests that it is wiser to retain the term "multinational corporation" although few firms qualify in the "pure" sense, much as Max Weber's ideal type of "charismatic" is used to describe authority figures who may not be charismatic in all senses of the word.

In terms of size, multinational corporations are traced back to the East India Company, chartered in London in 1600, which established "outposts of progress" overseas. Ultimately, the British East India Company had its own private army to protect its stakes and employees in unpredictable environments abroad. From the nation of small shopkeepers (and local pin factory) of Adam Smith, to the national corporation, to international representation for trade abroad, to direct investment in manufacturing and the emergence of multinational corporations with global strategies, the development of multinational strategies has been evolutionary, often catching government policymakers by surprise. Business managers are compulsively future-directed (although not necessarily long-term oriented); technology is inherently unpredictable (although not necessarily always absorbable); and foreign competitors are enigmatic (but not undecipherable). Thus, to get at some of the universals in multinational development despite historical or cultural differences is not easy. A brief comparison of business systems emerging from significantly different cultural traditions illustrates the possibility and complexity of pinning down such principles.

The Emergence of U.S. versus Japanese Multinational Corporations

From the English, French, and Dutch mercantile families of the seventeenth century, the Americans learned that to succeed at international trade it was necessary to have representatives overseas. Typically, the Americans would either send independent agents or family members abroad to represent their businesses as foreign commerce grew in the colonial era. Up until the time of the American Revolution, American business development was conditioned by the control of British mercantile policy: This policy aimed to keep a favorable balance of payments for the mother country, to discourage manufacturing within the colonies, and to constrain the colonists to trade within the British Empire.[1] True to their independent nature, the Americans openly disregarded such restrictions.

Individuals Go Abroad: Entrepreneurship Multinationalized

At the turn of the nineteenth century, cotton became the greatest American export and the basis for establishing an important American textile industry (relying, of course, upon inexpensive slave labor). In the early third of the century, canals were built to link the interior of the country with the coast. The mood became one of "Manifest Destiny." However, perhaps due to the tradition of rugged, laissez-faire individualism, many of the businesses started abroad by Americans in the middle of the nineteenth century lasted only for their lifetime or that of their sons. They found themselves heavily under pressure in the developing countries by host governments, and their concessions were often cancelled. This contrasted with more benign treatment in countries like Canada. The Panama Railroad and Nicaraguan carriage-steamboat line were the most important American direct foreign investments preceding the Civil War.

American experience in Nicaragua and elsewhere taught U.S. business people that they had to vary their plans for different cultures. In the second half of the nineteenth century American business abroad came into increasing competition with the British, particularly in third-country regions such as Mexico and Central America. Transportation and communication developments within the United States increasingly made it possible for companies to become *national* enterprises—the first step toward becoming multinational concerns. *When a U.S. company decided to go abroad, true to the laissez-faire tradition of American liberalism, the government usually had little involvement, leaving the company on its own. In the late nineteenth century, surplus output and the desire to benefit from economies of scale led many U.S. companies to seek export markets. However, again true to the American belief in free trade, there is little evidence of "dumping" by American businesses. Rather, there was a rough adherence to the principle of comparable prices.* Communication innovations led to automatic international extensions as the Western Union Telegraph Company was founded in 1856. The International Ocean Telegraph Company installed the first cable to Latin America between Florida and Havana in 1866. By the 1880s, Tropical American Company had acquired the telephone rights in South America and was selling parts to Latin American telephone companies. At the same time, the Edison Electric Light Company exported to Brazil, Chile, and Argentina and started installing lighting systems in Latin America. But after reaping few profits, Edison withdrew from foreign markets in disappointment.

By the last decade of the nineteenth century, American inventors, manufacturers, and marketers were involved in international business, led by men such as Isaac Singer, Alexander Graham Bell, Thomas Edison, George Westinghouse, George Eastman, John D. Rockefeller, and J.P. Morgan. What Mira Wilkins has termed the "American Invasion" era was in full swing.[2]

The thrust of American international business activity was directed toward forward integration into sales or into horizontal integration—generally in the industrial or industrializing countries. The American government, in turn, was pulled into becoming more involved. It passed the Sherman Antitrust Act of 1890 (forbidding agreements that restrained trade) and conquered the Philippines (which government policymakers thought would become a base for U.S. trade in the Orient). In the chaotic Third-World markets, the U.S. government was particularly likely to provide American businesses with information and assistance. *Rather than directly competing with the Americans, the Europeans preferred a policy of "negotiated environments." For example, American and European gunpowder industries negotiated market boundaries, some exclusive, some shared, and some free. In coming to terms with European traditions, many American businesses found they had to cooperate with European companies rather than act independently as they were naturally inclined to.* Thus, multinational corporate alliances emerged.

German hostility to foreign enterprise at the time, not to mention high tariffs and restrictive patent laws, led American firms to set up manufacturing facilities there (much as the Japanese were motivated out of similar concerns to make direct investments in the United States a century later). For somewhat different reasons (but including high tariffs), American companies also started local manufacturing in France. In Russia the American multinational ran into a stiff nationalism: Businesses operated under close government scrutiny with the Finance Minister monitoring almost every deal and with the Russian government serving as virtually the exclusive customer for some companies (such as Westinghouse Air Brake Company). To cope with nationalism abroad, American multinational strategies focused on incorporating in a joint venture with host companies, shifting from sales operations to manufacturing and refining so as to bypass tariffs, hiring local people, buying locally, taking on "national" titles and, if necessary, making security deposits (in the case of insurance companies).

In the U.S., multinational corporations emerged primarily from an entrepreneurial strategy—businesses and families sending their agents abroad to make foreign trade possible; innovations in transportation and communication facilitating the emergence of national companies that sought export markets on their own *for surplus production and economies of scale; and protectionist international relations leading to high-risk direct investments to avoid tariffs and cultural obstacles.* The state or government followed with supportive policies long after entrepreneurs had led the way, many businesses going bankrupt abroad within one or two generations for lack of assistance and continuity. Contrast this with the way Japanese multinational companies evolved, something we will now examine.

Zaibatsu and Sogoshosha: How Japanese Maintenpreneurial Multinationals Emerged

The rise of Japanese corporate groups, the **zaibatsu** *(literally "financial clique"), stemmed from the Meiji Restoration of 1868. Prior to this radical change in government form toward centralization (which helps to explain the "tight-ship-in-a-storm efficacy" of "Japan Inc." in the world economy today) Tokugawa Japan possessed a government (the* bakufu*) of decentralized personal bonds that linked the shogun, the* *daimyo, and the samurai, bonds that were more important than institutions. The impetus for changing the governmental structure came largely from abroad.* In 1853 and 1854 U.S. Commodore Matthew Perry forced open Japanese ports to the West. Foreign trade interests began to invade the country, imposing a 5 percent limit on the tariffs the Japanese could put upon imports. The foreigners went so far as to demand the right to **"extraterritoriality"** so that their citizens could be governed by their own laws rather than those of the Japanese while they resided in Japan. The resentment of the Japanese helped to bring down the shogun who ran the country, theoretically returning power to the Emperor—Meiji—whose name is used to identify the 1868–1912 consolidation of the Japanese political system.[3] In *Imitation and Innovation* (1987) sociologist Eleanor Westney details how Western organizational forms were emulated in Meiji Japan: "collective learning" at work.

As in Great Britain and the United States, mergers were a favored form of business restructuring in Japan in the second half of the nineteenth century. Many of the largest businesses in the early to mid-Meiji era were single-industry businesses. By 1896, of the fifty largest manufacturing and mining companies, twenty-eight were cotton textile companies—firms that were to become even more dominant because of the merger movement. In the early twentieth century, the number of cotton-spinning companies fell from seventy-eight to forty-six.[4] Such Japanese industrial companies were less integrated than American firms and were more comparable to British companies. The insular state depends upon companies abroad for sources of raw materials and markets for finished goods, resulting in a relative lack of vertical integration. Japan had a reasonably well-developed marketing system dating back to the early nineteenth century. Manufacturers did not have to set up their own marketing networks. Foreigners (to this day) have found it difficult to penetrate this marketing arrangement.

Thus, huge diversified companies—*zaibatsu*—soon assumed a hegemonic position over the industrial and other business sectors in Japan. *More diversified than American or British multinational companies, the* zaibatsu *typically included manufacturing, a bank to finance manufacturing activities, and a trading company to market the products abroad (the* sogoshosha*). By 1914, Japan was dominated by eight major* zaibatsu. *Three of these (Mitsubishi, Mitsui, and Sumitomo are still among the largest of the nine main* sogoshosha *(trading companies) that helped to steer Japanese business in the late twentieth century.* By the early 1920s, a great deal of the mining, shipbuilding, banking, foreign trade, and industry of Japan was controlled by the *zaibatsu*.

Almost all Japanese firms specialize in a single sector—a specialization nurtured in part by **MITI**—Japan's governmental ministry of industry and trade, which seeks to create appropriate conditions for the competitiveness of the country's major companies over the long run. (See Chapter 5.) This specialization contrasts with the loose American conglomerate, made up of businesses from different sectors that may be added or dropped depending upon short-term market fluctuations. Either companies from a single industrial sector organize for collective learning and clout, or one strong firm from each sector is incorporated into a *zaibatsu*, which is centered around large banks and linked to non-*zaibatsu* groups. The twentieth-century tradition of the *zaibatsu* was to have a holding company at the top, directly controlling the specialized firms in the *zaibatsu* group. Although these holding companies were forbidden and dispersed during the occupation following World War II, the *sogoshosha* or trading companies, remaining still operate along the lines of the *zaibatsu* much as the large companies supposedly broken up in Germany after the war have been recast and predominate in the German economy.[5] The five largest of the nine major **sogoshosha** are not just trading companies but utilize a strategy aimed at securing sources of basic raw materials and maintaining world market share. For example, the largest of the five (Mitsubishi, Mitsui, C. Itoh, Marubeni, and Sumitomo) alone account for about one-third of the energy (gas and oil) imported by Japan.[6]

The *sogoshosha* serve not only the big organizations but also the small: They eliminate difficult barriers to entry into new foreign markets for small manufacturing firms that would not normally have the financial or managerial resources to support international ventures. Brazil, Korea, and the Southeast Asian political economies have developed their own forms of *sogoshosha* based upon the Japanese model, so convinced are they that these organizations are engines of export-led economic growth. *Overcoming the static concepts of comparative-advantage theories of international trade, the* sogoshosha's *key strength is to gather foreign marketing intelligence from all over the world, to sift through the information, and target it for the right company at the right place at the right time.*

As information increasingly becomes the basis for power and competitiveness in the international economy, the Japanese trading company intelligence networks are strategically placed and traditionally cultivated to be highly efficient information processors for both Japanese multinational companies and the Japanese nation. Using something of a "tribal clan mode of organization," the *sogoshosha* serve as large and loyal clearing houses for companies offering diverse goods and services, hooking ultimately into the *senmonshosha*—thousands of specialized, wholesale distributors trading in specific sectors. The *sogoshosha* are flexible organizations, highly leveraged (in terms of debt-equity ratio), and thrive on both dynamic and static economies of scale given a national and worldwide network of market contracts. They are able to barter goods and services among themselves for significant savings and can move in and out of specific markets quickly with the effective collective learning capacity made possible by territorial knowledge bases cultivated over decades.[7] (See also Chapter Five.)

Perhaps the most significant contrast between the American and Japanese multinational management cultures is the traditional laissez-faire antagonism between the (government) maintenance base and the entrepreneurial company on the one hand, and the cooperation between big government and big business in Japan on the other. Early in the twentieth century, American antitrust legislation led the U.S. government to break up Standard Oil of California, for example, into eleven parts. Each part ultimately became larger than the initial company. In comparison, MITI and the *Keidanren,** the government trade and industry bureaucracies, actively cultivate mergers between weaker companies to consolidate firms into large, competitive units to make Japan more effective in international trade. The laissez-faire system encourages individualism and entrepreneurial innovation, whereas the maintenpreneurial approach stresses long-term targeting and collective adaptation with an institutional structure that assures follow-through on national strategies.

INTERPRETATIONS

Regardless of which culture one observes, the trend in multinational organization or global direct investment in the twentieth century has been one of mergers organizationally and towards foreign direct investment led by **oligopolistic industries** (that is, those controlled by a few competing sellers). Not only did the influence of the state on national political economies grow greatly in the twentieth century, but the impact of multinational corporations also expanded: The turnover of the largest multinational companies is greater than the GNP of some eighty countries. What made this national and international growth of corporations possible is the growing importance of *imperfect* competition. In a world of perfect competition—the utopia of Adam Smith—there would be many small competitors in each nation supplying all the goods and services demanded and no impetus for direct foreign investment. But in the real world economy, the imperfection of competition provides irresistible payoffs for companies with special access to scarce resources or specialized knowledge or technology for which there is great demand. The chaos of imperfect markets, reasserted incessantly by the creative destruction of capitalist innovation, creates the motivation for oligopolistic organizations to maximize their global market share. They merge or form cartels with their counterparts to make entry into their markets difficult through economies of scale and cooperative pricing. In the process, observers have noted that the world economy has become increasingly structured into developed and uneven developing regions—metropoles and peripheries epitomizing the inequality between rich and poor nations in the late twentieth century.

---

*The *Keidanren,* the peak industrial association made up of the 700 or so largest companies, works closely with MITI.

Direct Investment: Oligopoly and the Law
of Uneven Development

In tracing the development of companies from workshop to factory to national corporation to multidivisional corporation to multinational corporation, economist Stephen Hymer argued that oligopolies were the leaders in direct investment, which is concentrated in the metropolitan centers (or metropoles) of advanced developed countries leaving everywhere else—the periphery—underdeveloped.[8] It is not just a question of increase in size: Corporate growth is qualitative as well as quantitative, evolving increasingly complex administrative and communication systems, or "brains." By the early 1980s, of the top fifteen recipients of direct investment only four were generally not classified as developed countries: South Africa, Brazil, Mexico, and Hong Kong. The less developed countries (LDCs) accounted for only about 31 percent of foreign-owned affiliates, 54 percent being in Europe.[9] Thus, the statistics support Hymer's argument. The thrust of his interpretation is that *money and new plant construction from the rich nations will continue to flow disproportionately to the most developed sections of the rich countries, financing technological and economic innovation and development there at the expense of all the other peripheral areas of the world where the investment could have gone but did not. Because of the "learning-by-doing" effects of this deepening of capital, two different worlds of education and economic sophistication emerge as the gap between them grows.*

Hymer's vision is one of an emerging imperial economic hierarchy headed by oligopolistic multinational corporations that eventually reach an "oligopolistic equilibrium" following an acute competitive phase aimed at increasing global market share. This "Imperial System" will follow the "Law of Uneven Development" as it creates poverty as well as wealth, underdevelopment as well as development. The division of labor between geographic regions corresponds to the vertical division of labor within the company. High-level decision making in the system will be centralized in the metropoles—a few key cities in the advanced countries. The metropoles, in turn, are surrounded by a number of regional subcapitals. The rest of the world (the periphery) is confined to low levels of activity and income—having the status of villages or towns in the Imperial System. The metropoles monopolize income, status, authority, and consumption. They share some with the regional subcapitals but with declining curves of these values as one moves from the (metropole) center to the periphery, perpetuating a pattern of inequality and dependency. Thus, New York, London, Tokyo, Berlin, Paris, and Beijing become the major centers of high-level strategic planning in the Imperial System, while lesser cities deal with day-to-day operations. And the "best" and highest-paid professionals—administrators, doctors, lawyers, scientists, educators, government officials, actors, and servants—will be concentrated in or near the metropoles.

Hymer's vision is astutely prophetic in terms of the concentration of economic and political power. Statistically, the metropoles and their suburbs are responsible for being the greatest producers of new patents—the indicator of cutting-edge research and development. *Corporate, government, and academic institutions in the metropoles often have a leadtime of at least six months in receiving information on new technological and economic innovations, giving them an often decisive competitive edge in a fast-moving global economy and perpetuating their dominance over subsidiary and lesser institutions located in the periphery.* If information is power in the emerging high-tech/high-information global economy, then sitting at the source of new information is a prerequisite to political and economic competitiveness. And the most sophisticated technologies for processing information—for sorting out the quick from the dead—are often concentrated in the metropoles in such quantity as to make a qualitative difference in the levels of information flows received by inhabitants of these privileged areas. Collective learning happens faster here and in a concentrated, high-tempo manner, thus intensifying the learning and experience curves hypothesized by economist Kenneth Arrow and the Boston Consulting Group.[10] The metropoles, in short, are staging grounds for static and dynamic economies of scale that propel institutions there ahead of others.

Host Country versus Home Multinational Bargaining Power

Having one's headquarters in one of the world's key metropoles can help maximize the bargaining power of a multinational corporation in dealing with host countries in the periphery where it makes direct or portfolio investments. Theodore H. Moran identified three other variables perhaps even more crucial in determining the negotiating balance of power between multinational corporations and host countries: (1) the extent of competition in the industry (or, How unstable are the oligopolies?); (2) the changeableness of the technology (or, How fast is it changing?); and (3) the importance of marketing and product differentiation. *Bargaining power for the multinational corporation is high relative to the host country if competition is low, if technology is changeable, and if the importance of marketing is high. On the other hand, host countries can be expected to have high bargaining power if competition is high, if technology is stable, and if marketing is of little importance. Moran projects increasing power for Third-World host countries as bargaining power changes over time, as the host countries move up a learning curve, and as the viability of economic nationalism in Third-World countries increases.*[11]

The shift in bargaining power from First-World-based multinationals to Third-World host countries began in the 1970s with the success of OPEC. Stimulating Third-World economic nationalism and largely frustrated efforts at forming other commodity cartels, host governments became more sophisticated in their bargaining conditions. However, with the widespread debt crisis in developing countries in the 1980s, bargaining power shifted back the other way. Desperately in need of new capital, many developing countries had to make major concessions—particularly on initial corporate tax rates—in order to lure First-World multinational companies into uncertain political and economic environments. Standing to gain from better use of production factors and idle resources and the possibility of upgrading resources and production with new technology and investment, developing countries bent over backwards to attract foreign companies to their soil.

The risks involved—the exploitation of their prime resources, the replacement of local firms by the multinationals, the potential destruction of local entrepreneurship—not to mention increasing dependence upon foreign influence—were often understated for the sake of short-term economic gains that could bolster the power position of elected officials in the Third World.

In the late 1980s and 1990s a strategy emerged in the Third World aimed at consolidating the gains in bargaining power of the nation-state made in the 1970s with the economies of scale made possible through organizing large multinational enterprises by subsidizing the creation of Third-World-based multinationals.[12] The success of such efforts to use homegrown multinationals as arms of the state's economic policy depends not just upon obtaining start-up financing but upon the previous success of critical transfers of technology.

The Product Cycle and Technology Transfer

That which has been called "the product cycle" almost always begins in the developed countries where high-income market economies provide an environment conducive to both technological innovation and the flexibility and maintenance risk insurance facilitating the commercial applications of technological change. The United States is the prime example. Its large domestic market; loose, flexible labor structure; high-income consumption; and collective tendency to try out, develop, or purchase "the new" make it an optimal testing ground for new products. The entrepreneurial culture spawns new product innovation. It also serves as a basis for the hegemonic role of the United States (as the entrepreneurial culture *par excellence*) in the world economy since World War II, attracting direct foreign investment and portfolio investment with combinations of a multitude of inventive investment options, political stability, attractive interest rates, receptiveness to innovation, a skilled and mobile labor pool, and multiple sources of capital and technology.

The product life-cycle theory—sometimes called the neotechnologist school*—is divided into four stages: introduction or innovation; growth; maturation; and decline.* At the **introductory stage,** a new product is created in a developed market economy where the cost of innovation is not a problem and the innovator does not have to worry about the product having a high initial price. Then, if the product has a certain amount of success, the **growth stage** commences and the product becomes widespread in the national market. When the product reaches the **maturity stage,** its production has become standardized and, therefore, cheaper to produce with unskilled labor. At this stage the product is exported, having satiated the domestic market. But given the standardization of production it soon becomes cheaper to produce the product in developing countries where the wages are lower than in the home country. Competition emerges as the technology is copied or adapted or bought. The foreign developing country then starts exporting the same product back into the home, developed country where it was born—the final **phase of decline.**[13]

Product-cycle theory assumes that information does not flow freely across national borders: Key technological processes related to production and marketing are concentrated and protected in certain developed countries—at least initially. Moreover, it assumes that each country has its own peculiar milieu, which is more or less conducive to technological change and which steers the direction of that change. Finally, the theory assumes that international trade is often directed by the particular stages that products happen to be in during their life-cycles combined with the changing matrix of international marketing opportunities for the product.

The product life-cycle theory applies to many but not all products.[14] For example, the fashion industry moves so quickly, the creative destruction occurs so fast, that the product life-cycle theory hardly applies as the new is constantly replacing the old.[15] But if it can eventually be established that the theory covers most products, a major cause for the inequality between the developed and developing countries will have been confirmed. For the rich, developed countries where the innovations initially take place get the most profits and mileage out of the products in the early phases of their life cycle. By the time the products are in decline, the multinationals in the metropoles have more innovative replacements ready to launch on the markets in order to maintain market leadership, if not domination. The developing countries are given recycled technologies by the developed countries after quite a bit of the juice has been drained from them.

Benjamin Franklin argued that technological innovations of any kind should be shared freely with mankind. But that was in the eighteenth century. He would never have dreamed that the United States might one day attempt to live more off of selling the patents for technological innovations and their servicing than from producing agricultural or manufactured goods. In service-sector-dominated developed economies, the control of technology transfers to potentially competitive economies has become a key to maintaining economic, if not political, hegemony.

To understand the dynamics of the multinational corporation in a global context, it is not sufficient just to focus upon the product cycle and technology transfer. Longer-term economic and business cycles are significant as well for managers who seek to cope effectively with change by system-atically reducing uncertainty into calculable risk. A failure to understand these cycles—or the error of mistaking one for another—tempts corporate managers to become preoccupied with mere maintenance strategies rather than those of the dynamic entrepreneur. And the larger the corporation, the more tempting it is to be predominated by maintenance strategies. The U.S. manager, for example, is shackled with the short-term scrutiny of stockhold-ers (unlike longer-term bank-financed Japanese managers). The stockhold-ers block the U.S. manager from "going for broke" with everything in terms of innovation or the direction of the highest long-term payoff. So the Ameri-can manager "satisfices"—maintaining low risks in some areas while taking high-risk gambles in others.*

Short-term, Intermediate, and Long-term Business Cycles

Corporate plans and strategies succeed or fail depending upon the ac-curacy of assumptions that managers make concerning the frequency and nature of business cycles. Such cycles, together with power transitions, can also be used to anticipate wars between states.† *In everyday usage, the concept of* **"business cycle"** *refers to three- to eight-year patterns of rising and falling economic activity, of expansion and recession, peaks and troughs. However, many economists have found these short-term, fluctuating modes of behavior alone to be insufficient to explain and predict business patterns. Therefore, they have combined short-term "busi-ness cycles" with intermediate-term (fifteen to twenty-five years) "long-swing" invest-ment (or Kuznets) cycles, and long-term or "long-wave" (forty-five to sixty years) Kon-dratieff cycles.*

Expansionary economic phases can be viewed as part of a **syntropic process,** a building up of production, employment, incomes, stock market prices, and construction. Periods of recession or decline, on the other hand, may be seen as a form of **entropic process,** of obsolescence and disintegra-tion. Business or corporate survival depends upon anticipating syntropic and entropic shifts in the economy, at least in terms of the key sectors upon which the lifeblood or cash flow of the business depends. But such economic forecasting is a precarious undertaking. It depends upon where one is stand-ing and upon whether one is preoccupied with short-term, intermediate-term, or long-term cycles when analyzing change.

For example, focusing upon the interconnection between short-term

---

*Economist and Nobel laureate Herbert A. Simon used "satisficing" to combine "satisfy" and "suffice": the tendency to choose an alternative that looks like it will make do, rather than the best one.

†For political management perspectives on the relationship between economic cycles, power transitions, and wars, see "Special Issue: The Economic Foundations of War," *International Studies Quarterly* 27, No. 4 (December 1983), particularly the article by Raimo Väyrynen, pp. 389–418.

and intermediate-term cycles, Harvard economist Alvin Hansen concluded that from 1795 to 1937 in the American economy there were seventeen cycles of an average duration of 8.35 years. One to two minor peaks occur regularly between the major peaks of these eight-year cycles, each minor cycle lasting less than half the duration of the major or "normal" business cycles. However, in looking at the key sector of building construction, Hansen noted that the cycle in this area averaged between seventeen or eighteen years in length, or about twice the length of the normal business cycle. He concluded: "American experience indicates that with a high degree of regularity every other major business boom coincides roughly with a boom in building construction, while the succeeding major cycle recovery is forced to buck up against a building slump. . . .[T]he depressions which have fallen in the interval of the construction downswing are typically deep and long. And the succeeding recovery is held back and retarded by the unfavorable depressional influence from the slump in the building industry."[16]

In illustrating the interconnectedness of short-term business cycles and **intermediate-term Kuznets cycles** (referring to the 1971 Nobel economist Simon Kuznets, who discovered them in 1930), Hansen makes clear that a corporate strategy dependent upon the building construction sector would most likely come to grief if it failed to consider the perspective of the intermediate-term cycle, if it focused, for example, only upon short-term cycles. But what about the opposite danger? It is also possible to go wrong in strategic planning by unduly stressing long-term cycles lasting half a century or so at the expense of neglecting short-term fluctuations.

Russian economist Nikolai D. Kondratieff fathered the concept of the **long-wave cycle** in capitalist economies of some fifty years in length, only later to die in solitary confinement in one of Stalin's concentration camps.[17] Kondratieff discovered two-and-a-half cycles in a series of price, wage, interest rate, and value-affected data, with troughs in 1790, 1844–1851, and 1890–1896; and peaks at 1810–1817, 1870–1875, and 1914–1920.[18] Although production data do not always fit well into Kondratieff's framework, the "idealized" Kondratieff Wave approximates the actual behavior of U.S. wholesale prices closely enough to suggest to long-wave observers that the American economy may descend into a depression, as Figure 9–1 suggests.

Several critical objections can be raised to long-wave forecasts of a probable depression. First and foremost, a preoccupation with entropic processes of long-wave decline may blind the forecaster to counter-cyclical syntropic processes of economic growth and technological innovation. These positive developments may balance out the entropic processes sufficiently to keep what might have become a depression within the bounds of what may be a series of limited recessions. The long-wave model may also suffer from what Karl Popper called the "poverty of historicism" by basing future projections upon past behavior, whereas we can never know what people in the future will know and therefore cannot predict what their options will be. Another

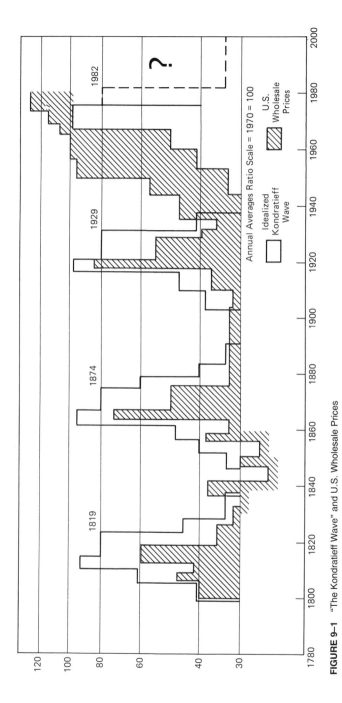

FIGURE 9–1 "The Kondratieff Wave" and U.S. Wholesale Prices

Source note: This line drawing is the author's rough conception of the original "Kondratieff Wave." The original chart was published in the international MONEYLINE, a financial newsletter.

277

objection to the long-wave depression thesis is that it could become a negative self-fulfilling prophecy, having a **reverse Pygmalion effect**—increasing the odds of extraordinarily bad economic outcomes by projecting such negative expectations.

The difficulty for the corporate strategist who overemphasizes the long-wave is the tendency to miss the healthy trees by taking a distant view of the dark forest: Not all sectors decline in any particular recession. The astute entrepreneur may be far better off looking for hidden positive opportunities in familiar territory in a situation of economic turbulence. Otherwise he or she may go bankrupt by accepting a fatalistic, cyclical determinism and waiting for a decade or more to pass in order to catch the next long wave as it begins to make its "inevitable" ascent. For example, by ignoring market cycle timing and by focusing on specific company situations he knew from interviewing or personal experience, Peter Lynch was able to maintain the highest average returns for his Fidelity Magellan Fund portfolio of stocks throughout the 1970s and 1980s, transforming it into the largest American mutual fund (see Lynch's *One Up on Wall Street*). The long-term wave has the flavor of the material determinism against which Benedetto Croce warned us two years after the onset of the Great Depression of 1929: "The sterility of matter will not bring forth and cause to blossom either morals or religion or poetry or philosophy, and not even economics itself, which requires the glow of life, keen intelligence, and eagerness."[19]

In sum, in using short-term, intermediate-term, and long-term business cycles as a basis for corporate or business planning, one must be wary of the errors that result from overemphasizing any one time-frame or cycle. One must be wary of assuming that a general, macrolevel cycle will necessarily affect a specific microlevel sector or economic situation. To become preoccupied with cyclic thinking may inadvertently lead to a conservative maintenance bias in strategic planning and snuff out the sparks of individual enthusiasm and risk-taking without which the entrepreneur is but a straw man blowing in the wind.

Corporate Strategy

Step, for a moment, into the shoes of the corporate manager who is responsible for strategic plans, which assure not merely the corporation's survival but also a significant return on investment for owners and shareholders. It is easy to understand why a conservative maintenance strategy is tempting in an era of erratic change and uncertainty. The timing of business cycles often appears to be inscrutable. International markets and sources of supply are politicized. Flexible exchange rates and money-market funds have revolutionized the international monetary system. Productivity growth is erratic. Technological breakthroughs often appear to be in capital-intensive rather than labor-intensive sectors. Future inflation hovers like a black cloud above the aspirations of industrial democracies where most multinational corporate headquarters are based. It almost seems reasonable under such circumstances to think in terms of Social Darwinism—the strong survive, the weak go under. And it is tempting to adopt a defensive strategy to preserve the value of existing assets and investments, to shore up existing bulkheads in the structure, and to tighten up on efficiency controls within the organization.

An examination of corporate strategies that were employed to fight inflation in the 1970s in terms of four Weberian ideal types—the Defeatist, the Free-rider, the Maintenance Man, and the Entrepreneur—revealed that the maintenance strategy predominated. These four types of strategies were classified according to risk orientation, time horizon, guiding motive, consumption pattern, and characteristic portfolio mix as illustrated in Table 9–1.[20]

Table 9–1 is not meant to be exhaustive either in the number of strategy types or in the range of portfolio mixes. **Weberian "ideal types"** are just typical patterns or typifications of striking features in social reality, like the tips of icebergs that serve to indicate the massive structure that lies invisible beneath the surface. Actual corporate behavior patterns usually draw from more than one strategy type, and sometimes from all of them. Nevertheless, particular strategy types appear to be dominant in specific organizations at certain historical moments. Organizational survival in the past decade, for example, appeared to depend upon the company's ability to transcend defeatist and free-rider strategies. But the international climate of uncertainty did not stimulate healthy, risk-taking behavior. Concerns about losing because of change or inflation reinforced a normal conservative bias of organizations that favors maintenance strategies and penalizes the entrepreneur in an environment calling for the opposite.[21]

To understand the rationale for the defensive, risk-avoiding attitude that prevails in many corporations and institutions, it is helpful to recall economist Mancur Olson's thesis in *The Logic of Collective Action: Unless the number of individuals in a group is small, or unless there is coercion or some other incentive to make individuals act in their common interest, rational, self-interested individuals will not act to achieve their common or group interests.*[22] *There has to be some principle or policy of motivation and deterrence that cuts through large organizations and corporations to constantly remind individuals to maximize the organization's interest, not just their own.* In capitalist free-market systems or mixed economies, this is no easy task and management can never be sure of the effectiveness of efforts to assure company loyalty. Moreover, in the large, anonymous group context of the corporation, the individual is often tempted to become a free rider (or a defeatist). There is a rational temptation to settle for mediocre group compromises in which strategies are targeted not for high gains (entrepreneurial strategies) but are rather spread to reduce risks and to keep things going as they are for the sake of job security or promotion (maintenance strategies). Thus *the corporation in turbulent times appears to be caught in a*

TABLE 9-1 Corporate Strategies

Strategy Type	Risk Orientation	Time Horizon	Dominant Motive	Consumption Pattern	Portfolio Mix
DEFEATIST	Low	Past	Passive	Thrifty	*Security-oriented:* divest weak holdings insure areas of vulnerability consider declaring bankruptcy exploit cash cows/mature products
FREE-RIDER	High	Present	Active/Passive	High when others pay	*Cheap credit-oriented:* refinance at cheaper interest rate relocate where taxes are lower and public transportation and infrastructure can be exploited relocate abroad for cheap labor speculate in exchange markets
MAINTE-NANCE	Medium	Present short-term	Passive/Active	High	*Stable return and diversity-oriented:* maximize short-term profits reorganize business units within firm, targeting for specific markets buy back company's own stocks shorten reaction time within business units with limited computer planning develop better inflation indicators diversify in firm to cover risks mergers with large companies in similar fields
ENTREPRE-NEUR	High	Future long-term	Aggressive	All or nothing	*High return orientation:* acquire smaller companies to reduce resource dependence & increase innovation and technology R&D bring in outside consultants to plan better financing and R&D increase individual payoffs in company for those who create plans for long-term gains foreign expansion to follow or create customers, increase world market share, overcome international currency and tax fluctuations or government regulatory barriers lobby in government for tax subsidies for R&D, capital formation, and less regulation

double bind: For organizational survival certain "maintenance" rules and conventional loyalty codes must be established, but healthy organizational growth depends upon entrepreneurial risk-taking, which is obstructed by this very maintenance activity. Security and stable returns become the predominant concerns in an era of economic uncertainty. And stockholders in American firms reinforce the problem by annually pushing for short-term profits rather than cultivating long-term world market share and research and development (R&D).

There is one obvious way out of this corporate dilemma in theory, despite numerous variations in practice: The corporation must clearly define limited maintenance objectives for the sake of organizational and group stability (which in many cases may be centralized within the organization) and simultaneously select a number of entrepreneurial target areas and creative pilot tests aimed at high returns and adaptation to change in the long term (which may well be decentralized).

In looking at Table 9–1 and comparing the portfolio mixes of the maintenance and entrepreneurial strategies, it is clear that *maintenance thinking has a low or medium risk orientation, with a focus upon cutting costs and maximizing benefits* within *the firm, whereas entrepreneurial strategies focus on long-term planning and investment in new areas of greatest potential growth with a high risk orientation, seeking to maximize benefits or cut costs by investing* outside *the firm either nationally or internationally.* This observation, based on the analysis of corporate strategies in the inflationary environment of the 1970s, is consistent with Peter Drucker's well-known (but often neglected) thesis in his book *Management: Within* the organization the focus is upon *efficiency,* whereas *outside* the organization the focus is upon effectiveness, and that corporate strategies cannot be effective unless they go from the inside out.[23]

To survive and expand, corporations require a maintenance base from which to take long-term entrepreneurial risks in the search for new technologies, markets, and sources of resource supply. The Japanese, for example, have become hypercompetitive on the world market in many sectors, such as automobiles, through a unique blend of maintenance and entrepreneurial strategies (or maintenpreneurial strategies). For example, according to the maintenance principle, about one-quarter of Japanese workers are guaranteed that once hired they will not lose their jobs until they are "retired" in their mid-fifties.* This and other conservative maintenance preconditions built into the Japanese culture give company managers a freer hand in times of change or crisis, permitting them to introduce radical reorganization and

---

*At this point, they typically either accept more difficult (and usually less desirable) assignments abroad or live off of personal savings until their pensions start at 65 (thus stimulating the Japanese savings rate throughout the life-cycle). The earnings of Japanese are more conditioned by the number of dependents, age and seniority than those of American workers. See Arne Kalleberg and James Lincoln, "The Structure of Earnings Inequality in the United States and Japan," *American Journal of Sociology,* supp., 94: p. S149 (1988).

technical innovation—such as the introduction of robots on the assembly line.

In the mid-1970s, when major automakers were threatened with bankruptcy, governments stepped in to bail out companies like Chrysler and British Leyland with mixed results, whereas in Japan a "postliberal," communitarian culture integrating companies and banks permitted Toyo Kogya (the producer of Mazda cars) of Hiroshima to radically shift its strategy, restructure, double its productivity, cut its debt, and to fire no one for five years. The "maintenance base" was provided by the traditional loyalty of the Japanese local community, labor force (given job security), and private creditors. Thus, the Sumitomo Bank appointed six of its people to major management positions in the auto company, including chairman (a standard practice in Japan where banks usually own companies and supply managers). These personnel shifts together with worker-participation groups offering suggestions gave Mazda both the financial basis and flexibility needed for effective entrepreneurial adaptation to the changed environment. Parts inventories were cut back, even given the risks of stopping assembly lines; new equipment was purchased to improve efficiency (including robots); new hiring was frozen; workers agreed to accept smaller wage rises; and several thousand unneeded workers on the assembly line were rerouted to serve temporarily as Mazda car salespeople at distribution centers and from door-to-door. In the 1992–93 recession, Mazda successfully repeated this strategy, shifting managers to production lines.[24]

Whereas the development of Western industrial societies involved the evolution of separate institutions with autonomous spheres of influence and it was assumed that the spiritual and social life of the individual should reside *outside* the workplace, this is not the case in Japan or China.[25] The Japanese company concerns itself with the worker's full range of social and spiritual needs, creating a maintenance base that is tightly knit and integrated with the culture. For example, Toyota Motor Company, Japan's largest automaker, has created an entire town ("Toyota City") to satisfy needs of its workers ranging from houses, dormitories, baseball fields, gymnasiums, swimming pools, tennis courts, and sumo rings, to a company stadium. This is perhaps the most efficient automobile production center in the world. Toyota managers long resisted the temptation to attempt to apply their manufacturing formula outside Toyota City before reluctantly setting up a plant with General Motors in California in the 1980s.[26] By strictly adhering to three manufacturing objectives, the efficiency of the maintenance base of Toyota allowed the company in 1982 to manufacture and ship small cars to the United States for $1,300 to $1,700 less than American automakers could produce a similar car. These three manufacturing objectives were: (1) keep inventories to a bare minimum, (2) ensure that all phases of the manufacturing process are completed correctly the first time even if it slows down the assembly line, and (3) reduce the amount of human labor expended on each automobile. *This efficient maintenance base of Japan's incredibly effective entrepre-*

neurship is grounded on a "shame culture." Kenichi Ohmae, former managing director of McKinsey & Company in Tokyo, observed: "The Toyota system is based on shame culture—that it is shameful to stop the whole plant. It would be risky in the United States. One guy could sabotage the whole plant. A lot of Toyota's advantage is not directly transferable."[27] The resulting Japanese advantage over American automobile manufacturers is sharply revealed in the statistics in Table 9–2, which compare Japanese, American, and European automobile assembly plant performance.[28] The **just-in-time** delivery of parts to the point of assembly by a few, well-trained suppliers reduces the costs of storing inventory in Japan and in Japanese firms in the U.S. The high percentage of Japanese workers in teams on the work force increases productivity and reduces defects (through Deming-derived "quality control circles").

The ways in which a culture or society such as Japan is able to create such an efficient maintenance base, which permits such effective entrepreneurial strategies in the world market, remain somewhat mysterious. However, an hypothesis can be suggested. When the samurai of Japan lost status in the disintegration of their feudal society, they turned to business to recover their sense of purpose.[29] A similar pattern of entrepreneurial reaction resulted from the downward mobility suffered by the Balinese aristocracy.[30] *The hypothesis is that acute downward mobility or outright disaster in a feudal society brings maintenance and security needs to the surface if the society is to survive, forcing upper-class elites into focused entrepreneurial patterns initially oriented toward reconstructing an efficient maintenance base.* This hypothesis (complemented with the

TABLE 9–2   Comparisons of Japanese, U.S., and European Automobile Assembly Plant Performance

	Japanese in Japan	Japanese in N. America	American in N. America	All Europe
INVENTORIES (days for 8 sample parts)	.2	1.6	2.9	2.0
QUALITY (defects per 100 autos)	60.0	65.0	82.3	97.0
PRODUCTIVITY (hours to make a car)	16.8	21.2	25.1	36.2
PERCENT OF WORK FORCE IN TEAMS	69.3	71.3	17.3	.6

investment of U.S. capital and technology) could explain the incredible Japanese and German economic reconstructions after World War II.[31] A disturbing corollary to this hypothesis may be that societies that have skipped the feudal stage and have largely avoided acute downward mobility or wartime destruction on their own soil, such as the United States, may not be sufficiently motivated to reconstruct a modern, efficient maintenance base. As a consequence, such nations will become increasingly less competitive against societies, such as the Japanese and German, which have succeeded in reconstituting a modern basis for effective entrepreneurial strategies.

However, despite its feudal past, the British case following World War II provides another contrast to the German and Japanese, given that most of the outdated British industrial plant was not destroyed during the war. Hence there was less incentive to reconstruct a modern and efficient maintenance base (meaning the British had to compete with old factories and equipment). Many of the British upper class were led to believe they could preserve their status without having to modernize their industries or to stoop to become merely upwardly mobile entrepreneurs.[32] The limits of Anglo-Saxon liberalism in Britain and the United States played a role in fragmenting domestic power and their success in World War II made them complacent.

If a society, because of downward mobility or destructive experience, "takes care of" creating and sustaining an efficient maintenance base (through, for example, the Japanese culture of shame or the German culture of order), the business sector is free to focus its energy upon export-oriented growth and entrepreneurial strategies. This assumes that government policies permit the corporate flexibility they have in West Germany and Japan. In short, there are numerous cultural and maintenance-base preconditions to "the German economic miracle" and the efficiency of Japan's global "laser beam" market analysis. Such prerequisites also facilitate corporations from these countries in *hedging* and *positioning* strategies aimed at ensuring against the risk of downturns in the business cycle on the one hand, and at preparing them to be in the right place at the right time for upturns in the cycle on the other.

Thus, in terms of "hedging," in 1982 Toyota sought a more international stance by going into negotiations with General Motors Corporation concerning the possibility of jointly producing small cars in the United States. Although the negotiations succeeded, this was less important for Toyota than the fact that they were held. For such cooperative gestures ease American protectionist pressures aimed at keeping American cars out of the American market, whether by tariff or "voluntary restraint." However, there may be a limit to which the Americans will be satisfied with symbolic gestures. Between 1970 and 1994, the cumulative U.S. trade deficit with Japan was over a trillion dollars. In 1993, alone, the U.S. trade deficit with Japan reached $59 billion, over one-half of the overall $116 billion U.S. trade deficit for that year. In 1994, the Clinton administration demanded quantitative quotas to prove results in changing this deficit, but the Japanese refused on the grounds of pushing for deregulation at home and advocating voluntary solutions. The probability of a U.S.–Japanese trade war significantly increased. The U.S. was no longer as concerned with not offending the Japanese for fear they would dump their holdings of U.S. Treasury securities (which help to finance the U.S. deficit) since Japanese banks, strapped by recession, only bought about 10 percent of the securities offered by early 1994 compared to about 25 percent in 1988.[33]

Apart from "talking compromises" to postpone conflicts, other corporate hedging strategies include concentric and conglomerate diversification. **Concentric diversification** is expansion related to an organization's existing line of business or "strategic fit." **Conglomerate diversification** branches out into lines of business or markets unrelated to existing ones. Finally, corporations can also hedge against risks by insuring assets against loss due to exchange-rate fluctuations or high interest rates by buying foreign currencies or shares in money funds.

As for "positioning" strategies, an example *par excellence* is the Japanese strategy of shifting away from additional future investment in the politicized sector of automobiles and turning increasingly to microchips and other related high-tech sectors. (By 1982 the Japanese 64K RAM microcomputer chip had 70 percent of the world market share, and Japanese market share remains high despite increasing international competition.)

IMPLICATIONS

This analysis of corporate strategy suggests many reasons why corporations are tempted to adopt maintenance strategies to assure their survival. If a country does *not* have a secure and efficient maintenance base—the case of most countries in the world including most developed industrial nations—companies may be more tempted than otherwise to focus on a maintenance strategy rather than a high-risk entrepreneurial approach. Indeed, companies in many countries may have to establish certain infrastructural maintenance prerequisites, which they cannot take for granted that their culture or government will provide.* One cross-cultural study concluded that Japanese managers place social and security needs higher than self-actualization needs because these needs are less well satisfied than in British and American cultures.[34]

At a certain stage of development, industrial societies with a maintenance or conservative set of value biases may socialize or indoctrinate man-

---

*This may explain why business interests in capitalist cultures ask the government both for subsidies (maintenance prerequisites) and freedom.

agers and companies with maintenance strategies to such an extent that entrepreneurial long-term risks cannot break through. Such collective learning patterns and their effect on strategies of social planning have been substantiated cross-culturally by anthropologist Gregory Bateson.[35] Both the theorist and the corporate strategist would like to know what the role of big companies is compared to small business in this process of collective adjustment within particular cultures in terms of global economic change. For this last question, at least, some tentative answers have emerged.

Big-Business Buffers
and Small-Business Flexibility

The trade-offs between big business and small business in a modern society involve extreme claims of both sides: "Bigger is better" versus "Small is beautiful." Let us assume that the survival of the business enterprise is a common value that all firms share, whether they be large or small. The question is then whether large or small companies best assure survival at the end of the twentieth century. And further, which size firm has greater advantages in addition to mere survival?

Big business, ultimately incorporated in the multinational organization, is an organizational form that emerged from the Industrial Revolution, illustrated by enterprises such as the Hudson's Bay Company and British East India Company and later, in the 1890s, by American companies such as Singer, Standard Oil, and American Bell. The promise of bigness was the promise of combining maintenance and entrepreneurial strategies in an organization large enough to buffer its interest against the storms of creative destruction in the world economy on the one hand, and providing the base for research and development, and investment risk-taking on the other. In a famous chapter on "Monopolistic Practices" economist Joseph Schumpeter argues that *the very imperfection of the world market creates conditions appropriate for large corporations since the big company can use its resources strategically, adapting to change through its research and development capacity while buffering against unexpected change with its very size and ability to set or control prices.*[36] *Economies of scale given corporate size and large world market share allow big companies to deter new competitors from entering the market, thus assuring the stability afforded by a limited number of suppliers of a goods or service.* Investors are attracted by the security of bigness, particularly when governments are reluctant to permit large corporations to go bankrupt because of the increase in the unemployment rate that would result or because of the strategic nature of certain industries in terms of the national interest (the steel industry, for example).

Paradoxically, as the world economy becomes more interdependent, mercantilist state philosophies are stimulated that view major corporations as critical arms of state economic objectives in the competition for world trade, resources, and development. Some have even gone as far as to claim the corporate era is an improvement over earlier eras since "corporate pluralism" is more viable and progressive than the rugged individualistic pluralism upon which democratic Western state ideologies were founded.[37] Many multinational corporations have the communications, technological, financial, and personnel capacity to have a global view of change and collective interests. Ultimately, some even have a corporate foreign policy that transcends that of any particular nation-state, ideology, or region.

However, not everyone is pleased with "the global bargain" struck by the multinational corporations abroad or the monopoly effects of the big corporation at home. The opposing viewpoint was elegantly expressed by economist E.F. Schumacher in his populist classic *Small Is Beautiful.* Schumacher argued that the "bigger is better" thrust of the corporate economies of advanced industrial states has contributed to the error of treating capital as income, particularly "natural capital" (such as fossil fuels) as if it were expendable without limits. Developing countries, accordingly, should not aim for this insatiable big business model of capitalist Westernization but wisely accept the limits of nature and the earth's resources and utilize **intermediate technologies** targeted for their own unique capacities and situation. Economic growth per se is not a higher priority for Schumacher than the dignity of man or the respect for the natural environment: "The substance of man cannot be measured by the Gross National Product. Perhaps it cannot be measured at all, except for certain symptoms of loss."[38]

On a philosophical level, *who can deny that small is beautiful, that humans should "cultivate their gardens," that human dignity resides in the creation of one's own limited niches, and that in small, limited, but carefully targeted plans lie flexibility as well as independence?[39] The motivational allure of independent small business entrepreneurship is, of course, one of the classical seeds of the capitalist economic model. One "Eureka" or "ah ha!" experience transformed into a marketable product or niche and one has the future key to all individual happiness*—is this not the New World dream of going into business for oneself, becoming independent of any boss, becoming free, and one day becoming rich (which is what "making it" means in capitalist society)?

Moreover, small young businesses are where most of the jobs are created in advanced stages of capitalist society, contrary to "bigger is better" mythology. The M.I.T. Program on Neighborhoods and Regional Change discovered where the net new jobs emerged in a sample of 5.6 million businesses in the United States between 1969 and 1976: Two-thirds were created by companies with twenty or fewer employees, and about 80 percent were created by companies with 100 or fewer employees! As David L. Birch observes: "Smaller businesses more than offset their higher failure rates with their capacity to start up and expand dramatically. Larger businesses, in contrast, appear rather stagnant."[40] In addition, the M.I.T. study indicated that 80 percent of replacement jobs are created by firms four years old or younger. So large companies are no longer the major providers of new jobs for Americans. Nor are old companies. And in Italy, where macroeconomists were surprised at the economic recovery and growth rate in the late 1970s, the basis for the growth was found to be in small- and medium-sized firms. Evidently, at a certain advanced stage of capitalist development, *as a national economy shifts increasingly away from the manufacturing and toward the service sector, small young businesses become the engines of economic growth and job creation as large corporations seem to reach a point of stalemate or diminishing returns.*

Centralization and Decentralization

Of course the *either-or* thinking behind the split between big and small business organizations is a Western habit or pattern of collective learning that may be more a part of the economic problem than of the solution. Not surprisingly, Schumacher saw through this in his chapter entitled "Towards a Theory of Large-Scale Organisation." Here he notes that *while large-scale organisation is here to stay, the fundamental task is to achieve smallness* within *large organisation. A large organisation normally goes through alternating phases of* centralizing *and* decentralizing, *like swings of a pendulum:* "Whenever one encounters such *opposites,* each of them with persuasive arguments in its favour, it is worth looking into the depth of the problem for something more than compromise, more than a half-and-half solution. Maybe what we really need is not *either-or* but *the-one-and-the-other-at-the-same-time.*"[41]

This non-Western approach of simultaneously centralizing and decentralizing within the large organization, or as the Zen sage might put it, seeing the *yin* and *yang,* big and small, black and white, good and evil as interdependent, appears to be one of the reasons for the effectiveness of Japanese management in competing on world markets in spite of the turbulence of global change. For example, take the world's largest manufacturer of electrical appliances, Matsushita. In the 1930s, Matsushita combined four decentralized functions with four centralized functions within the organization. The four decentralized functions included independent managers and distinct product categories; strong consumer orientation on the part of these self-sufficient managers; the flexibility of small companies; and the cultivation of specialized expertise among these managers to allow them to mature rapidly.

At the same time, Matsushita countered these characteristics with four centralized functions: controllers reporting to a centralized accounting system at headquarters; a company bank that took in divisional profits and gave out funds for capital improvements; centralized personnel recruitment; and centralized training. The managerial genius of Matsushita (the founder) resided in the fact that he refused to choose "once and for all" between decentralization and centralization (the trap of Western either-or rigidity). Rather, he accepted the uncertainty of an unresolvable conflict between these organizational alternatives. This allowed Matsushita to view centralization and decentralization as a kind of alternating spiral, and he could draw on one aspect or the other depending upon what each particular historical moment called for.

Thus, in the confusion following World War II, Matsushita replaced his decentralized divisional organization with strong centralization under himself. He headed the advertising department personally to stimulate consumer confidence in his products. In the early 1950s, with greater need for flexibility to match increasing competition, he shifted the company back to a phase of decentralization, bringing back independent product groups. In the late 1950s he recentralized to adjust to the turbulence of an historical stage of growth and increasing interdependence in international markets. But when the business cycle in the early 1960s swung into recession and stagnation, he decentralized again to give his people in the field more flexibility and initiative. Following the oil crisis in the early 1970s, centralization was again instituted as a buffer against this disruptive rush of creative destruction.[42]

Thus the astute corporate manager can use centralization as a means to solidify maintenance objectives in times of historical crisis or disruptive change and can shift to decentralization to stimulate entrepreneurship among his people when the business cycle permits. Effective corporate strategies depend upon managers getting the feel for the relativity of unexpected change; upon sensing when to shore up the maintenance base and when to throw all energies toward entrepreneurial risk; upon knowing when to take a business cycle downturn or upturn seriously and how to react without overreacting: *both-and,* not either-or, *big-small,* not big or small, *long-short-term planning,* not long-term or short-term, *centralization and decentralization,* not centralization or decentralization. Governments can promote, or retard, such strategies of corporate adaptation by providing information, subsidies for sunrise industries, and protection for sunset industries. But from the corporate management perspective, rather than relying upon the uncertainty of government aid, it is usually best to try to reduce some of the uncertainty in planning by trying to anticipate business-electoral cycles that can have a significant impact upon economic growth and consumption.

The Politics of Business Cycles

Not only must corporate managers find a balance between long-term and short-term planning, between centralization and decentralization, between bigness and smallness, and between maintenance efficiency and entrepreneurial effectiveness, but they must develop an acute sense of political as well as economic timing in order to take advantage of business-electoral cycles. When asked in 1982 why he predicted a world economic recovery in 1984 given the global recession and widespread pessimism about the economic future, William W. Crouse, president of the Latin American Region of Revlon Health Care Group, answered: "Because a number of major countries have elections in 1984 and the economy picks up before elections."[43] In

Western democracies, the dependence of corporate planning upon governmental policies takes on a certain wavelike form that usually follows the pattern of national elections.

In an analysis of electoral-economic cycles in twenty-seven countries between 1961 and 1972, Professor Edward Tufte discovered that in nineteen of them short-run accelerations in real disposable income per capita were more likely to occur in election years than in years without elections. Tufte concluded: "The politicians' economic theory of election outcomes gives great weight to economic events in the months before the election; thus the politicians' strategy is to turn on the spigot surely and swiftly and fill the trough so that it counts with the electorate."[44] And other studies have confirmed that upswings in real disposable income per capita are highly correlated with greater electoral support for incumbents.[45]

By using instruments of economic policy like tax cuts, money creation, and transfer payments, politicians up for reelection can stimulate spending, economic growth, and job creation in the months before the election. Managers of multinational corporations seeking to maximize corporate interests and to buffer themselves against unfavorable change can systematically use their "international election portfolio" in order to take advantage of these spurts of economic growth, spending, and credit availability. And they can disinvest or lower their vulnerability in the off-years between elections. Even if the presence of a multinational company in a country is more or less permanent, the management can shift its funds and tax vulnerability according to the electoral-economic cycle of democracy so as to maximize its financial interests.

Of course these general electoral-economic cycle schedules must be counterbalanced by the real possibility of government incompetence in the management of macroeconomic tools for its own interest. Such government incompetence has become more apparent as changes in the global economy narrow the options of state economic policymakers—such as the rise of OPEC and the Euro-credit market. The mismanagement of the U.S. economy in terms of the electoral economic cycle in the late 1970s and the early 1980s is a striking example. President Jimmy Carter perfectly mistimed the recession his economic advisors had been coordinating, believing that Americans would stop spending once they anticipated hard times ahead, while in fact they kept spending out of an accurate sense that Carter's anti-inflation policy would prove ineffective in the short term and that dollars should be used up before they lost even more value. Thus, the belated recession preceding the 1980 presidential election was timed to the advantage not of the incumbent, as it should have been, but of the challenger, Ronald Reagan. President Reagan, however, initially appeared to be equally unable to manage the electoral-economic cycle. Waging an excessive battle against inflation, which resulted in record-high interest rates, the recessionary effect overwhelmed the stimulation provided by general tax cuts and tax advantages for high-income investors, and this dampened the electoral chances of

Reagan's fellow Republicans up for election in the fall of 1982, who had been promised an economic recovery in time to lift their sinking boats. The Reagan recovery followed but at a high cost in federal deficits pushed up by Keynesian defense spending.

Neither President Carter nor President Reagan had enough knowledge of the global economy to anticipate accurately the limitations of their efforts to influence the timing of macroeconomic events. The overemphasis on anti-inflation policy through tight money and high interest rates caused the international value of the dollar to rise to such an extent that the resulting U.S. trade deficit brought about a "structural recession" in 1981, which could no longer be easily arrested by short-term economic levers.[46] Both Carter and Reagan proved to be incapable of predicting the economic behavior of their fellow citizens: Carter overestimated the American propensity to save (even given a dismal past record) and Reagan overestimated the willingness of the rich to make long-term capital investments upon which his promised economic recovery depended.[47] Finally, President George Bush complacently overestimated the electorate's willingness to believe in an economic recovery that *was* actually in progress, resulting in Bush's loss to Clinton in 1992.

The failure of corporate strategists to appreciate the bias that electoral cycles can have upon business cycle projections in democracies such as the United States may help to explain the short-term motives and pressures for immediate results that have served to undermine American competitiveness in world markets in important sectors. Politically unwary, corporate planners too often take government projections at face value, which must necessarily be overly optimistic for the sake of reelection prospects. For similar reasons, corporate strategists may not take sufficient advantage of short-term economic boomlets that tend to occur before national elections, while simultaneously overstressing short-term *business* cycles, which appear to have been rendered more erratic by technological and global developments since the 1940s than they had been previously. Thus, the Hayes-Abernathy thesis of the Harvard Business School, which contended that American management had gone astray by drifting away from basics such as the factory floor and assembly line, focusing upon short-term financial management rather than long-term investment in technology and production facilities, may have been more of a symptom than the root cause of American industrial decline.[48] Global changes in technology and finance have been revolutionary in the late twentieth century, making the long-term future so uncertain that the maintenance-oriented manager is tempted to stress the short-term and low-level risks out of insecurity. The contribution of Professors Robert Hayes and William Abernathy lies in pointing out the *abstract* nature of the short-term thinking of American management in contrast, for example, with the "zero-defect" objective of the Japanese production process. *The entrepreneurial American culture is good at innovative beginnings, mass marketing and consuming the new. These very characteristics, however, mitigate against its ability to compete with the more conservative German and Japanese cultures in terms of systematic follow-through in managing programs, meeting perfectionist zero-defect standards and martialing and targeting resources, for effective competitiveness.*[49] (See Chapter Five.)

But long-term thinking must be motivated by more than mere error-elimination and assembly-line efficiency. Investing in technology and plant capacity for the twenty-first century implies seeing through the red herrings provided by short-term electoral and business cycles, anticipating intermediate and long-term business waves, and choosing strategic areas for concrete development in which a particular national political economy or corporation is apt to be able to maintain a comparative advantage in the future. From the long-term perspective, it is more a time to cut the quick from the dead than a time to become preoccupied with reviving the dead on the assembly line. The maintenance base of industrial manufacturing in a country may best be served by a "postliberal" culture in which the state targets growth areas for long-term economic support and helps to consolidate weak sectors essential to the national interest. The key is public management to create long-term conditions conducive to corporate competitiveness and low national unemployment through indirect means rather than direct intervention. As the Zen masters put it: "To point at the moon a finger is needed, but woe to him who mistakes the finger for the moon."

THOUGHT QUESTIONS

1. Compare and contrast how American and Japanese multinational companies emerged.

2. What is "The Law of Uneven Development" and how does it relate to the bargaining power of multinational companies based in rich, as opposed to poor, countries? How does the product cycle fit into this?

3. Describe the short-term business cycle in comparison with the intermediate-term cycle and long-wave. Give examples.

4. Compare Table 9–1 (p. 280) with Table 8–1 (p. 249). Is the dilemma that the state has to motivate and provide for its people the same as that of the corporation?

5. There are problems associated with extremes of any organizational type. For example: centralized vs. decentralized decision making in a corporation; free-market vs. socialism (welfare state) for a nation, but there are advantages as well. The thesis in the text, whether it be state or corporation, seems to be that one *can* have it all, humankind just has not yet quite figured out how! Preparation for *group project in class:* Begin formulating a theory for the corporation (a mature one that tends towards maintenance) that you think would allow the corporation to "have it all"—it would motivate the people and provide for

them! (Optimally, the theory could be used for a nation as well.) What do you think is the maximum size of group in which entrepreneurship is apt to function effectively and why?

NOTES

1. Mira Wilkins, *American Business Abroad from the Colonial Era to 1914* (Cambridge, MA: Harvard University Press, 1970), p. 6. Wilkins serves as the basic source for this section on the American evolution.

2. Ibid., p. 70.

3. Mansel G. Blackford, *The Rise of Modern Business in Great Britain, the U.S. and Japan* (Chapel Hill: University of North Carolina Press, 1988), p. 35.

4. Ibid., p. 80.

5. See Georg H. Küster, "Germany," in Raymond Vernon, ed., *Big Business and the State: Changing Relations in Western Europe* (Cambridge, MA: Harvard University Press, 1974), p. 138.

6. Anonymous personal interview with manager in Mitsubishi, November 26, 1988.

7. Yoshi Tsurumi, *Multinational Management: Business Strategy and Government Policy*, 2nd edition (Cambridge, MA: Ballinger, 1984), pp. 107–20.

8. Hymer made the oligopoly-leading-direct-investment argument in his 1960 doctoral dissertation at the Massachusetts Institute of Technology. For the relation of this argument to the "Law of Uneven Development," see Stephen Hymer, "The Multinational Corporation and the Law of Uneven Development," in J. Bhagwati, ed., *Economics and World Order from the 1970s to the 1990s* (New York: Collier-Macmillan, 1972), pp. 113–40.

9. United Nations Centre on Transnational Corporations, *Transnational Corporations in World Development*, Third Survey (New York: United Nations, 1983), pp. 318–26.

10. See Y. Tsurumi, *Multinational Management*, pp. 193–96.

11. Theodore H. Moran, "A New United States Policy Toward Multinational Enterprises," a paper presented at the Faculty Seminar on International Political Economy at Columbia University, New York, November 19, 1975.

12. For initial efforts at forming such Third-World companies, see David A. Heenan and Warren J. Keegan, "The Rise of Third World Multinationals," *Harvard Business Review* (Jan.–Feb. 1979): 102, 103; and Louis T. Wells, Jr., "Guess Who's Creating the World's Newest Multinationals?" *The Wall Street Journal*, December 12, 1983, p. 22.

13. See Raymond Vernon, "International Investment and International Trade in the Product Cycle," *Quarterly Journal of Economics* LXXX (May 1966): 190–207.

14. See James M. Lutz and Robert T. Green, "The Product Life Cycle and the Export Position of the United States," *Journal of International Business Studies* XIV, No. 3 (Winter 1983): 77–94, and Alicia Mullor-Sebastian, "The Product Life Cycle Theory: Empirical Evidence," *Journal of International Business Studies* XIV, No. 3 (1983): 95–106.

15. See Ian Giddy, "The Demise of the Product Life Cycle Model in International Business Theory," *Columbia Journal of World Business* (Spring 1978): 90–96.

16. Alvin H. Hansen, *Fiscal Policy and Business Cycles* (New York: W.W. Norton, 1941), pp. 18–24.

17. Alekandr Solzhenitsyn, *The Gulag Archipelago* (New York: Harper & Row, 1973), p. 50 fn.

18. N.D. Kondratieff, "The Long Waves in Economic Life," *The Review of Economic Statistics* XVII (November 1935). Also see George Garvy, "Kondratieff's Theory of Long Cycles," *Review of Economic Statistics* XXV (November 1943), and W.W. Rostow, "Kondratieff, Schumpeter, and Kuznets: Trend Periods Revisited," *Journal of Economic History* 35, No. 4 (December 1975). Also see W.W. Rostow, *Why the Poor Get Richer and the Rich Slow Down* (Austin: University of Texas Press, 1980), Chapters 1 and 2. For a recent version of long-wave thinking see Jay W. Forrester, "A Great Depression Ahead?" *The Futurist,* December 1978, pp. 379–385.

19. Benedetto Croce, *History of Europe in the Nineteenth Century* (New York: Harcourt, Brace and World, Inc., 1963, originally published in 1933), p. 37.

20. Robert Isaak, "Modern Reactions to Inflation: Private and Public Strategies," Part II in Wilhelm Hankel and Robert Isaak, *Modern Inflation: Its Economics and Politics* (Lanham, MD: University Press of America, 1983). German version: *Die moderne Inflation* (Köln: Bund-Verlag, 1981). Also see R. Isaak, "Inflation Strategies in the 1980s," *The Adherent* 9, No. 1 (March 1982): 32–47.

21. Ibid. For the conservative bias of organizations, see Ruth Mack, *Planning on Uncertainty* (New York: Wiley, 1971); Robert Townsend, *Up the Organization: How to Stop the Corporation from Stifling People and Strangling Profits* (London: Michael Joseph Ltd., 1970); and Peter Drucker, *Managing for Results* (New York: Harper & Row, 1964). On being overenamored with the process of management stressing order, efficiency, and predictability (what I have referred to as the 'maintenance syndrome') see Abraham Zaleznik, *The Managerial Mystique* (N.Y.: Harper & Row, 1989).

22. Mancur Olson, *The Logic of Collective Action* (Cambridge, MA: Harvard University Press, 1965), p. 2.

23. Peter F. Drucker, *Management: Tasks, Responsibilities and Practices* (New York: Harper & Row, 1973).

24. Andrew Pollack, "Japan Finds Ways to Save Tradition of Lifetime Jobs," *The New York Times,* Nov. 28, 1993.

25. Richard Tanner Pascale and Anthony G. Athos, *The Art of Japanese Management* (New York: Simon & Schuster, 1981), Chapter 1, pp. 19–27. For the global implications from a Japanese perspective, see Takashi Inoguchi and Daniel I. Okimoto, *The Political Economy of Japan* (Stanford, CA: Stanford University Press, 1988).

26. For a critical view see Mike Parker and Jane Slaughter, "Behind the Scenes at Nummi Motors," *The New York Times,* December 4, 1988.

27. Steven Lohr, "The Company That Stopped Detroit," *The New York Times,* March 21, 1982, Section 3, p. 26.

28. These statistics are from James P. Womack, Daniel T. Jones, and Daniel Roos, *The Machine That Changed the World* (New York: Macmillan, 1990), pp. 92, 118.

29. See Everett Hagen, *On the Theory of Social Change* (London: Tavistock Publications, 1964), Chapter 14.

30. See Clifford Gertz, *Peddlers and Princes: Social Development and Economics in Two Indonesian Towns* (Chicago: University of Chicago Press, 1963).

31. For the German case interpreted from this perspective see R. Isaak, *European Politics: Political Economy and Policy Making in Western Democracies* (New York: St. Martin's Press, 1980), Chapter 2, pp. 27–62.

32. Ibid., Chapter 4: "Great Britain: A Socialized Economy in Crisis," pp. 99–125.

33. Bob Davies and Jacob M. Schlesinger, "Trade War? Unlikely, but Shifting Relations Do Increase the Risk," *The Wall Street Journal,* February 18, 1994.

34. Mason Haire, Edwin Ghiselli, and Lyman W. Porter, *Managerial Thinking* (New York: Wiley, 1966). But also see C.J. McMillan, "Social Values and Management Innovation: The Case of Japan," in *Management under Differing Value Systems,* edited by Günter Dlugos and Klaus Weiermair (Hawthorne, NY: Walter de Gruyter, Inc., 1981).

35. Gregory Bateson, "Social Planning and the Concept of Deutero-Learning," *Steps to an Ecology of Mind* (New York: Ballantine Books, 1972), pp. 159–76. It may be time to take one step backwards in order to take two steps forward and learn how non-human animals learn collectively. For example, big horn sheep transmit home range knowledge from generation to generation *if* individual lambs are not dispersed from their home range (see Valarius Geist, *Mountain Sheep: A Study in Behavior and Evolution.* Chicago: University of Chicago Press, 1971). And wolf pups raised without the social structure of a wolf pack adapt poorly to life in the wild (see Barry Holstun Lopez, *Of Wolves and Men.* New York: Charles Scribners' Sons, 1978). Individual freedom (that is, mobility) is not always the recipe for health, survival or collective adaptation to global change. The cultural constraints upon mobility in West Germany and Japan may help to explain their efficacy at collective learning.

36. Joseph Schumpeter, *Capitalism, Socialism and Democracy* (New York: Harper & Row, 1950), pp. 87–106.

37. See Neil H. Jacoby, *Corporate Power and Social Responsibility* (New York: Macmillan, 1973).

38. E.F. Schumacher, *Small Is Beautiful: Economics as if People Mattered* (New York: Harper & Row, 1973), p. 20.

39. See, for example, Kempe Ronald Hope, "Self-Reliance and Participation of the Poor in the Development Process in the Third World," *Futures,* Vol. 15, No. 6 (December, 1983), pp. 455–462. And Charles Hampden-Turner, *From Poverty to Dignity* (Garden City, NY: Anchor-Doubleday, 1974).

40. David L. Birch, "Who Create Jobs?" *The Public Interest* 65 (Fall 1981): 7.

41. Schumacher, *Small Is Beautiful,* pp. 242–43. International Management consultant Stanley Davis confirms the need to overcome false either/or, centralization/decentralization dichotomies and to deal with the simultaneity of business opposites: see S. Davis, *Future Perfect* (Reading, MA: Addison-Wesley Publishing Co., 1987), p. 188.

42. Pascale and Athos, *Art of Japanese Management,* Chapter 2, "The Matsushita Example," pp. 28–57.

43. William W. Crouse, "Future Trends in International Business." Panel at conference on The Increasing Internationalization of Business, Pace University, White Plains, New York, March 6, 1982.

44. Edward Tufte, *Political Control of the Economy* (Princeton, NJ: Princeton University Press, 1978), pp. 10–11.

45. See Gerald Kramer, "Short-Term Fluctuations in U.S. Voting Behavior, 1896–1964," *American Political Science Review* 65 (March 1971): 131–43; and Ed-

ward Tufte, "Determinants of the Outcomes of Midterm Congressional Elections," *American Political Science Review* 69 (September 1975): 812–26.

46. See C. Fred Bergsten, "The Main Cause of the Recession," *The New York Times,* Op Ed, December 21, 1981. Also see interview with Bergsten in the March/April 1982 issue of *Challenge,* pp. 25–32.

47. See R. Isaak, "On Unstuffing the Turkey and Making Jobs from the Wishbone," *The Adherent* 9, No. 2 (Fall 1982).

48. Robert Hays and William Abernathy, "Managing Our Way to Economic Decline," *Harvard Business Review* (July–August 1980). See Martin K. Starr, ed., *Global Competitiveness* (N.Y.: W.W. Norton, 1988) and Lester C. Thurow, ed., *The Management Challenge: Japanese Views* (Cambridge, MA: The MIT Press, 1985).

49. See R. Isaak, "The Conservative Tradition of American Liberalism," *American Political Thinking* (Fort Worth, TX: Harcourt Brace, 1994), pp. 1–13.

CHAPTER TEN

SUMMING UP

In social manipulation our tools are people, and people learn, and they acquire habits which are more subtle and pervasive than the tricks which the blueprinter teaches them.

Gregory Bateson, *Social Planning and the Concept of Deutero- Learning* (1972)

When it comes to the future, the task is not to predict it, but simply to enable it.

Antoine de Saint Exupéry

A collective learning approach to international political economy assumes that a people's competitive behavior on the one hand and sense of participative fair play on the other are not just individual or abstract phenomena. Rather they result from a social learning pattern with a specific organizational context and cultural pattern. We learn not just from the teacher but from the milieu in the classroom. Our values are shaped not just by the ends or objects obtained by those to whom we grant deference, but by the rules of the game or means that our leaders use to get to their ends. Collectively, the Japanese would not symbolize such a well-navigated, tight ship in the turbulent storm of the global economy without the backdrop of a neo-Confucian, hierarchical culture. Nor would the Swedes be so generous with foreign aid and willing to sacrifice great ranges of personal income if the neo-corporatist culture of their society did not place equality of economic opportunity before individual self-aggrandizement.

This book started with the analogy of a tale by O. Henry. The political authority of a society broke down not because of the economic asymmetry or inequality itself but because of the collective learning by the people when foreign goods were introduced in a situation of high demand and structured scarcity. The inequality was the fuel; but the recognition that desired goods were being arbitrarily withheld was the match. The book ends with a similar moral: While capitalist models of political economy may win in the short and medium run as means to maximize economic growth, standards of living and individual freedom, the legitimacy of elites in such societies will be undermined to the extent wealth gaps or ratios between high and low incomes become too extreme. Or, as Lord Overstone put it, "No warning can save a people determined to grow suddenly rich." Aristotle argued that stable democracy requires a large middle class. Extremes of wealth and poverty and of economic opportunity undermine the legitimacy of democratic societies— *and* the stability of global political economic systems.

For if an undemocratic world economy is envisioned as one large, *potential* democratic society, extremes of rich and poor and blatantly unequal economic opportunities in different nations undermine the legitimacy of the existing world order, destabilizing it. Transnational terrorism is motivated, in part, by a sense of being declassed and marginalized by the existing system: The rules appear to be heavily loaded not only against one's self but against one's people. While this general diagnosis of the consequences of extreme inequality seems obvious, effective political economic recipes to do something about the situation are not.

*   *   *

DEFINING THE SITUATION

International political economy is the study of the patterns of positioning and collective learning between nations and peoples that either preserve or change the inequality between them.

Anglo-Saxon ideology structured the institutional context of international economic exchanges during the nineteenth and twentieth centuries through a *pax Britannica* followed later by a *pax Americana*. The socialist antithesis to this hegemony—whether in its Soviet or Chinese or nonaligned manifestations—failed. However, the cold war struggles during the twentieth century did serve to undermine the legitimacy and financial soundness of the Anglo-Saxon order.

Great Britain was already financially crippled by the end of World War

II. But U.S. military spending, hyped-up to fever pitch during that war, led the way to push the Americans into becoming the world's greatest national debtor (four times that of Brazil) in absolute terms by the end of the 1980s. This was mitigated only by the fact that the U.S. debt was in its own currency and that currency happened still to be the world's key reserve currency.

As the superpowers could no longer afford their strategic arms race, the bipolar world became increasingly multipolar. International change became increasingly unpredictable: The greater the number of major players, the greater the uncertainty in global outcomes. Not only did a number of other nations obtain nuclear weapons, but Japan, Western Europe, and newly industrializing countries became world-class economic competitors in a number of fields. Ideologically, First, Third, and Fourth Worlds proliferated. Second (socialist) Worlds diminished. And *within* these "Worlds" the trend was toward disintegration within states for the sake of the ethnic autonomy of small, self-contained units. Those used to viewing world affairs with *bi*noculars now were looking through a kaleidoscope.

With the spread of multipolarity—militarily, technologically, economically, and ideologically—the primacy of global logic was countered with ethnic revolts. But the old, industrialized countries boosted their arms sales to feed the frenzy of local and regional conflicts away from home. The inequality between nations and peoples became more pronounced as technological developments and socioeconomic change accelerated both the tempo of life and the collective adaptations necessary to remain internationally competitive.

THE MAINTENANCE THESIS: MANAGING ECONOMIC RISK

The more dependent a country is in the world economy, the more its managers usually tend to seek control and stability. Or at least they strive for the appearance of equilibrium, which keeps them in power and makes their domestic situation seem predictable enough to outsiders to attract foreign aid and investment. Managers in wealthier or more independent countries, in contrast, can take this equilibrium or *maintenance base* for granted, using it as a springboard for entrepreneurial risk and technological innovation. Financial credit, too, flows more automatically to stable collectivities to support their risks.

Many managers in such a well-maintained milieu, however, do not take advantage of this dynamic management potential inherent in their privileged position. They prefer to minimize their risks for the sake of preserving a comfortable routine and a status quo friendly to their interests, falling into a maintenance syndrome. Thus, there are distinctive but understandable conservative tendencies on the part of managers in both rich and poor countries to embrace stability and to optimize existing balances of power rather than to make policies aimed at radical change or long-term risk to adjust their collectivities to the competitiveness required in the rapidly changing global economy.

The maintenance base is a boundaried social system or organization oriented toward internal stability, security, efficiency, and risk-reduction. The "inside" perspective of the maintenance base contrasts with the "outside" efforts at entrepreneurial innovation, risk-taking, adaptation, and effectiveness in terms of changing external markets in the global environment. Effective collective learning in the world economy involves going from the inside out once the efficiency of the maintenance base can be taken for granted and can help to target entrepreneurial risks in new global markets. To become too self-preoccupied within the maintenance base is soon to be passed by as global competitors aggressively pursue new global opportunities from their home bases.

On the other hand, to diffuse oneself in too many risk-taking ventures at once at the expense of neglecting the maintenance base is similar to having too many irons in the fire, or to attacking with too many figures at once in a chess game without backing them up with protection. All risks need not be hedged, but they need to be collectively thought through. Risk-taking must be targeted after careful positioning and follow up. Extraordinary economic success over time demands a flexible yet tightly coordinated institutional infrastructure capable of backing up collective entrepreneurial targeting.

In the late twentieth century, economic advantages have gone to nations with a feudal, hierarchical tradition and taken-for-granted maintenance base of order that have experienced an entrepreneurial break from this order. Typically their security needs were covered by others and they found ready access to finance and technology in a growing world economy: West Germany, Japan and South Korea—for example. The past hierarchical traditions of these countries underscore the importance of education and respect for those older and wiser with more experience. Consensus-building cultural schemata such as "shame" (in Japan) and "order" (in Germany) steered collective learning. In short, a deep-seated social consensus exists at the maintenance base that permits such societies to concentrate their collective energies on adapting to opportunities and innovations abroad. Indeed, in feudal societies of the past, the elites, whose landed status and legitimacy have been displaced by modernization and democracy, attempt to recover their status through entrepreneurial efforts, thus bringing new economic life to the maintenance base of their countries as well as to their families. Recall the cases of the Balinese aristocracy, the samurai of Japan, or, more recently, the restoration of the Minsheng Shipping Company family as the first large private company allowed to operate outside the state-planning system in the People's Republic of China. The resurrection of large German firms after World War II and the reincarnation of the Japanese *zaibatsu* as *sogoshosha* in postwar Japan are other cases in point. In times of economic crisis or structural stalemate, political economy managers call on the support of old elites and successful economic organizations of the past, taking calculated entrepreneurial risks to breathe new life into their national economies.

Whereas nations with "industrialized" feudal or hierarchical pasts often represent tight ships of order in the international chaos of global political economy, the United States represents the maintenance of domestic disorder or chaos for the sake of individual freedom and dynamic markets. This stable chaos keeps the Americans from being "ordered" around by hierarchical authorities and stimulates innovative creativity as people cast off relationships, careers, businesses, homes and lifestyles like unfashionable clothing in a restless, nonstop environment of mobility. Small wonder that savings rates are low, consumption high, markets innovative, and debt mushrooming in a country whose basic behavioral ground rules are freedom of action and the individual desire to freely choose to do well that which others in the society tell them is fashionable or appropriate. The possibility of exporting this consumer-led, democratic chaos of innovative mobility to other countries seems remote, despite American foreign policy efforts to the contrary. The absence of a feudal experience in American history sets the nation apart from many others, making it as hard for Americans to understand those with feudal pasts as it is for citizens of countries with former feudal ties to understand a nation without them. It should come as no surprise that the United States should have become the dynamic source of global innovation, security, and credit in the twentieth century for other nations constrained by feudal/hierarchical pasts and defeats given the different resource bases and cultural heritages.

SPEED LIMITS AND INFORMATION OVERLOAD: ACCELERATION VERSUS RETARDATION

The tempo of socioeconomic and technological change has greatly speeded up in the atomic century. Peoples all over the earth have found themselves future-shocked and overloaded with information. The Russian scientist Pavlov discovered that animals could be driven crazy if given too much stimulation or choice. The tempo of socioeconomic change threatens to have this Pavlovian effect upon the human animal. There are clear limits to how much information a human being or group of human beings can absorb and how fast a human being or group of human beings can be asked to think or to move without making irrational choices or breaking down.

In a high-technology, high-information global economy information has become power, but not just any information. The key to collective learning for economic and political effectiveness is to slow the information flow down, analyze it, select only the critical data for a clearly defined purpose, and to act on this targeted information, getting as much feedback as quickly as possible once action has been taken. *Significant information is that "ah ha" phenomenon which radically changes how we see the world and shakes us out of old routines or beliefs. Such a meaningful "information storm" (brainstorm) or breakthrough causes the socialist to realize one cannot stimulate economic growth without creating explicitly unequal material incentives, or causes the capitalist to see that the social control of violence or maintenance of social harmony depends upon explicit limitations upon human freedom and upon extreme income disparities.* Clearly it is more comfortable for such socialists and capitalists to maintain their conventional worldviews without having such information-storm breakdowns (or lighting ups). But the tempo of global economic change and the pervasiveness of international communications guarantee that data overloads and information storms are inevitable for those who continue to function as fully rational human beings capable of learning.

Speed control is perhaps the most underestimated phenomena in international political economy. Speeding up and slowing down are equally important strategic concepts, which can sometimes be used simultaneously in different sectors. Gorbachev tried desperately to get the Russian people to accept the concept of *uskorenie* (acceleration) in order to bring collective learning up to speed in furthering his *perestroika* (restructuring) program. But the integrity of the Russian soul depends upon an extensive view of time, as eternal patience for the sake of eternal values, if you will. The unhurried pace of life, which was the charm of Russian culture in the nineteenth century (the Chekhov *cachet*), became a stumbling block for Gorbachev's (and then Yeltsin's) desire for acceleration. Local ethnic communities want autonomy for their cultural way of life first, distrusting state-sponsored programs of modernization.

West German Chancellor Helmut Kohl sped up the pace of German unification in February 1990 in order to outmaneuver the domestic political opposition and to present the world with a fait accompli. President Carlos Salinas de Gortari of Mexico did all he could to push NAFTA through quickly in 1993. And Prime Minister Mahathir Mohamad of Malaysia used state financial disincentives to slow down speculative stock investment into his economy in 1994, which threatened to raise the inflation rate.

On another front, no insignificant part of the success of the Japanese political economy is its ability to slow down the decision-making process by use of *nemawashi*, or the informal shaking down of ideas among those who will be affected by them in order to prepare the ground or consensus for effective innovation. This slowing down process permits each individual in the company to make suggestions and point out weaknesses before a change becomes official, refining and targeting adaptations before they are instituted and getting everyone on board before innovation is launched. Such a slowing-down-in-order-to-follow-through-with-all-on-board process would be a good one for Americans to learn from: The traditional U.S. chief executive officer typically rams changes down the throats of subordinates in memos from the top of the hierarchy, thus putting his status on the line before the flaws are removed or before the soil has been properly prepared for change among his subordinates. On the other hand, in the same organization there are no doubt individuals who have to be motivated to accelerate their work processes—indeed, people whose slowness may be a hidden protest against the arbitrary authority represented by impulsive orders from the top.

Take a positive example of the use of strategic *retardation* (or slowing down): During the 1987 stock market crash, the head of the New York Stock Exchange prohibited computer programming for a few hours, requiring brokers to make buy or sell orders by hand. Slowing down the system meant that it did not have to be shut down, cooling off panic. The international manager can use a deliberate policy of retardation not only as a cooling off device, but also to focus attention upon the quality of results. On the other hand, the strategy of *acceleration* speeds up the process of change by identifying with it and positioning oneself on the cutting edge (as did Yeltsin) or pushing through fait accompli policy (such as German unification by West Germany).

COLLECTIVE LEARNING AND CULTURAL RESISTANCE

Information overload implies that collective learning is most effective when it is arbitrarily delimited and targeted but in a way that breeds consensus and high morale rather than polarization and resistance. If knowledge is the orderly loss of information, the critical prerequisite to collective learning is to create a consensus upon the criteria for sorting the wheat from the chaff. Ideology is only an abstract and imperfect criterion in this regard as those who tried to apply the Stalinist model of political economy discovered. What we are dealing with here is a dynamic link between the micro and macro levels of analysis, which enables groups of people to learn things efficiently and to apply them effectively in the context of a rapidly changing global economy. Cultural *schemata* or prototypes of learning consolidate "legitimate" information.

Collective learning is social learning with a specific organizational context and cultural gestalt: It is a process of differentiating legitimate patterns of adaptive behavior to manage environmental change without losing cultural integrity. The concept gets beyond the overly psychological notion of social learning theory—the result of reciprocal interactions among person (cognition), behavior, and environmental situation. Collective learning accepts these elements of social learning theory, and particularly its assumption that

individuals can learn from others vicariously or from modeling their own behavior after others whom they have observed. But collective learning emphasizes the collective gestalt or organizational pattern that delimits the
schemata for learning or for resistance to change. Such a collective gestalt or
cultural context presupposes the legitimacy of specific learning models,
structures, and paradigms and the exclusion of others. It emphasizes
deutero-learning or how people learn learnings, what they pick up from the
learning process and milieu, not just the content of learning.

For example, in Bulgaria during the cold-war era, the successful manager of the state-owned company was traditionally the one with enough clout
with his superiors in the party hierarchy to get a *reduction* in the annual production quota for his factory, even though this behavior contradicts the functional purpose of the enterprise. For the socialist manager learned that lower
quotas were easier to reach, meaning bonuses for himself and his workers.
Less work also means more free time and a higher quality of life. The collective schemata in such a political economy encouraged the most "successful"
individuals to reduce their output—a learning pattern picked up fast but not
exactly a recipe for increasing international competitiveness.

To take another example, the American worker is often stimulated to
dance the Olsonian rag: Behavior is guided by the assumption that the interests of one's self and one's own small group are different from the interests
of the larger organization.* The worker quickly learns to maximize his or her
own personal interests, income, and job prospects regardless of the costs to
the organization or firm since in any case he or she will cut and run and take
a job soon with another firm. The critical cultural schemata are short-term,
self-interest maximization and "learning by burning." The job mobility built
into the cultural context of the system means that large organizations get left
holding the bills for the opportunity costs left behind by workers whom they
have trained and nurtured.

The Japanese and, to some extent Europeans, have reduced such opportunity costs by assuring core workers of formal or informal lifetime job security. This breeds an atmosphere of trust and social community in the organizational and cultural context, which often serves to nip labor disputes in
the bud and encourages management to invest in lifetime training programs
for workers who will be with them a lifetime. However, the drawback in this
motivational milieu is that once again the worker will catch on to the tricks
or real rules behind the formal commitments: Lifetime security may dampen
the enthusiasm for extraordinary achievement or taking innovative risks. In a
culture like that of the Japanese, "where the nail that sticks up gets hit," consensus can mean complacent followership and a deterrent to creativity. Even

*Refers to Mancur Olson's *The Logic of Collective Action* (Cambridge, MA: Harvard University Press, 1965).

the remarkably effective Japanese quality circles (modeled on W. Edwards Deming's criterion of quality being the reduction of variation) may best serve the function of improving processes already in place by cutting costs, reducing hazards, eliminating defects, rather than nurturing the "anti-system" mentality that leads to creative, technological breakthroughs.

THREE TYPES OF COLLECTIVE LEARNING

In comparing different cultures and their key schemata or protypes of legitimatized learning, three universal types of collective learning emerge that are critical for economic competitiveness:

1. Reduction of error within a rigid frame
2. Open, synergistic networking based on trust
3. Radical quantum leaps for technological breakthroughs

Reduction-of-error learning is that of W.E. Deming: increasing quality by reducing variation or error. It also fits Kenneth Boulding's definition of knowledge: the systematic loss of information. The aim is to reduce costs and risks. Uncertainty is reduced by rigid rules within a narrow framework, which systematically eliminates the possibility of errors in the production process. Type One, reduction-of-error learning, is appropriate for firms producing standardized products for large markets with long product life-cycles. Its focus is upon systematically making the maintenance base more efficient.

Open, synergistic learning is based upon a leap-of-faith within and between organizations to brainstorm and create just-in-time products for the business cycle. Type Two, or open-synergistic learning, is appropriate for customized, short product life-cycle products that are on the cutting edge of technology. Careful partner selection and trust are bases to coopt technological innovations, cut restructuring costs, and expand global market share. The focus is on teamwork for targeted entrepreneurship and risk-taking, transcending mere error reduction to anticipate markets that may not even exist yet. Interactive telecommunication mergers to monopolize markets in advance for interactive television and video use in the home is an example of this type of collective learning. It characterizes *virtual organizations* or collective learning networks that can instantaneously produce and deliver products for a specific customer at any time, in any place, and in any variety—anticipating reality that is almost there and making it concrete.

Radical, quantum-leap learning breaks down old paradigms and results in technological breakthroughs and unpredictable creativity. There is often the hope that Type Two open-synergistic learning will spill over and result in Type Three radical, quantum leap breakthroughs. But the preconditions are often missing for such extraordinary outcomes. What is required is to find the best people in the world and let them run free in a semi-controlled, highly motivated environment with broad targets. Two German scientists won the Nobel Prize in physics in 1988 with research done secretly, behind the back of their scientist manager in their IBM laboratory in Zurich. They feared this manager might prevent them from putting in time on such an heretical idea. Type Three, radical-quantum-leap learning, requires a creative environment in which gifted people are given the freedom to revolt against the rules of the very system that managers have put them in.*

Of course finding the "right people" presupposes a cultural as well as a functional selection that may leave the majority outside the system or could even systematically discriminate against the most brilliant individuals. A person who believes that *Ogni mattina io rinasco* (Each morning, I am born anew) may have to work for himself or herself to find a superior willing to put up with this first principle. Yet firmly held first principles are essential to individual and cultural integrity. A person with "character" is one willing to fight the fashionable trends or repressive laws even to the death if necessary for some higher value. Antigone thus insisted on the right to bury her brother, despite the law forbidding it. And Lech Walesa, the leader of the once-outlawed Solidarity trade union in Poland, took his stand so firmly and persistently that by 1989 the Polish government reversed itself and opened talks with him, recognizing Solidarity's right to exist and Solidarity moved front and center into government power.

Throughout Eastern Europe there is a caldron of national movements to defend the cultural and political rights of autonomy for ethnic minorities. Cultural resistance to collective learning patterns directed from party officials and government leaders may be the key to the existential integrity of many peoples, even though their struggles have high collective costs. Collective adaptation for more economic gain is not the ultimate end of human existence.

The successful national manager of a political economy must read through the unmovable schemata of resistance scattered throughout the culture and give those marginal people of integrity a legitimate part in the process of collective economic transformation or watch desired reforms die of inertia. The extreme conservative reactions to the "shock therapy" economic reforms in Russia and Poland are telling illustrations of resistance to counterthreats to traditional cultural integrity.

*This learning typology was first presented in R. Isaak, "Virtual Organizations: From Entrepreneurial Networks to Strategic Alliances," a paper presented at an International Symposium, "Networking of Human Relations and Technology," at Tokyo Keizai University, October 25, 1993 in Tokyo; and later revised and given at the international seminar "Training for Change" at the *Institut d'Administration des Enterprises* May 5, 1994 in Aix-en-Provence.

CLOSURE VERSUS AMBIVALENT BELIEF SYSTEMS

Effective collective political economy strategies depend upon anticipating the tendency of the human mind toward closure and countering it, or unlocking it before it is too late. Collective organizational efforts can take on a life of their own and continue to the point of self-destruction unless they are derailed or side-tracked. An example of this "edge effect" gone mad, the momentum for the sake of aesthetic completion regardless of human consequences, is the World War II Manhattan Project, which developed the atomic bomb in the United States. Participants in the project found that they were so caught up in the collective learning process after three years of night-and-day struggle to achieve the breakthrough that even though they knew Nazi Germany had surrendered they had to continue to completion. The result was the dropping of two atomic bombs on Japan. Once "group think" gets rolling and is stimulated with patriotism, money, honor, status and wartime frenzy, the temptation for closure becomes almost irresistible.

Moreover, closure is often a much more attractive political style in a highly uncertain world situation than an ambivalent belief system. Stalin knew this. So did Mao Tse-tung. President Ronald Reagan benefitted from this effect in the simplicity of his creed, although thankfully he turned out to be a pragmatic compromiser in practice. People want their great communicators to have simple, firmly held beliefs. Closure, in short.

Not that all closure is necessarily a bad thing. If one considers those few modern cases of success in transforming authoritarian state-controlled economies to market-oriented, democratic economies one finds a moment of closure in historical time in which things are suddenly reversed, the price system decontrolled. Such was the case in the spring of 1948 in West Germany when the Reichsmark was almost without value, long lines surrounded stores, and black markets proliferated. German Economic Minister Ludwig Erhard with the cooperation of the American occupation forces (in Operation Bird Dog) obtained a few wagonloads of paper money printed in the United States and declared "the Currency Reform" overnight. Each German citizen was at first permitted to receive forty new Deutsche Marks (DM) in a 1:1 exchange for the next to worthless Reichsmark. No one was to receive either more nor less than forty DM. A little later, each citizen was permitted to receive twenty more. Thus began the Social Market Economy and West German economic miracle. And all done with a simple act of closure.*

Other forms of closure, however, are incompatible with collective adap-

---

*Of course it must be recalled that this currency reform was done under a military government that could force the people who lost their savings to swallow it—not exactly a democratic recipe. Poland's 1990 "shock therapy" policy of removing price controls while keeping wage controls, ending subsidies for goods and services, privatizing state-owned companies, postponing foreign debt repayment and getting aid from the World Bank, IMF and friendly governments bordered on short-term closure. But the people soon grew tired of sacrifices and voted to bring hard-line Communists back into power (See Chapter Two).

tation for either the sake of international competitiveness or for the sake of more widespread economic opportunity or social justice. This form of closure, for example, closes off the opportunity of becoming a U.S. Senator unless one has already been elected to that office and happens to have raised an average of $4 million. The closure of thinking against truly democratic election financing in the United States is turning a democracy quickly into an oligarchy with over 90 percent of those elected to the Senate and House of Representatives typically being incumbents. Or the closure of unions, which refuse to compromise with management even given the greater competitiveness and flexibility of workers abroad in the same industry. Or the closure of management in not granting the union workers meaningful lifetime security and health benefits. Or the closure of protectionism bills passed in Congress to put such managers and workers in a "greenhouse" until they use their time to become competitive.

But with the exceptions of infant industries, short-term import substitution, strategic and high-tech sectors, the greenhouse strategy often backfires in its collective learning effects. By putting their electronics companies in a state-subsidized greenhouse program, the French in the 1950s, for example, encouraged managers and workers alike to believe the comfortable support would go on forever. So they grew complacent and when the subsidies were withdrawn the French electronics industry went into a major crisis: It could not compete in real terms on the world market. And East Germans, used to guaranteed jobs and subsidized housing under the closure of a Communist Party state up until the fall of 1989, found the "cold shower" of market uncertainty and competition painful as they joined the West German collective learning process in the reunification of the 1990s. Closure, in short, can lull one into thinking uncertainty and risk have been licked and that one has it permanently made (despite the positive sense of social security which this provides). Closure is usually too comfortable to work for long.

The opposite of closure is targeted, strategic openness. This is the essence of the open-synergistic type of collective learning. As composer John Cage put it in *A Year from Monday* (1967): "In music it was hopeless to think in terms of the old structure (tonality), to do things following old methods (counterpoint, harmony), to use the old materials (orchestra instruments). We started from scratch: sound, silence, time, activity. In society, no amount of doctoring up economics/politics will help. Begin again, assuming abundance, unemployment, a field situation, multiplicity, unpredictability, immediacy, the possibility of participation." Not the cynical closure of Stalin nor the naive openness of democratic reformist ideology of the 1960s, but a yin/yang rhythm between the closure of necessary semi-control and targeting and the openness of spontaneous innovation and options for widening participation. The 1990s bring a realization of the systemness of the global economy, an in-house Keynesian system where international demand and supply can be stimulated or depressed with consequences for everyone on the earth.

But within this realization of the earth's closure and delicate ecological shield is the serendipity of chaotic markets, opening and closing markets depending upon innumerable liberating uncertainties and repressive structural obstacles, the rise and fall of petty protectionisms and heuristic innovations. If the Western markets continue to be partially closed to the exports of "the South," the South will have less currency to pay for goods from the Northern industrialized countries and the global economy will slow down. As the developing economies of the South work beyond temporary greenhouse and import substitution strategies to restructure and compete with Northern industries, the world economy will grow and more people will be employed. The radical restructuring in Eastern Europe towards market economics and emerging multiparty democracy bodes well for long-term world economic growth. Meanwhile, the East Asian NICs, NAFTA-inspired Latin American economies, the European Union, and improving U.S. productivity will stimulate world economic growth in the 1990s.

MODELS AND MODELING

The late twentieth century can be characterized as the Era of the Non-automatic Pilot Experiment. The scientific method and techniques of social learning have spread throughout the globe, including the notion of vicarious learning, modeling, and the pilot experiment. What characterizes the economic organizational models that have succeeded? On the national level these include the Japanese and the Swedish political economies. On the regional or international level, the European Union and OPEC come to mind. None of these political economy organizations succeeded overnight and all are imperfect still today (note the austerity policy with which Sweden has weathered the 1990s). All have in common a long history of frustrated consensus-building.

The dream of European unification goes back to Julius Caesar's conquests of France, England, and the Lowlands, which were added to the Roman territories of Italy, Spain, and the Balkans. The first book on European federation was Pierre Dubois's *On the Reconquest of the Holy Land* in 1306. Later both Edmund Burke and Immanuel Kant argued for the necessity of cultural similarity, if not homogeneity, for successful European integration (a strategy of exclusion). In the twentieth century progressive business leaders actually led the way to the formation of the European Economic Community, which could not, however, have been born without the cold, strategic calculations of French and German leaders when they joined forces in the European Coal and Steel Community. A history of collective action, a striving for homogeneity to the point of a strategy of exclusion, geopolitical strategic calculation, members with economic clout and leadership by both business and government leaders are behind the success of the European

Common Market—not to mention a benign American hegemony which not only let the bloc form, but helped to finance it. The 1989 expansion of the European Union (EU) of twelve nations to include six European Free Trade Association (EFTA) countries in a "European Economic Zone" provided a model for accepting Eastern European countries (such as Poland and Hungary) into a European bloc without having to admit them immediately to the more exclusive EC club.

OPEC, too, represented a coming together of members with economic clout (based on oil), a strategy of exclusion, hard strategic calculations, and an assumption that American hegemony would not stand in their way. And OPEC, too, created loose joint ventures with other oil producing nations to expand its influence without diluting its core. The timing of both the European integration and OPEC ventures was perfect. The leaders were sophisticated enough politically to suggest that such timing was no accident. Both were no doubt motivated to some extent by the desire for regional independence from the influence of the American hegemon. Other commodity cartels inspired by the OPEC model were based upon more diffuse membership, a less scarce or demanded commodity (bauxite, bananas and copper), and inappropriate timing and were not successful. The prerequisites for successful economic organizations (such as market share, organizational leadership, consensus, and timing) must be studied before they can be applied effectively as models.

Both the Japanese and Swedish models represent deep-rooted traditions of neo-corporatist consensus (the Japanese "without labor" and Sweden often almost labor-dominated), homogeneous populations, small states, and geographical locations on the periphery of American hegemony (that is, more protected by it than contributing to it). The literacy rate of both countries is high, and both are committed to maintaining a high level of intelligent participation by citizens in the economy (although the Japanese tendency to exclude women versus the Swedish tendency to include them is notable). Very little is left to chance when it comes to organizational networks in these countries. Control over population growth is also a similar characteristic. The extreme hierarchical nature of influence and information processing distinguishes Japan from the extreme focus upon egalitarianism, particularly when it comes to economic opportunity, present in Sweden. Both countries have maintained legitimate roles for traditional, noble families, who are expected to contribute in the form of public service. Both cultures stress limiting the range of incomes between those earning the most and those earning the least as a principle necessary for social harmony and consensus (in marked contrast with the United States, for example). Both target the industries they specialize in with great care and use government institutions and subsidies extensively in this task, thus striving for international competitiveness while yet preserving the integrity of their national cultures, social commitments, and some modicum of security at home.

In terms of the critical modeling phenomenon in the collective learning approach to international political economy one must also highlight the heavy reliance upon the strategy of the pilot experiment in the former socialist bloc—the capitalist zones and privatized factories near Hong Kong in the People's Republic of China, the Russian companies designated by the government to be permitted to make trade deals directly with Western firms in order to create "model" joint ventures (the cutting edge of *perestroika*), the experiments with stock markets in Hungary and China, and so forth. The initial aim in all cases appeared to be to graft market mechanisms on an outdated Stalinesque economic structure in order to make the political economy more competitive, attract Western hard currency and technology, and still not lose their integrity as socialist states.

Given the ability of China to transcend the Stalinist focus on heavy industry and to become self-sufficient in agriculture, it seems likely to be more successful in its economic reforms sooner than the Russian republics, even given China's 1989 authoritarian crackdown. Both of these regions have fostered economic growth by carefully targeting key industries in strategic regions for pilot experiments, which are designed to serve as models or "signals" for the rest of the country should they succeed. Similarly, the East Asian NICs learned from Japan as their "model."

One collective learning problem here is that it may always be more motivating to be part of a pilot experiment than it is to be a secondary copy of someone else's experiment making the initial experiments more successful than their clones. On the other hand, to the extent bugs are worked out, going second may be better than going first (as Japan has illustrated to the West in many industries).

Inequalities are necessary for economic purposes. What we have learned from "postliberal" successes is that such inequalities must be *targeted* for the overall strategic economic benefit of the nation.

STRATEGIES AND CYCLES

The success of political economy models in terms of economic growth depends upon the ability of their managers to adapt them, using appropriate strategic mixes at opportune moments in short-term, medium-term, and long-term business cycles. The key strategies associated with the maintenance thesis or maintenance model used in this book are the defeatist, the free-rider, the maintenance, and the entrepreneurial. One reason why so few successful economic models emerge from the developing world is that the global economy is structured to give them a choice between the least desirable of these two strategies: the defeatist and the free-rider. This is one reason why managers in developing countries dream of being able to pursue a maintenance strategy—that is, dream of being able to keep control of a self-sustaining system of equilibrium in which economic growth keeps up with the business cycle and the nation does not fall further behind. So if a country such as Mexico opts for a free-rider strategy in taking on as much debt as it can (as it did in the 1970s under the advice of the Cambridge School), one must understand this decision as one of the few choices realistically available to Mexico at the time. Bolivia's suspension of payments on its international debt in the 1980s is another free-rider variation. But, as we have noted, entrepreneurship can spring from free-rider "boosts" in the right circumstances.

The dilemma of advanced industrialized countries is markedly different. They can more or less take the maintenance of their existing political economy and its legitimacy for granted and have a choice between different risk-portfolios—or entrepreneurial strategies—depending upon whether they prefer maximizing the objectives of economic growth and job creation, or prefer the objectives of more equal distribution of economic opportunities and increasing the quality of life for those in the present generation. To a certain extent these are future versus past and savings/investment versus consumption trade-offs from the economist's viewpoint. But the cases of Sweden and West Germany illustrated that for fairly long periods (between periodic maintenance base restructurings for efficiency) it is possible for political economies to be able to have their cake and to eat it too (at least as long as the American protector protects).

No matter where one stands on these issues, they can be described in terms of maintenance-entrepreneurial (maintenpreneurial) strategy mixes. The economic threat to advanced industrial countries is more apt to come from risk-aversion or risk-shy behavior (or the maintenance syndrome) than it is from overdoing entrepreneurial risk-taking.

A case in point is the failure of West European countries to develop their own microchips in time to compete with the Japanese and Americans in the microelectronics business globally, making them dependent for some time to come on foreign chips. We can conclude that the optimum strategy is a maintenance-entrepreneurial mix heavily loaded toward the entrepreneurial *if* the tempo of socioeconomic and technological change continues at a rapid rate.

The cycles that all managers must face whether in the public or private sector are short-term, medium-term, and long-term. Since political economy strategies depend upon future assumptions concerning global economic growth or recession, energy prices, exchange rates and so forth, competent managers of international economic change must master the global cycles that will affect all their decisions and pay particular attention to the medium-term cycles specific to their own industry or national comparative advantage. Long-term, one must decide whether to side with those who believe the twentieth century will end with a bust—or with a boom—or with a wash between bust and boom. The depression scenarios tend to highlight a gap between existing technological developments and the ability commercially to apply and to sell these technologies, or a scarcity of liquidity given a debt-load meltdown globally, or both. But the debt crisis appears to have been restructured out of the limelight . . . .

From our collective learning perspective the information-overload, risk-shy maintenance thesis suggests that there are definite limits to the ability of people globally to absorb existing technology (that is until people start throwing out computers every year like an old-fashioned pair of shoes). But it is important to recall that the markets tend to discount this absorption problem well in advance, giving Silicon Valley its own private recession (in 1984) without necessarily contributing to a massive cyclical downturn.

The boom hypothesis has its own flaws, but perhaps not so many as the depression scenario. The optimists accurately forecast that the world's public and private financial institutions would ease the global debt crisis by informally writing off most of the developing country loans from the 1970s through longer terms and lower interest rates. They also argue that although the disinflationary trend may reverse, the rise of inflation will be gradual, thus providing the perfect elixir for global economic growth—stable growth with increasing liquidity. The baby-boom generation will spark consumption growth in the U.S. International peace will presumably break out throughout the world (led by Soviet and American weapons cut-backs and troop withdrawals), giving the stability argument further plausibility. But there are some drawbacks to this rosy scenario when one looks at specific sectors of the global economy (leaving the overcapacity problem in technology aside). If peace really succeeds, fewer weapons would be produced and sold, dampening these parts of the economy in those countries specializing in the weapons business. (With high-flying conventional weapons sales this seems unlikely.) With well over half of the aerospace military market in the world, the U.S. economy may be struck hard with readjustment problems, followed by European countries. (This, however, assumes that the United States and Europe put peace before economic growth, which is not their present priority.) A number of oil analysts project a significant rise in oil prices in the mid-1990s, which could undermine the moderate inflation assumption of the boom hypothesis.

When one descends from the level of the long-term, Kondratieff boom-or-bust genre of cycle projections (fifty years) to middle-range Kuznets cycles (fifteen to twenty-five years) or short-term "business cycles" (seven to nine years), the need for the manager of global economic change to be up-to-date in key sectors becomes even more compelling. If the manager should have corporate or national stakes in the global construction business, for example, it becomes important to know that the Hansen/Kuznets cycle projects that every other short-term business cycle will be a real boom in the construction cycle in the United States. And the alternating recessions are apt to be particularly deep when they coincide with the construction slump (the construction cycle being seventeen to eighteen years in length, about twice the length of the normal business cycle). When the manager anticipates a short- to medium-term recession coming on in a specific sector, he or she should adopt a maintenance strategy of consolidation or efficiency cutbacks, while an anticipation of boom might well trigger a higher risk, entrepreneurial strategy of expansion. Another option is to ignore market timing altogether, like Peter Lynch, manager of the most successful (long-term) stock mutual fund, Fidelity Magellan, and to invest systematically in concrete situations that one is very familiar with (which also seems to be the Japanese Research and Development investment strategy). This systematic, close-to-the-ground entrepreneurial strategy permits one to gain from economies of scale (as one's investment portfolio becomes ever larger). Simultaneously, one maintains quality by reducing variations through limiting oneself to industries one knows and experiences higher growth than average macro investment cycle returns by focusing upon the micromanagement of undervalued situations.

Since public managers are responsible for forecasting levels of unemployment and for attempting to encourage workers to shift from areas of low demand to areas of growing demand, such sector-specific short- to medium-term economic cycle research and micro-management analysis becomes invaluable to them as well. The economic aim of collective learning is to restructure the maintenance base of the organization or state with efficiency, cultural integrity and equal participation in order to position and target the collectivity for entrepreneurial niches and export-oriented growth. The following guidelines spell out how this might be done.

RECIPES FOR COLLECTIVE LEARNING

1.   Each individual has a *maintenance base* of home living expenses. *Encourage each person to cut these living expenses in half and to use this savings for voluntary investment in entrepreneurial undertakings or investment in the stocks of small, young companies (the job producers).* Individual wealth and economic growth will result. Entrepreneurs will emerge and the maintenance base will become more efficient, positioning the collectivity for competitiveness. The organization or state may need to provide social incentives for this savings and investment or cash from loans, grants, or taxes.

2.   The corporation or state should cut expenditures *within* their organizations and automatically shift this savings into *strategically targeted* investments *outside* the organizations according to comparative advantage in terms of return on investment, growth, and job creation. Social justice demands the maximum participation of the members of the collectivity in both the process of strategic targeting and in the jobs and rewards stemming from

economic growth. Such participation should be guided by an open, meritocratic elite.

3. To find savings and strategic investment targets:

- Do a survey of what people in the local community and immediate region
  want.
- Specialize in what customers want, using any comparative advantage at
  hand.
- Add value to products, processes, and raw materials to satisfy the needs identified by the people, using import substitution and training to increase the
  quality of jobs and products created in the community.
- Improve the aesthetics of where you live and work.
- Bring out the local cultural heritage, involving everyone with enthusiasm
  and community spirit.

View the local community as Jack McCall does in his *Small Town Survival
Manual (1988):* as a bucket where much may be poured into the top but the
bucket never overflows until the leaks are plugged in the bottom in order to
keep money and jobs at home that otherwise leak out.

4. Grassroots democratic organization can help to create a consensus
for teamwork, contributing to an efficient maintenance base by making
everyone a stakeholder through participation. In an authoritarian state, the
citizen has but "one boss" and must go underground for autonomy and creative freedom (work often going underground in the black market economy
as well). Democracy provides a choice between at least two potential "bosses"
or alternative parties, allowing the individual's energy to shine forth above
ground in community and market efforts in which he or she feels a part
"owner." To limit the factional instability of "too many bosses" (one strong
opposition party being better than two weak ones), adopt a rule requiring a
party to receive five percent of the vote in order to have representation in
parliament. Defend human rights, particularly the rights of minority groups
and factions, in order to coopt the energies of all individuals in the community to work enthusiastically towards collective goals.

5. Identify which collective behavior patterns need to be changed in
order to modernize the agricultural sector and to make it productive enough
to release surplus capacity for the manufacturing and service sectors.

6. Identify mature standardized industries that the state should subsidize *directly* and protect to assure resource availability and national security
independence (water, electricity, and so forth). Use joint ventures in these
sectors to transfer the cost of maintaining them to other states, firms, or organizations (a systematic free-rider strategy that can foster entrepreneurship). Target entrepreneurial innovations for modernization and rationaliza-

tion to further reduce costs. *For the reduction of costs in the maintenance base is the basis for the increase in the quality of life.* Elimination of variation, economies of scale, and strategic import substitutions can increase competitiveness and quality by creating savings for investment and retooling. "Cold shower" restructuring of the maintenance base is also required periodically of advanced welfare states that come to take their subsidies and standard of life for granted at the cost of noncompetitive tax rates and bureaucratic regulation that stifle entrepreneurial growth.

7. The state should stimulate emerging, high-growth "sunrise" industries through tax incentives and *indirect* subsidies in order to sharpen long-term competitiveness. But first calculate the timetable and market share that will enable the state to step out of the way of firms in these sectors once the infant industry stage has been passed (with the exception of continuing support for research and development). Set many of the initial import substitutions for self-destruct as comparative advantage shifts with development (but only provided that core community and cultural integrity can be kept).

8. Introduce monetary reform to assure a stable national currency and to restructure international credits to increase collective independence in the long-term. At the ripe moment in terms of economic cycles and changing value structures, shift for a quick, sharp break to move the society from a vicious to a virtuous economic circle (cutting inflation, stabilizing money, postponing foreign debt repayment, soliciting foreign loans, grants and investment, privatizing state-run firms, and stimulating small-business enterprise). But prepare the population for this shift in advance with a *policy of positive transparency* presenting facts with a hopeful blueprint for improvement. Let this policy aim at sustainable "green growth" to support ecological integrity at home and to attract environmental financial assistance from abroad. Anticipate political reactions to change for the sake of preserving traditional values and culture, demonstrating how these changes can be targeted to consolidate cultural integrity and competitiveness. Look for free rides and appropriate foreign policies to ease this transition.

9. The government and major companies should work together to cultivate educational and knowledge structures critical for training future workers in agricultural, mature, and emerging economic sectors. Institutionalize a targeted synthesis of the three types of collective learning: reduction-of-error within a rigid frame, open synergistic networking based on trust, and radical-quantum-leap learning for technological breakthroughs. Match appropriate portfolios of learning based on these types with clearly separate training tracks for general education versus apprenticeship versus high-tech professional development. In this educational reform, accent models that further economic adaptation for competitiveness while preserving a sense of equity and the integrity of core cultural values. Cultivate "a sense of agency" or enthusiastic self-determination in the people—both as individuals and as teams. Transform entrepreneurship into a moral act.

   10.   *The overall collective learning objective should be to establish a structural harmony that increases efficiency by reducing unnecessary variations and costs in the maintenance base while yet maximizing equal participation and preserving core cultural integrity, simultaneously promoting the effectiveness of entrepreneurial targeting, export-oriented growth, and job creation with fast feedback and systematic follow-through.*

SELECTED
BIBLIOGRAPHY

AGMON, TAMIR, *Political Economy and Risk in World Financial Markets*. Lexington, MA: Lexington Books, 1986.

ALBERT, MICHEL, *Capitalism Contre Capitalism*. Paris: Edition de Seuil, 1991.

AMIN, S., *Imperialism and Unequal Development*. New York: Monthly Review Press, 1988.

ANDERSON, JAMES E., *The Relative Inefficiency of Quotas*. Cambridge, MA: MIT Press, 1988.

ARGYLIS, CHRIS, *On Organizational Learning*. Oxford: Blackwell, 1992.

ARON, RAYMOND, *Progress and Disillusion: The Dialectics of Modern Society*. New York: Praeger, 1986.

BALASSA, B., ed., *Newly Industrializing Countries in the World Economy*. New York: Pergamon Press, 1981.

BANDURA, ALBERT, *Social Learning Theory*. Englewood Cliffs, NJ: Prentice-Hall, 1977.

BATES, R.H., *Rural Response to Industrialization: A Study of Village Zambia*. New Haven, CT: Yale University Press, 1976.

BATES, ROBERT A., ed., *Toward a Political Economy of Development: A Rational Choice Perspective*. Berkeley: University of California Press, 1988.

BATESON, GREGORY, *Steps to an Ecology of Mind*. New York: Ballantine Books, 1975.

BAUER, P.T., *Equality, the Third World, and Economic Delusion*. Cambridge, MA: Harvard University Press, 1977.

BECKER, J.F., *Marxian Political Economy: An Outline*. Cambridge: Cambridge University Press, 1977.

BELL, DANIEL, *The Cultural Contradictions of Capitalism*. New York: Basic Books, 1982.

BERGER, SUZANNE, & MICHAEL PIORE, *Dualism and Discontinuity in Industrial Societies.* New York: Cambridge University Press, 1980.

BERGSTEN, FRED, ed., *Global Economic Imbalances.* Washington, DC: Institute for International Economics, 1986.

BERRY, R.A., AND W.R. CLINE, *Agrarian Structure and Productivity in Developing Countries.* Baltimore: Johns Hopkins University Press, 1978.

BHAGWATI, JAGDISH, *New International Economic Order: The North-South Debate.* Cambridge, MA: MIT Press, 1977.

—, *The World Trading System at Risk.* Princeton, NJ: Princeton University Press, 1991.

BILLET, BRET L., *Investment Behavior of Multinational Corporations in Developing Areas: Comparing the Development Assistance Committee, Japanese, and American Corporations.* New Brunswick, NJ: Transaction Publishers, 1991.

BLOCK, F.L., *Origins of International Economic Disorder: Study of United States International Monetary Policy.* Berkeley: University of California Press, 1979.

BOTKIN, JAMES, DAN DIMANCESCU, & RAY STATA, *Global Stakes: The Future of High Technology in America.* Cambridge, MA: Ballinger Publishing Co., 1982.

BOULDING, KENNETH E., *Conflict and Defense: A General Theory.* New York: Harper and Row, 1962.

—, *Economy of Love and Fear.* Belmont, CA: Wadsworth Publishing Co., 1973.

—, *The Image: Knowledge in Life and Society.* Ann Arbor: University of Michigan Press, 1956.

BRADFORD, COLIN I., AND WILLIAM H. BRANSON, eds., *Trade and Structural Change in Pacific Asia.* Chicago: University of Chicago Press, 1987.

BRANDT, WILLY, et al., *North-South: A Program for Survival.* Cambridge, MA: MIT Press, 1980.

BRAUDEL, F., *Capitalism and Material Life.* New York: Harper and Row, 1973.

—, *The Structures of Everyday Life: The Limits of the Possible.* London: Collins, 1981.

BROWN, LESTER et al. *The State of the World 1994.* New York: W.W. Norton, 1994.

BROWN, MICHAEL BARRATT, *The Economics of Imperialism.* London: Penguin Press, 1974.

BUCHANAN, J.M., AND G. TULLOCH, *Calculus of Consent: Logical Foundations of Constitutional Democracy.* Ann Arbor: University of Michigan Press, 1962.

BURRUS, DANIEL, *Technotrends.* New York: HarperCollins, 1993.

BURSTEIN, DANIEL, *Turning the Tables: A Machiavellian Strategy for Dealing with Japan.* New York: Simon and Schuster, 1993.

CALLEO, DAVID, *The Bankrupting of America: How the Federal Budget Is Impoverishing the Nation.* New York: Avon Books, 1993.

CALLEO, DAVID, AND BENJAMIN ROWLAND, *America and the World Political Economy: Atlantic Dreams and National Reality.* Bloomington: Indiana University Press, 1973.

CAPORASO, JAMES A., *A Changing International Division of Labor.* Boulder: Lynne Rienner Publishers, 1987.

CASTANEDA, J., AND E. HETT, *El Economismo Dependentista.* Mexico City: Siglo XXI, 1978.

CHENERY, H.B., M.S. AHLUWALIA, C. BELL, J.H. DULOY, AND R. JOLLY, *Redistribution with Growth: Policies to Improve Income Distribution in Developing Countries in the Context of Economic Growth.* London: Oxford University Press, 1974.

CHILCOTE, R.H., ed., *Dependency and Marxism: Towards a Resolution of the Debate.* Boulder: Westview Press, 1982.

CIPOLLA, CARLO M., *The Economic Decline of Empires.* London: Methuen, 1970.

COHEN, BENJAMIN, *Organizing the World's Money: Political Economy of International Relations.* New York: Macmillan, 1978.

COHEN, S. S., AND J. ZYSMAN, *Manufacturing Matters: The Myth of the Post-Industrial Economy.* New York: Basic Books, 1987.

CORNWALL, JOHN, *Modern Capitalism: Its Growth and Transformation,* Oxford: Martin Robertson and Co., Ltd., 1977.

DAHRENDORF, RALF, *Lebenschancen.* Frankfurt: Suhrkamp Verlag, 1979.

DAVIDOW, WILLIAM H., AND MICHAEL S. MALONE, *The Virtual Corporation: Structuring and Revitalizing the Corporation for the 21st Century.* New York: HarperCollins, 1992.

DEMING, W. EDWARDS, *Quality, Productivity and Competitive Position.* Cambridge, MA: MIT Center for Advanced Engineering Study, 1982.

DENISON, E.F., *Accounting for United States Economic Growth, 1929–1969.* Washington, DC: Brookings Institution, 1974.

DENT, HARRY S., *The Great Boom Ahead.* New York: Hyperion, 1993.

DEO, SOM, *Multinational Corporations and the Third World.* Columbia, MO: South Asia Books, 1986.

DERESKY, HELEN, *International Management: Managing across Borders and Cultures.* New York: HarperCollins Publishers, 1994.

DE SILVA, S.B.D., *The Political Economy of Underdevelopment.* London: Routledge Chapman & Hall, 1982.

DICKEN, PETER, *Global Shift.* New York: The Guilford Press, 1992.

DIETRICK, WILLIAM S., *In the Shadow of the Rising Sun: The Political Roots of American Economic Decline.* University Park, PA: Pennsylvania State University Press, 1991.

DOUTHWAITE, RICHARD, *The Growth Illusion.* Tulsa, Oklahoma: Council Oak Books, 1993.

DRUCKER, PETER, *Innovation and Entrepreneurship.* New York: Harper and Row, 1985.

—, *Post-Capitalist Society.* New York: HarperCollins, 1993.

DUCHENE, FRANCOIS, AND GEOFFREY SHEPHERD, *Managing Industrial Change in Europe.* London: Francis Printer, 1987.

EELLS, RICHARD, Introduction by GEORGE W. BALL, *Global Corporations: The Emerging System of World Economic Power.* New York: Free Press, 1987.

FABER, MALTE, AND JOHN PROOPS, *Evolution, Time, Production and the Environment.* 2nd edition. Berlin: Springer-Verlag, 1993.

FLORA, P., AND A.J. HEIDENHEIMER, eds., *The Development of the Welfare States in Europe and America.* New Brunswick, NJ: Transaction Books, 1981.

FRANK, ANDRE, *Crisis in the World Economy.* New York: Holmes and Meier Publishers, 1980.

FREY, BRUNO, *International Political Economics.* Oxford: Basil Blackwell, 1986.

FROHLICH, N., AND J.A. OPPENHEIMER, *Modern Political Economy.* Englewood Cliffs, NJ: Prentice-Hall, 1978.

GALTUNG, J., *The True Worlds: A Transnational Perspective.* New York: Free Press, 1980.

GARDNER, RICHARD, *Sterling-Dollar Diplomacy in Current Perspective: The Origins and Prospects of Our International Economic Order.* New York, Columbia University Press, 1980.

GEIGER, THEODORE, *The Future of the International System: The United States and the World Political Economy.* Boston: George, Allen & Unwin, 1988.

GEISST, CHARLES R., *Entrepreneurial Capitalism: Foreign Investment and the American Dream in the Twentieth Century.* Westport, CT: Praeger Publishers, 1992.

GEOGESCU-ROEGEN, NICHOLAS, *The Entropy Law and the Economic Process.* Cambridge, MA: Harvard University Press, 1971.

GERTZ, CLIFFORD, *Peddlers and Princes: Social Development and Economies in Two Indonesian Towns.* Chicago: University of Chicago Press, 1963.

GHOSH, PRAPID K., *Multi-National Corporations and Third World Development.* Westport, CT: Greenwood Press, 1984.

GILPIN, ROBERT, *The Political Economy of International Relations.* Princeton, NJ: Princeton University Press, 1987.

GOUREVITCH, PETER, *Politics in Hard Times: Comparative Responses to International Economic Crisis.* Ithaca, NY: Cornell University Press, 1986.

GUNBERG, L. *Failed Multinational Ventures: The Political Economy of International Divestments.* Lexington, MA: D.C. Heath, 1981.

HAGEN, EVERETT, *On the Theory of Social Change.* London: Tavistock Publications, 1964.

HAITANI, KANJI, *Comparative Economic Systems: Organizational and Managerial Perspectives.* Englewood Cliffs, NJ: Prentice-Hall, 1989.

HALL, EDWARD, *Beyond Culture.* Garden City, NY: Anchor Press, 1976.

HAMPDEN-TURNER, CHARLES, AND ALFONS TROMPENAARS, *The Seven Cultures of Capitalism.* New York: Currency/Doubleday, 1993.

HAMPDEN-TURNER, CHARLES, *Gentlemen and Tradesmen: The Values of Economic Catastrophe.* London: Routledge Chapman & Hall, 1984.

HANCOCK, GRAHAM, *Lords of Poverty.* New York: The Atlantic Monthly Press, 1989.

HANKEL, WILHELM, *Die sieben Todsünden der Vereinigung.* Berlin: Siedler Verlag, 1993.

HANKEL, WILHELM, & ROBERT ISAAK, *Modern Inflation: Its Economics and Its Politics.* Lanham, MD: University Press of America, 1983. German version: *Die moderne Inflation.* Köln: Bund-Verlag, 1981.

HANKEL, WILHELM, *Weltwirtschaft.* Duesseldorf: Econ Verlag, 1977.

HANSEN, ROGER D., ed., *The Global Negotiation and Beyond: Toward North-South Accommodation in the 1980's.* Austin, TX: Lyndon B. Johnson School of Public Affairs, 1981.

HANSSON, GOTE, *Social Clauses and International Trade: Economic Analysis of Labour Standards in Trade Policy.* London: Croom Helm, 1982.

HARDIN, GARRET, & J. BADEN, eds., *Managing the Commons.* San Francisco: W.H. Freeman & Co., 1977.

HAYEK, F.A., *Monetary Nationalism and International Stability.* New York: Macmillan, 1937.

HEWLETT, S.A., *The Cruel Dilemmas of Development.* New York: Basic Books, 1980.

HICKS, J.R., *Monetary Theory and History: An Attempt at Perspective*. Oxford: G.B. Clarendon Press, 1967.

HIRSCH, FRED, *Social Limits to Growth*. Cambridge, MA: Harvard University Press, 1976.

HIRSCH, FRED, & JOHN GOLDTHORPE, eds., *The Political Economy of Inflation*. Cambridge, MA: Harvard University Press, 1978.

HIRSCHMANN, ALBERT O., *National Power and the Structure of Foreign Trade*. Berkeley and Los Angeles: University of California Press, 1980.

HOFSTEDE, GEERT H, *Cultures and Organizations*. New York: McGraw-Hill, 1991.

HOLLIS, W., & F. LAMOND TULLIS, eds., *An International Political Economy: International Economy Yearbook*. vol. 1, Boulder: Westview Press, 1985.

HOPKINS, R.F., & D.J. PUCHALA, *The Global Political Economy of Food*. Madison: University of Wisconsin Press, 1979.

HOPKINS, TERENCE K., & IMMANUEL WALLERSTEIN, eds., *Processes of the World-System*. Newbury Park, CA: Sage Publications, 1980.

INOGUCHI, TAKASHI, AND DANIEL I. OKIMOTO, *The Political Economy of Japan*. Stanford, CA: Stanford University Press, 1988.

ISAAK, ROBERT, *European Politics: Political Economy and Policymaking in Western Democracies*. New York: St. Martin's Press, 1980.

—, ed., *American Political Thinking*. Fort Worth, TX: Harcourt Brace, 1994.

JAMES, HARVEY S., JR., AND MURRAY WEIDENBAUM, *When Businesses Cross International Borders: Strategic Alliances and Their Alternatives*. Westport, CT: Praeger Publishers, 1993.

JANOSKI, THOMAS, *The Political Economy of Unemployment: Active Labor Market Policy in West Germany and the United States*. Berkeley, CA: University of California Press, 1990.

JOHNSON, CHALMERS, *MITI and the Japanese Miracle: The Growth of Industrial Policy, 1925–1975*. Stanford, CA: Stanford University Press, 1982.

JONES, R.B., *Perspectives on Political Economy*. London: F. Pinter, 1985.

KATZENSTEIN, PETER J., ed., *Between Power and Plenty: Foreign Economic Policies of Advanced Industrial States*. Madison: University of Wisconsin Press, 1978.

KATZENSTEIN, PETER J., *Small States in World Markets: Industrial Policy in Europe*. Ithaca, NY: Cornell University Press, 1985.

KENNEDY, PAUL, *Preparing for the 21st Century*. New York: Random House, 1993.

KEOHANE, ROBERT O., *After Hegemony: Cooperation and Discord in the World Political Economy*. Princeton, NJ: Princeton University Press, 1984.

KEOHANE, ROBERT O., AND JOSEPH S. NYE, *Power and Interdependence*. Boston: Little Brown, 1977.

KEREN, MICHAEL & GUR OFER, *Trials of Transition: Economic Reform in the Former Communist Bloc*. Boulder, CO: Westview Press, 1992.

KEYNES, JOHN MAYNARD, *General Theory of Employment, Interest and Money*. New York: A Harbinger Book, 1965.

—, *Laissez-faire and Communism*. New York: New Republic, Inc., 1926.

KINDLEBERGER, CHARLES, *Power and Money: The Economics of International Politics and the Politics of International Economics*. New York: Basic Books, 1970.

—, *The World in Depression, 1929–1939*. Berkeley: University of California Press, 1986.

KORNAI, JANOS, *Economics of Shortage.* vol 1, Amsterdam: North Holland, 1981.

KOVES, ANDRAS, *Central and East European Economies in Transition: The International Dimension.* Boulder, CO: Westview Press, 1992.

KRASNER, STEPHEN D., *Structural Conflict: The Third World against Global Liberalism.* Berkeley: University of California Press, 1985.

KUZNETS, SIMON, *Modern Economic Growth.* New Haven, CT: Yale University Press, 1966.

LINDBLOM, CHARLES, *Politics and Markets: The World's Political-Economic Systems.* New York: Basic Books, 1980.

LINDER, STAFFAN B., *The Harried Leisure Class.* New York: Columbia University Press, 1970.

LODGE, GOERGE C., *Perestroika for America.* Boston: Harvard Business School Press, 1991.

LOMBRA, RAYMOND E., AND WILLIAM E. WITTE, eds., *The Political Economy of International and Domestic Monetary Relations.* Ames, IA: Iowa State University Press, 1982.

LUTTWAK, EDWARD, *The Endangered American Dream.* New York: Simon and Schuster, 1993.

MADDOX, ROBERT C., *Cross-Cultural Problems in International Business.* Westport, CT: Quorum Books, 1993.

MAKIN, JOHN H., *The Global Debt Crisis: America's Growing Involvement.* New York: Basic Books, 1984.

MARRIS, PETER, *Loss and Change.* New York: Pantheon, 1974.

MARX, KARL, AND FREDERICK ENGELS, *Communist Manifesto.* Chicago: Charles H. Kerr, 1946.

MASUDA, YUJI, ed., *Human-Centered Systems in the Global Economy.* London: Springer-Verlag, 1992.

MAZRUI, ALI A., *The Moving Cultural Frontier of World Order: From Monotheism to North-South Relations.* New York: World Policy Institute, 1982.

MCCALL, JACK, *Small Town Survival Manual.* Columbia, MO: University of Missouri, 1988.

MCCLELLAND, DAVID C., *Roots of Consciousness.* New York: D. VanNostrand, 1964.

MCROBIE, GOERGE, *Small Is Possible.* New York: Harper and Row, 1981.

MICHIE, JONATHAN, ed., *The Economics of Restructuring and Intervention.* Brookfield, VT: Edward Elgar, 1991.

MILL, J.S., *Principles of Political Economy.* New York: Penguin, 1986.

MORAN, THEODORE H., *Investing in Development: New Roles for Private Capital.* New Brunswick, NJ: Transaction Publishers, 1986.

MORGAN, GARETH, *Riding the Waves of Change.* San Francisco: Jossey-Bass, 1988.

MUNDELL, ROBERT A., *Monetary Theory: Inflation, Interest and Growth in the World Economy.* Pacific Palisades, CA: Goodyear Publishing Co., 1971.

MYTELKA, LYNN, ed., *Strategic Partnerships and the World Economy.* Rutherford, N.J: Fairleigh Dickinson University, 1991.

NEWFARMER, RICHARD, *Transitional Conglomerates and the Economics of Dependent Development.* Greenwich, CT: Jai Press, 1980.

NOHLEN, DIETER, AND FRANZ NUSCHELER, eds., *Handbuch der Dritten Welt, Band 2: Suedamerika: Unterentwicklung und Entwicklung.* Ludwigsberg, W. Germany: Hoffman und Campes, 1985.

NURKSE, RAGNER, *Equilibrium and Growth in the World Economy.* Edited by Gottfried Haberler and Robert M. Stern. Cambridge, MA: Harvard University Press, 1961.

OHLIN, BERTIL, PER OVE HESSLEBORN, AND WIJKMAN PER MAGNUS, *The International Allocation of Economic Activity.* New York: Holmes & Meier, 1978.

OLSON, MANCUR, *Logic of Collective Action: Public Goods and the Theory of Groups.* Cambridge, MA: Harvard University Press, 1971.

—, *The Rise and Decline of Nations: Economic Growth, Stagflation and Social Rigidities.* New Haven, CT: Yale University Press, 1982.

PACKENHAM, ROBERT A., *Liberal America and the Third-World: Political Development Ideas in Foreign Aid and Social Science.* Princeton, NJ: Princeton University Press, 1987.

PANIC, M., *National Management of the International Economy.* New York: St. Martin's Press, 1988.

PARKIN, FRANK, *Class Inequality and Political Order: Social Stratification in Capitalist and Communist Societies.* New York: Praeger, 1975.

PERKINS, DWIGHT H., *China—Asia's Next Economic Giant?* Seattle and London: University of Washington Press, 1986.

POLANYI, K., *Great Transformation: The Political and Economic Origins of Our Time.* Boston: Beacon Press, 1957.

POLLARD, ROBERT A., *Political Economy of International Change.* New York: Columbia University Press, 1987.

PUTNAM, ROBERT D., AND NICHOLAS BAYNE, *Hanging Together: The Seven Power Summits.* Cambridge, MA: Harvard University Press, 1984.

RADICE, H., ed., *International Firms and Modern Imperialism.* Harmondsworth, U.K.: Penguin, 1975.

RAVENHILL, JOHN, *Collective Clientelism; The Lomé Convention and North-South Relations.* New York: Columbia University Press, 1985.

RAWLS, JOHN, *Political Liberalism.* New York: Columbia University Press, 1993.

REICH, ROBERT, *The Work of Nations.* New York: Alfred Knopf, 1991.

RICARDO, DAVID, *Works and Correspondence of David Ricardo: Principles of Political Economy and Taxation.* London: Cambridge University Press, 1981.

RIDDLE, D., *Service-Led Growth: The Role of the Service Sector in World Development.* New York: Praeger, 1986.

ROSECRANCE, RICHARD, *The Rise of the Trading State: Commerce and Conquest in the Modern World.* New York: Basic Books, 1987.

ROSTOW, W.W., *Stages of Economic Growth.* London: Cambridge University Press, 1971.

—, *Why the Poor Get Richer and the Rich Slow Down: Essays in the Marshallian Long Period.* Austin: University of Texas Press, 1980.

ROTHSTEIN, ROBERT L., *Global Bargaining: UNCTAD and the Quest for a New International Economic Order.* Princeton, NJ: Princeton University Press, 1979.

ROWLAND, BENJAMIN, ed., *Balance of Power or Hegemony: The Interwar Monetary System.* New York: New York University Press, 1975.

RUGGIE, JOHN GERARD, ed., *The Antinomies of Interdependence: The Political Economy of International Change.* New York: Columbia University Press, 1983.

SANDLER, TODD, ed., *The Theory and Structures of International Political Economy.* Boulder: Westview Press, 1980.

SAUVANT, KARL P., AND HAJO HASENPFLUG, eds., *The New International Economic Order: Confrontation or Cooperation between North and South.* Boulder, CO: Westview Press, 1977.

SCHELLING, THOMAS C., *Micromotives and Macrobehaviour.* New York: W.W. Norton, 1978.

SCHOR, JULIET, *The Overworked American.* New York: Basic Books, 1992.

SCHUMACHER, E.F., *Small Is Beautiful: Economics as if People Mattered.* New York: Harper & Row, 1975.

SCHUMPETER, JOSEPH, *The Theory of Economic Development: An Enquiry into Profits, Capital Interest and the Business Cycle.* Cambridge, MA: Harvard University Press, 1984.

SENGE, PETER, *The Fifth Discipline.* New York: Doubleday, 1990.

SMITH, ADAM, *An Inquiry into the Nature and Causes of the Wealth of Nations.* New York: Modern Library, 1937.

SMITH, PETER H., *The Challenge of Integration: Europe and the Americas.* New Brunswick, NJ: Transaction Publishers, 1993.

SMITH, TONY, *The Pattern of Imperialism: The U.S., Great Britain, and the Late-Industrializing World Since 1815.* New York: Cambridge University Press, 1981.

STRANGE, S., *Casino Capitalism.* Oxford: Blackwell, 1986.

—, ed., *Paths to International Economy.* London: George Allen & Unwin, 1984.

STRANGE, S., AND R. TOOZE, eds., *The International Politics of Surplus Capacity: Competition for Market Shares in the World Recession.* London: George Allen & Unwin, 1981.

THUROW, LESTER, *Head to Head: The Coming Economic Battle Among Japan, Europe, and America.* New York: William Morrow, 1992.

TOLCHI, MARTIN, AND SUSAN TOLCHI, *Buying into America: How Foreign Money Is Changing the Face of Our Nation.* Washington, DC: Farragut Publishing Company, 1993.

TRIFFIN, ROBERT, *Gold and the Dollar Crisis: The Future of Convertibility.* New Haven, CT: Yale University Press, 1960.

TROMPENAARS, FONS, *Riding the Waves of Change.* London: Economist Books, 1993.

TSURUMI, YOSHI, *Multinational Management: Business Strategy and Government Policy.* (2nd ed.) Cambridge, MA: Ballinger, 1983.

TUCKER, ROBERT W., *The Inequality of Nations.* New York: Basic Books, 1979.

TUFTE, EDWARD R., *Political Control of the Economy.* Princeton, NJ: Princeton University Press, 1980.

TYSON, LAURA D'ANDREA, *Who's Bashing Whom?: Trade Conflict in High Technology Industries.* Washington, DC: Institute of International Economics, 1992.

VERNON, RAYMOND, ed., *Big Business and the State: Changing Relations in Western Europe.* Cambridge, MA: Harvard University Press, 1974.

—, *The Promise of Privatization: A Challenge for U.S. Foreign Policy.* New York: Council on Foreign Relations, 1988.

VOGEL, EZRA, *The Four Little Dragons: The Spread of Industrialization in East Asia.* Cambridge, MA: Harvard University Press, 1991.

—, *One Step Ahead in China: Guangdong under Reform.* Cambridge, MA: Harvard University Press, 1989.

VON BEYME, KLAUS, *Der Vergleich in der Politikwissenschaft.* Munich: Piper, 1988.

WADE, ROBERT, *Governing the Market: Economic Theory and the Role of Government in East Asian Industrialization.* Princeton, NJ: Princeton University Press, 1994.

WALLERSTEIN, IMMANUEL, *The Capitalist World Economy.* Cambridge, MA: Cambridge University Press, 1979.

—, ed., *World Inequality: Origins and Perspectives on the World System.* Montreal: Black Rose Books, 1975.

WALTZ, KENNETH, *Theory of International Politics.* Reading, MA: Addison-Wesley, 1979.

WEBER, MAX, *Economy and Society: An Outline of Interpretive Sociology.* 2 vols. Berkeley: University of California Press, 1978.

WEISBAND, EDWARD, ed., *Poverty Amidst Plenty: World Political Economy and Distributive Justice.* Boulder: Westview Press, 1989.

WICKSELL, KNUT, *Lectures on Political Economy.* 2 vols. London: Routledge & Kegan Paul Ltd., 1934.

WILDENMANN, RUDOLF, ED., *The Future of Party Government, vol. 3: Managing Mixed Economies.* Ed. by Francis G. Castles, Franz Lehner, and Manfred G. Schmidt. New York/Berlin: Walter de Gruyter, 1988.

WILKINS, MIRA, *The Maturing of Multinational Enterprise: American Business Abroad from 1914–1970.* Cambridge, MA: Harvard University Press, 1974.

ZYSMAN, JOHN, *Government, Markets and Growth: Financial Systems and the Politics of Industrial Change.* Ithaca, NY: Cornell University Press, 1983.

INDEX

Savings, 315
  American dislike of, 156
Scharpf, Fritz, 257
Schemata, 20, 303, 306
Schmidt, Helmut, West German
  Chancellor, 93
Schmidt, Manfred, 256
Schumacher, E.F., 41, 286–88
Schuman Plan, 136
Schuman, Robert, 136
Second World, 58
  See also Eastern bloc
Security
  defined, 30
Self-sufficiency, 20, 27
  economic, 51, 124
  of nation-state, 37
Semiconductor industry, 168
Senmonshosha Japanese wholesale
  distributors, 269
Serlen Bruce, 245
Serra, Antonio, 116
"Seven Sisters," 141
Shame culture, 282
Sharjah, 142
Shell Oil Company, 141, 299
Sherman Antitrust Act of 1890, 266
Shock therapy:
  Poland, 307
Shougan Contract System, 70
Shumpeter, Joseph, 17, 21, 244,
  255, 286
Simon, Herbert A., 275
Singapore, 4, 11, 140, 200, 201,
  204, 231
Singer Company, 286
Singer, Hans, 129
Singer, Isaac, 266
Slater, Phillip, 254
Small Is Beautiful (Schumacher),
  41, 286
Smith, Adam, 5, 6, 7, 8, 16, 17, 99,
  117, 125, 126, 166, 265, 270
  invisible hand, 99
Smith, M. Brewster, 71
Smoot-Hawley Tariff Act of 1930,
  121
Snake. See Exchange rate in EEC
Snow, C.P., 217
Social capital, 69
Social Democratic Parties:
  (German and Swedish), 246,
  247, 256
  Social Democratic tradition, 256
Social learning theory (Bandura),
  19, 297
Social market economy, 160,
  251–52
  economic order, 252
  economic process, 252
  in West Germany, 307
Social planning and the concept
  of deutero-learning
  (Bateson), 297
Socialism, 8, 10, 21, 29, 50, 53,
  232, 238, 241
  of China, 65
  extreme socialist, 196
  socialist system, 54, 55
Socialist bloc. See Eastern bloc

Socialist market economy, 69
Socialist Party
  Hungarian, 61
Socialist Workers Party in
  Hungary, 56
Soft currency, 252–54
  depreciation, 254
  strategy, 247–54
Sogoshosha (trading company), 67,
  160, 268–69, 300
Solidarity union movement, 62, 306
Solidarity Union, Poland, 61, 65, 306
South Africa, 36, 140, 271
Sovereignty, 30, 50, 135, 140, 192
  EEC countries and European
  monetary system, 96
Sozialdemokratische Krisenpolitik
  (Scharpf), 257
Spain, 11, 137, 214, 243, 246, 309
Special Drawing Rights (SDR), 83,
  85
  and debt crisis, 91
  dollar in disguise, 34, 87
  the introduction of, 84
Speed:
  as the most underestimated phe-
  nomenon in international
  political economy, 301–3
Sri Lanka, 215
STABEX system, 182
  defined, 183
  See also Lomé Convention
Stability
  political, as a competitive edge
  of the U.S., 155
Stabilization
  macroeconomic, 63
Stabilization Fund, 80
Stages of economic growth. See
  Economic development
  theory
Stages of Economic Growth (Rostow),
  The, 238–41
Stagflation, 42
Stagnation, 196, 288
Stalin, Joseph, 5, 52, 56, 307, 308
Stalinesque economic model, 34, 50,
  54, 55, 56, 57, 59, 60, 67
  in China, 65
  in Hungary, 56
Stalinist political economy, 53–55
Standard Oil of California, 141,
  270, 286
State corporation, 246
  See also Economic development
  theory
State strategy, 231–57, 292
  of economic development,
  233–36, 250
  of soft-currency country, 252–57
  state capitalism, 233
  typology, 247–54
  See also North-South, East-West
  and separate state listings
Static economics of scale, 244–45,
  269
Statism. See Nationalism, economic
Status recognition, 242–43
Status society, 234
Stock market crash

of 1929, 121
of 1987, 114, 303
of 1989, 108
Strategic arms race, 299
Strategic Defense Initiative (SDI),
  44
Strategic openess, 308–9
Strategic petroleum reserve of
  U.S., 188
Strategic triangle, 88
Strategy mix, 201, 311–14
  maintenance-entrepreneurial,
  44, 67
Strategy:
  defined, 33–35
  of exclusion, 309–10
  strategic behavior, 33–35
  strategic fit, 284
  See also Defeatist, entrepreneurial, free-rider, maintenance, maintenpreneurial,
  state strategy
Structural adjustment (Lomé Convention), 183
Structural constraints, 173
Structural deficit, 37
  See also Structural surplus
Structural positioning. See
  Positioning
Structural stalemate, 301
Structural surplus, 36, 39, 44
Structuralism, 102
  interpretation of balance of payment adjustment, 99–100
  interpretation of world trade
  system, 128–31
  structuralist foreign aid, 192
  structuralist school, 4, 128
  structuralist strategy of import
  substitution, 194
Structure, North-West, 199, 200
  defined, 173–75
  foreign aid. See Foreign aid
  the Lomé strategy, 181–84
  origin, 175–76
  of pressure group, 184
  the South, 308, 309
  and World Bank, 177–80
  See also Asymmetry, Developing
  countries, Periphery
Structure, 13, 199–200
  of education and class, 254
  interpretation, 216–24
  of class system, 224
  of national economy, 292
  of OPEC, 180
  primary structures of states in
  world political economy,
  35–36
  of an object, 214
  and strategy, 255
  structural change, 244
  of value framework, 224
Structured scarcity:
  and high demand, 298
Structure, East-West, 13, 50–53,
  173, 200
  the East, 308, 309
  interpretation, 58
  origin, 53–58